D1677489

Principled Pragmatist

Principled Pragmatist
The Political Career of
Alexandre Millerand

Marjorie Milbank Farrar

BERG

New York / Oxford

Distributed exclusively in the US and Canada by
St Martin's Press, New York

First published in 1991 by
Berg Publishers Limited
Editorial offices:
165 Taber Avenue, Providence, RI 02906, USA
150 Cowley Road, Oxford OX4 1JJ, UK

Library of Congress Cataloging-in-Publication Data
Farrar, Marjorie Milbank.
  Principled pragmatist: the political career of Alexandre
Millerand / Marjorie Milbank Farrar.
    p. cm.
  Includes bibliographical references.
  ISBN 0–85496–665–X
  1. Millerand, Alexandre, 1859–1943.   2. Presidents–France
–Biography.   3. France–Politics and government–1870–1940.
4. Socialists–France–Biography.   I. Title.
DC393.M55F37 1990
944.0815092–dc20   89–18016
                                                                    CIP

British Library Cataloguing in Publication Data
Farrar, Marjorie Milbank.
  Principled pragmatist: the political career of Alexandre
  Millerand.
  1. France. Politics. Millerand, Alexandre 1859–1943
  I. Title
  944.081

  ISBN 0–85496 665–X

Printed in Great Britain by
Billing & Sons Ltd, Worcester

For
Lance
Olivia and Avery
Shepard and Eric

What seems to me essential is to recognize in the great man an outstanding individual who is at once a product and an agent of the historical process, at once the representative and the creator of social forces which change the shape of the world and the thoughts of men.

E.H. Carr

Contents

Acknowledgements

In the course of writing any book, an author incurs many debts to the individuals or institutions which have assisted. It is a great pleasure to acknowledge those obligations and express gratitude for that aid.

Several libraries and archives in Paris were particularly gracious in making their collections available for consultation. Mlle. Dorsemaine, archivist for the Millerand papers originally held by the Bibliothèque Nationale, guided me in the initial stages of my research. After the papers were moved to the Archives Nationales, Mme. Bonazzi, conservator of the private archives, gave me special access to the documents which were still not officially open. I benefited from the assistance of the staffs at the Archives Nationales, Bibliothèque Nationale, Ministère des Affaires Etrangères at the Quai d'Orsay, Ministère de la Guerre at Vincennes, the Assemblée Nationale, the Sénat, the libraries at the Fondation Nationale des Sciences Politiques, the Bibliothèque Historique de la Ville de Paris, the Bibliothèque de l'Hôtel de Ville, and the Bibliothèque de l'Institut.

A grant from the American Philosophical Society provided the funds for the initial research in Paris. Portions of the manuscript were published in different form in *French Historical Studies* and the *Proceedings* of the American Philosophical Society and appear here with the permission of those journals.

I would also like to record my appreciation to the friends and colleagues who actively aided my task. My thanks go above all to the late Jacques Millerand and his wife. I was privileged to have several lengthy discussions with the former about his father and to borrow his father's unpublished autobiographical memoir. The Millerands graciously extended personal invitations to me and later to my husband. One of the great joys of writing this book has been the continued contact with Mme. Millerand. Two historians, David Pinkney and Leslie Derfler, read the manuscript in an earlier version and offered detailed, constructive suggestions which assisted me enormously in the final revisions. Jean-Baptiste Duroselle, Jean-Nöel Jeanneney, Michel Rouffet, and Charles Maier guided me to new sources. James Joll, John Gillis, William Hoisington, and Karl Bottigheimer took particular interest and aided in the book's publication. I would like to thank them for all their assistance and also note my appreciation to the many friends and family who over the years showed an interest in the book's progress and fate.

Finally, to my husband, daughters and sons-in-law, I would like to record my gratitude for their interest and concern over the decade that this book has been part of my life and our conversations. As a small token of appreciation and in the hope that the final product may partially repay their loyal support, the book is dedicated to them.

Chestnut Hill,
Massachusetts

Abbreviations

A.E.	Ministère des Affaires Etrangères
A.G.	Archives du Ministère de la Guerre
A.N.	Archives Nationales
C.D.A.	Archives de la Chambre des Députés
D.B.F.P.	*Documents on British Foreign Policy*
D.D.F.	*Documents diplomatiques français*
F.M.	Fonds Millerand (Archives Nationales)
J.O.	*Journal Officiel*
P.B.	Papiers Barrère
P.M.	Papiers Millerand (Affaires Etrangères)
Sénat	Archives du Sénat

Introduction

This study of the political career of French politician and statesman Alexandre Millerand (1859–1943) is the first full-length scholarly examination of one of the most important Third Republic figures. It utilizes primary, documentary resources only recently available to scholars and heretofore largely unexplored, the Millerand papers at the Archives Nationales and the Quai d'Orsay as well as records of parliamentary debates and commission sessions and the war and foreign ministry archives. The vast collection of Millerand documents was, however, almost exclusively of a public nature: speeches, despatches, memos. With the exception of an autobiographical memoir written at the end of Millerand's life, personal letters or reminiscences were not available. Furthermore, the paucity of contemporary evaluations of his personality or achievements is as notable as the scant attention given his career by historians.

Millerand, who was first elected to the French Chamber of Deputies in 1885, served as either a deputy or a senator for fifty-five years (until the fall of France in 1940) with the exception of his four years as president of the Republic (1920–4). The length and diversity of Millerand's political career and the nature of the evidence available dictated the focus of this study and the decisions not to examine his equally long and active legal career or to devote much space to his youth, personality or private life. Personality traits are discussed only where they clearly affected his political activities or fortunes. Since he did not record his intimate thoughts or comment in his memoir about such major events of his political life as his expulsion from the Socialist party, a responsible historical discussion of his personality was not possible. Even his son described him as an exceptionally taciturn, private man, reticent about his political past. Viewing the historian's task as the presentation of as accurate and balanced an account as possible of the evidence in the documents, this study seeks to present a neutral rather than a partisan analysis. As Zeev Sternhell admonishes, the historian does not moralize; his role is to explain things, not to pass value judgements.[1]

Millerand, whose political activities spanned most of the Third Republic, began his career as a Radical, moved to socialism, and then gradually to a moderate, right of center nationalist stance – a progression that many notable Third Republic figures followed. His career is instructive because of the insights it provides on crucial events and on the nature of the successful politician. The fundamental characteristic of a significant political figure's career is the multiplicity of specific, practical decisions he confronts. Whether in the legislature, the ministry or the president's office, a political representative like Millerand has to take stands as he did on issues as varied as the Franco-Russian alliance, the role of the Bank of France, workers' pensions, or the production of shells for the 75mm gun. Although Millerand had principles to which he re-mained more true than many politicians, he was essentially a pragmatist rather than an ideologue. This observation is as true of 'leftists' as of 'rightists,' which illustrates the difference between 'insiders' and 'outsiders,' those bearing political responsibility as opposed to those outside the system.

Precisely because Millerand's political career covered such a long period and included numerous different responsibilities, there is no single theme which explains it. By shedding light on several important issues, his political activities refute the traditional view of him as simply an opportunist who abandoned socialism for conservative nationalism. Although his relationship to socialism was important, he was officially a socialist for only ten of the fifty-five years he spent in politics (1893–1903). Since that part of his career was relatively brief, the focus of the book is elsewhere, namely on the period of his greatest influence after 1903 and particularly after 1912.

Millerand's relationship to socialism, both its ideological varia-tions and its contending factions, was nonetheless an important stage in his career. His position of leadership within the parlia-mentary socialists affected his nomination as minister of commerce (1899–1902) in the national unity cabinet that emerged from the Dreyfus crisis. As the first Socialist to achieve cabinet rank in the

1. Zeev Sternhell, *Ni droite ni gauche. L'idéologie fasciste en France* (Paris: Editions du Seuil, 1983), p. 13.

Third Republic, Millerand won a place in the relatively small group of *ministrables* (those capable of holding ministerial rank) who dominated republican history and lent stability to the seemingly unstable political system. His choice marked the increased importance of parliamentary socialism but split the party, which eventually expelled the reformist Millerand and adopted a revolutionary orientation. As a deputy and as minister of commerce and later as minister of public works (1909–10), Millerand pressed for social reform. His concern for social justice, in the egalitarian tradition of the French Revolution, may have stemmed from his own modest background and his representation of a largely working-class district, but nonetheless his proposals for strike arbitration, unemployment, old-age and accident insurance, and a reduced work day made significant contributions to France's social legislation. They demonstrated his insistence that social change should be implemented peacefully through legislation, not by such violence as the strikes of the early twentieth century, which he termed a form of social warfare. Millerand's legalism, perhaps influenced by his legal training and career as a lawyer, would frequently affect the positions he took politically, as, for example, in the Du Paty de Clam affair of 1913.

For Millerand, however, national interests always retained priority over social reform. His republican patriotism would dictate both his opposition to Boulanger and his support for the Franco-Russian alliance. The nation in danger, whether due to domestic division as in the Dreyfus Affair or to foreign threat as in the First World War, required republican unity. Indeed, a dislike of internecine partisan politics, social strife or anti-patriotic behavior would frequently elicit from Millerand demands for unity among his countrymen, an echo of the fraternal slogan of the revolutionary heritage. This concern for national interests would lead Millerand as minister of public works to mobilize striking railroad workers (1910), a dramatic shift of position from the young lawyer and deputy who had defended strikers in the 1880s. Similar motives prompted his actions as minister of war (1912–13; August 1914 to October 1915) to foster military preparation by strengthening military discipline, depoliticizing the army, and encouraging the public's martial spirit. His tenures of the war ministry shed light on the relationship of civil–military powers in peace and war. Concern about national survival encouraged him to reorganize the war ministry and command structure, increase military and industrial strength, but triggered conflict with civilian politicians who saw democratic liberties threatened by Millerand's attribution of near invulnerability to the military hierarchy in wartime.

The devastating human, material and psychological impact of the First World War on France forced its postwar leaders to protect national interests from a defensive position. As leader of the victorious Bloc National, Millerand became premier and foreign minister (January–September 1920) with a goal of enforcing the Treaty of Versailles, particularly its disarmament and reparations clauses, over German recalcitrance and British hesitation. Despite acute Franco-British tension after the French occupation of the German Maingau towns, inter-Allied conferences like the one at Spa solved few problems related to the Treaty of Versailles. Concern for French security would dictate both Millerand's firmness toward Germany and his anti-Bolshevism, which was demonstrated by his refusal to deal with the Soviet Union, his support for Poland and his recognition of the White Russian General Wrangel. The empire, which always represented a source of French greatness for Millerand, would become particularly important in a world where France's prestige was less secure. While new resources would be important to the war-ravaged nation, France needed the proof of its greatness that colonies or mandates like Syria provided. Since national interests would take priority over ideological commitments like national self-determination, as they had over social reform, Millerand would ignore local wishes in Syria or disregard ethnic demands in Eastern Europe. Repression of domestic social unrest would reflect his conviction that strikes were part of a revolutionary political movement that threatened the republican unity essential to France's recovery. Nationalism therefore would assume an increasingly conservative, defensive posture after the war, as Millerand's activities illuminate.

Millerand's career focuses attention on the relationship between legislative and executive powers in a democratic state, a problem that the Third Republic failed to resolve satisfactorily. Although he would strongly oppose Casimir-Périer's 'personal' policy in 1894 and would always reject any form of dictatorship, Millerand would increasingly denounce the imbalance of power in favor of the Chamber of Deputies. Since he was convinced that the single-member constituency voting system, the *scrutin d'arrondissement*, was not only responsible for the corruption and narrow-mindedness of France's elected representatives but also contributed to the legislature's domination of the political system, he persistently advocated electoral reform from the 1890s onward. He would increasingly portray the unbalanced relationship between the legislative and executive powers as a dictatorship. Since freedom in all its forms would be a constant theme of Millerand's career, his opposition to legislative domination reflects his libertarian orientation. Convinced that a healthy democracy required a balance of powers, Millerand would advocate a stronger executive to balance legislative prerogatives, as his Evreux speech of 1923 did. As president of the Republic (1920–4), Millerand sought to transform that normally titular post into a more active executive role. He intervened particularly in foreign policy, most notably in opposing Premier Briand's policy at Cannes (1922), in persuading a reluctant Premier Poincaré to occupy the Ruhr (1923), and in assuming leadership of the Bloc National in the elections of 1924. Yet his actions won Briand's lasting hostility, failed to get Poincaré to follow up on the German surrender in the Ruhr, and made him the inevitable target of the Cartel des Gauches after its electoral victory. The ministerial strike which would force Millerand's resignation would avert a constitutional crisis but condemn France to continued cabinet instability and parliamentary dominance. While Millerand's actions would end his own effective career, they foreshadowed aspects of Charles de Gaulle's constitution for the Fifth Republic. Consequently, a study of Millerand's career not only fills a gap in French history but contributes to a comprehension of a significant and complex period. It provides a synthesis from the perspective of a notable individual that illuminates significant republican political developments.[2]

2. Joseph Konvits, 'Biography: the missing form in French historical studies,' *European Studies Review*, 6, 1976, pp. 9–20; David Pinkney, 'The dilemma of the American historian of modern France,' *French Historical Studies*, I, No. 1, 1958, pp. 11–25.

Part I

The Formation of a
Political Leader

1
Youthful Libertarian and Social Reformer

Born in Paris on 10 February 1859, Etienne-Alexandre Millerand came from a modest, lower-middle-class background. His father, a draper in the rue de la Jussienne, was the son of a wine merchant of peasant origins who came to Paris from Roche-sur-Vanon in the Franche-Comté. Except for an eight-month stay in Brittany during the 1870–1 siege of Paris and summer vacations in the Franche-Comté, Millerand spent his youth in the capital, where his studies at the prestigious *lycées* of Vanves, Louis le Grand and Henri IV, facilitated entry into a professional career considerably above his modest family origins. Education thus opened a channel of upward social mobility from which his own intelligence and perseverance benefited. Strongly drawn to politics, Millerand considered Pierre Bonaparte's acquittal by the High Court at Blois in spring 1870 of the murder of a radical journalist to be a denial of justice. Contemporaneously, he responded to Gambetta's plea after the fall of Metz for Frenchmen to confront the terrible challenge facing their nation. Even at the age of eleven, his patriotic dedication to republican France and his hatred of dictatorship, guiding influences on his political career, were clear. Although the future Cardinal Lavigerie impressed the young Millerand, who was himself a prize-winning catechism student, his religious faith did not survive his reading of Renan's *Life of Jesus*.

An interest in politics probably influenced Millerand's decision to seek a law degree at the University of Paris after his baccalaureate in letters. He later argued that his exposure to men from all backgrounds during his year of military service in Brittany provided an apprenticeship for public life. Although the demands of military life were not burdensome, he returned enthusiastically to his legal

studies, which culminated in his inscription in the Ordre des
Avocats of the Paris bar in 1881. Anxious to find uncontroversially
valid general principles, he was especially influenced by John Stuart
Mill and Herbert Spencer. An initial acceptance of liberty as the
greatest good was eroded by increasing dismay at *laissez-faire*
economic liberalism's inhuman consequences, which eventually led
him to socialism. His basic ideas and rhetorical skills were, however, developed between 1881 and 1885, when he was both an
active young lawyer and a budding journalist and politician.

The early 1880s were a period of general economic depression
which produced numerous strikes in French mines. Using his
recently acquired legal skills, Millerand defended the miners at
Montceau-les-Mines in 1882, and subsequently often backed strikers
against the large companies' stranglehold. Georges Laguerre, an
active participant in the Conférence Molé and chief defending
counsel for the strikers at Montceau-les-Mines, as well as legal
correspondent for Georges Clemenceau's newspaper *La Justice*,
strongly influenced the young Millerand. The Conférence Molé,
which represented all republican nuances, permitted informal discussion between lawyers and politicians, thereby bridging the legal
and political worlds. In fact, Millerand replaced him on *La Justice*
when Laguerre became a deputy. Laguerre thus linked the three
worlds of politics, law and journalism, as would Millerand. Despite its limited subscription, *La Justice* attracted talented young
journalists because of its director's disproportionate influence. To
Millerand, the governing Opportunists represented the politics of
favoritism. Although subsequently disillusioned, he expected a
Radical victory to end the manipulation and executive abdication
encouraged by the current confusion of powers.

Millerand entered elected politics in 1883 when the Radical–
Liberal committee appointed him as secretary to Jehan de Bouteiller,
Chamber of Deputies candidate for the sixteenth *arrondissement*.
Despite de Bouteiller's loss to a reactionary, Millerand gave his first
political speech during the campaign demanding the separation of
church and state. Though shy, he proved an able public speaker.
The next year, he launched his own political career as a Parisian
municipal councillor for the Muette district. His slim, eighty-vote
victory in the second round on 11 May 1884 permitted him, as a
member of the Seine's General Council, to participate in the senatorial elections. High unemployment in the Paris region and the
general depression contributed to the Radicals' electoral success and

probably encouraged Millerand's concentration on social and edu-cational issues as a municipal councillor. Nonetheless, he always sought pragmatic and legal solutions. For the young lawyer, how-ever, municipal politics served only as a stepping-stone to national politics. As municipal councillor, he sought political visibility in the Paris region by speaking for the separation of church and state. In the national elections of 1885, Millerand chose the Seine con-stituency because of his familiarity with the Parisian area and the prominence he had achieved as municipal councillor. Defeated on 4 October, Millerand was elected to the Chamber of Deputies in the second round of a by-election on 27 December 1885. The list-voting electoral system (*scrutin de liste*) permitted multiple candi-dacies that required by-elections to fill vacated seats. At the age of twenty-six Millerand, who took his seat on 29 December, began a national political career lasting fifty-five years.[1]

The elections of 1885, which coincided with economic hardship and colonial setbacks, benefited the unified Right as did the *scrutin de liste* electoral system. However, republican discipline in the second round preserved a republican majority (367 to 202 votes). The potential monarchist victory forced the republicans to end their wrangling and, briefly, their bitter attacks, led by Clemenceau, against Jules Ferry's colonial policy in the south-central China region of Tonkin. The Radicals feared that an active colonial policy would distract France from vital European issues. Although the Opportunists won Grévy's reelection as President of the Republic in December, they had to share power for the first time with the Radicals, whose electoral success gave them nearly a third of the republican seats (120). The young Millerand entered the Chamber of Deputies as a Radical and Clemenceau's disciple. His patron, the power behind the new Freycinet cabinet, dictated the choice of the dashing republican General Georges Boulanger as minister of war.[2]

The emergence, growth, and collapse of Boulangism, which coincided with the 1885–9 legislature, challenged the new Radical

1. Leslie Derfler, *Alexandre Millerand: The Socialist Years* (The Hague: Mouton, 1977), ch. 1; Alexandre Millerand, 'Mes souvenirs (1859–1941) – contribution à l'histoire de la Troisième République,' Versailles, 22 April 1941, pp. 3–22bis (unpublished manuscript in the possession of the Millerand family, Sèvres, France), hereafter cited as Millerand, 'Souvenirs;' Raoul Persil, *Alexandre Millerand (1859–1943)* (Paris: Société d'éditions françaises et internationales, 1949), pp. 11–12; Jules Basdevant, 'Notice sur la vie et les travaux de Alexandre Millerand,' *Publications de l'Institut de France* (Paris, 28 November 1955), p. 3.
2. Millerand, 'Souvenirs,' pp. 22–4; Paul A. Gagnon, *France since 1789* (New York: Harper & Row Publishers, 1972), pp. 239–43: the death of the Bourbon

deputy, Millerand. Though both Radicals, Millerand and the new war minister were soon separated by an unbridgeable gap. Indeed, Boulangism not only divided Millerand and Clemenceau but prompted the former's departure from the Radical party and postponed his move toward socialism. While Millerand did not officially break with his former patron until 1889, he quickly perceived the potential danger posed by the new war minister's anti-republican tendencies. Always hostile to dictatorship, Millerand later recalled his apprehension at the spectacle he witnessed at one of the war minister's evening receptions. He denounced the specter of dictatorship which the crowd's response to Boulanger's demagogy raised. Overwhelming popular adulation of Boulanger, reminiscent of Bonapartism, at the Longchamps review of 14 July 1886 made the dashing blond general on his famous black horse into a hero later memorialized in laudatory songs and poems. To Millerand, this idol of a new national movement rehabilitating the French army threatened his beloved republican system. He and his fellow Seine deputy Jean Marie de Lanessan organized what he later described as the first French anti-Boulangist meeting at Chalon-sur-Saône in late 1886.[3] With Boulanger still Minister of War, however, and supported by most Radicals, Millerand's stance separated him from his party.

The new legislature, worried about a possible conservative revival after the Right's strong electoral performance, voted to expel from France members of the former ruling houses and to forbid them to serve in its military forces. To eliminate royalist and clerical influences from the army and to win Radical approval, Boulanger went further and forcibly retired his former superior, the Orleanist Duc d'Aumale. At the same time, he sought rank-and-file army support with improvements, long in preparation, of daily military life, such as food, clothing, and housing, and restored morale with martial music and colorful parades – reforms similar to Millerand's of 1912 but done in Boulanger's more flamboyant style.[4]

pretender the Comte de Chambord in 1883 had allowed the monarchists to unite; Derfler, *Millerand*, pp. 21–4; Alfred Cobban, *A History of Modern France* (Baltimore, Maryland: Penguin Books, 1967), III, pp. 31–2. François Goguel, *La Politique des partis sous la IIIe République* (Paris: Editions du Seuil, 1946), pp. 58–60, gives the election results as 201 Conservatives to 383 Republicans.

   3. Millerand, 'Souvenirs,' pp. 26–7; Derfler, *Millerand*, p. 38.

   4. Gagnon, pp. 242–3; D.W. Brogan, *The Development of Modern France,*

While the government moved forcefully to avert a monarchist restoration, it had still not made its peace with the Left. The general amnesty granted the Communards in 1879 and 1881 left a few extremists in prison. Millerand's maiden speech to the Chamber of Deputies of 6 February 1886 urged an extension of that pardon to the remaining prisoners. To Millerand, it was a measure of clemency and appeasement that satisfied the official objective of democratic reform. Continued punishment, which rural groups supported, jeopardized republican unity because urban forces opposed it.[5]

In January 1886, shortly after Millerand became a deputy, coal miners in Decazeville went on strike. Millerand's sympathy for the Decazeville workers brought him into opposition to the government. The use of government troops in the Decazeville and later Vierzon strikes of 1886 undoubtedly fueled Millerand's hostility since it smacked too much of Second Empire procedures. Asserting his attachment to the common people, Boulanger nonetheless opted for order in crises like Decazeville and denied Socialist charges that the army had attacked the miners. While Millerand did not specifically tie the military's action in industrial disputes to the war minister, acknowledging the general governmental nature of the decision, he still saw the general as standard-bearer for a policy harmful to those social groups he sought to protect.

Defense of freedom was Millerand's thesis in the Decazeville miners' strike, a libertarian position that often characterized his political stances. In Decazeville, a strike, triggered by salary cuts and compulsory use of the high-priced company store, led to violence against the management and use of troops to restore order. When journalists were arrested for articles that allegedly used news of the strike to provoke social unrest, the issue expanded from worker rights to freedom of the press. Defending all types of freedom from the press' liberty to publish strike reports to the right of assembly and finally to the freedom to strike, Millerand insisted on 10 April 1886 on the need to protect the workers' right to strike as well as their access to those capable of instructing them; they

1870–1939 (New York: Harper & Row, 1966), I, pp. 183–7; Cobban, III, pp. 32–3; Goguel, pp. 60–1; Gordon Wright, *France in Modern Times* (Chicago: Rand McNally, 1974), pp. 244–5; Theodore Zeldin, *France, 1848–1945*, (Oxford: Clarendon Press, 1973), I, pp. 641–5.

5. *Journal officiel de la République française, Débats parlementaires, Chambre des Députés*, 6 February 1886, hereafter cited as J.O., *Chambre*; Derfler, *Millerand*, pp. 26–7.

must not be isolated by barriers (*cordon sanitaire*) from their more knowledgeable compatriots. To Millerand, the Great Revolution's ideal of liberty justified not only workers' rights to protest against unjust treatment but also society's to information. Although sympathetic to the situation causing the agitation, he focused on freedom rather than social justice. Nonetheless, his opposition to governmental action influenced his adherence to a worker group (*groupe ouvrier*) in the Chamber. His official alignment with socialism did not follow this first formal step for another five years.[6]

Millerand, who always opposed violence whether by the authorities or the workers, wanted official neutrality in conflicts between labor and capital. He particularly disliked the use of troops to maintain order; military intervention, generally beneficial to management, elevated the level of violence. On 18 October 1886, Millerand claimed that the presence of troops in Vierzon on 5 October had caused unnecessary bloodshed since the crowds, sympathetic to the strikers protesting against the company's arbitrary dismissal of their colleagues and reduction of the work day, had in turn become violent. Indeed, the state's intervention, arresting those counselling moderation and increasing the violence it sought to forestall, had been clumsy.[7]

Boulanger's chauvinistic patriotism was provoking alarm across the Rhine. In January 1887, Chancellor Bismarck justified a larger military budget by citing the threat of 'General *Revanche*'. In April, Boulanger's demand for a partial mobilization and an ultimatum in response to Germany's arrest of French customs' official Schnaebele, supposedly within French territory, hampered the government's effort to settle the issue peacefully. Frightened by Boulanger's chauvinism, the Opportunists sought his resignation. When the cabinet fell in May 1887, a new Right–Center combination led by financier Maurice Rouvier replaced it. The moderates, abandoning their alliance with the Radicals, turned back to the Right, and Boulanger left Paris to assume a provincial command in Clermont-Ferrand.[8] On 31 May, Millerand attacked the new government, arguing that its rightist support would jeopardize its republican

---

6. J.O., *Chambre*, 10 April 1886; A. Zévaès, *Histoire de la IIIe République, 4 septembre 1870–21 octobre 1945* (Paris: Editions de la Nouvelle Revue Critique, 1946), p. 160; Derfler, *Millerand*, pp. 27–9.

7. J.O., *Chambre*, 18 October 1886; Derfler, *Millerand*, pp. 30–1.

8. Goguel, pp. 61–2; Brogan, I, pp. 189–90; Gagnon, pp. 243–4; Wright, *France*, p. 245.

commitment. The absence of any leftists proclaimed its limited appeal. He pleaded for a focus on economic and social reforms, not risky colonial adventures.[9]

The autumn and winter of 1887–8 witnessed both the growth of Boulangism and the revelation of republican corruption – phenomena which were undoubtedly linked. The sordid Wilson scandal over Legion of Honor decorations brought graft and greed to the doors of the Elysée through the person of President Jules Grévy's son-in-law, the deputy Daniel Wilson. It eventually triggered Grévy's own resignation in December 1887 and the collapse of Rouvier's government under attack from both Radicals and Conservatives. Millerand supported Clemenceau's denunciation of Grévy and his obstruction of Jules Ferry as the next premier. For Millerand, Ferry, the man responsible for the Tonkin disaster, was as dangerous as Boulanger, even though he later apologized for the insulting slogan of 'neither Boulanger nor Ferry'.

Disenchantment with republican morals probably contributed to the contemporaneous growth of Boulangism. However, Millerand and some Radicals disliked Clemenceau's continued support for the general. The Right also viewed him as an anti-republican weapon. Although his military status made it illegal for him to hold political office, supporters still entered his name in by-elections. When he won, he resigned the seat. An unofficial, piecemeal, national Bonapartist-type plebiscite was launched. It accelerated in 1888 after the government retired him from the army, thereby legitimizing his political campaign.[10]

As a deputy, Millerand could not ignore national crises like the Wilson scandal and Boulangism, but he still spent much time on less flamboyant matters. As a reporter on prison administration for the Chamber's budget commission, he analyzed the role of places of punishment in national life. To him, their goal should be education as much as repression in order to allow criminals to return to normal society. Since the vast majority of condemned prisoners were illiterate or barely educated (only 8 percent had completed a primary education), he blamed their crimes generally on misery or ignorance. Even though some hardened criminals were beyond redemption, the low level of schooling meant that the

9. J.O., *Chambre*, 31 May 1887; Derfler, *Millerand*, p. 31.
10. Millerand, 'Souvenirs,' pp. 23, 28; Derfler, *Millerand*, p. 31; Brogan, I, pp. 192–9; Gagnon, pp. 244–5; Goguel, pp. 62–3; Frederic H. Seager, *The Boulanger Affair* (Ithaca: Cornell University Press, 1969), pp. 58, 130.

penal system should seek social reparation through education. If the criminal were to rejoin society a better person than he left it, he must gradually adapt to the outside world. Opposed to both segregation into individual cells and the more drastic option of deportation, Millerand considered isolation suitable for monks but not citizens, and the overseas penal colonies an even greater obstacle to the desired transformation. He wanted criminals gradually reintegrated through a secular educational program that included a moral dimension. His humanitarian concern for society's underdogs, the underprivileged of the mines and factories or the poor, uneducated criminals in the prisons reflected also an optimism about legislative reform from above and educational redemption from below.[11]

While Millerand advocated official neutrality in industrial conflicts, particularly avoidance of military repression, he wanted the state to intervene for better industrial working conditions. Less contradictory than it seemed, this position illustrated his sympathy toward the poor and suspicion of the rich. His dislike of force in labor disputes applied to government troops in quelling strikes or workers demanding changes. He always wanted social reforms instituted legally. Discussing a law designed to regulate industrial working conditions for women and children, he maintained that freedom of contract had not granted workers true equality in industrial negotiations. Since workers faced unemployment in reprisal for strikes or union membership, an unequal bargaining relationship required state intervention. 'What have you done? You have made instruction free and obligatory, you have taught the worker to think, to conceive of an ideal which yesterday he could not have perceived, and you do not understand that as you raise him above his condition and enlighten him with a higher ideal, you make his actual condition even more unfortunate.' To Millerand, the Republic's intellectual and moral elevation of the working class through education gave it a concomitant responsibility to supply the leisure for intellectual activities and performance of civic duties. A reduced work day, which would alleviate the degeneracy inflicted on France's citizens by overly long factory hours, would not, he argued, lead to socialism. Rather, it reflected the spirit of

11. Archives Nationales de France, C5381, Chamber, Budget Commission for 1888, 12 October 1887, hereafter cited as A.N.; J.O., *Chambre*, 25 February 1888; Derfler, *Millerand*, p. 32; Gordon Wright, *Between the Guillotine and Liberty* (New York: Oxford University Press, 1983), pp. 143, 146.

the Revolution's Declaration of the Rights of Man with its advocacy of spiritual freedom. The reform, which would redound to the Republic's credit, was thus an act of both social justice and patriotic foresight.[12]

By late 1888, General Boulanger's mounting popularity made a *coup d'état* genuinely possible, and Boulangism a central political concern. The stunning electoral success of the general's plebiscitary strategy, notably in the north, linked the Republic's enemies of the Left and the Right, the so-called *politique du pire*. Hatred of the Republic made odd bedfellows of Royalists and Socialists who hoped Boulanger could precipitate its demise. Despite Boulanger's erratic behavior, he continued to win by-elections; the Republic's doom appeared as certain as his victory. The climax came with his dramatic success in the Paris election of 27 January 1889, but he was reluctant to launch the *coup d'état* which would have secured his dictatorship. Instead, he waited for an overwhelming victory in the September legislative elections to give him the position legally. In fact, that January night represented his movement's peak, for rumors that he faced a trial for treason led him to flee to Belgium in April, and Boulangism quickly collapsed.[13]

Fears of a march on the Elysée and a scarcely survived Bonapartist threat led France's legislators to replace the *scrutin de liste* electoral system with the single-member constituency *scrutin d'arrondissement*. No future Boulanger should be able to capitalize on multiple candidacies or department level support to threaten the republican system. Even though he was an early and persistent foe of Boulanger, Millerand held the *scrutin d'arrondissement* in great contempt. It encouraged, he charged, those 'stagnant ponds' which were the 'fatal instrument of corruption,' and would surely betray its supporters' expectations. A list voting system, on the other hand, permitted voters to perceive such larger currents as the linkage between Boulangists and reactionaries. However, for his colleagues, a general fear of Boulanger and comparable dictatorial threats far outweighed anxiety about future corruption. Millerand's opposition could not prevent reinstitution of the old electoral system. Indeed, he soon had to find a constituency for himself.[14]

12. J.O., *Chambre*, 14 June 1888.
13. Millerand, 'Souvenirs,' p. 27; Brogan, I, pp. 199–207; Gagnon, pp. 245–6; Goguel, pp. 64–5; Seager, pp. 197–8.
14. Millerand, 'Souvenirs,' pp. 25, 28; J.O., *Chambre*, 11 February 1889; Derfler, *Millerand*, pp. 41–2; Brogan, I, p. 208.

Millerand's fears of dictatorship did not outweigh his reservations about manipulating the law so that the general's supporters could be tried. The struggle between the 'republican party' and a Boulangist-reactionary faction forced republicans to obey their guiding principles, not to adopt their adversaries' tactics. If they prosecuted Paul Déroulède's League of Patriots for supporting Boulanger they would have to use outdated penal code provisions that they had consistently opposed. Fidelity to its own past, notably a respect for principles, required the republican party not to pervert the law for political ends.[15]

Nonetheless, Millerand remained as strongly hostile to Boulanger as ever. His stance influenced his formal break with Clemenceau and other Radicals and his separation from those Socialists who used the general as a weapon against the governing Opportunists. Millerand faulted Clemenceau both for giving Boulanger an opportunity to gain power and for long failing to recognize the danger. Yet, when Clemenceau and many Radicals abandoned Boulangism in spring 1889 and joined the republican counterattack against Déroulède's League, Millerand castigated their arbitrariness. He thus broke with his former Radical colleagues over their anti-Boulangist tactics and their support for the Opportunists on the electoral system, but he held back from his future Socialist allies because of their support for Boulanger. The Boulangist episode therefore both delayed Millerand's adherence to socialism and illustrated traits that would characterize his entire political career – an independence from partisan politics and a commitment to principles at the expense of friendship and personal advancement.[16]

Millerand's anti-Boulangist speech in Mâcon on 11 May 1889 confirmed the breach with Clemenceau. Despite Boulanger's flight to Brussels on 1 April, it was not yet clear that the Boulangist menace was over. It took the Boulangist legislative defeat in September to demonstrate that fact. In May, therefore, the issue still seemed to be of vital interest. The forthcoming legislative elections prompted Millerand to examine the republican party's position. Critical of Ferry's Tonkin legacy and the recently restored *scrutin d'arrondissement*, he pleaded for more fundamental reforms

15. J.O., *Chambre*, 2 and 14 March 1889.
16. Millerand, 'Souvenirs,' p. 28; Derfler, *Millerand*, pp. 42–4; Leslie Derfler, *President and Parliament. A Short History of the French Presidency* (Boca Raton, Florida: University Presses of Florida, 1983), pp. 52, 103.

instead of simply reviving the old alliance with the Opportunists – a positive response to Boulangism and reactionism. Politically, he urged constitutional revisions to reorganize the judiciary and separate church and state – logical consequences of freedom of conscience and educational neutrality. Political reforms, however, were only a prelude to social changes designed to give a more enlightened and free citizenry a larger share of the national wealth. Among desirable social reforms, Millerand gave priority to a more just allocation of the tax burden – workers and farmers should pay according to their means and be spared taxes that left them with too few resources to provide for their families' essential comforts. Furthermore, the state should provide insurance for the sick and aged to shield the small and weak. While such revolutionary social reforms required political support, Millerand repudiated revolutionary or dictatorial methods. If the government peacefully introduced a reform program to improve the lot of workers and peasants, a revolution would be unnecessary. At Mâcon, therefore, Millerand outlined his tactics and goals for the next decade.[17]

Millerand consistently defended society's small and disadvantaged members. He urged the government to intervene and grant the 'wrongly-imprisoned' strikers in Decazeville an amnesty that would restore their civic rights as well as their physical freedom. On another occasion, he praised the government for guarding the small and weak against the potentially disastrous copper crisis, but insisted on prohibiting such speculations by large and powerful forces in the future. In that instance, the small artisan or worker who invested his hard-earned savings in the seemingly secure Comptoir d'Escompte, found himself penniless. To Millerand, such scandals required the government to insure that large companies not evade punishment for their misdeeds. The principle of equality before the law imposed on the government a duty to terminate privilege in France.[18]

A description of the thirty-year-old Millerand predicted that he would be one of the great personalities of the future. A man of medium build, he had an assured, vigorous manner, a penetrating

---

17. Archives Nationales, 470 Archives Privées, Fonds Millerand XI, Millerand's speech of 11 May 1889 in Mâcon, published in *La Justice*, 13 May 1889, including a letter from Millerand to Clemenceau of 11 May accepting the latter's decision not to publish those portions of the speech reflecting policy differences with Clemenceau, hereafter cited as A.N., F.M.; Derfler, *Millerand*, pp. 44–5.

18. J.O., *Chambre*, 9 March 1889; J.O., *Chambre*, 21 March and 24 May 1889.

regard, and a mocking smile, although his generally serious expression was almost severe. Already considered an eloquent speaker, his style was notably dispassionate and rational. His precise, severe, correct manner accompanied a keen evaluation of men and events. It is striking that a young deputy after only four years of national political experience had already achieved recognition and that his personal and professional traits were so clearly delineated.[19]

Forced by the new electoral system to select a constituency for the elections of 1889, Millerand chose the first district of the twelfth Parisian *arrondissement*, a poor area encompassing the furniture shops of the Faubourg Saint-Antoine and the wine merchants of Bercy, partly because of its resistance to the Boulangist appeal and partly because of family connections in the area. Lacking a party affiliation because of his break with the Radicals over Boulangism, he designated himself a 'republican socialist' for the 1889 elections but had no established party's endorsement. To his new constituents, Millerand stressed his legislative experience and defended his two fundamental goals: political freedom that gave citizens the right to speak, vote, think and publish counterbalanced by peaceful intervention to insure social justice. To him, universal suffrage and a recourse to violence were contradictory. Victorious in the run-off election of October 1889, Millerand returned to the Chamber as representative of the district that would support him consistently until 1920. The political composition of the new legislature was remarkably similar to its predecessor, despite the Boulanger and Wilson crises, but the Radicals were sufficiently discredited by their flirtation with Boulanger to enable the Opportunists to govern almost without interference for another decade.[20]

The legislative session of 1889–93 marked a significant political change for Millerand as he formally adopted socialism. Although he had termed himself a 'republican socialist' in the electoral campaign, the term denoted a commitment to republican and socialist principles, not a political affiliation. He also continued to support programs he had previously endorsed: constitutional revision, laicity, defense of the poor, workers' rights, opposition to privilege

---

19. A.N., F.M. XI, article on Millerand by Henry du Basty, *Revue d'histoire contemporaine*, 20 January 1889.

20. Millerand, 'Souvenirs,' pp. 28–9; Persil, p. 12; Derfler, *Millerand*, pp. 48–9.

and corruption. Although officially an independent, Millerand wavered neither in his commitment to the Republic nor in pressures for a unified republican party transcending partisan divisions. Urging a reformist program favoring the small and weak while progressively eroding the privileges of the wealthy, he demanded specifically an end to the Bank of France's special privileges and a tax reform that did not increase indirect contributions.[21] He also opposed tariffs, specifically wine and wood taxes that affected his constituents. Although he was clearly protecting his electorate's needs, his opposition to internal taxes on cheap wines derived from dried raisins reflected his conviction that such taxes harmed the working class that consumed large quantities of the less expensive beverage and benefited the large southern wine producers. They thereby accentuated the distinctions that the legislature should eradicate. To Millerand, a republican body could not augment the workers' already heavy charges. Yet, Millerand had to fight throughout the decade for his Bercy wine merchants against the large southern producers.[22]

More broadly, a nationalistic concern for French economic prosperity led Millerand to reject tariffs as harmful to French industry. Several times in 1891, he denounced French import tariffs. A tax on imported wood would raise prices in the construction and furniture industries that used imports and thus make French exports more expensive and less competitive. While penalizing French workers and consumers, the tariff would invite reprisals. Likewise, a tariff designed to exclude inexpensive Spanish wines might encourage comparable foreign duties that would hurt a major French export industry. Finally, he argued that a tariff on imported silk would increase production costs, make the finished French product less competitive in world markets, and create unemployment at home.[23]

Millerand always demanded a secular state which guaranteed freedom of conscience and expression. A strong supporter of secular education, Millerand had urged the elimination of religious

21. J.O., *Chambre*, 19 November 1889; Derfler, *Millerand*, pp. 56–7.

22. J.O., *Chambre*, 24 March 1890; J.O., *Chambre*, 24 June 1890; Derfler, *Millerand*, pp. 52–3; A.N., C5381, Chamber, Budget Commission for 1888, 8 April and 9 May 1887: already in 1887 before representing the Bercy district he had urged governmental economies and a tax reform not based on higher personal property and alcohol taxes.

23. J.O., *Chambre*, 23 June 1891; J.O., *Chambre*, 2 July 1891; J.O., *Chambre*, 16 July 1891.

instruction from secondary schools (the *lycées*) in 1887 arguing that they, like the primary schools, should be the exclusive refuge (*asile*) of science and closed to all dogmas and clerics.[24] In 1890, he opposed an amendment to the laws of 1880 and 1884 governing property of the religious orders, but his first concern was with the broader issue of governmental religious policy. To Millerand, the principles of a secular state and equality before the law logically led to separation of church and state in the schools and military conscription that made all citizens liable to pay a 'blood tax.' Perceiving military service as both a school for patriotism and a lesson in social diversity, he had rejected special dispensations for students at the Ecole Normale Supérieure in 1887.[25] Despite the defeat of the clerical party, the government had applied the law on 'congregations' so leniently that the banned religious orders had gradually returned to France. While the right of association was a fundamental freedom, along with freedom of conscience, it required legislative regulation to insure that wealthy religious orders did not benefit from special privileges that harmed all citizens' equal rights.[26] Furthermore, Millerand rejected censorship as an infringement of freedom of expression. The controversial subject of Edmond de Goncourt's play *La Fille Elisa* did not justify limiting that vital liberty. Millerand's sympathy for the play's social criticism of poverty and prostitution in comparison to frivolous tales of the salon world probably influenced his general opposition to official interference with free expression.[27]

During the 1889–93 legislature, Millerand focused on social issues, especially the use of force in domestic incidents and workers' political rights. Industrial labor unrest culminated in two episodes, the fusillade of Fourmies of 1891 and the Carmaux strike of 1892 that officially converted Millerand to socialism. At Fourmies, a northern textile area suffering economic difficulties and labor unrest, workers had assembled to express grievances and press for social reforms. Troops were brought in to preserve order. Pressed by the hostile crowds, they fired into the assemblage, killing several demonstrators. In a heated session on 4 May 1891, the Chamber of Deputies debated responses to such demonstrations. Millerand opposed the use of force in domestic disputes, as

24. J.O., *Chambre*, 25 January 1887; Derfler, *Millerand*, p. 31.
25. J.O., *Chambre*, 28 June 1887.
26. J.O., *Chambre*, 8 December 1890.
27. J.O., *Chambre*, 24 January 1891.

he had five years earlier in Decazeville and Vierzon. The army, he maintained, should be used only when absolutely necessary; every precaution should be taken to avoid arousing the public. While the army's involvement was most disastrous in Fourmies, unfortunate incidents also occurred in Lyons, Marseilles, and elsewhere. A less visible military presence, Millerand argued, might have produced less tragic results. Other nations handled such demonstrations less violently. Indeed, the legitimate demands of French workers for social reforms did not include violent means to achieve them. He discounted the role of anarchist agitators. 'What attitude is the government going to adopt? Is it an enemy or an ally? If the Republic exists and has endured, it is only because of these millions of workers from the factories, mines, and fields who today expect the social reforms to which they have a right. You make promises but you eradicate them with a policy of repression.' Millerand insisted that the government must reassure them by punishing those responsible for the deaths at Fourmies. The Chamber authorized some financial compensation to the victims and their families, but refused to set up a commission of inquiry.[28]

The Fourmies incident involved Millerand as both a lawyer and a legislator. The Marxist Paul Lafargue, charged with inciting disorder by his speech in April, asked Millerand to use the defense that he was a scientist convinced of capitalism's inevitable demise, and not a mob agitator. Millerand agreed, but did not convince the jury that a guilty verdict would simply buttress the socialism they feared. Lafargue was sentenced to a year in prison, but the issue revived in the autumn when he agreed to run as a Socialist for the Chamber to fill a vacancy due to the death of a deputy from Lille. On 31 October, Millerand urged his colleagues, as a measure of appeasement to implement ministerial promises of peace and eradicate memories of the bloody repression, to release Lafargue to campaign for the seat. Indeed, a refusal could be viewed as a declaration of war against republican socialism. If the route to peaceful pursuit of legitimate worker demands were closed by a ban on their candidate, they might, in exasperation, turn to revolutionary tactics. His pleas failed to sway the Chamber, but an active campaign by Guesdists, a barrage of pamphlets from Lafargue, and speeches by independents like Millerand won Lafargue's election to the Chamber on 8 November, and his release from prison the

28. J.O., *Chambre*, 4 May 1891; Derfler, *Millerand*, pp. 58–9.

following day. Although he described himself as a republican socialist for the 1889 elections and had earlier joined a worker group in the Chamber, Millerand's public support for Lafargue's candidacy marked his formal adherence to socialism – a gradual evolution, however, not a dramatic conversion. He continued, nonetheless, to defend an evolutionary route to social reform, especially the election of Socialists and passage of laws, within a republican context.[29]

At Calais on 13 March 1892, Millerand first defined the republican socialist principles that he accepted and the actions they implied. Independent of any formal group, he would seek social reform through legislation. Since the government had an obligation to assure all citizens of the greatest possible freedom and happiness, it must investigate relations between labor and capital and existing working conditions as a first step to reform. Mechanization and capital accumulation during the nineteenth century, which had undermined individual ownership and divided owners and workers, dehumanized the latter and threatened important human relationships such as the family. The machine should take the worker's labor, but pay him well enough for scientific progress to foster happiness, not misery. While the working class needed organization, its principal tools were education and suffrage, not violence. A legal, peaceful revolution must use universal suffrage to achieve the workers' program of social reform; a peaceful victory at the ballot-box alone could demonstrate their ability to manage affairs. Anxious for a Socialist party accessible to all who accepted its beliefs, notably intellectuals, bourgeois professionals, and the dispossessed lower middle class as well as workers, Millerand did not consider socialism the exclusive preserve of the industrial proletariat. He was, however, determined to exclude those privileged groups, notably the Catholic Church, which threatened the freedom of the underprivileged. Above all, social equality should complete political equality.[30]

Since workers had the same political rights as their employers, Millerand wanted them truly observed. For example, he argued

29. J.O., *Chambre*, 31 October 1891; J.O., *Chambre*, 9 November 1891; Derfler, *Millerand*, pp. 60–1; Alexandre Zévaès, *Ombres et silhouettes. Notes et souvenirs d'un militant* (Paris: Editions Georges-Anquetil, 1928), pp. 175–7; Claude Willard, *Les Guesdistes. Le mouvement socialiste en France, 1893–1905* (Paris: Editions sociales, 1965), pp. 88–9.

30. Alexandre Millerand, *Deux discours* (Paris: Librairie Marcel Giard, 1923) speech at Calais, 13 March 1892; Derfler, *Millerand*, pp. 62–4.

that a railroad worker, who was a candidate in a Parisian municipal election, should not have to choose between his job and a political position unless the latter interfered with the former. A company ultimatum interfered with the equal exercise of rights by all citizens. The Republic, therefore, had to shield the weak from the capricious, arbitrary behavior of the powerful.[31]

Since union activity potentially threatened capitalist control more than political representation, workers' syndical rights were particularly controversial. Although the law of 1884 permitted workers to join unions, membership was often an excuse for firing. To Millerand, freedom of association equalled freedom of conscience or the right to vote in importance. Unions were a source of education and professional emancipation for the workers, whose elimination would jeopardize social peace by seeming to close the door to change. Like their wealthy employers, workers should be free to organize without having to choose between their material existence and their legal rights. They should also be able to attend union congresses, even if they lost work time thereby. His libertarian approach undoubtedly prompted Millerand's efforts to transform legally guaranteed freedoms into reality, but he was also convinced that a legal, peaceful route to social reform had to be kept open if violent conflict were to be avoided. His support for the right to unionize reflected both his liberalism and his socialism.[32]

Millerand's bitter castigation of society's privileged élites matched his vehement defense of its underdogs. His opposition to renewing the Bank of France's privileges, originally granted in 1803, illustrated his view that the banking system should serve the whole nation and not just its wealthy segment. At issue was the Bank's right to print paper money which, in Millerand's opinion, permitted it to control France's commerce and industry, thereby exercising a pernicious (*néfaste*) influence. He pressed for a national bank instead of a private corporation to control the supply of money. He reiterated his charges in 1897 during the vote on the renewal of the Bank's privileges. To Millerand, opposition to the Bank of France constituted a Socialist victory in 1892 by forcing the Bank to renew its appeal to the new legislature.[33]

A miners' strike in Carmaux (Tarn) in 1892 permitted Millerand

31. J.O., *Chambre*, 13 May 1890.
32. J.O., *Chambre*, 22 March 1892 and 28 May 1892.
33. J.O., *Chambre*, 21 June 1892; Derfler, *Millerand*, pp. 67–8; *La Petite République*, 4 January 1893, article by Millerand, 'Notre bilan.'

to reiterate the view of a worker's right to hold both a job and political office that he had addressed in 1890. The Carmaux strike was declared in sympathy for the miner Calvignac, whose election as a municipal councillor and subsequently as mayor of Carmaux prompted the company to deny him time for his public duties and ultimately to fire him. Other workers, unsuccessfully defended by Socialist lawyers Millerand and René Viviani, received prison sentences for using force toward company officials. On 18 October, Millerand defined universal suffrage as the issue in Carmaux, claiming that Calvignac lost his job because he defeated the company's official candidate in the municipal elections. The company had exceeded its prerogatives in letting political considerations affect labor decisions. The government must, Millerand argued, counteract such financial feudalism so that economic power did not control the political system.[34]

Millerand blamed the company for prolonging the strike to give it an excuse to punish enterprising workers. His proposal for a governmental seizure of the mines encouraged Director Baron Reille's acceptance of Premier Loubet's arbitration. The verdict of late October was a compromise: the strikers, except those charged with violence, were pardoned and reemployed by the company; Calvignac received a leave of absence to perform his political functions; the company manager retained his post. The result was termed a victory for labor, although neither side was truly satisfied.[35]

The mine-workers scored a political victory of national importance when Jean Jaurès defeated the conservative deputy, the Marquis Jerome de Solages, with family connections to the mine-owners, in the legislative elections of 1893. To Millerand, the Carmaux strike held greater significance than the favorable settlement of the specific dispute. The strikers achieved their goals, the struggle unified the Socialists, and republican France generally backed the workers' political position. He considered it the first example of a political strike whose peaceful, orderly progress eventually defeated those capitalists who wanted to limit workers' political independence. Millerand interpreted Jaurès' election as the final

34. J.O., *Chambre*, 18 October 1892.

35. Jack D. Ellis, *The Early Life of Georges Clemenceau, 1841–1893* (Lawrence, Kansas: The Regents Press of Kansas, 1980), p. 168; Harvey Goldberg, *The Life of Jean Jaurès* (Madison: University of Wisconsin Press, 1962), pp. 104–5; Derfler, *Millerand*, pp. 64–7.

step in that victory. The developments of Carmaux, as well as the earlier municipal electoral success that gave Socialists control of numerous town halls and councils, proved to him France's readiness for socialism.[36]

In late 1892, the simmering crisis stemming from the desperate financial plight of the Panama Canal Company reached a climax with that organization's bankruptcy and revelation of shady operations. Launched in 1880 to dig a canal through the isthmus of Panama, the company initially attracted both money and attention because of its leader's reputation, the builder of the Suez Canal, Ferdinand de Lesseps. Local mismanagement and faulty engineering so augmented costs that the government authorized a lottery in 1888 to salvage the dying enterprise. Increasingly desperate efforts sought to conceal the problems and locate funds, but the loans were inadequate to avert bankruptcy or the ruin of thousands of small French investors. Evidence of the bribery of politicians brought the crisis to the doors of parliament, touching government ministers and prominent figures like Clemenceau. Although the parliamentary investigation and judicial procedures produced few convictions, the episode created a furor among French politicians.[37]

Millerand joined the attack against capitalist corruption epitomized by the Panama scandal. On 16 February 1893, he demanded that universal suffrage pass judgement on governmental behavior in the upcoming elections. He refused either to exonerate the government for its actions in the affair or give it a vote of confidence for the future. The Panama scandal proved how much corruption had infiltrated the government, police, judiciary, and financial worlds. Republicans must find ways to combat the church and high finance. How much longer, he wondered, would they have to wait for that separation of church and state so necessary for a genuine freedom of conscience? Even more important to resolve were those vital social questions that attracted peasants and workers to socialism. Indeed, the vices of capitalism, dramatized by disasters like the Panama débâcle, had attracted even small businessmen to socialism. To achieve their eventual goals, the Socialists first had to attack high finance, whose domination of public affairs stemmed

36. *La Petite République*, 4 January 1893, article by Millerand, 'Notre bilan.'
37. Wright, *France*, pp. 250–1; Goguel, pp. 69–71; Brogan, I, pp. 268–85; Gagnon, pp. 247–9.

from governmental weakness and complicity. Specifically, he urged nationalization of the Bank of France, the mines, and the railroads. He perceived two possible routes: a pragmatic republican alliance or a theoretical idealistic program. An alliance of republican factions often shielded the system's supporters because national representatives won power by using their personal influence to pacify the diverse factions. To Millerand, only a program of well-defined principles could combat this deplorably corrupt multi-party system. Republicanism's victory in France stemmed from its loyalty to the great revolutionary ideals of fraternity, liberty, and justice. The nature of the system was not at stake, he maintained, merely some of its personnel. Commitment to republican ideals must be reaffirmed so that workers and peasants could see the Republic as a symbol of emancipation unsoiled by the corruption around it. Millerand considered the bourgeoisie of 1893, the political leaders of the preceding fifteen years, similar to the nobility of the previous century, whose external respectability concealed internal corruption. Dedicated to giving the democratic republic a social dimension, he repudiated violent change in favor of the power of the vote, through which all citizens could promote that evolution permitting them to share in the ownership of the means of production.[38]

The national legislative elections of 1893 gave Millerand the opportunity to suggest electoral tactics and define political and social objectives. Convinced that a two-party system was essential to normal French public life, he wanted parties committed to the republican system. A conservative party that linked all groups seeking to preserve the existing economic state, including its vices and abuses, should face a progressive party that combined forces anxious for a fundamental, but peaceful, program of social and political reform. The latter party could include a Socialist organization expanded by disillusioned Boulangists and reform-minded Radicals. Thus far, change had been too slow; the discrepancy between theory and reality remained too great. For example, action on a law on industrial accidents had been postponed for more than a decade. The electoral system was partially to blame. Since deputies representing small districts were virtually sovereign for four years, they could ignore programs that they had been elected to pass into

38. J.O., *Chambre*, 16 February 1893; Derfler, *Millerand*, pp. 69–70; *La Petite République*, Millerand article, 'Entre deux mondes,' 15 March 1893.

law. Millerand, seeing petty interests obstructing the advancement of the public interest, concluded that constitutional as well as political reform was vital.[39]

Millerand, who worked to unify and strengthen the Socialists before the elections of 1893, undoubtedly contributed to their significantly larger political representation. When Socialists and Radicals agreed to an electoral collaboration, Millerand urged his colleagues to avoid divisive internecine quarrels. As he later recalled, the different Socialist factions had long fought each other. Unless all social reformers united, their views could not triumph. When he became editor of *La Petite République* during the summer of 1893, Millerand opened the journal to all shades of socialist opinion. He also helped found the Socialist Federation of the Seine in early 1893 and promoted the electoral coalition of Socialists, Radicals, and former Boulangists.[40]

The national elections for the Chamber of Deputies of 20 August and 3 September 1893 dealt a setback to the conservatives, preserved the moderate majority, and significantly increased socialist representation. Approximately fifty Socialists of various persuasions were elected to the new legislature, including Millerand, overwhelmingly returned by the 12th *arrondissement*, who emerged as a leading figure. As Millerand later recorded, the elections returned parliamentary veterans like himself, Jules Guesde, and Edouard Vaillant and promising newcomers like René Viviani and Marcel Sembat, with independent Socialists proving most successful. Although not formally unified, the Socialists became a significant political force for the first time in the 1893 legislature. Despite Clemenceau's defeat, the sordid revelations of parliamentary involvement with the Panama Company seemingly played little part.[41]

By 1893, Millerand, with eight years' experience as a deputy, had

39. Michel Offerlé, 'Les Socialistes et Paris, 1881–1900,' thèse en science politique, Université de Paris, I, 1979, pp. 255, 263, cites Millerand's article in *La Petite République*, 7 December 1892; *La Petite République*, 26 April 1893, article by Millerand, 'Tactique socialiste;' *La Petite République*, article by Millerand, 24 May 1893; A.N., F.M. 1, Millerand's speech to his electors prior to the elections of 1893.

40. Millerand, 'Souvenirs,' pp. 29–31; Persil, p. 13; Georges Lefranc, *Le Mouvement socialiste sous la Troisième République (1875–1940)* (Paris: Payot, 1963), p. 90; Zeev Sternhell, *Maurice Barrès et le nationalisme français* (Paris: Armand Colin, 1972), p. 189; Derfler, *Millerand*, p. 77.

41. Derfler, *Millerand*, pp. 82–3; Millerand, 'Souvenirs,' p. 32; Persil, p. 13; Goguel, pp. 71–2; Gagnon, pp. 248–9; Lefranc, *Le Mouvement socialiste*, pp. 91–2; Zévaès, *IIIe République*, p. 202.

completed the transition from radicalism to socialism. His different official affiliation, however, did not affect the consistency of his fundamental positions. A dedication to France and its republican system marked the 34-year-old parliamentarian as much as the 11-year-old boy. For the successful deputy, liberty was still a guiding principle as it had been for the young law student, whereas hostility to privilege, a concern for society's weak and underprivileged, motivated the Socialist leader as they had the Radical municipal councillor. Hatred of dictatorship, dedication to a republican democracy, patriotic devotion to France, love of freedom, and a commitment to social reform clearly delineated Millerand's basic views as he entered his third legislative session, and as they would for the remainder of his political career.

2
Progress to Socialist Leadership and Ministerial Candidacy

The years from 1893 to 1899 were crucial to Millerand's political career. He began his third legislative session as an acknowledged, but independent, Socialist with a legal and legislative record in industrial conflicts that had solidified his position with his Parisian electorate and won him national recognition. During that legislature, he not only emerged as the leader of parliamentary socialism but also helped forge Socialist unity behind a minimum common program. His new interest in foreign policy demonstrated a patriotism that thenceforth always characterized his socialism. By 1898, as leader of the parliamentary Socialists and a national figure, he was a logical choice for a cabinet position in the wake of the Dreyfus crisis. His progression from Socialist deputy to commerce minister testified both to the augmented political importance of socialism and to Millerand's own achievements.

Millerand's efforts to unify the diverse Socialist factions and formulate a common program were finally successful in 1896 when Socialists accepted his famous Saint-Mandé program. On 30 April 1894, he used a debate in the Chamber of Deputies on the government's attitude toward priests and religious propaganda to outline his reasons for endorsing socialism. Millerand agreed with clerical deputy Albert de Mun's charge that Socialist ideas and parliamentary representation were a menace, but only to de Mun's reactionary ideas. The Socialist party was a significant national force because its demands stemmed from a social situation in which mechanization and scientific progress had benefited economically an ever-smaller minority by depriving an ever-larger majority and forcing it into an increasingly miserable existence. That party would eventually win public power, not through revolution as the

reactionaries charged, but by the ballot-box. The Socialists' electoral success would make them reluctant to abandon the secure
route to social reform or let their enemies profit from the hazards of
violence. To Millerand, the validity of their ideas and the wisdom
of universal suffrage would eventually insure victory. Supporting
neither violence nor abolition of private property, the Socialists
simply wanted all workers to receive the fruits of their labor, not to
lose them to a privileged minority.[1]

Persistent social conflict did not persuade Millerand to opt for a
violent route to social reform, since legal methods had already
achieved much success. The Socialists' electoral victories had given
them significant representation in the Chamber, and their activities
outside parliament had aided strikers and the working class generally. To Millerand, greater Socialist influence reflected a degree of
unity. Lafargue's trial after the 'crime of Fourmies' and his election
to the legislature, which encouraged Socialists to bury their differences, contributed to the electoral success of 1893. All factions
agreed that a capitalism which pitted an ever-smaller and wealthier
plutocracy against an ever more miserable proletariat was doomed,
but recognized that the means of production must be gradually
transferred from the minority to the masses. Millerand insisted that
the Socialist party did not want to dispossess the small proprietor;
its targets were monopolies, primarily the mines, railroads, and
banks, and later large industries like the sugar refineries. This goal
of society's transformation was revolutionary, but its methods
were evolutionary, a gradual, legal change through unionization
and legislation. While capitalism was inevitably moving toward a
more egalitarian society, Socialists must foster a transformation
that completed the Radicals' program of political libertarianism
with economic justice. Millerand's endorsement of a collective
appropriation of the means of production was generally Marxist,
but his support for evolutionary means and legislative action deviated from orthodox Marxism.[2]

Millerand's efforts to define a common Socialist ideological
program were matched at the tactical level by trying to coalesce
opposition to the same foe. President of the Republic Sadi Carnot's
assassination at Lyons on 24 June 1894 by an Italian anarchist was

1. J.O., *Chambre*, 30 April 1894.
2. *La Revue socialiste*, July 1895, Millerand's speech of 28 June 1895, 'Evolution
socialiste,' to a group of collectivist students, pp. 1–13; Goguel, p. 101; Lefranc, *Le
Mouvement socialiste*, pp. 90–2.

the culmination of several years of anarchist violence. Earlier that year, after a bomb was thrown into the Chamber, parliament had passed several repressive security laws (*les lois scélérates*). While not condoning violence, Socialists bitterly denounced laws that restricted individual freedom and allowed judicial secrecy to violate the right of opposition. The Chamber's moderate majority, the Progressists, led by Premier Charles Dupuy and Chamber President Jean Casimir-Périer, played on the anarchist danger to pass the laws over Socialist and Radical opposition. To the Socialists, Casimir-Périer's election as president of the Republic after Carnot's assassination confirmed the anti-republicanism of the security laws. Scion of the millionaire Anzin mining family, Casimir-Périer epitomized the political and economic power that Socialists sought to undermine.[3]

Millerand and other Socialists viewed Casimir-Périer's election as a red flag and rejoiced when their constant attacks led to the new president's abrupt resignation within six months. In the *Petite République* of 5 July 1894, Millerand discussed Casimir-Périer's stated intent to use all constitutionally valid presidential prerogatives. Accountable only for high treason, the president refused to let his rights be misunderstood or restricted, thereby breaking with the apolitical presidential tradition. Denigrating him as a cudgel-bearer (*porteur du trique*), Millerand castigated him for serving as the agent for those hostile to social demands but hesitant about assuming leadership. Did they not have, he queried, a better candidate than the millionaire Anzin shareholder, beneficiary of generations of exploited miners? With the Elysée representing a policy and a will, those chosen by universal suffrage had a right and an obligation to pass judgement.[4]

Millerand, who continued to attack the president throughout the autumn, termed the choice of Casimir-Périer a challenge (*défi*) to democracy. He had accepted the position, Millerand charged, only to promote the conservative republican interests of a bourgeoisie responsible through its misdeeds and thefts for France's misery during the past century. Casimir-Périer, the living incarnation of those great legal bandits, who parasitically profited from the

3. Goguel, pp. 72–3; Brogan, I, pp. 301–3; Derfler, *Millerand*, pp. 84–6; Derfler, *President*, pp. 55–6; Gagnon, p. 255; Marcel Prelot, *L'Evolution politique du socialisme français, 1789–1934* (Paris: Editions Spes, 1939), p. 110.

4. *La Petite République*, article by Millerand, 'Politique personelle,' 5 July 1894; Derfler, *Millerand*, p. 86.

laborers' toil, was democracy's enemy, not its leader.[5]

The collapse of Dupuy's government finally led the frustrated Casimir-Périer to resign three days later, on 17 January 1895. To Millerand the resignation constituted a Socialist victory, as their charges of a personal presidential policy were gradually recognized to be valid. He considered it fortunate that Casimir-Périer's tenure ended without inflicting irreparable damage on the Republic.[6] The Socialists' victory did not, however, bring a more liberal replacement. The new president, Félix Faure, though less socially and economically distasteful to the Left and conforming to the image of a figure-head presidency, still represented the moderate tradition.

Premonitions of Socialist support for a reform-oriented cabinet came in November 1895 when Léon Bourgeois formed a Radical ministry backed by some Moderates, Radicals, and Socialists, with a program of income and inheritance taxes, workers' pensions, and arbitration procedures. As Millerand observed, Socialists, though loyal to their long-range objectives, would support the new ministry's pragmatic efforts to improve gradually existing conditions.[7]

Bourgeois's tenure was, however, short-lived; his government fell on 23 April 1896 because of conservative opposition, particularly in the Senate, to a graduated income tax with a maximum levy of 5 percent. Although Millerand strongly defended his Parisian constituents' interests, he considered that national concerns held final priority. In March 1896, for example, he supported his small proprietors against the burdensome tax proposals, rejecting a connection between voting rights and taxation that would deprive the poor, who paid no taxes, of their political rights. He also believed that the proposed revenue tax would primarily hurt large cities like Paris. Millerand's opposition to the fiscal proposals undoubtedly reflected a Parisian partisan stance, but he was ready to bury his reservations in the nation's interest. However, representatives of such diverse groups as large industrialists and small proprietors refused to accept official interference with their economic privacy. With the new premier, Jules Méline, considered to be a protégé of

5. *La Petite République*, article by Millerand, 'L'Ennemi,' 8 November 1894; Zévaès, *IIIᵉ République*, p. 207.

6. Derfler, *President*, pp. 56–7; Brogan, I, p. 303; Gagnon, p. 255; *La Petite République*, article by Millerand, 18 January 1895; *Revue socialiste*, July 1895, article by Millerand, 'Evolution socialiste,' of 28 June 1895, pp. 1–13; Derfler, *Millerand*, pp. 86–7.

7. J.O., *Chambre*, 18 November 1895; Gagnon, p. 255; Derfler, *Millerand*, p. 97; Goguel, pp. 74–5.

the anti-republican Right, the Socialists returned to the opposition and the experiment in republican concentration ended.[8]

Although nationalistic considerations sometimes outweighed social concerns for Millerand, he did not blindly accept all measures supposedly required by national interests. For example, he rejected unsound financial procedures to cover larger military expenditures. Nor did France's need for a strong army exempt the military hierarchy from obedience to the Republic's laws, specifically that of 1844 prohibiting soldiers from joining any associations, religious or secular. He rebuked the war minister for not reprimanding officers for violating the law and subjecting their subordinates to religious proselytizing. Finally, considerations of France's power and prestige did not justify, in Millerand's opinion, a disregard for ethics. Specifically, he denounced French capitalists who used Algerian phosphate concessions to cheat local owners, and suggested state ownership as a way to control private greed and exploitation of colonial victims.[9]

Millerand's constant preoccupation through the 1890s remained working conditions and workers' rights. He wanted parliament to investigate France's economic and social conditions and pass reform legislation. For example, an explosion in the Montceau mine prompted him to urge the Chamber's labor commission to visit the mine and assess the dangers inherent in exploiting the subsoil. On 14 December 1893, he attacked the government for attributing strikes in the Pas de Calais and elsewhere solely to the mineworkers when other factors, like deteriorating economic conditions and company efforts to increase profits through lower wages, played a part. Efforts to suppress the unions discriminated against those workers who were totally loyal to the organizations. Instead of negotiating or arbitrating reasonable worker demands, the companies had called in government troops, with violence as the inevitable result and a virtual state of siege restricting the workers' freedom. To Millerand, the strike in the Pas de Calais, which had broader implications of basic social reform and not simply company–worker relations, required the republicans generally to take

8. J.O., *Chambre*, 26 March 1896; *ibid.*, 30 April 1896; Derfler, *Millerand*, pp. 98–9.
9. A.N., C5548, Chamber Budget Commission, 24 May 1895; J.O., *Chambre*, 20 May 1895; *ibid.*, 23 December 1895.

an interest and not to let it degenerate into a partisan issue. His pressures for an investigation, however, did not convince the moderate majority.[10]

Millerand continued to oppose the use of government troops in industrial conflicts. Unless the government remained officially neutral in labor disputes, it would appear to back the strong and wealthy against the weak and poor. During a glassworkers' strike at Carmaux (Tarn) in 1895, Millerand personally experienced official repression when, after a speech to the strikers, police interrupted his conversation with friends in front of the hotel. In Carmaux, a short suspension of work had been declared in sympathy for a worker that the company fired after his election to the municipal council. The factory remained closed, however, not because the workers would not return to work, but because the owner refused to re-open it until the workers accepted lower wages, an unjust penalty in view of the company's continued payment of a 7 percent dividend. Furthermore, the prefect of the Tarn's partisan stance compounded the problem when he lent official support to one side by trying to persuade the workers that the company's position was valid, and told neighboring communities of his attitude. Since the strikers had violated no law, the prefect should, Millerand believed, have remained neutral instead of illegally lending administrative, and subsequently judicial, support to the wealthier and stronger side. Indeed, the judicial confiscation of their treasury menaced the strikers with famine. Anxious for an end to acrimonious social conflicts, Millerand did not want parliament to seem to abandon the working class.

In fact, Millerand was part of the arbitration commission that in January 1896 chose Albi over Carmaux for a new glassworks, but labor unrest in the Tarn did not end. Indeed, the choice of Albi illustrated the priority that Millerand assigned to general interests over loyalty to friends. Carmaux deputy Jean Jaurès and local militants urged Carmaux, but Millerand thought Albi's better facilities and larger manpower supplies would make it more successful. He thus backed the engineers and technicians against his friends' pressures.[11]

Again in 1896, Millerand criticized the use of government troops

10. J.O., *Chambre*, 14 December 1893; Derfler, *Millerand*, p. 85; A.N. C5613², Chamber Labor Commission, 8 February 1895.
11. J.O., *Chambre*, 26 October 1895; Derfler, *Millerand*, pp. 87–9; Persil, pp. 17–18; Goldberg, pp. 141–3.

to quell labor unrest in Albi and Carmaux. He saw Jaurès' and other Socialist electoral victories as popular mandates, invalidating the government's argument that troops had dispersed crowds 'hostile' to the Socialists. When the police disrupted a meeting attended by Jaurès they not only violated the law of 1881 which guaranteed the right of assembly but used precisely those violent, illegal tactics blamed on the Socialists. Since they knew that violence served as a provocation for repression, as it had at Fourmies, the Socialists had conducted an orderly meeting. The legal route to winning public power had been too productive for them to abandon it.[12]

The Franco-Russian Entente, signed in stages between July 1891 and January 1894, transformed both France's diplomatic situation and its domestic political alignments. By mid-1893, partly because of German military increases, most obstacles to the pact had disappeared. In October, the enthusiastic reception of the Russian fleet at Toulon symbolized France's relief at the end to twenty years of diplomatic isolation. A governmental exchange of notes formally ratifying the military convention of August 1891 by-passed the French constitutional requirement for parliamentary ratification of treaties. Despite secrecy about precise commitments, the French public, and especially its political leaders, clearly knew the general implications.[13]

An alliance with autocratic Russia forced Socialists to assess the relative importance of patriotism and socialism. Did loyalty to their nation transcend commitment to social reforms? In his famous speech at the Socialist electoral victory banquet of the Grandes Carrières on 1 October 1893, Millerand specifically discussed the Franco-Russian alliance and the general relationship between nationalism and socialism. Arguing that the Entente was a major public issue on which Socialists could not avoid taking a stand, he supported an alliance which ended French isolation. 'French Socialists are patriots, profoundly patriotic, patriots by sentiment and by reason.' The sole criterion was national interest, specifically the nation's external security. Like their predecessors, who courageously fought Germany in 1870, all Socialist factions considered

12. J.O., *Chambre*, 5 November 1896.
13. Brogan, I, pp. 311–17; Wright, *France*, pp. 301–2.

France's survival a prerequisite for social progress. Since defeat in the Franco-Prussian war dominated recent French history, French Socialists bore different responsibilities from their German counterparts, however innocent the latter. A dismembered and conquered France could not initiate moves that delivered it up to the 'appetite of its implacable enemies.' With the nation always ready for war, Socialists had an 'imperative duty' to accept the double burden of obligatory military service and a heavy war budget at the same time as they scrutinized military outlays and urged a two-year service obligation. Signature of an entente, which created an equilibrium with the Triple Alliance, did not, however, diminish France's control over its own destiny or subordinate its policy to a foreign power. As Millerand asserted, 'common institutions are not a sufficient reason for common international action and a difference in regimes is not always an obstacle to cordial relations between two governments.' To him, therefore, national security interests forced France to sign a defensive alliance that served as a mutual insurance policy with equal rights for both parties. Acceptance of this position by other Socialists testified to the dominance of reformism in the 1890s.[14]

Millerand's support for the Franco-Russian alliance as a counterweight to the German menace did not, however, encompass damage to national interests in order to satisfy France's ally. He thus opposed any action, however symbolic, that linked France and Germany. For example, French support for Russia in the Sino-Japanese conflict of 1895 could have led to a French naval action if the Japanese had proved less moderate. He would have preferred the government to use national interests as justification for a diplomatic stance that refused to let force triumph over law. Since China had proven itself incapable of maintaining order on its frontiers, the claim that French interests in Tonkin required Chinese territorial integrity was patently false. The Entente with Russia seemed to Millerand the true explanation for France's intervention, since Russia wanted Japan out of the Liao-Tung peninsula. Germany had also supported Russia. Common Far Eastern action had in turn prompted France's participation in the Kiel Canal celebra-

14. Millerand, 'Souvenirs,' p. 34; A.N., F.M.1, Millerand's speech at the banquet of the Grandes Carrières, 1 October 1893; Persil, p. 13; Derfler, *Millerand*, pp. 92–4; Carlo Sforza, *Makers of Modern Europe* (London: Ekin Mathews & Marrot, 1930), p. 209; Michel Winock, 'Socialisme et patriotisme en France (1891–1894),' *Revue d'histoire moderne et contemporaine* (Paris: July–Sept. 1973), pp. 406–9.

tions, thereby aligning it with the former enemy, Germany, and fostering the German emperor's goal of dissipating French distrust of Germany. Millerand compared the situation to Bismarck's encouragement of French colonial expansion, which, by siphoning men and money into overseas acquisitions, weakened France for an eventual continental encounter. France's anxiety for peace and social reform must not, Millerand insisted, override its memory of the iniquity which had deprived it of two provinces.[15]

Interest in foreign policy prompted Millerand to investigate France's commitments to Russia as they affected the Turkish Empire, specifically Greece. What form did France's alignment with Russia take: military convention, memorandum, or treaty? National honor and security dictated a suppression of partisan politics where vital interests were concerned. The reverses of 1870 meant that France could not disdain any useful alliance, even one binding a democratic nation to an autocratic empire. Indeed, an alliance that took over twenty years to materialize was predicted by Engels in 1870 as the inevitable consequence of Germany's 'crime.' Millerand considered the evolution which drew Russia to France as proof of the latter's revival, a tribute to its restored international prestige. The tsar had indicated his respect for France's republican system and a refusal to meddle in its domestic disputes. Likewise, French officials should not let the Entente dictate domestic political or ministerial decisions. Although the foreign ministry should be able to conduct negotiations discreetly, Millerand thought that in a democracy the public had a right to know about developments affecting the nation's destiny. In the Kiel celebrations, the Sino-Japanese conflict, and the Armenian massacres, France seemed to follow Russia's lead. Had the alliance perhaps compromised national interests and those human rights that gave France its moral stature? Fearful that commitments to Russia could lead to a war that infringed parliament's constitutional war-making powers, Millerand thus wanted a clarification of France's obligations.[16]

Chaos in the Ottoman Empire forced European intervention. Millerand worried about Foreign Minister Gabriel Hanotaux's confidence in the sultan's reform promises in the face of French

15. J.O., *Chambre*, 10 June 1895; Derfler, *Millerand*, pp. 95–6; E. Malcolm Carroll, *French Public Opinion and Foreign Affairs, 1870–1914* (London: Frank Cass & Co. Ltd, 1931), p. 164; Jacques Chastenet, *Histoire de la Troisième République* (Paris: Librairie Hachette, 1960), vol. 3, p. 91.

16. J.O., *Chambre*, 21 November 1896; Derfler, *Millerand*, p. 96.

Ambassador to Constantinople Cambon's pessimistic assessment. Cambon wanted the Concert of Europe to intervene in the revolutionary outbreaks in the Ottoman Empire, whereas Hanotaux ignored his ambassador's information and displayed a 'naive' confidence in the Turks. This disregard for diplomatic evidence stemmed, Millerand believed, from Entente considerations. Afraid to alienate its ally, which supported the Ottoman Empire in Crete, France took a position prejudicial to its own interests. For Millerand, however, the inevitable massive massacres that would result if the sultan regained control forced the European Great Powers to act together to forestall a restoration of Ottoman control. Dissolution of the Empire with the attendant intractable racial and religious problems, or preservation of the status quo, an invitation to revolts and punitive massacres as in Crete, both seemed unviable responses to Ottoman anarchy. The only other option, reform, required both European surveillance to insure that all Ottoman subjects benefited equally and Ottoman acquiescence, not subjection, to external force. A subsequent Greek request for Crete to be consulted about its fate led Millerand to demand parliamentary ratification of any decision to use French military force. Even in France, different pressures were exerted on foreign policy; financial considerations and humanitarian objectives were often at odds. Furthermore, its diverse world-wide commitments forced France to proportion its efforts to its obligations. Its victimization by force twenty-six years earlier forced France, however, to give humanitarian appeals serious consideration. Indeed, since moral strength was an important ingredient in France's material power, imponderable idealistic values should not, Millerand believed, be totally displaced by material considerations in foreign decisions.[17]

Since Millerand did not consider Great Power unity more important than French national interests or humanitarian values, he resisted Russia's pressures for France to adopt policies that violated its traditions and interests. After the sultan's massive massacres, instead of the promised reforms, the Greek fleet intervened in Crete to prevent more bloodshed. The Great Power threat of a blockade or coercive tactics unless Greece withdrew prompted Millerand to urge negotiations rather than imperious ultimatums, especially since Greece defended civilization's cause in the Ottoman Empire. If France did not join general European decisions, its international

17. J.O., *Chambre*, 22 February and 9 March 1897; Derfler, *Millerand*, p. 96.

status would undoubtedly be hurt, but its peaceful inclinations made it reluctant to ratify possibly bellicose decisions. Only if such intrinsically undesirable acts such as a blockade encouraged peace could Millerand back French participation. If, on the other hand, France could preserve its international influence and Eastern position without joining coercive measures that violated its traditional sentiments and pacific objectives, then it should abstain. Millerand urged that France follow the policy it had adopted in 1886, when it refused to join a blockade precisely because of parliamentary and public opposition.[18]

France's Mediterranean policy continued to evoke concern about commitments to Russia at the expense of sentimental ties to Greece. Seeking neither French neutrality in Eastern affairs nor a rupture of the European Concert, Millerand still wanted French policy to reflect its own interests rather than let foreign pressures use French financial involvement in Greece to dictate a forceful stance. Furthermore, military pressures contravened the general sympathy for Hellenism. Millerand attributed France's overly severe treatment of Greece to German influence. It had committed the irreparable error of joining Greece's adversaries, thereby reinforcing the sultan's position and making reform less likely. Furthermore, Germany had displaced France as the preponderant nation in Constantinople. To Millerand, the Franco–Russian Entente's commitments, which had profoundly altered France's foreign policy, might have encouraged Germany to discount France and undermine its influence in the East, as demonstrated by events like the Kiel celebrations, the Sino-Japanese war, or the Turkish conflict. A concern that the Russian tie had harmed French interests somewhat eroded Millerand's initial support. Although his arguments in 1898 may have reflected his general dislike of the conservative Méline ministry and concern about the forthcoming elections, they were consistent with his foreign policy statements over the preceding three years.[19]

Socialist municipal electoral victories in May 1896 were the occasion for a celebratory banquet in the Paris suburb of Saint-Mandé. Attended by all Socialist factions except the Allemanists and in-

18. J.O., *Chambre*, 15 March 1897; Derfler, *Millerand*, p. 96.
19. J.O., *Chambre*, 7 February 1898.

42 Principled Pragmatist

cluding such notabilities as the Marxist Jules Guesde, the Blanquist Edouard Vaillant, and Normalien Jaurès, the banquet gave keynote speaker Millerand an opportunity to outline a 'minimum' Socialist program which the Socialist Union subsequently adopted as its charter. His famous Saint-Mandé speech, in outlining criteria for socialism, paved the way not only for its author's leadership of the parliamentary Socialists but for his reception of a ministerial post three years later. To Millerand, Socialist unity was a prerequisite for success in the national legislative elections of 1898. The Socialists had to accept a general program, end their internecine quarrels, and unite against the common enemy, forcing weaker candidates to yield on the second ballot instead of competing with each other. Millerand's Saint-Mandé program, which suggested principles and means, was not innovative in terms of his own intellectual development. Since he had enunciated its themes for several years, particularly in 1895 to the collectivist students, its significance derived primarily from its acceptance by the various Socialist factions.[20]

The Saint-Mandé program, the charter of Socialist unity, had three basic themes: individualism, collectivism, and reformism. To allow each individual to develop fully his personality required both freedom and property. Recalling the French Revolution's 'Declaration of the Rights of Man and Citizen' of 1789 that characterized man's imprescriptible rights as liberty, property, security, and resistance to oppression, Millerand maintained that property insured security and individual development. Freedom was meaningless without it. His socialism was therefore rooted in the Revolution's individualistic, libertarian tradition.[21] The offspring of scientific development and capital accumulation, a new feudalism had expropriated the small owners and separated work from property. Inevitably moving toward a new tyrannical monopoly, capitalist society had created modern slavery that collectivism could end by transferring large enterprises from private to state control, such as the major banks, railroads, mining enterprises, and the sugar refineries. Their monopolistic character, concentration of capital, and high profits made them ripe for 'social appropriation.' Small property would, however, remain private.

Millerand took a pragmatic approach to collectivism – rigidity

20. Prelot, pp. 110–11.
21. Georges Lefebvre, *The Coming of the French Revolution*, translated by R.R. Palmer (Princeton: Princeton University Press, 1947), appendix, pp. 221–3, 'Declaration of the Rights of Man and Citizen' of 26 August 1789.

about ultimate objectives but flexibility about means. Large enterprises should be 'successively incorporated,' gradually transformed, not violently overthrown. Dedicated to the Third Republic's democracy, he wanted Socialists to achieve political power through universal suffrage. As republicans, they repudiated pretenders or dictators; as reformists, they sought working-class votes to alter the economic system by democratic, parliamentary means. While Millerand wanted an international entente of workers, he was primarily a patriot who considered France the instrument of material and moral progress. Millerand urged his colleagues to behave responsibly so that their actions as opposition would be consistent with those as government members. He was convinced, however, that only a major domestic or foreign crisis would open government ranks to the Socialists, as proved to be true in the Dreyfus crisis.[22]

Millerand attacked the Méline government for its clerical orientation and its political and financial corruption. His commitment to the separation of church and state, of which educational secularism was a key component, led him to argue that the school system was a republican institution that should be above partisan disputes. The Méline government had, he charged, supported the 'clerical army' by its complacent attitude toward priests, who had not been replaced by lay faculty, thereby delaying educational secularization. Furthermore, privileges based on wealth had no place in an egalitarian society. Money should not, he argued, dictate political choices. Electoral subsidies used to defame opposition candidates permitted financial corruption to affect election results. Likewise, renewal of the Bank of France's privileges would permit financial pressures to exert an influence on political life. The government's argument that French economic prosperity required the renewal did not convince Millerand, who viewed skeptically a secret agreement with the Bank's regents that would make its resources available in wartime, because of its refusal in 1870. He wanted all France's resources, financial and human, available in a national peril. Not only did he want to eliminate the Bank's privileged status, but also to exclude its officials from parliamentary positions so that private financial

22. A.N., F.M. 1, Millerand's speech to the banquet of Socialist municipalities, 30 May 1896, at Saint-Mandé, booklet published by the *Petite République française*; also in Millerand, *Deux discours*; Derfler, *Millerand*, pp. 101–5; Persil, pp. 13–16; Gagnon, pp. 255–6; Willard, p. 404; Brogan, I, pp. 298–9; Aaron Noland, *The Founding of the French Socialist Party (1893–1905)* (Cambridge: Harvard University Press, 1956), pp. 48–50; Basdevant, pp. 4–5; Millerand, 'Souvenirs,' pp. 33–4.

considerations did not exert an undue influence on the determination of national interests.[23]

Millerand not only faulted Méline's government for its subordination to large finance and industry and its conservative ties, but also for failing to institute the important fiscal reforms promised to the electorate. Electoral considerations were partially to blame for delays in altering the tax system. After fifteen months in power, the government had passed laws only on sugar and the Bank of France, both of which benefited large finance and industry. Official assistance to the rich accompanied additional fiscal burdens, like a wine surtax, on the poor. He argued that the measure would actually raise prices for Parisian consumers, instead of promoting domestic trade by eliminating internal barriers, as the government claimed. To Millerand, the measure was a governmental electoral maneuver that permitted Méline to claim credit for a tax reform and disregard its actual damage to the working class.[24]

Millerand's attack on the governing coalition clearly contained partisan rhetoric directed toward the 1898 elections. Nonetheless, he genuinely abhorred its anti-republican ties to conservatism and the church. In his view, the Méline ministry was a reactionary combination of clericals, disenchanted republicans, and conservatives, which played on fears of socialism robbing the peasant of his land and coming to power violently to maintain control. The Socialists would, however, demonstrate that the plutocracy represented by the government was the true source of exploitation and expropriation. Terming the ministry the Pope's and Pretender's protégé, he maintained that church financing refuted governmental denials of clerical or royalist support. To Millerand, official pressure on teachers was especially objectionable; they risked losing their jobs unless they became anti-republican clerical agents.[25]

For the national legislative elections of spring 1898, Millerand assessed his own and Socialist achievements over the preceding four years and outlined future objectives. His electoral program echoed his Saint-Mandé ideas. Local issues dominated an electoral

23. J.O., *Chambre*, 12, 25 and 26 November 1896; *ibid.*, 27 February 1897; *ibid.*, 10, 14 and 15 June 1897.
24. A.N., C5555, Chamber Budget Commission, 3 June 1897; J.O., *Chambre*, 12 July and 19 November 1897.
25. J.O., *Chambre*, 12 March 1898.

campaign in which the Dreyfus Affair played almost no part. To Millerand, parliamentary activity, along with union action, propaganda, and education, was important because political reforms were vehicles for social change, for example, laws on sanitation and length of the work day. The electoral campaign served to win converts and publicize Socialist ideals. The Socialist program defined desirable goals while its political muscle defended acquired rights. Although a republican government based on universal suffrage and fundamental freedoms should be above discussion, he suggested a single assembly renewable by thirds, greater decentralization of power, changes in the judicial system and Napoleonic codes, and a limitation of military service to two years. A formal separation of church and state would eliminate the church's budget and subject the clergy to secular laws. Education should be free and secular, with opportunities available through competition. His economic program included a reform that replaced consumption taxes with a graduated revenue tax and nationalization of mines, railroads, and monopolistic industries like the sugar refineries. For the workers, he wanted laws on working conditions, arbitration councils, union rights to intervene for factory safety, and pensions for sickness, old age, and unemployment. Finally, he urged an extension of political and economic rights to women as well as men. This genuine democracy he was still determined to achieve through reformist, parliamentary means, not by revolution.[26]

Whether they chose the program or Millerand the successful parliamentary figure, his electors overwhelmingly reelected him on 8 May 1898. Furthermore, his victory was a personal triumph and not part of a Socialist landslide, for the elections of 1898 encompassed some setbacks over the stunning Socialist success of 1893. Two of their most prominent representatives, Jaurès and Guesde, were defeated, leaving Millerand the clear leader of the parliamentary Socialists.[27]

26. A.N., F.M. 4, Millerand's speech of 12 February 1898 to the Republican Socialist committee of the 1st constituency of the 12th *arrondissement*, 'L'Action parlementaire,' booklet published by the Librairie of the *Revue socialiste*, 1898; Paul Louis, 'Une législature,' *Revue socialiste*, March 1898, pp. 299–326; Derfler, *Millerand*, pp. 128–9.

27. A.N., F.M. 1, Millerand's electoral program submitted to his electors in the 12th *arrondissement* for the elections of 8 May 1898. Noland, p. 67, argues that independent Socialists like Millerand avoided the unpopular Dreyfus controversy to avoid compromising their electoral chances. Derfler, *Millerand*, pp. 129–30, states that Millerand won 8,700 out of 9,900 votes. J. Jolly (ed.), *Dictionnaire des parlemen-*

While Méline's ministry emerged with a slight majority, its tenure was precarious. On 13 June, Millerand again attacked the Méline ministry's clericalism and conservatism and outlined Socialist objectives. As realists and not narrow-minded ideologues, Socialists sought a society in which peace and order would replace injustice and anarchy. Ironically, those financial and industrial magnates deriving their wealth from exploitation were precisely those who accused the Socialists of expropriating the poor. On the contrary, Socialists sought old-age insurance, working-conditions legislation, lower fiscal burdens, and a progressive revenue tax. A loyalty to their nation did not keep Socialists from recognizing that modern production conditions, with steam and electricity undermining international barriers, made an international workers' entente essential. In fact, an international workers' union would simply mirror the same international links that connected large financiers. Since all parties from extreme Left to extreme Right assigned the nation's grandeur and security top priority, none could monopolize the designation 'nationalist.' Although Millerand did not specifically mention Dreyfus, he repudiated the Affair's anti-Semitism, which violated the republican ideal of equality. Large Jewish fortunes were, however, as distasteful to him as gentile wealth. The ministry fell on 15 June 1898 after more than two years in office. A cabinet more acceptable to the Left, led by Radical Henri Brisson, replaced it. Millerand's denunciation of the governing coalition was probably not crucial to the ministry's collapse, but his suggestions of idealistic guidelines and concrete programs paved the way for a more constructive Socialist role in the new legislature.[28]

The defeat of Jules Guesde in the Lille area led Millerand to denounce electoral corruption. He used the incident to investigate broader issues, like political freedom and an independent suffrage. Eugène Motte, a large industrialist with about 6,000 employees at Roubaix, whom Méline strongly supported, had applied inexcusable electoral pressures on his workers, Millerand charged. Millerand blamed the textile crisis that cost 3,000 workers their jobs in

---

taires français (Paris: Presses Universitaires de France, 1972), vol. 7, p. 2465, gives the tally as 8,791 out of 9,905. Goguel, p. 91, argues that the Dreyfus Affair probably did not figure in the electoral campaign because it was not yet a parliamentary concern; Gagnon, p. 262.

28. J.O., *Chambre*, 13 June 1898; Derfler, *Millerand*, pp. 130–1; Gagnon, p. 262; Brogan, I, pp. 336–7; Goguel, pp. 91–2.

Roubaix on the Méline tariff. Since prices had become uncompeti-
tive, foreign rival industries like Motte's in Poland had been established. Yet Motte attributed local hardship to Guesde's revolutionary propaganda and accused him of dishonest self-enrichment as a
deputy. Motte not only spent exhorbitant sums on electoral propaganda, but also told his factory supervisors to lead workers to the
polls so that they received ballots with Motte's name. Job vulner-
ability made workers unable to resist this 'inexcusable employer
tyranny' and fearful of signing affidavits against Motte. To Miller-
and, the intimidation of the workers was an 'abominable' form of
civil war that proved the degeneracy of Méline's backers. Furthermore, support for Motte by *La Croix* and the clerical hierarchy
mingled politics and religion, whereas Guesde's ties to the German
socialists permitted charges of national disloyalty. Motte's election
was, nonetheless, validated, and he retained his seat until Guesde
finally recaptured it in 1906.[29] Undoubtedly, Millerand's own
consistent electoral success and Guesde's interrupted parliamentary
career affected the former's continued attachment to reformism and
the latter's reversion to a revolutionary ideology and disillusionment with the legislative route.

Although Captain Alfred Dreyfus was arrested and condemned for
treason in December 1894, the Dreyfus case only gradually became
a national crisis. In spring 1898, it was still neither a parliamentary
nor an electoral issue. Like most Socialists, Millerand was initially
neutral in this 'bourgeois' affair. As he later recalled, the Dreyfus
Affair confronted the Socialist party with a difficult decision. Was it
obliged to join the campaign for justice and humanity? While Jaurès
became an ardent Dreyfusard, Guesde was an equally strong adversary. The latter believed that socialism could not abandon its
struggle against capitalism to aid an officer condemned by his peers;
a change from neutrality to partisanship might undermine fragile
Socialist unity and jeopardize chances of social reform. As for
Millerand, he urged abstention until a judicial error was proved.
Colonel Henry's suicide and confession of August 1898 were the
decisive events which converted Millerand into a Dreyfusard.[30]

29. J.O., *Chambre*, 23 June 1898; Derfler, *Millerand*, p. 131.
30. Millerand, 'Souvenirs,' pp. 35–6; Persil, p. 19; Zévaès, *IIIe République*, p. 220;
Zévaès, *Ombres*, pp. 272–3; Derfler, *Millerand*, pp. 134–7; Leslie Derfler, 'Le "cas
Millerand": une nouvelle interprétation,' *Revue d'histoire moderne et contemporaine*,

The autumn of 1898 was difficult for France. Labor unrest and the political turmoil accompanying the Dreyfus Affair menaced the Republic's very existence. For Millerand, only a unity tied to such fundamental principles as the separation of church and state could save the Republic from the clerical, reactionary coalition which refused to reconsider Dreyfus' case. He linked the clerical menace to the expansion of large finance that gave fewer people greater financial and territorial power, creating a virtual state within the state – an anti-republican trend that republicans could only arrest by general laws, not by useless decrees.[31]

Millerand wanted to end the Dreyfus Affair quickly because the attendant unrest menaced republican unity and shunted aside social issues. His initial statements reflected primarily his outrage at the legal irregularities. On 28 November 1898, Millerand urged a postponement of Colonel Picquart's trial for revealing official secrets until review procedures for the Dreyfus case were settled. If Picquart were judged in that explosive atmosphere, national divisions would only be accentuated. In the national interest, the government should avoid a detrimental civil–military conflict.[32] Although the Chamber refused his request, Millerand's argument linked him to the parliamentary Dreyfusards.

Legal scruples also prompted Millerand's demand that the court evaluating Dreyfus' case should receive all relevant information. He feared the war ministry might withhold information prejudicial to national interests from the Cour de Cassation, but the court could not render a just verdict that would pacify the public unless it had complete independence. Information about conservative manipulations to change the judges so that the court gave an anti-Dreyfus verdict dismayed Millerand. Since he viewed the crisis as a battle between republican and anti-republican forces, he urged his fellow Socialists to rally to the threatened Republic and repudiate such arbitrary behavior. The Republic's danger made the Socialists into revisionists, and put Millerand in contact with such loyal republicans as Senator René Waldeck-Rousseau, subsequently a friend and political mentor. As he later recalled, they came from

April–June 1963, pp. 81–5. Although a single, formal Socialist party did not exist in the 1890s, Millerand often referred to the Socialists in the singular.
    31. Persil, p. 19; Derfler, '"Cas Millerand,"' p. 87; J.O., *Chambre*, 22 November 1898; Derfler, *Millerand*, pp. 138–9; Noland, p. 78.
    32. J.O., *Chambre*, 28 November 1898; Derfler, *Millerand*, p. 142; Pierre Sorlin, *Waldeck-Rousseau* (Paris: Armand Colin, 1966), p. 395.

two parties (Socialist and Moderate) seemingly at parliamentary
extremes, but Waldeck-Rousseau's responsibility for the law of
1884 on professional unions showed a greater sensitivity to social
questions than that of his colleagues.[33]

February 1899 has been called a turning-point in the Dreyfus
Affair. The Socialists rallied to the Republic by openly joining the
Dreyfusards, and representatives of all republican parties linked
revision to a defense of the Republic. The death of anti-revisionist
President of the Republic Félix Faure on 16 February 1899 and the
choice of leftist candidate Moderate Senator Emile Loubet to replace him rather than the anti-Dreyfusard Méline tilted the balance
symbolically toward the Dreyfusards. The failure of Déroulède's
attempted rightist *coup d'état* and the Court of Cassation's decision
for Dreyfus' retrial by court martial at Rennes were indications of
the Affair's eventual resolution, although the atmosphere remained
troubled for several months.[34]

The climax came in June 1899 with a rightist assault on President
Loubet at the Auteuil racetrack and his subsequent protection at
Longchamps by a large working-class crowd. The institution of the
presidency, and perhaps even the Republic, seemed to be in danger.
The collapse of the Moderate Charles Dupuy ministry on 12 June
1899 showed that the Chamber believed a government of republican defense was necessary to calm the tumultuous atmosphere.
Since February Millerand, along with Radicals and Moderates who
considered the Dreyfus Affair threatened the Republic, had pleaded
in parliament and newspaper articles for republican unity against a
common enemy. His demand indicated Socialist support and possibly even Socialist participation in a government of republican
concentration.[35]

A long ministerial crisis opened that ended only on 22 June 1899
when Senator René Waldeck-Rousseau's republican coalition cabi-

33. J.O., *Chambre*, 19 December 1898; *ibid.*, 10 February 1899; Derfler, *Millerand*,
pp. 142–4; Millerand, 'Souvenirs,' pp. 36–7; Sorlin, p. 395; Derfler, '"Cas Miller-
and",' pp. 87–9; Brogan, I, pp. 338–40, 346ff.

34. Brogan, I, pp. 346–7; Gagnon, pp. 262–3; Goguel, pp. 92–7; Derfler, *Miller-
and*, pp. 144–5.

35. Brogan, I, pp. 349–50; Goguel, pp. 95–7; Gagnon, pp. 262–3; Derfler,
Millerand, p. 144; Persil, p. 19; Millerand, 'Souvenirs,' p. 37; Basdevant, p. 9;
Zévaès, *Ombres*, p. 273; Jolyon Howorth, *Edouard Vaillant. La création de l'unité
socialiste en France* (Paris: Edi Syros, 1982), p. 243.

net finally won parliamentary ratification by a narrow 25-vote
majority. President Loubet first asked Millerand's friend and former classmate, the young Moderate lawyer, Raymond Poincaré, a
former minister of finance and education. Because of the gravity of
the situation, Millerand urged Poincaré on 16 June to include a
Socialist in his cabinet so that all republican factions would be
represented. He suggested his young colleague René Viviani, but
was not surprised by Poincaré's refusal. Poincaré later maintained
that divergent republican and Socialist interests made the combination impossible. To him, the majority of 'collectivists' were revolutionaries committed to violence. Although Millerand openly rejected such tactics, Poincaré did not consider him capable of re-
straining his colleagues. Jaurès' biographer attributed Millerand's
'unsolicited' visit to Poincaré to professional ambition. He hid
behind an unsuitable youthful Viviani candidacy to push himself
for a ministerial portfolio. For Millerand to defend Socialist participation in a cabinet of republican defense was entirely consistent
with his actions during the preceding months and his support over
the years for reformism, not simply the product of momentary
opportunism. The acknowledged leader of the parliamentary Socialists, he was the logical choice for a cabinet post. Possibly ambitious
for recognition, Millerand wanted above all Socialist representation
in the new cabinet. The Republic's salvation, which necessitated
unity, took precedence over his own career advancement. In fact,
Poincaré was unable to form a cabinet, not because of Socialist
exclusion, but because of the inclusion of his friend Louis Barthou,
whom the Radicals disliked for his participation in Méline's
cabinet.[36]

Loubet then appealed to Waldeck-Rousseau, who recognized
that the national crisis required a cabinet embracing all political
tendencies. He was thus ready to include a Socialist, and the
gradualist, reform-minded Millerand appeared most appropriate.
Progressist opposition initially defeated him, but when Loubet's
appeal to Léon Bourgeois also failed, Waldeck-Rousseau, persuaded by Millerand among others, agreed to try again. His efforts

36. Jean-Baptiste Duroselle, *La France et les français. Vol. 1. La France de la Belle
Epoque, 1900–1914* (Paris: Editions Richelieu, 1972), pp. 242–4; Millerand, 'Sou-
venirs,' p. 37; Raymond Poincaré, *Questions et figures politiques*, (Paris: Bibliothèque
Charpentier, 1907), pp. 167–8, 174; Jacques Chastenet, *Raymond Poincaré* (Paris:
René Julliard, 1948), p. 62; Goldberg, pp. 248–9; Derfler, *Millerand*, pp. 145–6;
Zévaès, *Ombres*, p. 274; Brogan, I, p. 350; Noland, pp. 89–90; Sorlin, pp. 401–2.

were successful. The subsequently famous cabinet of 22 June included Millerand as Minister of Commerce and the so-called 'Butcher of the Commune,' the Marquis de Galliffet, as Minister of War.

The formation of Waldeck-Rousseau's cabinet has received considerable retrospective attention, with timing and motivation seen as particularly controversial. Specifically, did Millerand know about Galliffet's inclusion before meeting the parliamentary Socialists? After President Loubet's second offer of the ministry to Waldeck-Rousseau, Millerand, at a dinner at Galliffet's chateau on 20 June, begged the senator to re-open negotiations. Waldeck-Rousseau agreed to try again, and they apparently drafted a cabinet list that included Galliffet's name, but did not reach any final decisions. Millerand was still unsure about a post and, more importantly, about Waldeck-Rousseau's success. He seemingly knew therefore about a possible Galliffet position and participated in the cabinet discussions at the general's chateau but did not deliberately deceive his Socialist colleagues the next day.

Millerand, who had indicated Socialist support for a possible republican reform-oriented coalition during the preceding year and had concretely discussed Socialist cabinet participation during the ministerial crisis, told only a few of his closest associates, notably Jaurès, about his thoughts and initiatives. He first notified his Socialist parliamentary colleagues about a possible cabinet post without mentioning Galliffet on 21 June. He did not indicate that negotiations were still in progress, merely the possibility of Socialist ministerial participation. The group's consensus was favorable to future offers if Millerand accepted in his own name and without committing the Socialist party. The theoretical issue of ministerial participation and socialism's commitment to a reformist over a revolutionary route were raised only after the cabinet's composition was announced. Nonetheless, even though Socialist ministerialism was treated as a matter without current implications, all segments of Socialist parliamentary opinion, Blanquist and Guesdist as well as reformist, supported it on 21 June.

Only after that meeting did Millerand learn from Reinach that he had the commerce ministry in a cabinet that definitely included Galliffet. While Millerand may not have known of the final decision on Galliffet, he clearly knew about the possibility. To him, however, the basic issue was not a given cabinet's composition but that of Socialist governmental participation. The gravity of the national crisis, which required the Socialists to back a government of republican defense, outweighed his preference for a cabinet without the general. He sought and received that theoretical ratification on 21 June. That some Socialists, specifically Blanquists and Guesdists, changed their theoretical position after hearing about Galliffet's appointment proved their inconsistency rather than Millerand's.

To Socialists, General Galliffet's heroism at Sedan was vitiated by his role in suppressing the Paris Commune of 1871. Reports of Waldeck-Rousseau's cabinet on 22 June outraged such revolutionary Socialists as the Blanquist Vaillant and the Marxist Guesde. Only the reformists, led by Jaurès, who in turn was influenced by Lucien Herr, the Socialist librarian of the Ecole Normale Supérieure, still defended Millerand's position in the new cabinet. They believed that the threat to the Republic required a strong government that included representatives of all political groups from the extreme Right to the extreme Left. While Galliffet's presence rather than ministerialism initially divided the Socialists, the dispute rapidly focused on the broader rather than the narrower problem. Guesdists and Blanquists withdrew from the Socialist union in the Chamber, insisting that governmental participation violated the principles of class struggle. Jaurès, however, strongly backing Millerand, persuaded numerous Socialists to vote for the ministry while the remainder abstained.

Nonetheless, Millerand's acceptance of a portfolio, a logical result of his Saint-Mandé speech, split the Socialist party and launched the famous 'Millerand Case' (*cas Millerand*). Possibly, jealousy of Jaurès' notoriety and prestige stemming from his Dreyfusard activities was the true motivation for Guesde's and Vaillant's overt break with reformism. However, doctrinaire Socialists had become increasingly dissatisfied with the Saint-Mandé position since 1896. Guesde's electoral defeat in 1898 may have influenced his opposition to Millerand in 1899, although the victorious deputy Vaillant did not have that motivation. Probably a mixture of personal and ideological factors contributed to the Guesdist and Blanquist reactions of June 1899.[37]

---

37. Millerand, 'Souvenirs,' pp. 38^1–40; Derfler, '"Cas Millerand"', pp. 81–102; Derfler, *Millerand*, pp. 145–60; Persil, pp. 19–20; Goldberg, pp. 248–54; Zévaès, *Ombres*, pp. 274–81; Basdevant, pp. 9–10; Vincent Badié, *Les Principaux Aspects du socialisme réformiste en France* (Montpellier: Imprimerie du progrès, 1931), pp. 35–6, 51–2; Chastenet, *Poincaré*, p. 66; Georges Bourgin, *La Troisième République, 1870–1914* (Paris: Armand Colin, 1967), pp. 131–5; Zévaès, *IIIe République*, pp.

Millerand's acceptance of the Ministry of Commerce was significant not only for his own political career but also for French and European Socialist history and French domestic political developments. For Millerand, a ministerial portfolio marked his arrival at the Third Republic leadership level occupied by a relatively small number of *ministrables*, those considered capable of holding cabinet posts. The republican political system's seeming instability concealed a surprising stability of the governing élite where power rotated among relatively few men. Although Millerand would probably not have achieved that position by 1899 without the national crisis of the Dreyfus Affair, once there he remained a republican leader. In fourteen years he had progressed from a young, unknown Parisian deputy to leadership of the parliamentary Socialists, sufficiently prominent for Waldeck-Rousseau to choose him for a ministerial post. Married the previous year, the forty-year-old Millerand had achieved a professional success that was compatible with his own legal background and reformist theoretical position, but shared little with the revolutionary theories of some of his Socialist colleagues.

The immediate impact of Millerand's move on French socialism was initially divisive and ultimately anti-reformist. Blanquist and Marxist denunciations of the cabinet ruptured the fragile unity of Saint-Mandé. Their opposition quickly altered from the specific cabinet's composition to repudiating any Socialist participation in a bourgeois cabinet. Their initial abstention from voting on Waldeck-Rousseau's ministry hardened into an irreconcilable opposition to ministerialism on the ground that the principle of class conflict precluded collaboration between Socialists and middle-class parties. Within the French parliament, therefore, the Socialists were divided into Millerand's supporters and opponents. In 1904, the reformists accepted the revolutionary wing's victory at the international Amsterdam Congress, thereby recreating French Socialist unity at the expense of reformism. Until the national

228–9; Noland, pp. 89–93; Duroselle, *Belle Epoque*, p. 229; Gustave Rouanet, 'La Crise du parti socialiste,' *La Revue socialiste*, August–September 1899, pp. 200–5; Howorth, pp. 243–57; Sorlin, pp. 401–3; J. Paul-Boncour, *Entre deux guerres. Souvenirs sur la IIIe République* (Paris: Plon, 1945), I, p. 93; Willard, pp. 423–44; Brogan, I, pp. 350–3; Gagnon, p. 263; Goguel, p. 97; Zeldin, I, pp. 771–2. Charles Andler, *Vie de Lucien Herr (1864–1926)* (Paris: Editions Rieder, 1932), pp. 148–50, notes Herr's approval of Millerand's acceptance of a cabinet post and his view that he was a great Socialist minister. To Herr, Millerand's subsequent evolution would have been different if the Socialist party had not rejected him.

emergency of the First World War, no member of the unified Socialist party again accepted a cabinet position. Only former Socialists like Millerand, Viviani, or Aristide Briand became ministers in the Third Republic. The sterile opposition role of the Socialists undoubtedly dictated their departure from socialism as much as personal ambition. Although Socialist parliamentary representation increased dramatically in the next decade, the party's resolute adherence to a revolutionary line left it permanently in opposition and deprived its working-class clientele of the concrete results that its growing strength might otherwise have achieved. France's inadequate record of prewar social reform stemmed at least partially from socialism's rejection of governmental participation.

The international impact of Millerand's decision was equally significant. Victory for the revolutionary position at the Amsterdam Congress of 1904 gave the Germans a clear dominance over international socialism. As strong patriots, appalled by German brutality, French Socialists were increasingly torn between their loyalty to France and to the international working class. Although they chose their nation in the crisis of 1914, they clearly were split in the preceding years between a desire to improve their compatriots' lot and obligations to a revolutionary line which gave international revolution priority over pragmatic local reforms. Internationalizing the issue of ministerialism determined the behavior of Socialists in democratic France on the basis of the political situation in autocratic nations like Germany and Russia. While revolution may have been the only option in dictatorial regimes because of the impossibility of reform, its adoption in France, where universal suffrage and a parliamentary system opened a legal route to change, was unfortunate.

Part II
The Social Reform Minister

3

Social Justice and Economic Prosperity: the Minister of Commerce's Goals

Waldeck-Rousseau's ministry, despite an initially precarious majority, defied logical expectations of a short existence to last for three years, the longest ministry of the Third Republic. Furthermore, it was one of the few to end by choice instead of reversal. Poor health prompted Waldeck-Rousseau to resign in June 1902, shortly after the national legislative elections, although his cabinet still had a majority. As Minister of Commerce, Millerand thus had an unparalleled opportunity to promote social reforms from a governmental post. While his accomplishments fell short of his goals, his record of social legislation in three years exceeded, Paul-Boncour argued, that passed during several decades of parliamentary discussion. Although many of his reforms were implemented by decree not law, they paved the way for subsequent French legislation. Indeed, as Sforza commented, no French social reform of the early twentieth century lacked Millerand's authorship.[1] These possibly too-adulatory assessments of Millerand's contribution counterbalance the criticism of Blanquist and Guesdist contemporaries, who argued that his collaboration with their capitalist foes undermined the working-class movement.

In August and September 1899, the court martial at Rennes focused public attention on the Dreyfus Affair. On 9 September, it again found Dreyfus guilty, but with 'extenuating circumstances,' and sentenced him to ten years in prison. Waldeck-Rousseau's cabinet was divided, although it supported the premier in trying to

---

1. Paul-Boncour, I, p. 94; Sforza, p. 208.

end the Affair rapidly. Millerand, who backed a presidential pardon as the most satisfactory juridical solution, even though it meant renouncing the right to appeal, finally convinced his colleagues. With the verdict of another trial uncertain, Dreyfus' health precarious, and public pressures for peace and order, the pardon granted on 19 September 1899 satisfactorily resolved the Affair, even though Dreyfus did not receive legal exoneration until 1906.[2]

Like his later Socialist counterpart, Léon Blum, Millerand launched a program of social reform during a period of severe social unrest. In 1899 and 1936, the arrival of a Socialist in power coincided with massive strikes; the working class may have hoped that the Socialist ministers would respond sympathetically to this demonstration of dissatisfaction by passing reform legislation. The peace and prosperity of the early twentieth century were in sharp contrast to the Depression's hardships, but the necessity for social change encouraged comparable expectations. While Millerand's and Blum's legislative achievements were considerable, they did not appease the working class. However, the fears which the unrest provoked were at least partially responsible.

The generalized worker discontent that accompanied Waldeck-Rousseau's assumption of office led to three times as many lost work days by strikes in 1899 and 1900 as were lost in 1898. Much debate has surrounded Millerand's responsibility for this working-class unrest. Since he had long urged the peaceful settlement of labor disputes instead of the resort to 'war,' as he termed strikes, he clearly did not encourage these work stoppages. The existence of a Socialist minister may, however, have persuaded the workers that strikers would be sympathetically treated. The strikes would also dramatize the need for reforms and reinforce pressures for labor legislation. Millerand received numerous requests from workers to negotiate with their employers. Expectations of a moderate governmental reaction may therefore have encouraged strikes actu-

---

2. Derfler, *Millerand*, pp. 170–1. David R. Watson, *Georges Clemenceau. A Political Biography* (London: Eyre Methuen Ltd., 1974), pp. 151, 153, cites Reinach, V, p. 558. Duroselle, *Belle Epoque*, p. 245; Douglas Johnson, *France and the Dreyfus Affair* (London: Blandford Press, 1966), pp. 163–79. Mathieu Dreyfus, *L'Affaire telle que je l'ai vécue* (Paris: Bernard Grasset, 1978), pp. 239–46, discusses the meeting at the commerce ministry where Clemenceau and Jaurès opposed a pardon as hampering the battle for justice, whereas Millerand and Reinach supported it on humanitarian grounds. Millerand finally won over Jaurès and Clemenceau and then threatened to resign unless President Loubet agreed. Although the cabinet unanimously favored a pardon, Loubet only acquiesced after hearing the doctors' report on Dreyfus' poor health.

ally stemming from more profound causes, like salary and working conditions. The strikes, particularly the Creusot strike of September 1899 that Waldeck-Rousseau successfully arbitrated, convinced Millerand that contacts between workers and employers were vital if peaceful, legal procedures were to replace violence.[3]

On his arrival at the rue de Grenelle (location of the commerce ministry), Millerand reorganized his administration in a more rational fashion. As he later commented, the Ministry of Commerce covered a vast area of activities, but its diverse responsibilities required a more logical and suitable organization to keep the constant internal conflicts from interfering with efficient operation. In addition to the department of commerce and industry which handled technical, commercial issues like customs legislation, he established three other divisions: technical education, insurance and social welfare (*assurance et prévoyance sociale*), and labor. The welfare department implemented the new law on work-related accidents and drafted a pension law; the labor department, predecessor of the labor and social insurance ministry established by Clemenceau in 1906, inspected the factories to insure hygienic and safe working conditions. Millerand's achievements in the area of labor were notable and innovative, although the head of the new labor department, Arthur Fontaine, also played a large role. Loyal collaborators, who admired their chief and were dedicated to their work, made feasible an otherwise overwhelming job. His administration, he believed, deserved Europe's generally high regard.[4]

Millerand's reputation as Minister of Commerce derives primarily from the so-called 'Millerand decrees' of 10 August 1899 and the law of 30 March 1900. Although the August decrees affected only state-employed workers, they provided a model for communes, municipalities, and private industry. The decrees gave workers a day off each week, set salary and work hours normal for the region, established proportions for foreign employees, and required auth-

3. Duroselle, *Belle Epoque*, p. 247: lost work days were 1,200,000 in 1898, 3,550,000 in 1899, 3,760,000 in 1900 and 2,000,000 in 1901; Zévaès, *IIIe République*, p. 237; Derfler, *Millerand*, pp. 173–6; Sorlin, pp. 470–2; Millerand, 'Souvenirs,' p. 42.
4. Millerand, 'Souvenirs,' pp. 40–40[1], 40[2]–41; J.O., *Chambre*, 23 November 1899; Persil, p. 21; Derfler, *Millerand*, pp. 166–8; Bourgin, p. 135; Lefranc, *Mouvement socialiste*, pp. 113–14; Alexandre Millerand, 'Les Origines française du B.I.T.', *Revue des deux mondes*, 1 April 1932, p. 593.

orization for subcontracting. Although the Chamber had long
debated a similar law, it had still not passed one when Millerand
became Minister of Commerce. He used governmental decrees
rather than legislation to institute the changes. Decrees were more
efficient but potentially less effective, since they lacked penal sanctions. Millerand, denying that decrees were illegal, argued that they
could modify earlier decrees on the same issue. The government
did, however, intend to seek approval from the Council of State.
He expected the decrees to be effective because entrepreneurs had to
observe civil law.[5]

The decrees reflected reforms long demanded by the Broussists
(reform Socialist disciples of Paul Brousse). These important and
innovative decrees extended the principle of a weekly day of rest to
all adult workers, not simply women and children, linked the
duration of work to the regional norm, protected salary levels by
tying remuneration to customary local wages instead of a minimum, and charged the employers if the state supplemented salaries.
Millerand wanted unions to transmit workers' views to employers
and represent them in salary and working-condition negotiations.
If working conditions in an entire area were regulated, private
industry would have a desirable model and abuses would be less
possible. The decrees, which proved official interest in the regulation of French economic life, gave democracy an increasingly social
dimension.

The decrees were nationalistic in the way they limited the proportion of the foreign workers to between 5 and 30 percent of the
employees in state enterprises, depending on regions, so that
French workers did not suffer unfair foreign competition. Previously, the entrance and employment of foreign manpower had
been virtually uncontrolled. The decrees were significant for large
public works like road, railroad, and port construction, all of which
used many foreign workers. After 1899, French workers, facing
reduced salaries or unemployment, cited Millerand's decrees to
pressure their employers. They thus satisfied the working-class
demand to shield national labor from foreign competition, as tariffs

5. Millerand, 'Souvenirs,' p. 40[1]; Persil, pp. 21–2; Badié, p. 102; Bourgin, p. 135;
Lefranc, *Mouvement socialiste*, p. 114; Brogan, I, p. 373; Lavy, *L'Oeuvre de Millerand.
Un ministre socialiste (juin 1899–janvier 1902)* (Paris: Librairie Georges Bellais, 1902),
pp. 7–14; J.O., *Chambre*, 4 July 1899; also in Alexandre Millerand, *Travail et
travailleurs* (Paris: Bibliothèque Charpentier, 1908), pp. 13–21; Derfler, *Millerand*,
pp. 168–70.

had protected French markets. In fact, they had little effect on the use of foreign manpower. Complaints about foreign competition had been most vociferous during the Depression of the 1890s, but by 1899 improved economic conditions reduced that competition. The Dreyfus Affair, however, which heightened national sensibilities, reinforced workers' hostility to foreigners and weakened international working-class solidarity.[6]

The law of 30 March 1900 was the fundamental piece of social legislation enacted while Millerand was Minister of Commerce. The so-called 'law by degrees' (loi des paliers) adopted an eleven-hour work day, to be reduced in two stages to ten hours after four years, for all workers in establishments employing men, women, and children. A law of 2 November 1892, which set a ten-hour work day for women and children, had not been observed, particularly in mixed establishments where different requirements for men, women, and children were difficult to enforce. In 1899, Millerand tried to secure compliance with the earlier law while drafting a new one. Inadequate inspection was partially at fault, since the supervisory commissions had often never met and included only employers' representatives. Unless the unions and the workers were equally represented, labor inspectors could not have accurate information about compliance. Millerand wanted workers' delegates, as well as employers', on the general councils that oversaw the law's observation. Professional unions should report violations to labor inspectors. Corporate groups like unions provided the most effective intermediaries for collaboration.[7]

The Minister of Commerce had, in Millerand's opinion, an 'imperative duty' to insure observation of the 1892 law, particularly Article 3 on working hours for women and children. In September 1899, he instructed labor inspectors and prefects to notify workers and employers of the government's determination to apply the law, but gave employers a grace period. When employers complained, he replied that they had fifteen days to notify the government of the time needed for the changes. On 5 November 1899, he gave

6. Pierre Milza, 'Quand Millerand restreignait l'immigration,' L'Histoire, No. 16, October 1979, pp. 96–9.
7. Badié, p. 101; Bourgin, p. 135; Zévaès, IIIᵉ République, p. 237; Brogan, I, p. 373; Millerand, 'B.I.T.', p. 594; Lefranc, Mouvement socialiste, p. 114; Millerand, 'Souvenirs,' p. 40[2]. The day was reduced to ten and a half hours after two years and to ten hours two years later, by 1904 therefore. A.N., F[22] 543, Millerand's circular to the prefects, 17 August 1899 on the law of 1892; A.N., F[22] 543, Millerand's circular to the secretaries of professional unions, 19 January 1900.

industry until 1 January 1900 to regulate matters or face penalties, but Chamber and Senate discussions of a general law postponed application of that requirement, first until 31 January 1900 and then to 31 March.[8]

Moves to enforce the law of 1892 did not weaken Millerand's determination to pass a new law that would set a common work day. It was virtually impossible for men, women, and children in the same firm to work different hours, but the Senate's pressures for an eleven-hour day conflicted with the Chamber's support for ten hours. Often, there were three or four different categories of workers in the same establishment who worked days ranging from twelve to ten hours. On 22 November 1899, Millerand suggested a compromise whereby an eleven-hour day would be reduced to ten within a specified period. Industrialists needed time to adapt their plants so that they could produce as much in ten hours as in eleven and so maintain salary levels. Rationalization and humanitarianism dictated Millerand's desire for a common working day of ten hours. Convinced that social reform must come through legislation, he maintained that acts rather than words were the best way to convert the working class.[9]

On 22 December 1899, the Chamber passed the law setting an eleven-hour work day for all personnel in mixed establishments with a two-stage reduction to ten hours within four years, but the Senate delayed ratification for another three months. The law proved unexpectedly controversial. The Left felt that an eleven-hour day for all workers violated the ten-hour day for women and children set by the 1892 law. Industrialists, however, accused Millerand of trying to ruin French industry. The same pay for a shorter day would reduce profits by increasing costs relative to output. Blanquists and Guesdists obviously suspected efforts to buy off the workers by modest improvements, whereas the industrialists resented governmental limitations on economic freedom.[10]

Under debate since 1892, the concept of a ten-hour work day was not novel. Since it was already the norm in many regions, its

---

8. J.O., *Lois et décrets*, pp. 6976–7, Millerand's circulars to the prefects, 21 October 1899; *ibid.*, p. 7238, 5 November 1899; *ibid.*, p. 8273, 22 December 1899; *ibid.*, p. 8292, 24 December 1899; A.N., C5673, Chamber, Labor Commission, audition of Millerand, 22 November 1899.

9. A.N., C5673, Chamber, Labor Commission, audition of Millerand, 22 November 1899; J.O., *Chambre*, 23 November 1899; also in Millerand, *Travail*, pp. 22–38.

10. Persil, pp. 23–4; Lavy, pp. 40–58; Derfler, *Millerand*, pp. 179–80.

legal ratification was simply at stake. Millerand was convinced that workers and industrialists would accept the law if they had time to adjust and if it applied to everyone. To him, the law was primarily an act of 'solidarity, moralization, and social pacification,' which removed those tensions in the work-place stemming from divisions based on sex and age, and also legislated more humane conditions. Although the law did not affect categories of workers such as industries employing only men, commercial, agricultural, or professional employees, it directly benefited nearly two million workers and provided a model for the rest of the economy. Once the principle of legislating working hours was accepted, a progressive reduction was merely a question of time.[11]

Millerand later portrayed the law of 1900 as a response to the 'imperative necessity' of eliminating the several different regimes within the same factory. The four-year transition period from eleven to ten hours permitted employers to adapt without cutting salaries. Millerand recognized that the costly social reforms needed a wealthy nation to sponsor them. In fact, arguments for the Méline tariff had originally stressed the inevitability of a ten-hour day; if employers had to bear that burden, they needed benefits to offset it. Yet the tariff was passed eight years before the ten-hour day was accepted in principle and four more before it was implemented. Considerable debate during the 1902 elections focused on the law, but Millerand insisted it was not opposed by the working class, nor was it responsible for a contemporaneous apprenticeship crisis that stemmed, instead, from increased labor specialization.[12]

The postal and telegraphic department (P.T.T.), a branch of the civil service, was under the commerce ministry's jurisdiction. As employer, the commerce minister could more readily reform those services than employer–employee relations in private industry, although parliament had to ratify any financial changes. A law of 30 March 1900 gradually introduced an eight-hour day for Parisian P.T.T. workers and then extended it elsewhere. Millerand also sought safer working conditions, better salaries, insurance coverage, and advancement opportunities. His numerous circulars covered such diverse matters as medical services, instructions about

11. J.O., *Senat*, 26 March 1900; A.N., C5673, Chamber, Labor Commission, 27 March 1900; J.O., *Lois et décrets*, pp. 3116–19, Millerand's circular to the prefects, 17 May 1900.
12. J.O., *Chambre*, 21 November 1902.

bicycles for postmen, mail delivery schedules, or disciplinary arrangements. The postal and telegraphic reforms indicated in microcosm Millerand's social reform objectives and gave private industry a model.[13]

Millerand continually tried to improve the workers' lot. He not only urged a shorter work day and higher salaries, but a safer and more hygienic working environment. A law of 9 April 1898, which indemnified workers for industrial accidents, took effect shortly after he became commerce minister. Its guiding principle was 'professional risk,' those dangers accompanying the normal performance of industrial tasks. Workers no longer had to prove that employer error was responsible for accidents. Previously, they did not receive compensation for accidents due to their own negligence. The enterprise now assumed the financial burden of industrial accidents instead of the workers, with product prices being raised correspondingly. To Millerand, the worker had as much right to an indemnity for work-related accidents as to a salary for his labor. Since compensation levels were set for specific accidents before the event, the personal element was removed. He considered this law of 'peace and concord' to be an important step in French social history, even though it affected only industrial, not agricultural or commercial, enterprises. The state set aside special funds to compensate bankrupt companies, but expected industry to establish an insurance system to pay for claims. The law, which covered only employment-related accidents, not illness due to prolonged exercise of unhealthy professions, indicated an awareness that the world's economic transformation entailed responsibilities as well as profits.[14]

Millerand also pressed for better working conditions so that accidents or illness would be less likely. He wanted existing hygiene and security laws as completely applied as possible. His reforms covered specific measures, like winter heating of workshops and seats for saleswomen, as well as the establishment of a general commission on industrial hygiene to formulate new regulations. The French governmental proposal to provide sufficient

13. Persil, pp. 34–5; Lavy, pp. 259–305.
14. J.O., *Lois et décrets*, pp. 5759–62, Millerand's circular to the prefects, 24 August 1899; Lavy, pp. 115–25, 391–8, Millerand's speech in Lille, 15 October 1899; Derfler, *Millerand*, pp. 171–3; Badie, p. 108.

seats behind the counters for all saleswomen in shops and work-shops would, he insisted, be observed only if inspectors checked the stores. A law of 29 December 1900 required stores to provide sufficient seats for all women employees, but strict application was problematical, since it depended on parliamentary approval of funds to pay inspectors. Millerand also demanded that violations by employers cease. Too often, labor legislation like safety require-ments or work hours for apprentices, women, or children was ignored. His numerous detailed instructions specified, for example, the weight a young worker could carry on a delivery bicycle, or the application of protective legislation on women and child work hours in food-related professions like baking, closer to domestic than industrial life.[15]

The Commission on Industrial Hygiene, established on 11 Decem-ber 1900, made a significant contribution to investigating industrial poisons and workers' hygiene. One study, for example, evaluated the use of lead paints. Millerand considered it vital to safeguard workers' health against the new and dangerous products which science had invented. Ideally, he believed, a concept of professional illness should complete that of work-related accidents to protect and indemnify workers for injury in the workplace.[16]

Millerand considered collaboration rather than confrontation between workers and employers most conducive to social peace and economic progress. This goal led him to reorganize the Su-preme Labor Council (Conseil Supérieure du Travail), which had been set up in 1891 as a consultative body attached to the commerce ministry. Millerand's decree of 1 September 1899 defined pro-cedures for electing labor and management delegates to the for-merly appointive committee. Workers had to be represented on a council that investigated those working conditions not covered by current legislation. Millerand's linkage of labor and capital under state auspices echoed Socialist thought, such as Benoît Malon's, but also Albert de Mun's Christian Socialist corporatist theory. The Supreme Labor Council, which played a significant role during the Third Republic, focused initially on legislation governing working hours and safe and hygienic conditions.[17]

15. A.N., C5673, Chamber, Labor Commission, 14 February 1900; *ibid.*, Miller-and's letter to Dubief, commission president, 28 June 1901 and Millerand's circular, 26 January 1901; Persil, p. 22; Lavy pp. 17–35.

16. J.O., *Chambre*, 4 February 1902; Lavy, pp. 105–15.

17. Millerand, 'Souvenirs,' p. 42; Persil, p. 24; Lavy, pp. 65–77, 397, Millerand's

The regional counterparts of the Supreme Labor Council, created by decree in late 1900, were less successful. Local labor councils supposedly offered both sides a chance to discuss problems so that a conciliatory approach might replace aggression. With labor and management equally represented, the councils permitted employees to defend their interests and express views on labor conditions to their employers so that pressing social problems might be peacefully and legally resolved. Millerand hoped to transform the normally hierarchic employee–employer relationship into one of equality. Since the relative strength of the two sides was so different, workers, as isolated individuals, were powerless to protect their jobs unless they joined unions. The government must, Millerand argued, encourage the formation of corporate associations, unions, which would protect individual workers against a vulnerable isolation and thus foster social peace. Millerand again used executive fiat rather than legislation to introduce a social reform, since ratification of local labor councils had been stalled in parliament for eight years. The decree, which implemented a long-demanded principle, made the councils purely consultative. Millerand did, however, reject universal suffrage for selecting the councils, since voter absenteeism had elsewhere invalidated the results and undermined the unions. A key motive for Millerand in setting up the local labor councils was greater union power. His conviction that strong unions would promote social reform essentially led him to disenfranchise the vast majority (four-fifths) of unaffiliated French workers.[18]

Since workers were often ignorant about the relevant legal provisions affecting them, Millerand wanted them to share in executing the legislation. Those inspectors who applied labor laws should come from the working class and maintain contact with the unions. Labor legislation could only be effective if working conditions were closely checked. A scarcity of inspectors meant that over half the industries had not been visited, which encouraged violations of the labor laws. Millerand's pressures did, however, increase the number of reported infractions. Inspectors required

speech in Lille, 15 October 1899; Derfler, *Millerand*, p. 187; Bourgin, p. 135; Goldberg, pp. 270–1; Millerand, 'B.I.T.,' p. 593; Sorlin, p. 475; Lefranc, *Mouvement socialiste*, p. 115.

18. Persil, pp. 25–7; J.O., *Lois et décrets*, pp. 6229–31, Millerand's report to the President of the Republic, 18 September 1900; Lavy, pp. 78–90; Derfler, *Millerand*, pp. 187–8; J.O., *Chambre*, 22 November 1900.

eye-witness information about violations, but workers were often hesitant to report them because of potential repercussions. To Millerand, the unions could best serve as intermediaries between individual workers and inspectors. The Creusot strike offered a model for worker participation, since the unions had transmitted working-class views to the management and had persuaded fellow workers to accept the final verdict.[19]

Existing legislation designated arbitration councils to settle industrial disputes, but was seldom used because the verdict lacked sanctions. However, the vast number of strikes, including the deaths of three demonstrators by police fire at Chalon-sur-Saône in June 1900, persuaded even Waldeck-Rousseau that procedures to resolve disputes peacefully were vital. He supported Millerand's draft law for a generalized system of obligatory arbitration. Referring to a weavers' strike at Saint-Etienne, Millerand claimed that maintenance of order was the government's primary concern. Although established rights should be freely exercised, conflicts harmful to national interests must be averted. Far from encouraging the strikers, Millerand used his influence to encourage a peaceful solution to disputes.[20]

On 15 November 1900, Millerand and Waldeck-Rousseau submitted a draft law on the amicable settlement of work-related disputes to the Chamber of Deputies. The idea of compulsory arbitration was not new for Millerand, but to be effective it required representation from both sides. Opening the Creusot pavilion at the Universal Exposition in Paris, he demanded an end to absolute monarchy in the monstrous modern factories. Since their smooth operation required mutual agreement more than authority,

19. Lavy, pp. 91–4, 394–5, Millerand's speech in Lille, 15 October 1899; Basdevant, p. 10; Badié, p. 94; Bourgin, p. 135; Millerand, 'B.I.T.,' pp. 593–4; J.O., *Chambre*, 24 November 1899; A.N., F²² 543, Millerand's circular to the divisional inspectors, 19 January 1900. Donald Reid, 'Putting social reform into practice: labor inspectors in France, 1892–1914,' *Journal of Social History*, Vol. 20, No. 1, 1986, pp. 67–8, 72–3, 79, argues that republican reformers like Millerand perceived the state as an intermediary between the workers and employers. Relying on the Labor Inspectorate, which he tried to make more accessible to workers, he met or corresponded with divisional and departmental inspectors and encouraged contact between them and union representatives.
20. J.O., *Chambre*, 18 January 1900; also in Millerand, *Travail*, pp. 39–45; Brogan, I, p. 373; Sorlin, pp. 477–8; Zévaès, *IIIᵉ République*, p. 237; Derfler, *Millerand*, pp. 175–6, 180–1.

they needed organizations to transmit worker grievances to management so that discontent did not erupt violently. Worker delegations that encouraged discussion, a sense of common interests, and respect for majority decisions were a preliminary solution. In the case of intractable conflicts, however, they should turn to an impartial outside authority instead of stopping work.[21]

Millerand sought to avert disputes with permanent institutions that facilitated peaceful discussions and to resolve unavoidable conflicts with legally defined obligatory procedures. The vast number of strikes, particularly the Chalon-sur-Saône tragedy, undoubtedly affected Millerand's statements at Lens on 7 October 1900, where he described strikes as civil wars that were harmful to all parties. Even if victorious, strikers paid heavily. As models, he cited the previous year's decision in Lens for worker and management representatives to discuss outstanding issues prior to a strike, and the recent national congress resolution at Montceau-les-Mines for a favorable majority vote by secret ballot before declaring a strike. Furthermore, a peaceful, preferably obligatory, arbitration mechanism needed to be set up in advance. Millerand suggested that the labor councils name the arbitrators. He linked his stance of 1900 on obligatory arbitration to his Saint-Mandé speech, which had urged a gradual, peaceful, social transformation not a violent one. Designating a mechanism to settle labor conflicts peacefully gave specific content to that 1896 position.[22]

Millerand, who considered his policy consistent with both his premier's and his own past, refuted Alexandre Ribot's charges of inconsistency. In 1900, as in 1893, he was convinced that social reforms would result from long and painful popular efforts rather than from a violent blow. Although a loyal Socialist, he was also committed to the government of which he was a part. Working-class organizations had a vital function in promoting social reform. The unions' majority rule, which permitted workers to express their true views, had led, for example, to public endorsement for continuing a miners' strike at Dourges, but a secret decision to resume work. To Millerand, unionization and arbitration were both preconditions for domestic peace.[23]

---

21. Lavy, pp. 150–3, includes Millerand's remarks at the opening of the Creusot pavilion, 29 June 1900; Derfler, *Millerand*, p. 182.

22. Lavy, pp. 410–15, Millerand's speech at Lens, 7 October 1900.

23. J.O., *Chambre*, 6 November 1900; also in Millerand, *Travail*, pp. 55–60; Persil, pp. 27–9; Lavy, p. 153; Millerand, 'Souvenirs,' p. 43; Badié, p. 88.

The proposed law on the peaceful regulation of labor disputes tried to avert strikes if possible or resolve them by arbitration if not. Permanent worker delegations presented grievances to employers; arbitrators handled insoluble problems; strikes required majority support. The law, which applied only to large establishments (over fifty employees) working for the state, made acceptance of the arbitral decision obligatory. Professional unions, Millerand insisted, were not threatened by the requirement for management and labor delegates to meet regularly. Such organizations would be strengthened if workers were used to the idea of collective contracts and to discussing common corporative interests with employers. To Millerand, strikes were often the result of frustration in communicating grievances. They drew attention to discontent while failing to articulate specific demands. The new arrangement permitted an exchange of views and a presentation of grievances. The strike, which became a measure of the last resort, also had to be renewed weekly. Often the majority suffered from strikes declared by a minority. They needed a legal system to replace the current anarchy with majority rule. The right to strike remained inviolable, but obligatory arbitration by technically competent arbitrators offered a peaceful way to settle insoluble disputes.[24]

Millerand, who stoutly defended the right to strike in principle, considered the reality to be responsible for such damage to all parties as to require the exhaustion of all other remedies first. Anxious for authoritative, competent, and impartial arbitrators, the government decided that labor council members should be chosen from both worker and employer unions before a conflict. Even without penal sanctions, the law could be effective because it facilitated industrial communication through regular labor–management contacts. Before a strike, workers must formulate their demands in writing; a strike required an obligatory delay and a majority vote by secret ballot so that an aggressive minority did not dictate the decision. Protection of belligerent rights did not justify damage to society's larger interests; a strike must be a regular procedure, not an unexpected explosion, which also envisaged arbitration of insoluble conflicts. To Millerand, government efforts to settle labor conflicts peacefully increased proletarian security and

24. Lavy, pp. 154–62, exposé des motifs, 15 November 1900; Derfler, *Millerand*, pp. 182–3.

restrained exploitation as much as laws on the length of the work day, working conditions, or social insurance.[25]

The arbitration bill, which never reached parliamentary committee during Waldeck-Rousseau's ministry, was opposed by labor and management. To the workers, it restricted their syndical rights and jeopardized a strike's significance by eliminating its unexpectedness. To the employers, it unacceptably restrained the freedom to work. Millerand subsequently often pressed for compulsory arbitration, but never overrode opposition to the obligatory aspect.[26]

While Millerand was anxious to resolve labor disputes peacefully, he preferred to forestall them. To this end, he considered unionization vital, since it allowed workers to express their wishes concretely instead of turning to inchoate unrest. He called the development of syndical organizations in the working class, unions and labor exchanges (*bourses du travail*), the principal theme of his administration because it was indispensable to social peace. Association promoted the workers' material and moral strength. Millerand and Waldeck-Rousseau introduced a bill to expand the right of association of the law of 1884 to allow the unions to have commercial subsidiaries. Denying that the change would increase economic competition, Millerand argued that for social and educational reasons unions should be able to defend their material and corporate interests. A powerful 'instrument of emancipation,' the proposed law would improve material conditions and foster civic education by letting unions accumulate capital and achieve a cooperative status without forming monopolies. For Millerand, a better working-class situation was intimately linked to that ability to comprehend and defend labor's interests, which unions encouraged.[27]

25. Derfler, *Millerand*, pp. 180–7; Duroselle, *Belle Epoque*, p. 249. Lavy, pp. 170–5, cites Millerand's speech of 12 January 1901 to the Chambre syndicale de papeterie and of 6 March 1901 to the banquet of the Alliance syndicale du commerce et de l'industrie. Millerand, *Travail*, introd. and pp. 61–86, speech to the Chamber of Commerce of Paris, 16 January 1901; Alexandre Millerand, *Le Socialisme réformiste français* (Paris: Librairie Georges Bellais, 1903), pp. 116–21, Millerand's preface to Jules Huret, *Les Grèves*, August 1901; Basdevant, p. 10; Bourgin, p. 135; Sorlin, pp. 477–8; Lefranc, *Mouvement socialiste*, pp. 115–16.
    26. Persil, pp. 27–30.
    27. Millerand, 'Souvenirs,' p. 44; Lavy, p. 229; J.O., *Chambre*, 1 June 1900; Lavy, pp. 397–8, Millerand's speech in Lille, 15 October 1899; Malcolm O. Partin, *Waldeck-Rousseau, Combes and the Church: The Politics of Anti-Clericalism 1899–1905*

Since Millerand believed man made his own destiny, the working class had to emancipate itself. It was the government's responsibility to promote union organization and effectiveness. He described the wage-earners as those nineteenth-century men who could best raise civilization to a new humanitarianism, but their efforts required guiding principles rather than individual saviors. To achieve genuine freedom, the workers must understand their responsibilities and not turn to hatred or violence. Since a sense of responsibility derived from power, the government should unite the workers into associations from which they could develop a sense of their strength and obligations. Unionization could secure better material conditions for the working class and educate responsible citizens who were committed to peaceful social reform and hostile to violent activity. Millerand's active endorsement of unionization while commerce minister may have partially affected the significant increase in union membership.[28]

Millerand often discussed the unions' potential role. In Nouzon on 29 May 1901, he urged that the working-class democracy (*la démocracie laborieuse*) be educated. Syndical associations promoted this goal by permitting workers to assume responsibilities and thus to recognize their duties as well as their rights. If they were shown the benefits of professional associations, they would be less likely to unleash those violent explosions that harmed all parties. Minimal material and moral security was, however, vital if society expected its least privileged members to behave with control and to trust that gradual and peaceful methods would improve their lot. Only association, Millerand was convinced, could transform the proletariat's weakness into strength and promote the recognition of its responsibilities.[29]

(Durham: Duke University Press, 1969), p. 23; Derfler, *Millerand*, pp. 177–8; A.N., C5673, Chamber, Labor Commission, 5 December 1900.

28. Millerand, *Socialisme réformiste*, pp. 110–15, speech to the banquet of the Cooperative Associations of Production, 12 July 1900; Lavy, p. 230; Persil, p. 30; Derfler, *Millerand*, p. 178; J.O., *Chambre*, 10 December 1900. Also in Millerand, *Travail*, pp. 53–4, which noted, however, that the law of 1884 did not permit civil servants to unionize. Mailmen could form an ordinary association but not a professional union. Since civil servants worked for the state, a professional syndicate to defend their interests threatened the nation. As employer, the state was different from a commercial enterprise. Millerand consistently opposed unionization of state employees on nationalistic grounds.

29. J.O., *Lois et décrets*, pp. 3349–50, Millerand's speech at Nouzon (Ardennes), 29 May 1901, at the distribution of prizes to students in the professional course; Lavy, p. 231; Millerand, *Socialisme réformiste*, p. 47, speech at Carmaux, 12 October 1902.

Millerand considered education, which expanded the horizons of the salaried workers, the key to a better working-class position. Since only educated people could effectively perform their civic rights and duties, he strongly supported a technical education which increased a worker's skills and economic value. Millerand expanded existing technical schools, set up new ones, and added trade union representatives to their governing bodies. In the arts and crafts schools (*écoles d'arts et métiers*) he promoted pedagogical reforms that gave students the practical, technical instruction required by industry and also exposure to general culture to promote a sense of dignity and responsibility as free citizens. He added a course in civic and moral education to the technical school curriculum and relaxed the rigid, disciplinary tone in hopes that a more normal educational environment would foster the instruction of students by persuasion rather than by compulsion.[30]

Millerand wanted not only to improve working conditions but to aid workers outside the active labor force, specifically the old and unemployed. The state had an obligation to support those citizens who could not work. An early proponent of social insurance measures, Millerand supported the law on accident insurance and urged a pension program and, later, unemployment insurance. Although the legislation was not passed while he was Minister of Commerce, the later laws owed their initiative to Millerand's projects.[31]

The Paris Exposition of 1900, which brought many workers to the capital, confronted the government with an unemployment problem after it ended. To Vaillant, Millerand argued that the issue was less to end unemployment than to mitigate its effects. If the central administration and provincial authorities developed a public works program, like naval and port construction, and centralized information about projects needing manpower, they could shift unemployed workers to the provinces. The unions could pass on work information to their members. It was, however, more important to investigate the causes of unemployment so that remedies could be suggested. Better working conditions, like a shorter work day, greater safety, and stronger unions to promote inspection

---

30. Persil, pp. 39–40; Lavy, pp. 360–75; J.O., *Sénat*, 2 April 1900.
31. Badié, pp. 108–13; Lefranc, *Mouvement socialiste*, pp. 115–16.

would also, he thought, ease the problem. Municipal funds might furnish financial aid to the unemployed. In suggesting governmental and syndical assistance to the unemployed, Millerand hinted at unemployment insurance. His endorsement of governmental intervention in the market economy took the form of outlays for public works projects and assistance to unemployed laborers.[32]

Reforms in the legislation on placement offices also affected unemployment. The abuses that characterized the existing system of paid agencies led Millerand to urge that the local government inform workers about job openings in their region, but not charge them for the service. To pay for job information would accentuate the hardships of the unemployed. Millerand's stance on placement offices demonstrated his desire to decentralize responsibilities as well as to alleviate unemployment.[33]

Old-age pensions were key to any social insurance program. Other drafts predated Millerand's proposal of 1901 and the actual program was not ratified for another decade, but his project was a significant step in that history. To the commerce minister, the nation owed a debt to workers who had devoted a lifetime of work to society. A law that insured their survival constituted a 'primordial right to life.' Workers at age sixty-five, or earlier if injured, were entitled to a pension derived from obligatory contributions by workers and employers, linked to salary levels. The state would guarantee a 3 percent interest rate. A prosperous nation could, Millerand believed, increase the social component of the republican budget. The obligation was as legitimate and necessary as educational, military, or taxation commitments. For society could not let its work-force suffer the worst agonies of illness and old age any more than it could let its machinery and material deteriorate. The scheme, which preserved man's essential dignity, guaranteed the minimal material and moral security to enable the worker to perform effectively. As the home of revolution, France could not lag behind its rival Germany's leadership in social insurance coverage. Millerand endorsed Mirabeau's view that the poor and their misfortunes belonged to the nation, which must help them rise above the servitude to daily necessities so that they could enjoy a complete spiritual existence as human beings and citizens. Miller-

---

32. J.O., *Chambre*, Vaillant interpellation, 1 June 1900; Lavy, pp. 175–8.
33. Lavy, pp. 180–1; J.O., *Chambre*, 22 November 1900; A.N., C5673, Chamber, Labor Commission, 21 November 1900; Persil, p. 30.

and's impassioned pleas did not win over the opposition, but his project still represented an advance in defining that system of social legislation which France would institute before the First World War.[34]

Although labor issues were an important part of the commerce ministry's responsibilities, commercial matters also fell to Millerand. As its principal administrator, Millerand expended time and derived prestige from the Universal Exposition of 1900 in Paris. The previous year, he had urged the prefects to provide public assistance to worker delegations visiting the Exposition because the international exhibits would enlarge their horizons and foster their theoretical and practical development. Since the principal goal was worker education, no entry fees, or at most token ones, should be charged so that its principal beneficiaries were not kept out. Millerand thought that the Exposition might transmit innovative currents to French industry, thereby serving as a school of economic initiative and technical education and promoting France's peaceful struggle against foreign competition. In his opinion, the Exposition permitted France to display its technological achievements and to benefit from unparalleled educational opportunities.[35]

The Exposition, which opened in Paris on 15 April 1900, was the product of years of planning encumbered by innumerable delays and much opposition. Calling it primarily a 'democratic effort,' Millerand noted the unfavorable circumstances, including opposition to the concept, that its organizers had had to surmount. As a result, construction of the Grand Palais started only in 1897 and of the Palais des Machines in 1899. Nonetheless, Millerand wanted it to remain a national endeavor, not the object of partisan disputes. The Exposition was a huge enterprise which demonstrated the revolutionary impact of science and technology. To Millerand, the miraculous ability to tour the world in minutes linked races and nationalities in a common legacy of science and beauty, despite different educations, customs, and prejudices. As the Exposition proved, the economic revolution of the preceding three generations

34. Millerand, 'Souvenirs,' p. 40[2]; Persil, pp. 30–4; J.O., *Chambre*, 13 June 1901; Lavy, pp. 189–221; Lefranc, *Mouvement socialiste*, pp. 115–16; Sorlin, p. 479; Derfler, *Millerand*, pp. 200–3.

35. Lavy, p. 242; J.O., *Lois et décrets*, pp. 5427–8, Millerand's circular to the prefects, 11 August 1899; Millerand, 'Souvenirs,' p. 43.

had so tamed the forces of nature that the character of the world
was totally altered. The machine had made human labor the auxili-
ary of iron and steel. Although reduction of distances, cure of
diseases, and technological advances had altered human relations,
ignorance and misery remained to be conquered. The benefits of
economic progress must therefore be spread throughout society.
On a conservative note reminiscent of Edmund Burke, Millerand
noted the 'solidarity' which tied the current generation to the past
and the future despite these revolutionary changes.[36]

The composition of the Exposition's jury allowed Millerand to
rebuke those strident nationalists who opposed it. While political
preferences had not dictated his jury nominations, he admitted a
preference for loyal republicans over those anti-republican
nationalists of a royalist or dictatorial bent who had actively campaigned against the Exposition. To him, they had selfishly disregarded the interests of the thousands of small people and, more
significantly, of the nation. Furthermore, as he later observed, the
Exposition provided another source of influence on the large
industrialists.[37]

A conviction that economic prosperity was a prerequisite for
social reforms guided Millerand's specific commercial decisions.
Since reforms required money, public finances needed competent
management so that the nation's productive wealth was augmented. All Frenchmen had a stake in France's strength and
prosperity.[38] He tried to apply existing commercial laws and draft
new legislation to remedy existing problems. Commercial and
navigational complaints led him to propose a new statute for
France's decadent merchant marine. A law of 1893 to subsidize
construction of sailing vessels at the expense of steamships had been
a retrograde economic decision which ignored scientific progress.
As a result, France's tonnage and equipment had declined relative
to that of foreigners. During the 1890s, French steamship production had fallen from 88 percent to 42 percent compared to foreign
construction. That law, which had driven foreign clients from
French shipyards, deprived France of the revenue from foreign

36. J.O., *Chambre*, 3 April 1900; Jacques Chastenet, *Cent ans de République* (Paris: Jules Tallandier, 1970), vol. 3, p. 239; Millerand, *Travail*, pp. 7–12, speech inaugur-ating the International Exposition, 15 April 1900; Derfler, *Millerand*, pp. 197–8.
37. J.O., *Chambre*, 10 July 1900; Millerand, 'Souvenirs,' p. 43.
38. Millerand, *Socialisme réformiste*, pp. 54–5, speech to the 12th *arrondissement*, 3 December 1902.

sales and a modern transportation system for its own merchandise. In a decade when French steam tonnage remained virtually stationary, construction of sailing vessels increased by 25 percent. This 'absurd' and 'deplorable' phenomenon, which forced France to pay for foreigners to transport its merchandise, essentially subsidized foreign construction and navigation – an annual tribute by French commerce to its overseas competitors. Millerand blamed the specific merchant marine legislation on the isolationist and autarkic economic regime of the 1890s whose tariff and subsidy decisions had damaged foreign economic relations. Railroad rates, France's inadequate fluvial system, and insufficient funds for large port development had encouraged freight to go abroad, and France's limited emigration deprived it of compatriots who could defend its commercial interests abroad. France had lost the advantages of its geographical position, since larger steamships and rapid transportation eliminated intermediary disembarkation ports. Since foreign ships no longer had to stop at French ports, they did so only to fill empty cargo space with France's luxury exports.

Reform of the merchant marine was an aspect of the larger objective of augmenting French national wealth. While French industry lost a significant industrial asset and had to pay for foreign transportation, larger national interests were also at stake. Wherever a foreign ensign displaced the French flag, the nation's prestige and power diminished relative to that of its rivals. Foreign and colonial policies required both a strong navy and a prosperous merchant marine. No aspect of the nation's wealth could languish in outdated or underdeveloped status, since social reform and French international prestige both depended on economic prosperity.[39]

Millerand's principal commercial and industrial goal was to maintain and develop France's rich natural resources. He promoted legislation to improve French communication routes, railroads, navigable rivers and canals, and maritime port facilities. Germany's system of navigable waterways was significantly more developed. Not to lag behind, France must improve its land and water transportation systems to provide requisite fuels and raw materials for its industrial centers and facilitate the despatch of exports. For

---

39. Persil, p. 36; J.O., *Chambre*, 23 November 1899; also in Millerand, *Travail*, pp. 22–38; J.O., *Chambre*, 29 October 1901; also in Lavy, pp. 317–25; J.O., *Sénat*, 24 February 1902; also in Millerand, *Travail*, pp. 279–93.

example, linking the canals of the Chiers and the Escaut to the Meuse would connect the port of Dunkirk with the Longwy industrial region. Frenchmen should bury their divisions and unite to promote French power and grandeur. In the ever-fiercer struggle for existence between nations, France must do everything possible to foster its victory, including a full utilization of natural resources and swifter, less costly transportation. He hoped his investigations would encourage a vast public works program of railroad, canal, and port construction that would provide domestic employment and eventual industrial advantages. Millerand's commercial proposals contained a strong nationalistic competitiveness that linked France's international status to economic prosperity and modernization as much as to military force.[40]

Commercial and nationalistic concerns also made communication with France's overseas colonies a high priority. As part of the large public works program designed to improve the nation's communication routes, Millerand wanted to expand underwater cables between the metropolis and its distant colonies. In the Far East, cables were laid between China and Indochina (from Tourane to Amoy) and in the Mediterranean, between Oran and Tangier. An inadequate network threatened national defense and commercial relations. Millerand's legislation expanded the telegraphic system to link France and certain colonies and connect parts of North Africa. To him, cables maintained and expanded France's influence and demonstrated its industrial prowess.[41]

Economic nationalism led Millerand to support export tariffs and to punish monopolies and speculation that hurt economic exchanges. Since the goal of the 1892 tariff was a defense of French exports, Millerand was cautious about modifying it. A crisis in the silk industry had prompted requests for higher tariffs, but the commerce minister was reluctant to agree. Because the problems stemmed from industrial mechanization, the transition from hand to machine labor, rather than an altered demand for the finished

40. Lavy, pp. 312–16, cites Millerand's speech to the annual banquet of the Alliance syndicale du commerce et de l'industrie, 6 March 1901, and a projet de loi of 1 March 1901. Persil, p. 36; J.O., *Lois et décrets*, Millerand's speech to the Conseil superieure du commerce et de l'industrie, 19 January 1900; *ibid.*, circulars to the prefects and presidents of the Chambers of Commerce, 17 February 1900; *ibid.*, pp. 3349–50, Millerand's speech at the prize distribution to students in the professional course at Nouzon (Ardennes), 29 May 1901.
41. J.O., *Chambre*, 26 March 1902; Lavy, pp. 305–7; J.O., *Lois et décrets*, pp. 3349–50, Millerand's speech in Nouzon, 29 May 1901.

product, aid in the necessary transformation seemed more appropriate than tariffs that excluded foreign competitors. Considering tariff stability indispensable to French prosperity, Millerand made few changes in the regime as Minister of Commerce.[42]

Millerand refused to endorse aspects of industrialization that benefited the rich over the poor, specifically monopolistic or speculative practices that increased prices. Did the high prices in the three large trusts for alcohol, sugar, and metals stem from price-fixing in violation of the penal code or from independent economic factors? It was in the state's interest to prevent an artificial inflation, since higher copper prices, for example, would increase the P.T.T. budget. Large industries had to comply, he argued, with existing laws against monopolistic price-fixing. He also denounced speculation in the public sales of worsted wools at Roubaix. A general dislike of speculation did not, however, override his legalism. Only if speculators or monopolists broke the law could they be penalized. Parliament alone could modify unjust legislation. In the case of large depositors using savings banks rather than current bank accounts, he also supported strict application of the law that provided a grace period to reduce those accounts. When concessionaires wanted to increase freight charges on goods transported to and from Algeria because of higher fuel costs, Millerand only accepted a modest increase to offset the 'exceptional situation' of high coal prices. Careful scrutiny characterized his response to specific incidents involving possibly illegal or inequitable prices.[43]

Not opposed to monopoly *per se*, Millerand was determined to pursue legally those industrialists guilty of monopolistic misdemeanors. Industrial syndicates, trusts, and cartels had proliferated with industrialization because of mechanization and scientific progress and the concomitant expansion of communication and transportation facilities, not because of a protectionist regime. The consequent overproduction and price reductions encouraged producer combinations to restrict output and protect prices. Millerand wanted the government to take steps to offset the higher consumer

42. Lavy, pp. 333–7, cites Millerand's speeches of 15 March 1900 to the Association générale des tissus, of 6 March 1901 to the banquet of the Alliance syndicale de commerce et de l'industrie, and of 18 January 1901 to the Chamber of Deputies. J.O., *Lois et décrets*, pp. 393–4, Millerand's speech to the Conseil supérieure du commerce et de l'industrie, 19 January 1900.

43. J.O., *Chambre*, 23 November 1899; also in Millerand, *Travail*, pp. 22–38; J.O., *Chambre*, 9 July 1900; *ibid.*, 27 November 1900; *ibid.*, 18 January 1901.

prices and profits obtained at labor's expense. It could even repeal the protective tariffs or sue the industrialists if they used their power fraudulently. While such economic groups were useful, they were also potentially dangerous and needed supervision. Millerand also regularized legislation affecting commercial and industrial property by altering patent laws to give inventors greater protection and provided more extensive export and exposition information for businessmen and traders. Throughout, his goal was to foster economic prosperity and a stronger commitment to the Republic.[44]

For years before joining the government, Millerand had defined the Socialist party's political goal as the peaceful conquest of public power. As its influence grew, so did its chances of achieving its social reforms. During the 1890s, he worked to unify the Socialist party, to divert it from violence, and to promote its political success. Effective political influence would allow it to spread socialist ideas and identify basic problems. France, a nation endowed with traditional values linked to the progress of human civilization, could only be converted if Socialists were prepared to assume the responsibilities of power. Since all loyal republicans had a 'primordial' duty not to shirk the dangers or the honors of a governmental post, Millerand had accepted that responsibility as a republican duty and an opportunity to institute social reforms.[45]

Millerand reflected on socialism's governmental collaboration at Firminy on 13 January 1902. Although the Socialist party joined a government of all republican factions in the wake of the national crisis of 1899, its views and actions during the preceding decade made that move logical. In a republic based on universal suffrage, it was clearly futile to disregard majority opinion. Socialist efforts to educate the public and to win power legally made it paradoxical to seek victory through a chance act of force. Their ideals, however, implied individual liberation from the bonds of ignorance and economic deprivation – a freedom won by human endeavor and not through any external religious or autocratic power. Dedicated to society's transformation, Socialists could not evade the responsi-

44. J.O., *Chambre*, 22 March 1901; also in Millerand, *Travail*, pp. 269–78; Lavy, pp. 339–54; Millerand, 'Souvenirs,' pp. 44–5; Persil, p. 36.
45. Lavy, pp. 391–8, Millerand's speech in Lille, 15 October 1899; Derfler, *Millerand*, pp. 172–3.

bilities of governmental collaboration, and within the reformist republican coalition they had to define their foreign and domestic objectives. For Millerand, freedom, reform, and power were not antithetical but complementary.[46]

Millerand consistently linked socialism and republicanism. As the avant-garde of the republican army, he viewed the Socialist party as the proponent of peaceful tactics and solutions for foreign and domestic issues. Since science had made wars so devastatingly destructive, all men, Socialists included, were compelled to avert that nightmare by promoting the international and domestic victory of reason, peace, and justice. The peaceful translation of doctrines into pragmatic reforms required, however, Socialist participation in governmental decisions, an acceptance of republican responsibilities as well as advantages. Democracy, a legacy of the French Revolution, allowed socialism to end the industrial revolution's inequities for the working class. To Millerand, French Socialists, in seeking the economic liberation of the working class, had to remember their involvement in the larger Republic of all democratic Frenchmen. The solidarity of classes was complementary to the idea of class struggle. In 1902 Millerand, still a staunch social reformer and patriot, believed the democratic Republic encompassed a positive role for a reformist Socialist party.[47]

Although Waldeck-Rousseau's republican coalition triumphed in the national legislative elections of 1902, Millerand had the greatest electoral difficulties of his political career. Only when the revolutionary Guesdists abstained did he narrowly defeat his nationalist opponent in the run-off election of 11 May 1902. He was opposed by both Left and Right. Nationalists attacked him as part of a government that had punished the army and the church for their activities in the Dreyfus Affair. They also rejected him as a Socialist who wanted to abolish those economic injustices from which they benefited. The revolutionary Socialists, on the other hand, faulted his collaboration with a 'bourgeois' government and his defense of reformism. They could forgive neither his collaboration with Galliffet nor his acquiescence in suppressing the strikes. To the Left, he

---

46. Millerand, *Socialisme réformiste*, pp. 36–40, speech at Firminy, 13 January 1902.

47. *Ibid.*, pp. 43–7, speech at Carmaux, 12 October 1902; *ibid.*, pp. 54–6, speech to the 12th *arrondissement*, 3 December 1902.

was not sufficiently radical; to the Right, he was a revolutionary threat. Their common opposition made odd bedfellows but nearly brought about Millerand's political demise. Furthermore, his constituents were not entirely happy about his ministerial position; they wanted a deputy who would protect their particular interests rather than a prominent national statesman. His electoral difficulties stemmed from specific personal issues, such as his effectiveness in defending local vested interests and his position among the Socialists, and larger national matters such as his membership in a ministry aiming to republicanize the army and restrain clericalism.[48]

On the national level, the elections focused on religion, particularly the government's Associations Law of 1 July 1901. The Right considered it a violation of religious freedom; the Left supported its attack on clericalism. That much-discussed law required that religious congregations receive authorization and forbade members of unauthorized orders to teach. Anxious to curb the active anti-Dreyfusard religious order, the Assumptionist Fathers, Premier Waldeck-Rousseau wanted to guarantee freedom of association while controlling the religious orders. Most liberal republicans supported the freedom of association, but their fears of a 'clerical invasion' because of the church's behavior in the Dreyfus Affair reinforced their anticlericalism. A social dimension accentuated religious divisions, since the lower middle and working classes blamed the church, with its links to the aristocracy and wealthy middle class, for their economic exploitation. The Associations Law, which focused these antipathies, became a major electoral issue. The victory of the republican bloc made it likely that it would receive an anticlerical application despite the premier's plan for moderation.[49]

48. A.N., F.M. 4, Millerand's speech to his electors prior to the elections of 27 April 1902; Millerand, 'Souvenirs,' p. 46; Derfler, *Millerand*, pp. 210–12.

49. Duroselle, *Belle Epoque*, pp. 249–51: anxiety about Millerand's social goals may have affected Waldeck-Rousseau's policy toward the congregations, but the premier's Dreyfusard position and his responsibility for the Associations Law of 1884 made logical his dissolution of the Assumptionist Order and his freedom of associations bill. Coincidence of timing, however, encouraged speculation about the connection between Millerand's objectives and Waldeck-Rousseau's anticlerical moves. Immediately after Millerand's speech in Lille of 15 October 1899 about the law on work-related accidents and Socialist goals, Waldeck-Rousseau dissolved the Assumptionist Order and presented a draft law on freedom of association, at least partly because of pressures from industrialists. The following year, after Millerand's speech at Lens on 7 October 1900 that called strikes a form of warfare and proposed a system of compulsory arbitration, Waldeck-Rousseau promised business leaders

The disciplining of the army was another direct effect of the Dreyfus Affair; some segments of the army, especially the officer corps, had been prominent anti-Dreyfusards. The ministries of interior, directed by the premier, and war under General Galliffet were preeminent in liquidating the Affair. Close links between the Catholic Church and the upper echelons of the army, to the degree that priests influenced military promotions and Catholic aristocrats held a disproportionate place in the military leadership, meant that a republicanization of the army would accompany restrictions on the church's influence in education. While Waldeck-Rousseau's successor, Emile Combes, adopted the most draconian measures, the former initiated the campaign against the church and the army. Waldeck-Rousseau's Associations Law was the vehicle for harnessing the church's activities; Galliffet and later General Louis André radically altered the general staff and the promotion system so that loyal republicans supplanted Catholic monarchists in the military's upper ranks.[50]

Millerand played a peripheral role in the attacks on the church and the army, but his anticlericalism and Dreyfusard sympathies aligned him during the Waldeck-Rousseau ministry with the premier's position. Later, Combes' and André's extremism pushed him into the opposition. Although Millerand had been at the dinner at Galliffet's chateau that drafted the Waldeck-Rousseau cabinet list and later served in a cabinet that included the general, his relations with the war minister deteriorated during the next year. By late 1899, Millerand urged Waldeck-Rousseau to find a war minister who would institute more stringent republican restrictions on the army. In May 1900, the general told the premier he would have to choose between himself and Millerand. The commerce minister's antipathy, which reflected general Socialist views, undoubtedly predated the cabinet's formation, but Socialist denunciations of the war minister during the autumn and winter contributed to his poor

he would deal immediately with the congregations. Gagnon, p. 265; Cobban, III, pp. 58–9; Goguel, pp. 112–17; Brogan, I, pp. 360–1; Lavy, pp. 391–8, Millerand's speech in Lille, 15 October 1899; *ibid.*, pp. 410–15, speech in Lens, 7 October 1900; Partin, p. 23. Williams, p. 24, argues that the attack on the congregations served to distract 'dangerous firebrands' like Millerand from social reform. Derfler, *Millerand*, pp. 172–3, 206, 210. While Waldeck-Rousseau rejected collectivist aspects of Millerand's program and reluctantly accepted some social reforms, he wanted cabinet unity. His ministers, therefore, could only make statements that reflected general governmental policy. Basdevant, p. 9.
  50. Gagnon, p. 268; Brogan, I, p. 379.

relations with Galliffet. Friction with Millerand may have influenced Galliffet's resignation on 29 May 1900, although he cited the government's position toward an alleged nationalist plot. A close friend of the premier, Galliffet may also have been jealous of Millerand's apparent influence in the cabinet. Since the new war minister, General André, a known anticlerical republican, was more acceptable to the Left, that specific difficulty between Millerand and the Socialists was removed.[51]

Millerand's social reform program did not heal the split between Guesdists and Blanquists on the one hand and Millerand's supporters on the other that the news of Galliffet's appointment had triggered. On the contrary, it deepened, although the climax occurred two years after Millerand's departure from the commerce ministry. Shortly after the cabinet took office, militant Socialists drafted a manifesto which repudiated the Saint-Mandé program by denouncing ministerialism and insisting that the party remain in the opposition. Under Jaurès' influence, the diverse factions convened a 'unity' congress at the Japy gymnasium in Paris in December 1899. Ministerialism, represented by the 'Millerand case,' however, defeated hopes of restoring Socialist unity. Jaurès, Briand, and Viviani strongly defended ministerial participation, but Guesde, Vaillant, and Lafargue persuaded the congress to endorse Guesde's resolution that the class struggle precluded Socialist participation in a bourgeois government. Adjustments for exceptional circumstances left a slight possibility of reconsideration.[52]

Despite this seeming restoration of Socialist unity, opposition to Millerand and ministerialism continued. Revolutionary Socialists opposed virtually all his reforms. The government's repression of the strikes increased the hostility, so that the socialists joined the ministry's nationalist opponents, a connection that partly explained Millerand's own electoral difficulties in 1902. Although rank-and-file Socialists did not fully endorse the militant leaders' program, the related issues of unity and ministerialism troubled Socialist party discussions in France and in the Second International. Socialist unity formally ended when the Guesdists and Blanquists seceded from the Socialist Congress at Lyon in 1901. Millerand's speeches

51. Douglas Porch, *The March to the Marne. The French Army 1871–1914* (Cambridge: Cambridge University Press, 1981), pp. 66, 72; Derfler, *Millerand*, pp. 199–200; Duroselle, *Belle Epoque*, pp. 245–6.

52. Rouanet, pp. 210–14, 349, 369; Derfler, *Millerand*, p. 191; Duroselle, *Belle Epoque*, p. 229; Badié, p. 36; Prelot, p. 141.

and ministerial programs remained consistent with the reformist socialism defined the previous decade. The Guesdists' and Blanquists' change from support to hostility illustrated, not Millerand's inconsistency, but their own.[53]

Although Waldeck-Rousseau retained his majority after the elections of 1902, he resigned on 4 June for reasons of health. The premier persuaded President Loubet to choose Radical senator Emile Combes as his successor. Millerand later recalled that Waldeck-Rousseau told him, but wondered what reason he should give for his resignation. The former apparently suggested health as the least controversial. While Waldeck-Rousseau did die of cancer two years later and was perhaps already ill, a political rather than a medical explanation appears reasonable. Since the Radicals were the largest group in the victorious leftist coalition after the elections and Waldeck-Rousseau's Progressists were split among ministerial supporters and opponents, it was more logical to have a Radical premier. Waldeck-Rousseau's republican coalition was designed to pacify the nation during the Dreyfus crisis. After that danger passed, the combination of incompatible groups was less necessary, and the premier was increasingly uncomfortable with the majority's leftist orientation. When Millerand left the Ministry of Commerce, he resumed his seat among the parliamentary Socialists but no longer as their leader. While his goals remained unchanged, Millerand's ministerial experience had given him a taste for power and a sense of authority, and the decline of his influence among the Socialists added to his stature as a national figure.[54]

Millerand's retrospective assessment of his ministry reflected a continued dedication to his former patron, Waldeck-Rousseau, and frustration at management's and labor's obstruction of social reform. The premier's support for commerce ministry projects had increased his admiration and respect. Time (a passage of approximately forty years) and France's later problems may, however, have distorted Millerand's memory, for Waldeck-Rousseau seemingly accepted social reforms to appease working-class unrest rather than to make social relationships more equitable. The two

53. Derfler, *Millerand*, pp. 191–7, 203–7.
54. Duroselle, *Belle Epoque*, pp. 251–4; Millerand, 'Souvenirs,' pp. 46–7; Derfler, *Millerand*, pp. 212–13; Lefranc, *Mouvement socialiste*, pp. 116–17.

men clearly established a compatible relationship, and the ministry's long tenure allowed the minister of commerce to draft and pass more social legislation than in several previous decades.[55]

Employers and workers disliked Millerand's attempt to substitute peaceful methods for confrontation. His frequent meetings with large industrialists elicited only incomprehension and inertia. They, like the workers, were not persuaded that French production would benefit more from peaceful collaboration than from bellicosity. Unions were happy to accept the benefits of their stronger position, but refused to abandon violence as the necessary counterpart. To Millerand, this stubborn adherence to their respective positions resulted in unnecessary social strife and hampered legislative reforms. It was probably utopian to expect groups with radically different social stakes and expectations to abandon their respective rights, but Millerand correctly defined those social changes needed for a more equitable and prosperous social environment. His social programs were neither unique nor innovative, but he was a more realistic visionary than many of his contemporaries, and had a power base for three years that allowed him to execute more reforms than others with similar concerns.[56]

Assessments of Millerand as minister of commerce reflected the orientation of his critics, whether contemporary or modern. To the revolutionary Socialists, his acceptance of a cabinet position alongside Galliffet provoked a hostility that none of his subsequent actions could mitigate. For Socialists to participate in a bourgeois cabinet undermined that sense of class conflict needed for an eventual proletarian victory. Piecemeal reforms, instead of improving the workers' position, simply anesthetized their sense of injustice, and made them accept less fundamental changes. Several of Millerand's specific programs actually hurt the working class; his law on the number of hours in a work day, for example, lengthened the day for women and children during the transition period. More significantly, his position in a government that had repressed strikes at the cost of human life constituted an unforgivable reinforcement for the opponents of the working class.

All political groups to the right of the Socialists considered that Millerand's presence in the cabinet legitimized revolution. His reforms, however modest or partial, evoked fears of radical

55. Millerand, 'Souvenirs,' pp. 40²–41.
56. *Ibid.*, pp. 43–4; Badié, pp. 57–88, 103–26; Derfler, *Millerand*, pp. 213–19.

changes in the social structure. Industrial and business groups saw his social legislation as infringing on their economic freedom and reducing their profits. They resented paying the same wages for shorter work days, compensating workers for accidents, unemployment, or old age, or sharing factory control with union representatives. They did not find persuasive Millerand's logic that social peace and a happier, more prosperous work-force would enhance the entire nation's economic well-being.

Even moderates like Millerand's old classmate, Raymond Poincaré, saw him as representing a possible Socialist tyranny. To Poincaré, Millerand's decrees were the opening wedge of a collectivist infiltration of government policy. He blamed the severity of social unrest, reflected in the number and duration of strikes, on Millerand's presence in the government; Socialists used the unrest to push the government to enact social reforms. Despite his relatively modest actual achievements, Millerand was faulted for too great a focus on social reform.[57]

To the extreme Right, especially the new group of bellicose nationalists, Millerand's Dreyfusard stance and his social views were an anathema. His persistent opposition to all anti-republican movements since Boulanger, along with his interest in social change, insured the dislike of those nationalist, conservative forces determined to protect the institutions of the church and the army that were identified with the past.

Millerand's support came mainly from those working-class groups that benefited from his reforms and fellow reformist Socialists, but even they did not admire him totally. The workers appreciated better working conditions, but could not pardon Millerand's anti-strike stance. Reformist Socialists, like Jaurès, endorsed Millerand's social legislation but disliked the idea of social collaboration.

Millerand has sometimes been described as a corporatist rather than a Socialist.[58] His interest in social justice and efforts to enact social reforms that would allow the working class to share in the economic benefits of its labor identified him with certain Socialist currents. On the other hand, his belief that labor–management

---

57. Poincaré, *Questions et figures*, pp. 202–4, speech in Rouen, 9 March 1902, denounced Millerand and the 'Collectivists.' The speech exhibited exaggerated electoral rhetoric, but Poincaré had always opposed Socialist participation in the cabinet and had rejected Millerand's suggestion to that effect in 1899.
58. Goldberg, pp. 270–1.

collaboration under state supervision would increase society's peace and prosperity linked him to corporatist theory. Corporatist and Socialist, which validly describe Millerand's theories and actions, are complementary, not antithetical. For Millerand, an atmosphere of labor–management collaboration and economic prosperity rather than class warfare was most propitious to the implementation of social reforms. Only a narrow definition of socialism based on revolutionary Marxism eliminates Millerand from its ranks. In the context of 1899–1902, that rigid, scientific definition was commonly accepted neither by society at large nor by many Socialist groups. The revolutionary wing's victory at the Amsterdam Congress of the Second International in 1904, which prompted the French Socialist factions to unite in 1905 in a single Socialist party (S.F.I.O., Section française de l'internationale ouvrière), produced a Marxist triumph at the theoretical and tactical levels without eliminating other forms of socialism or persuading independents like Millerand to abandon the designation Socialist. Millerand's record as commerce minister was significant for the history of French social reform and his own political advancement, even though his achievements did not live up to his aspirations.

4
The Social Reformer as Party Outcast and Government Critic

Change and continuity marked the seven years between Miller-and's departure from the commerce ministry in June 1902 and his return to the cabinet as Minister of Public Works in Briand's ministry of July 1909. He still urged social reforms, like old-age pensions, and social theories that opposed violent change. Yet his official expulsion from the French Socialist party and his attack on a Combes government backed by the republican bloc moved his position closer to the center of the French political spectrum. Still terming himself a socialist, he added 'republican' to his political title. During the years between his two social reform ministries, Millerand, who was less active in the Chamber of Deputies, concentrated on his commission activities and his legal practice.

Millerand played a peripheral role in the major issues that France confronted during the early twentieth century. In the years after Waldeck-Rousseau left office, church–state relations were the principal domestic issue. Critical of Combes' obsession with anticlericalism, Millerand took little part in the debates about the congregations, the rupture of diplomatic relations with the Vatican, or the separation of church and state. He was active only as a lawyer in liquidating the congregations' financial assets. A period of severe domestic unrest, with frequent strikes and much violence, found Millerand still opposed to revolutionary tactics. Still a republican devoted to France, Millerand seldom addressed publicly such important diplomatic and colonial events as the conclusion of the Entente Cordiale, the first Moroccan crisis, or the serious Balkan tensions. Despite this relative political inactivity, Millerand had become a leading republican figure who was often suggested for ministerial positions, even the premiership.

Millerand's acceptance of a cabinet post had ruptured fragile Socialist party unity, which membership in a government that repressed social disorders had confirmed. Although revolutionary Guesdists and Blanquists considered improvements in the working-class situation to be contrary to the principle of class struggle, reformists defended Millerand's program despite a dislike of governmental repression. The years from 1899 to 1902 had divided Millerand and the reformists from the revolutionary Socialists. The year 1903 isolated him from the reformists; his expulsion from the French Socialist party and the open breach with Jaurès followed the next year, which was also the year of the revolutionaries' victory in Amsterdam.

Millerand's votes in the Chamber of Deputies, rather than ministerial participation, brought the *cas Millerand* to a head in 1903. Although his positions, specifically on military and religious questions, were consistent with his own earlier views and with those of the Waldeck-Rousseau government, they were unacceptable to the parliamentary Socialists. Doctrinal purity and party discipline were at issue, but the Socialist position had evolved in a more rigidly anticlerical and antimilitarist direction.

Several of Millerand's votes in January 1903 offended the parliamentary Socialists and the Socialist Federation of the Seine. Although a supporter of church–state separation, he thought the momentous and delicate change required time to prepare. He voted against Socialist proposals to terminate the church's budget and the Vatican Embassy not, as he argued to the national Socialist Congress in Bordeaux, because of loyalty to the previous ministry but because church–state separation needed preparation, and could not be achieved spontaneously by sterile manifestations. He was also the only Socialist to support the war ministry's prosecution of trade union leaders from the Bourse du Travail for the *Manuel du soldat* pamphlet encouraging young soldiers to desert. An advocate of labor exchanges, Millerand wanted them open to working-class soldiers, but repudiated their non-professional propagandizing of antimilitarism. In the current European situation, preservation of the army's strength and integrity had to be maintained, which imposed on all Frenchmen the patriotic duty to perform their military service.[1]

1. Persil, p. 45; Noland, p. 148; Derfler, *Millerand*, pp. 233–7; *Revue socialiste*, May 1903, pp. 538–50, 601–8, Millerand's speeches to the Socialist Congress at Bordeaux, 12–14 April 1903; Basdevant, p. 11.

In Bordeaux, Millerand's defense went beyond his parliamentary votes to a general policy statement that acknowledged the reality of class struggles, but stressed class solidarity and common participation in a national entity. Respectful of the party's position and a regular participant in its parliamentary group meetings, he insisted that his views had remained the same since he became a Socialist in 1893. Still anxious for Socialist cohesion based on realism, he wanted the party to achieve its goals of freedom, justice, and well-being through universal suffrage in the Republic, not by revolutionary promises of miracles. Human efforts alone could gradually transform social and economic conditions. Access to municipal and national power had significantly furthered the cause of peaceful, legal reform. He pleaded with the Socialists to repudiate those programs that deviated from their ten-year commitment to using democratic means for society's progressive transformation.[2]

Although revolutionary Marxists and Blanquists were not at Bordeaux, those reformists, led by Pierre Renaudel and Gustave Hervé, who opposed Millerand's parliamentary votes almost won his exclusion from the party. Jaurès' spirited defense of Millerand's ministerial achievements and denunciation of unjust sectarian campaigns modified the decision from exclusion to a reprimand.[3] Millerand remained a party member and agreed to accept Socialist discipline, but did not believe loyalty to socialism required him to abandon individual initiative or freedom of thought. Given his commitment to reformism and an increasingly militant party, it was only a matter of time before another divisive issue emerged.

Millerand's votes of October and November 1903, though similar to January, illustrated his independence and again placed him in opposition to his Socialist parliamentary colleagues. He supported the government against charges stemming from a police raid on the Paris Bourse du Travail; he did not vote for a Socialist resolution cutting off the Ministry of the Interior's funds for secret agents; and, most importantly, he was the only Socialist to vote against deputy Gustave Hubbard's resolution of 23 November for France to initiate international disarmament proposals. Millerand agreed with Foreign Minister Théophile Delcassé that a defeated France could not be the first to disarm. Millerand's votes, which supported the

2. *Revue socialiste*, May 1903, pp. 538–50, 601–8, Millerand's speeches to the Bordeaux Congress of April 1903; Persil, p. 48; Lefranc, *Mouvement socialiste*, p. 131; Paul-Boncour, I, p. 95.
3. Derfler, *Millerand*, pp. 237–9; Noland, pp. 149–56; Persil, pp. 46–7.

government, were consistent with his earlier stand on national security and domestic order. For the Socialist Federation of the Seine, which excluded him from its ranks and from the French Socialist party on 4 January 1904, however, they were the final straw.[4]

To the Federation, Millerand's independence was incompatible with Socialist discipline. Given its increasingly revolutionary orientation, the Federation's expulsion of Millerand was less surprising than the reformists' acceptance of that position at the Amsterdam Congress of the Second International in August 1904. German Marxists won international repudiation of the reformist route to gradual, legal, social change, and adoption of the revolutionary program seeking a proletarian victory in the inevitable class war with bourgeois society. The hostility of the French reformists to Millerand's parliamentary activities paved the way for their acceptance of this uncompromising stance. Despite his legislative contributions, Millerand thus fostered the increasingly sterile opposition role that the French Socialist party adopted after the Amsterdam Congress and the formation of the unified Socialist party (S.F.I.O.) in March 1905.[5] Millerand's official exclusion from Socialist ranks did not, however, lead him to abandon social reform or alter his political views. He still called himself a socialist, retained working-class support, and often collaborated with his former colleagues in the Chamber.

Millerand focused his parliamentary activities during the 1902–6 legislature on the Chamber's Commission on Insurance and Social Welfare of which he was president. Its primary task was to draft a law that would provide a system of old-age and sickness insurance. As Minister of Commerce, Millerand had sponsored a pension bill, but opposition from unions and industry had buried it in committee. To Millerand, the state had an obligation to aid the aged and infirm. It must establish a public service that recognized the legal rights of old and sick citizens without funds and an insurance system for former workers. All citizens should support the cost of this public service of 'social solidarity,' not charity. The fundamental human right to life was at the root of the specific details.[6]

4. Noland, pp. 157–8; Lefranc, *Mouvement socialiste*, p. 131; Persil, p. 51; Derfler, *Millerand*, p. 241.
5. Derfler, *Millerand*, pp. 254–5.
6. Millerand, 'Souvenirs,' pp. 47–8; A.N., C7278, Chamber, Commission d'as-

The Insurance and Social Welfare Commission, which met frequently during 1903, drafted a pension law that Millerand defended in the Chamber of Deputies on 12 June 1903. The law sought to establish a 'right to life' for all citizens by providing the old and sick with payment from the state, either locally or nationally, of the debt created by their existence. He pleaded with the legislature to endorse a law, under discussion for fifteen years, whose revolutionary effects would constitute a legislative landmark for the Third Republic.[7]

Millerand's commitment to the pension law influenced his opposition to the Combes ministry from November 1903 to January 1905. The premier's determination to curb the congregations and separate church and state had distracted him from social reform, even though his ministerial statement of 10 June 1902 had listed workers' pensions as a principal goal. Millerand was frustrated by his inability to win ministerial support for the retirement proposals and angered by Combes' distortion of the 1901 Associations Law into a general attack on the French Catholic Church.[8]

In July 1902, the government closed 300 religious orders for not filing authorization requests; in November, requests were categorized and decided on by blocks. Authorization for the five congregations that Combes supported were sent to the Senate, the rest to the Chamber. In the first half of 1903, virtually all requests for authorization from teaching orders were denied. In June, Waldeck-Rousseau accused his successor of violating the spirit of the Associations Law with his group rejections. He again attacked Combes in the Senate in November 1903, at which time his former collaborators, including Millerand, joined the opposition.[9]

Millerand's famous speech of 17 March 1904 denounced the premier for permitting his anticlerical campaign to displace social legislation, specifically workers' pensions. As he later commented, he would have been derelict in his duty had he not stopped an

surance et prévoyance sociale, sessions of 28 November and 5 December 1902.

    7. A.N., C7278, Chamber, minutes of the Commission, 16 January–8 June 1903; *ibid.*, 1 July, 27 October and 17 November 1903, detailed discussions of the pension funds to finance workers' retirement insurance, specifically the retirement age, proportions of state, employer, and employee contributions, percentage of workers' salary to be contributed and budgetary ramifications; J.O., *Chambre*, 12 June 1903; also in Millerand, *Travail*, pp. 151–6; Persil, p. 51; Derfler, *Millerand*, p. 246.

    8. Duroselle, *Belle Epoque*, pp. 256–7.

    9. Goguel, pp. 118–20; Persil, p. 52.

enterprise that sacrificed major social reforms to sectarian passions. He noted that the Insurance and Social Welfare Commission had repeatedly sought an official reaction to the proposed law, but the premier and the ministers of finance and commerce continually postponed their auditions and their verdict. This 'dilatory' treatment was unacceptable from a cabinet that had formally promised to promote the program. The commission had drafted a pension law by January 1903, but Combes' constant postponement of his audition had created a stalemate. Finally, in July, he commented that the government planned to study the commission's proposals and not to present its own. The premier's subsequent actions even invalidated his remarks to the commission because official instructions had made communication with the finance minister impossible. Since the commission could not complete the retirement project without financial collaboration, it faced the 'lamentable' situation of postponing the law until 1905. Millerand, who understood Minister of Finance Maurice Rouvier's reservations, insisted that the commission was flexible. Rouvier would have collaborated, he was convinced, if Combes had assigned a sufficiently high priority to the pension law's expenses. However important the anticlerical struggle against the congregations, Millerand refused to accept it as the cabinet's sole objective.

> Ever since the cabinet has been on these benches, I have given to the necessary struggle which it has pursued against the congregations, a support without reserve . . . but I would never have believed that any government as profoundly convinced as it was of the necessity of this battle could limit its horizons and its ambitions to the struggle against the congregations . . . Even at the most critical moments, the premier of 1899 never separated social action from republican defense. The more harsh and keen is the battle against the forces of the past, the more tightly it imposes on the republican power the obligation to pursue with equal vitality as the necessary destructions those constructions so impatiently attended.

Only the Republic's enemies would benefit if the workers' needs were ignored. A persistent proponent of church–state separation and a Dreyfusard hostile to the congregations' activities, Millerand still viewed the Combes ministry's monomaniacal anticlericalism as excessive.[10]

10. Millerand, 'Souvenirs,' pp. 49–50; J.O., *Chambre*, 17 March 1904.

With Combes unprepared for Millerand's attack, only Jaurès' impassioned defense saved the government from reversal. The premier, who maintained that his government had passed reforms other than religious, noted that Millerand had been no more successful in passing a pension bill while he was commerce minister. Jaurès, who stressed that the religious threat justified the cabinet's treatment of the congregations, attributed Millerand's attack to personal ambition and faulted him for abandoning the government at a time when republican solidarity was vital. Indeed, it was this attack on Combes rather than Millerand's exclusion from the French Socialist party that created an irreparable breach between him and Jaurès. Combes later defended his record and blamed Millerand for undermining the government. He refuted Millerand's charges of official inactivity where the Insurance and Social Welfare Commission's proposals were concerned. Those complex issues, which were slow to investigate, required additional information. Combes, who was surprised by Millerand's interpellation, called his opponent's maneuver an 'ambush' that simplistically equated too many anticlerical laws with too few social reforms. Careful planning, he argued, had insured the presence of all ministerial opponents from the Right and Center and the absence of many republican supporters. The government won by a narrow eleven-vote majority and lasted another ten months, but its tenure was precarious thereafter.[11]

The republican steering committee, the Délégation des Gauches, not being forewarned about the attack was unable to avert it. Since Combes' activities had already created dissension within the republican majority, division on the Left reinforced support for Millerand from the Right and Center to explain the close vote. Some Moderates and Radicals, former supporters of Waldeck-Rousseau's republican coalition, had become disenchanted with Combes' policies. Although Socialist support saved his government, it was weaker in March 1904 than his retrospective apologia implied. If planning occurred on one side, it was not absent from the other.

11. Goguel, p. 122; Derfler, *Millerand*, pp. 246–9; Abel Combarieu, *Sept ans à l'Elysée avec le Président Emile Loubet* (Paris: Librairie Hachette, 1932), pp. 272–4; Mermeix, *Histoire du franc depuis le commencement de ses malheurs* (Paris: Albin Michel, 1926), pp. 146–9; Chastenet, *Poincaré*, p. 72; Partin, p. 215; R.A. Winnacker, 'The Délégation des gauches: a successful attempt at managing a parliamentary coalition,' *The Journal of Modern History*, IX, No. 4, December 1937, p. 466; Jacques Millerand, 'Alexandre Millerand,' *L'histoire*, No. 8, 1979, p. 109; Emile Combes, *Mon ministère Mémoires, 1902–1905*, (Paris: Librairie Plon, 1956), pp. 150–6.

While former Waldeck-Rousseau ministers like Millerand, Leygues, and Caillaux sounded out known anti-ministerial deputies on their social views, Combes also used civil servants and journalists to pressure wavering deputies. Indeed, the failure of Millerand's interpellation has been attributed to the blackmailing tactics of Eugène Etienne (leader of the Gauche Démocratique).[12] Blackmail and planning may have influenced the final balance between the two sides, but larger issues of governmental policy, particularly anticlericalism, explained the cabinet's precarious position.

The cabinet's narrow victory in March 1904 did not silence Millerand, who denounced the ministry on 10 June for certain legal changes that benefited the wealthy but harmed those subject to jurisdiction and to the treasury. The old rates of 1807 had to be modified, but not by raising costs. When parliament tried to assign responsibility, the government responded that its actions had to be inviolate to protect the laic and social program, even though it had consistently postponed workers' pensions to an unspecified date, presumably after the clerical danger had ended and a budgetary equilibrium been achieved. The social gains, which Combes cited, like aid to foundlings or primary and secondary education laws, were actually made against official opposition or were criticized as inadequate and incoherent. Millerand viewed the government as an impotent administration that was detrimental to republican interests, and that had resorted to a personal denigration in order to defend itself.[13]

The Combes cabinet, though shaken by Millerand's attack in the spring and insinuations of corruption in the early summer, preserved its increasingly fragile majority into the autumn. The Amsterdam Congress of the Second International's verdict that Socialists must not collaborate with bourgeois parties further weakened it. The French Socialists withdrew from the Délégation des Gauches, thereby depriving Combes of formerly loyal backers. Shady espionage practices linked to the war ministry and civil service revealed anti-democratic characteristics, reminiscent of earlier anti-Dreyfusard tactics, that compromised the Republic's reputation for integrity and justice. In October 1904, a nationalist interpellation mentioned a war ministry espionage system, aided by the masonic lodges, that compiled evidence on French officers' religious beliefs and practices

12. Duroselle, *Belle Epoque*, p. 261; Persil, pp. 52–4; Derfler, *Millerand*, pp. 246–9.
13. J.O., *Chambre*, 10 June 1904; Derfler, *Millerand*, pp. 257–8; Persil, p. 54.

to insure that only anticlerical officers were promoted. Officers who attended mass or sent their children to religious schools were accused of republican disloyalty and suffered professional disadvantages.[14] Although War Minister General André may not have known the system's details, he set the goal of republicanizing the army on which it was based.

Revelations of the war ministry's tactics, first publicized by the nationalists, attracted a broader spectrum of governmental opponents. During a stormy session on 4 November 1904, Millerand condemned the war ministry for soliciting information on individual behavior under the guise of fighting the religious orders. To republicanize the army did not validate dishonorable methods that bred hatred and division in the army and the nation.[15] Although the ministry survived the vote of confidence, General André had little choice but to resign on 15 November.

Millerand again interpellated the government on its dishonorable practices the following month, applying the subsequently famous epithet of 'abject regime' to the Combes government. Anxious to have loyal public servants, the government had solicited prefects' information on the political views of all civil servants and candidates for public office. Such tactics would, Millerand charged, make the Republic an odious and uninhabitable abode for Frenchmen. His attack had shifted from a criticism of governmental neglect for social reform in the spring to a denunciation of military and civilian espionage tactics in the autumn. Although Combes again survived, his ministry's position was too precarious to operate effectively. When its opponent, Paul Doumer, was elected president of the Chamber, Combes finally conceded and resigned on 18 January 1905. His anticlerical and military programs primarily destroyed the secure majority of 1902. Millerand's interpellations, which drew attention to the government's inadequacies and delinquencies, played a significant part in its demise.[16]

Various motives have been attributed to Millerand for his attacks on Combes. To the Left, especially to Jaurès' supporters who

14. Duroselle, *Belle Epoque*, pp. 262–3; Goguel, pp. 122–3; Derfler, *Millerand*, p. 260.

15. J.O., *Chambre*, 4 November 1904; Derfler, *Millerand*, p. 260; Duroselle, *Belle Epoque*, p. 263; Goguel, p. 123.

16. J.O., *Chambre*, 9 December 1904; Derfler, *Millerand*, pp. 260–1; Gagnon, p. 268; Chastenet, *Poincaré*, p. 72; Lefranc, *Mouvement socialiste*, p. 131; Robert Cornilleau, *De Waldeck-Rousseau à Poincaré* (Paris: Editions Spes, 1927), pp. 104–9; Porch, p. 98.

approved their leader's loyalty to the Combes government, Millerand sought a ministerial collapse to return to the cabinet. Calling him an ambitious loner (*isolé ambitieux*), they believed that Millerand's political ambitions had led him to join former Waldeck-Rousseau ministers, such as Leygues and Caillaux, and disenchanted Radicals and Moderates, like Ribot and Doumer, in order to undermine Combes' position.[17] His opposition has, however, been interpreted in a less self-interested light. It reflected a genuine dismay at governmental neglect for social reform, shady police state procedures, and distortion of Waldeck-Rousseau's religious and army programs. Loyalty to a former patron and ideological integrity influenced his behavior at the expense of possible political harm or isolation. Certainly, Millerand's actions were the final wedge between him and his former Socialist colleagues. Indeed, they may have finally alienated Jaurès from ministerial collaboration and persuaded him to accept a revolutionary orientation for a unified Socialist party.

After Millerand's attack on Combes in March 1904, he was mentioned as a possible replacement. The dying Waldeck-Rousseau, who appreciated his former colleague's denunciation of Combes for making the Associations Law an anti-religious crusade, still wrote to President Loubet on 24 March that he admired Millerand but did not consider appropriate a cabinet led by him. For the president, Millerand's 'dangerous' political and social doctrines outweighed his obvious courage and intellectual skills. In January 1905, Doumer and Dubost proposed a Millerand cabinet. While the suggestion was unrealistic, Millerand was obviously sufficiently prominent to be a conceivable choice as premier.[18]

While personal ambition may have partly influenced him, Millerand did not win immediate political benefits from his attack on Combes. It further undermined his relations with the Socialists, with whom he identified even after his official exclusion, and did not win him supporters elsewhere. Although the Right disliked Combes, it did not yet welcome a renegade Socialist. Millerand considered it his duty to stop an enterprise that sacrificed social reforms to sectarian passions. For Combes had used Waldeck-Rousseau's peaceful Associations Law as a militant anticlerical

17. Bourgin, p. 141; J. Ries, 'Combes, Millerand et Jaurès en 1904,' *La Revue socialiste*, July 1964, pp. 213–16; Cornilleau, *De Waldeck*, pp. 104–6.

18. Combarieu, pp. 272–4, 299; Cornilleau, *De Waldeck*, pp. 104–9; Ries, p. 216; Derfler, *Millerand*, pp. 249–52.

weapon that relied on odious police tactics.[19] Millerand's reputation for independence, and perhaps integrity, undoubtedly enhanced his prestige among some politicians, but an equation of his attack with political ambition is too simplistic. While it may have yielded future career benefits, its motives were a mixture of loyalty to Waldeck-Rousseau, commitment to social reform, and a genuine republican libertarianism that viewed anticlerical and dictatorial procedures as detrimental to national interests.

Millerand stressed to his constituents the republican crisis which the Combes ministry's weakness and corruption had provoked. He had loyally backed the government from June 1902 until March 1904, even though Waldeck-Rousseau had disavowed his successor in July 1903. The Chamber had finally voted for obligatory assistance to the old and the ill in May 1903, but opposition in the Senate and, later, governmental financial reservations had blocked its implementation. The ministry should have informed the social welfare commission about its financial questions and not unexpectedly proposed to raise the requisite 30–40 million francs by increased taxes, which would surely bring about a parliamentary veto. Millerand cited the successful German system of borrowing the money from a retirement fund (approximately 300 million in yearly contributions), created by employer and employee payments, which the budget could easily support. He had also persuaded parliament to ratify an unemployment fund that would shield workers from that common but cruel insecurity. Millerand particularly faulted the government for its incoherent and vacillating behavior in the difficult matter of church–state separation. The Republic had gradually achieved a spiritual and temporal separation with its laws on free, obligatory, and secular education, associations, and public assistance. The question of religious behavior, which had still not been settled, contained such vast problems that it would either brutally arouse legitimate protests or insure that religious associations allowed all citizens to enjoy freedom of conscience. Instead of treating that complex situation skillfully, the Combes government had displayed an irresponsible frivolity that even encompassed personal calumny toward the opposition. Loyalty to the Republic and its fundamental objectives lay at the root of Millerand's opposition to Combes.[20]

19. Millerand, 'Souvenirs,' pp. 48–50.
20. A.N., F.M. 5, Millerand's speech to the Fête du cercle républicain du XIIe, 17 December 1904, published in *Le Douzième*, 22–28 December 1904, Persil, pp. 54, 58.

Combes' program toward the congregations triggered a series of charges of bribery and corruption that made a complex situation particularly sordid. To handle requests for authorization, the government had divided the orders into three groups: teaching, preaching, and commercial orders, specifically the Chartreux, the Carthusian monks of the Grande Chartreuse who were noted for their liquor. Late in 1902, it was rumored that the premier's son, Edgar Combes, had agreed to let the Chartreux make a donation of 2 million francs, the famous *million des Chartreux*, to avert eviction. Millerand, who questioned Edgar Combes' integrity on 10 June 1904, accused the premier of shifting from the political to the personal level. The charges and countercharges led the Chamber to appoint a special parliamentary commission of investigation. To the commission, Millerand maintained that the 'Chartreux incident' had been exaggerated. While the Chartreux had seemingly offered money to the government, corruption was not involved. A contribution to republican electoral funds was not related to the Chartreux affair, as had been charged. He minimized the incident and did not charge Edgar Combes with accepting a bribe from the congregation.[21]

The waters were, however, muddied by countercharges accusing Millerand of receiving funds from religious orders during the 1902 elections. Millerand, who defended himself in the Chamber of Deputies, stressed public over personal issues. His personally painful treatment jeopardized, he insisted, all citizens' vital interests. Such police tactics were a 'scandalous abuse of power' that violated individual privacy. He attributed the charges of corruption to a wish to damage the credibility of the cabinet's political adversary, even though the evidence was distorted and without a factual basis. The government's charges of financial corruption were a shady form of revenge for his political opposition. Although no evidence proved that Millerand had questionable business dealings either as Minister of Commerce or as a lawyer, mention of his name created suspicions. While the personal attack clearly outraged him, he was more concerned about the broader political implications of a government capable of slander in order to protect its existence.[22]

Combes later portrayed the affair of the Chartreux millions as yet

---

21. Goguel, p. 102; J.O., *Chambre*, 10 June 1904; Derfler, *Millerand*, pp. 257–60; Duroselle, *Belle Epoque*, p. 259; A.N., C7310, Chamber, Parliamentary Inquests, 15 June 1904; A.N., C7311, Parliamentary Inquests, 22 June 1904.
22. J.O., *Chambre*, 1 July 1904; Derfler, *Millerand*, p. 260.

another maneuver against his ministry. Accusing Millerand of using any possible chance to reverse his defeat on 17 March, Combes viewed the interpellation of 10 June as a 'ridiculous pretext' to attack the premier whose moral sacrifice led him to adopt the previous government's position in the Chartreux affair. Maintaining that he and his son had not behaved shamefully, as the investigative commission had confirmed, he accused Waldeck-Rousseau's government, and particularly Millerand, of distributing secret funds and legion of honor decorations. While he did not link Millerand to the Chartreux millions, he charged him with hiding a subordinate's secret financial transactions. For Combes, personal ambition explained Millerand's opposition to the cabinet, including insinuations of bribery or dishonesty.[23]

From the murky, confused tale of the Chartreux millions, it was a short step to the famous billion of the congregations (*milliard des congrégations*), the wealth which the orders' liquidation should have yielded to the state. However, the exile of the orders proved considerably less lucrative than anticipated; the *milliard* for social reform failed to materialize, at least partly because of the slow and costly liquidation process. Rumor claimed that a substantial portion was siphoned off into the pockets of lawyers like Millerand who defended the congregations. Combes' charges that Millerand had amassed such a fortune from the numerous cases as to even make him repugnant to his friends undoubtedly fueled the allegations. He cited sources from the justice ministry as evidence of Millerand's exhorbitant liquidation fees, but his accusations did not hold up under scrutiny. A court-appointed receiver termed an 'absurd legend' the accusation that lawyers like Millerand were paid outrageous fees. On the contrary, remuneration, which was generally below normal levels, was tied to the specific case's complexity. In the beginning, it was necessary to set general principles for applying the Associations Law. Millerand, who took the legally significant or difficult cases, charged considerably less than his normal rates and received a fraction of the amounts cited by the critics.[24]

Millerand did indeed establish a substantial legal practice after he

23. Combes, pp. 166–7, 181; Winnacker, p. 466.
24. Duroselle, *Belle Epoque*, p. 260, gives a figure of 35 million for the amount the state finally received from the liquidation process. Brogan, I, p. 366; Combes, pp. 168–9; E. Nast, 'A propos de la liquidation des biens des congrégations,' *Revue politique et parlementaire*, LIV, 10 October 1907. Persil, p. 56, noted, for example, that Millerand testified thirty-two times before the liquidator Duez for a total of 65,000 francs, a derisory figure of 2,000 francs per case.

left the commerce ministry. His political experience, including his ministerial legacy, probably attracted clients. He may have inherited some of Waldeck-Rousseau's large industrial clients after the latter's death, but his substantial income came primarily from his civil legal practice, not from liquidating the religious congregations. Nonetheless, Combes' slanderous implications left a pernicious legacy. When the rumors reached parliament, Millerand could no longer disregard them. On 14 March 1910, while Minister of Public Works, he noted that except for the congregations' affairs, he had always refused political cases. In that instance, he broke his rule because the Associations Law posed such difficult and sensitive legal issues that most lawyers avoided the cases. Loyalty to his former mentor and an obligation to apply an important piece of republican legislation had guided his decision to accept those cases that raised questions of principle. Although he had not naively expected his scrupulous treatment to silence calumnious accusations, he had disregarded such ludicrous charges as fees of 300,000 francs or a shameful tithe extracted from his collaborators until they surfaced in parliament. Duty to his colleagues then required him to speak out and deny any unethical behavior. For example, one charge of excessive fees for a single case in fact represented a year of advice and trial defenses.[25] Scandalous charges of graft and greed, which tainted the innocent as well as the guilty, finally forced the state to take over the liquidations in 1910. No evidence, however, justified including Millerand in the story of shady dealings and unscrupulous individuals which accompanied that complex process. If Millerand was active in Combes' fall, the former premier's slanderous accusations of greed and corruption had a surprisingly lasting impact on his opponent's career.

Millerand's opposition to the Combes ministry diverted him from social reforms and the working-class plight. His concern to enact a

25. Georges Bonnefous, *Histoire politique de la Troisième République*, I, *L'Avant-Guerre* (Paris: Presses Universitaires de France, 1965), p. 174; Brogan, II, p. 424; Paul-Boncour, I, p. 95; Derfler, *Millerand*, pp. 226–8; Persil, pp. 54–6; J.O., *Chambre*, 14 March 1910; also in Millerand, *Politique de réalisations* (Paris: Bibliothèque Charpentier, 1911), pp. 349–53; Duroselle, *Belle Epoque*, p. 344. Georges Suarez, *Briand: sa vie – son œuvre* (Paris: Librairie Plon, 1938), II, pp. 257–60, comments on Briand's response to Jaurès that Millerand was one of his best collaborators and a friend that he would not abandon. He cites Millerand's letter to Briand of 25 July 1910 from Carlsbad transposing his personal gratitude to a general appreciation for being able to collaborate in the noble and necessary enterprise of political renovation.

pension law even made him reluctant to formulate other programs, such as unemployment insurance. A national unemployment fund, a precursor to unemployment insurance, seemed preferable to emergency relief efforts. He recognized, however, that it was not possible to justify a fund costing 18 million francs a year at the same time as making provision for an old-age and sickness program. The French should instead adopt the Ghent model, an unemployment fund joining state and private efforts by contributions from unions and communes. Although this program would be only a temporary solution, it would reinforce private initiative, encourage worker associations, and provide local and national official support. Millerand was clearly sympathetic to the harsh fate that was suffered by many individuals in modern society, but he realistically recognized that the state could not tackle all the problems at once.[26]

Pressures for a retirement program linked Millerand's nationalism and socialism. In 1905–6, he frequently demanded a pension law at a time when the separation of church and state and the first Moroccan crisis were the focus of national attention. In July 1905, just after the vote on church–state separation, Millerand pleaded with his colleagues to consider workers' pensions. In November, he described the law as important for the proletariat's moral and material advancement; greater working-class security would benefit the whole nation. Since economic prosperity and social change were closely related, it would be contradictory to expect an impoverished nation to pass reforms. The government required a financial plan, including efforts to stimulate production, so that the workers' situation could be gradually and peacefully improved.[27]

Millerand's eloquent speech of 22 February 1906 finally won the Chamber's passage of the pension law, although the Senate did not ratify a somewhat modified version until 1910. To Millerand, the pension law represented the victory of foresight and solidarity inherent in republican ideals. The law set pension figures for workers aged over sixty and a payment schedule for active laborers. Funds derived from a percentage of workers' salaries and

26. J.O., *Chambre*, 30 November 1904; also in Millerand, *Travail*, pp. 137–50.
27. J.O., *Chambre*, 3 July 1905; *ibid.*, 29 November 1905; also in Millerand, *Travail*, pp. 203–14; Sanford Elwitt, *The Third Republic Defended. Bourgeois Reform in France 1880–1914* (Baton Rouge: Louisiana State University Press, 1986), pp. 144, 147, terms Millerand a 'social liberal' who linked defense of national interests to enactment of social reforms to improve workers' conditions.

matching employers' contributions. The program might eventually include small businessmen, shopkeepers, farmers, the infirm, and families without breadwinners. He praised republican accomplishments like the freedom of the press, meetings and association, and free, obligatory education, but added that French greatness also needed a social program to insure that civilized and peaceful behavior would avert violence and disruption. Millerand believed that a retirement system, by encouraging unity and happiness, fostered national greatness as much as did military hardware. The pension system's obligatory character reflected democratic self-discipline. Despite diversity, a common faith bound Frenchmen in a disciplined union capable of confronting any external menace. A solidarity that transcended internal divisions was as necessary to peacetime prosperity and greatness as it was to wartime military success.[28]

Despite Millerand's primary interest in a social insurance program, he was still involved in French technical education and the merchant marine. As president of the Arts and Crafts Conservatory's administrative council, he publicized its contributions to industry and science and urged it to adapt to contemporary production needs. For example, he sponsored a testing laboratory that checked products and machines for industrialists. It was mechanization and the division of labor, rather than legislative decisions, that had produced a French apprenticeship crisis which made practical professional education especially important. The worker had become simply a cog in a machine, endlessly performing the same task. A process that dehumanized workers and producers would inevitably lead to national decadence. France must, Millerand argued, reverse a process that reduced vital national forces, prosperity, and moral power. A technical education that encouraged workers' professional capacity provided the best solution, as nations like Germany had already recognized.[29]

28. J.O., *Chambre*, 22 February 1906; also in Millerand, *Travail*, pp. 215–26; Millerand, 'Souvenirs,' p. 52; Derfler, *Millerand*, pp. 202–3, 246–7; Millerand, *Travail*, pp. 227–44, speech in Bordeaux, 20 October 1906, to the departmental union of the Sociétés de secours mutuels de la Gironde; *ibid.*, pp. 108–34, Millerand's speech in Lyon, 14 May 1907, to the Lyonnaise section of the republican committee on commerce and industry.
29. Millerand, *Travail*, pp. 251–5, Millerand's speech of 1 July 1903 at the Conservatoire des arts et métiers; *ibid.*, pp. 256–67, speech of 4 June 1907, to the

Millerand was also president of a special commission appointed to study the merchant navy and propose changes in naval and armaments construction. Since France needed a formidable army and navy to be independent, it also had to have a stronger merchant marine. All citizens still had a patriotic duty to perform their military service, as Gambetta had proclaimed long ago. Only a 'deadly rhetoric,' that most Frenchmen resisted, denied that obligation. Even a passionately peaceful and democratic France did not exist in isolation. The preservation of peace required a clear demonstration that France did not fear war. Millerand believed that a better mercantile navy would enhance France's chances of survival in that atmosphere of armed peace which had characterized Europe for thirty-five years.[30]

On a theoretical level, Millerand remained true to the ideas he had supported for two decades. Unionization, education, and opposition to revolution were the constant themes of his speeches. Education liberated humanity from internal and external constraints and offered hopes for the future. Unions also performed an educational function by teaching workers to defend their professional interests and giving them a sense of their rights and obligations. Furthermore, the organization of workers in factories could facilitate a peaceful settlement of disputes by applying the democratic principles of a majority vote to avert strikes and to settle disputes peacefully by arbitration. Since only orderly, persistent human endeavor could emancipate the workers, education, in which unions played a vital role, best prepared the proletariat to assume its proper tasks and responsibilities.[31]

Millerand also took stands on major domestic and foreign issues. In late 1903, for example, he argued that church–state separation was a logical consequence of the Republic's secular policy, but wanted to avoid persecuting the church while freeing the state. The measure was one of freedom and not one of financial expediency. In 1905, Millerand investigated the positive and negative effects of

Conservatoire des arts et métiers; J.O., *Chambre*, 3 December 1904.

30. A.N., F.M. 5, extra-parliamentary commission report on the merchant marine, 4 May 1904; *ibid.*, Millerand's speech to the banquet of the Dunkirk pilots union, 28 August 1905; Derfler, *Millerand*, p. 228.

31. Millerand, *Socialisme réformiste*, introduction, pp. 6–15; *Revue socialiste*, June 1903, pp. 641–50, Millerand's speech 'L'organisation ouvrière' of 16 May 1903 at the Université populaire du Faubourg Saint-Antoine.

the first Moroccan crisis: more cordial French ties to Italy and Great Britain but almost overt hostility toward Germany. The Moroccan crisis proved that France could not preserve its independence or defend its lofty ideals without a strong and disciplined army and navy and close alliances, and not by pacifist statements.[32]

Millerand was still convinced that national wealth was a prerequisite for social reforms. He urged public works projects and particularly an expanded communications network to provide work for the proletariat and to augment national wealth. The French should construct a link to the new Simplon Pass so that commerce could profit from the new route. He also supported international collaboration, such as common legislation to set the length of the work day or protect workers' hygiene. Such social cooperation between nations, which matched the domestic solidarity of classes, fostered peace. Millerand's specific projects, like the laws on working hours or pensions, were part of a large program designed to eradicate industrialization's inequities and promote more harmonious relations among Frenchmen and nations.[33]

For Millerand, economic expansion abroad and domestic productivity both enhanced national strength. Urging industrialists and merchants to expand their intellectual and economic horizons, he suggested studying foreign languages and investigating foreign business opportunities. Since the struggle for world power had shifted to the economic domain, commercial attachés should be attached to the foreign ministry. To preserve peace, diplomats should focus on economic areas like international technical conventions. Although merchandise followed the flag, national influence expanded with the sale of goods. Traders therefore exported French theories and innovations as much as products; French greatness and prosperity grew along with the traders' personal wealth.[34]

Republican unity was a constant theme for Millerand. In 1908, he perceived syndicalist violence as an attack on the nation. The resort to violence through strikes, which harmed all parties, was generally due, Millerand believed, to agitators. Regular communication be-

32. A.N., F.M. 5, Millerand's *compte-rendu du mandat*, 24 October 1903; *ibid.*, 14 June 1905.

33. *Ibid.*

34. Millerand, *Réalisations*, pp. 31–42, Millerand's speech of 3 April 1908, 'L'organisation du commerce extérieur,' at the Ecole des sciences politiques.

tween workers and employers could best resolve problems and avoid industrial violence. Solidarity of classes implied that all members of society had a common stake in a better way of life. National solidarity, an important ingredient of national greatness, required the elimination of disruptive forces and ideals and creation of a political system that encouraged common interests to transcend divisive particular concerns. Anxious to reform the parliamentary regime, Millerand considered the electoral system of single-member constituencies, the *scrutin d'arrondissement*, to be the fundamental problem. It made deputies advocates of local vested interests. This narrow-minded mentality, *esprit de clocher*, perniciously obscured the recognition of national needs. Urging adoption of a list-voting system and proportional representation, Millerand viewed electoral reform as the key to other changes.[35]

The separation of church and state and the first Moroccan crisis dominated French attention after the fall of the Combes ministry, but Millerand did not take an active part in either issue. Maurice Rouvier, Combes' successor, was reversed in March 1906 ostensibly because of the religious battles due to the separation. Since France was preoccupied with the Algeciras Conference to settle the Moroccan situation, a governmental crisis was hardly opportune. Foreign and domestic tensions made a government of luminaries seem appropriate but impossible to constitute. Paul Doumer suggested Millerand for premier, but President of the Republic Armand Fallières preferred Radical deputy Jean Sarrien, who chose Georges Clemenceau as Minister of the Interior. Clemenceau took over that key ministry just as a new wave of strikes and labor unrest hit France.[36]

Although the national legislative elections of May 1906 took place in an atmosphere of religious and social unrest, the results left the balance between Left and Right in the Chamber of Deputies remarkably unchanged. The Radical-dominated leftist block retained its majority; Nationalists and right-of-center Moderates lost

35. A.N., F.M. 7, Millerand's speech to the Cercle Voltaire of Bordeaux, 7 November 1908; *ibid.*, Millerand's speech of 28 February 1909 to the republican circle of Versailles (Albert Joly); also in Millerand, *Réalisations*, pp. 1–15. Persil, pp. 60–2, also notes the linkage of social reforms and national prosperity in Millerand's speech of 14 May 1907.
36. G. Bonnefous, I, pp. 8–11.

slightly; Socialists, both unified and independent, gained. The March strikes in the north and Pas de Calais seemingly did not alienate the electorate from the revolutionary Marxists of the S.F.I.O. Nor did the earlier violence, provoked by efforts to establish inventories of church wealth, weaken the Radicals or benefit the Conservatives. Nonetheless, the government's actions in 1906 to control social unrest officially divided the Radicals and the Socialists, and ended the latter's support for a leftist block dating from 1899.[37]

Millerand, who was easily reelected in 1906, still wanted the government to concentrate on social reform rather than anticlericalism. Supporting the law separating church and state, he called it a law of freedom that gave all sects the right to practice their faith along with independence of the state and the churches. Public authorities should end their sectarian quarrels and focus instead on national wealth and greatness. France should not only protect its citizens against life's risks but also provide humane urban and agricultural working conditions. Since such reforms were costly, the tax system should be modified to cover national needs. An indispensable ingredient of a nation's power was its wealth relative to other states. Economic tactics were therefore part of the national arsenal. Denouncing the Socialists' opposition to military service as anti–patriotic 'criminal madness,' he insisted that no state, however committed to peace, could neglect military preparedness or abandon its alliances. In the tradition of Gambetta and Waldeck-Rousseau, Millerand denounced the *scrutin d'arrondissement* voting system and urged the *scrutin de liste* with proportional representation. Millerand, who had long opposed the *scrutin d'arrondissement* despite its personal benefits, became, along with Doumer and Paul Deschanel, a determined advocate of electoral reform in the elections of 1906. He later joined the parliamentary electoral reform group, which first met on 20 March 1907 in Paris and supported proportional list-voting. Electoral reform transcended partisan divisions as membership spanned the political spectrum from Conservative Denys Cochin to Socialist Jean Jaurès. The issue did not, however, reach the floor of the Chamber until 1909 when Briand was premier and Millerand was Minister of Public Works.[38]

37. *Ibid.*, pp. 6–9, 17–20; Goguel, pp. 123, 129–30; Duroselle, *Belle Epoque*, pp. 274–6.
38. Persil, p. 60; A.N., F.M. 6, Millerand's speech of 23 February 1906 at the Salle Vierney to his constituents of the 12th *arrondissement*; *ibid.*, summary of his achieve-

Radical leader Georges Clemenceau's government, which replaced the short-lived Sarrien ministry in October 1906, lasted
almost three years, the second longest of the Third Republic.
Clemenceau, who kept the Ministry of the Interior, offered Miller-
and the Ministry of Justice. Millerand, who would have liked the
foreign ministry already assigned to Stéphen Pichon, declined the
offer because his activities as Minister of Justice might aid his future
legal career. It did not seem ethically correct to appoint, as Minister
of Justice, magistrates before whom he might later plead as a
lawyer. Owing their positions to him, they might render overly
favorable judgements. Committed to an independent magistrature,
Millerand, who was never to be Minister of Justice, was always a
lawyer, who retreated to his legal career in times of political adversity.[39]

Ethics also dictated Millerand's response to the increased parliamentary stipend that the Chamber passed in November 1906.
Nationalists and Socialists in general opposed the raise, but the
issue split parties. The Chamber, which significantly increased the
annual parliamentary remuneration (from 9,000 to 15,000 francs),
gave the unfortunate impression of official incompetence except in
defending its own interests. Millerand, who decided to give his
own annual supplement to the indigent children of his *arrondissement*, asked for the gift to be treated anonymously. Although he did
not seek political capital from his magnanimity, Millerand was
obviously uncomfortable about official readiness to expand public
outlays for personal advantage instead of passing expensive social
reforms.[40]

Severe social unrest plagued the Clemenceau ministry. The
government responded repressively to the almost constant strikes,
often using troops to preserve order. Not only did the number of
strikes increase significantly, but they were so dispersed through
the industrial and agricultural sectors that the proportion of striking
workers to the work-force at large augmented radically.[41] As

ments since 1899 by the Comité républicain socialiste; G. Bonnefous, I, pp. 18, 58;
Millerand, 'Souvenirs,' pp. 55–6.

39. G. Bonnefous, I, p. 36; Persil, p. 59; *Le Parlement et l'opinion*, 1920, pp.
1658–62, article by Jean Melia on the character and personality of Millerand.

40. Duroselle, *Belle Epoque*, p. 283; Goguel, p. 134; G. Bonnefous, I, pp. 45–7;
A.N., F.M.6, letter from Millerand to A. Sabot, mayor of the 12th *arrondissement*, 2
December 1906, and Sabot's reply, 5 December 1906.

41. Wright, *France*, p. 265; Gagnon, pp. 274–5; Goguel, pp. 129–32. Duroselle,
Belle Epoque, p. 283, cited one striker for every 121 industrial workers in 1866
compared to one for 16 in 1906.

Millerand observed in June 1906, there were as many strikes between 1900 and 1905 as in the preceding ten years (4,360), and the situation worsened dramatically between 1906 and 1911. Since the existing optional arbitration system was used infrequently, the conflicts increased as the resort to peaceful solutions declined. France experienced a period resembling social warfare as the century's first decade neared an end.

Millerand continued to press for passage of the Waldeck-Rousseau ministry's draft law of 15 November 1900 on the peaceful settlement of labor disputes. France was not the only nation to confront the menace of strikes, but others had already passed appropriate legislation. Inspired by New Zealand laws, the French draft required a regular vote of the labor force to precede any strike decision. A democratic majority decision would replace a minority dictatorship, but workers feared that internal factory organization would jeopardize union prerogatives, and management feared a potential rival authority. Workers were so attached to the principle of the right to strike that it could not be eliminated. Strikes, however, threatened the public as much as the workers and industrialists. To Millerand, they were a 'detestable' form of warfare, which legislation to establish conciliation procedures sought to eradicate. Harmful in private industry, strikes could not be permitted in the public services because they threatened national interests. Since Millerand considered a strike to be the suppression of the labor contract, he wanted its declaration made as difficult as possible. His view that all warfare, whether international or domestic, was a measure of last resort clearly influenced his hostility to strikes, despite his support for social reform.[42]

During the spring of 1907, overproduction in the southern wine industry produced an almost revolutionary crisis. Fraudulent procedures and unprofitable sales triggered large-scale demonstrations (an estimated 700,000 at Montpelier on 9 June) to which the government responded harshly: the result was injuries and military mutinies, the latter unknown since the Paris Commune. On 21 June 1907, Millerand criticized Premier Clemenceau for encouraging a movement that he subsequently repressed. Government subsidies paid for demonstrators to reach the protest site, where

---

42. Millerand, *La Grève et l'organisation ouvrière* (Paris: Felix Alcan, 1906), speech of 29 June 1906; Millerand, *Le Contrat de travail* (Paris: Felix Alcan, 1907), speech of 18 January 1907; Millerand, *Réalisations*, pp. 16–30, speech of 10 January 1909 to the Comité des études professionelles; J.O., *Chambre*, 22 March 1909.

troops forcefully dispersed them. The government easily survived a vote of confidence, but with a reduced majority. Although opposed to strikes and social disorders, Millerand blamed the government for not taking precautions after being informed about plans for meetings and the demands of agricultural groups. Despite official encouragement of the demonstrations, the government was seemingly surprised when the meetings became unruly. This 'vacillating and whimsical' behavior, Millerand argued, had undermined public confidence in the government's effectiveness. Declaring that its impotence and lack of foresight had produced a state of anarchy, he opposed the ministry he had been invited to join.[43]

After nearly three years, the troubled Clemenceau premiership ended almost by accident on 20 July 1909. It was just retribution for the fiery 'Tiger' that the author of his demise was Delcassé, whom Clemenceau had cruelly censured a few years earlier. The premier had blamed the former foreign minister for France's 'humiliation' at the Algeciras conference; Delcassé accused the Clemenceau ministry of irregularities in the naval construction program, and a general neglect of military preparation. Not expecting a governmental challenge on the eve of the parliamentary recess, the government was overthrown by a narrow sixteen-vote majority because nearly a third of the deputies, including many of its supporters, were absent.[44]

While the actual circumstances of Clemenceau's fall were accidental and illustrative of the Third Republic's capricious political system, three years of social unrest had exhausted his regime. Its popularity had declined even though he preserved his majority on important issues. His ministry would probably have survived had the full Chamber been present, but France was ready for a change. The new Briand government again opened the door to ministerial influence for Millerand. Over the next six years, he would be in the government for more than three years. By the summer of 1909, therefore, Millerand had clearly joined France's governing élite.

43. J.O., *Chambre*, 21 June 1907; G. Bonnefous, I, pp. 68–75; Duroselle, *Belle Epoque*, pp. 285–6; Porch, p. 119.

44. Millerand, 'Souvenirs,' p. 53; G. Bonnefous, I, pp. 130–8; Goguel, p. 135; Duroselle, *Belle Epoque*, pp. 288–9, 341–2.

5
National Interest as Motivation for the Minister of Public Works' Reforms and Repression

The subtle Aristide Briand had a very different style from his combative predecessor Georges Clemenceau, but did not alter radically French policy or the composition of the parliamentary majority.[1] Millerand, who was Minister of Public Works from 24 July 1909 to 2 November 1910, was one of three independent Socialists in the new cabinet, along with the premier, who was also Interior minister, and Labor Minister René Viviani. As Minister of Public Works, Millerand tried to maintain social order so that France could exploit fully its natural resources, enact necessary reforms, and preserve social peace. In 1909–10, he was more actively involved in the repression of strikes, especially those in the public sector, than he had been seven years earlier as commerce minister. He again reorganized his departmental services. His continued support for electoral reform even divided him from his cabinet colleagues, but reflected a similar nationalistic desire for a better political system. Two major disasters particularly occupied him: the floods of 1910 that inundated the Paris region and the railroad strikes that started in the south, moved north, and culminated in an abortive general strike. In both instances, he sought to maintain normal activity in vital services. To him, the government was a watchdog which tried to alleviate the effects of disasters, natural or human. His interventionist view of the government aligned him with the Socialists and the Conservatives, although the former clearly disliked official repression of social conflicts. To

1. Duroselle, *Belle Epoque*, pp. 342–3.

Millerand, however, the government was obliged to promote social improvements like the pension law, finally enacted in March 1910, and economic developments like port autonomy and modern communication routes and to avert disruptions like strikes that harmed national interests.[2] Millerand's Ministry of Public Works, an epilogue to his career as social reformer, was a bridge to his subsequent activities as nationalist war minister and premier. His 55-year political career can be divided roughly in half: from 1885 to 1912, his focus was on social reforms within a republican context; from his war ministry of 1912 until the Third Republic's collapse in 1940, it was on nationalism, with social reform subordinated to France's international concerns.

An efficient administrator, Millerand wanted harmonious relations with his subordinates and a more efficient departmental organization. On 30 July 1909, he told his personnel that he hoped their collaboration would be productive. As he later recalled, he initiated at the Ministry of Public Works regular weekly meetings with departmental directors that he later used in the war ministry and at the commissariat in Strasbourg. On Mondays, he investigated all pending issues with the directors of the public works, railroad, and P.T.T. departments, listened to their opinions, and made decisions. He wanted consensus and personal involvement in the ministerial subdivisions. He was evidently an effective and popular administrator who won his collaborators' loyalty.[3]

Millerand reorganized his departments and drastically altered responsibilities to make the telephone, telegraph, and postal departments autonomous. In April 1910, he separated bridges and highways from mines and assigned the latter the responsibility for railway lines and electric energy. He added railroad directors to the general council of the bridges and highways and included six representatives each of the company and the employees on the railroad's technical development committee.[4] He sought autonomy for his services, but contact between personnel performing similar tasks. Vertical collaboration accompanied horizontal separation –

2. G. Bonnefous, I, pp. 167–73, the Senate passed the pension law on 22 March 1910 and the Chamber on 31 March.

3. Millerand, 'Souvenirs,' pp. 57–8; Persil, p. 65; Millerand, *Réalisations*, pp. iv–x.

4. Persil, p. 65; Millerand, *Réalisations*, pp. v–x; Stéphane Rials, *Administration et organisation, 1910–1930* (Paris: Editions Beauchesne, 1977), p. 158; A.N., C7349, Chamber, Budget Commission, audition of Millerand, 17 September 1909.

increased communication within an enterprise combined with autonomy for disparate activities.

Millerand introduced administrative and technical reforms in the postal and telegraphic section of his ministry to adapt the P.T.T. to modern requirements. Taking office shortly after a postal strike, Millerand investigated individual situations and, as an act of clemency, gradually reintegrated all suspended postal workers. His postal reforms included simpler procedures to distribute mail more rapidly, rates for postcards and letters, a service for active accounts and money orders, machines to weigh letters or distribute stamps, and bicycles or trams for mail deliveries. In the telephone and telegraph services, Millerand increased and improved lines and equipment, renovated the Parisian underground wires, laid additional underwater cables between France and Algeria, and expanded wireless telegraphic networks and stations.[5]

Millerand, who considered harmonious relations between all national service employees vital, streamlined the P.T.T. organization, which was previously characterized by a 'confused centralization' that fostered mutual recriminations among the sections. As Minister of Commerce, he had dealt with only three large associations, but by 1909 nearly thirty specialized self-seeking organizations had supplanted those groups. So many associations made effective collaboration between employees and the minister impossible and also weakened their bargaining power. Elected in February 1910, P.T.T. employees' delegates, who met regularly with Millerand and departmental representatives, conveyed civil service views on working conditions, promotion, and discipline. Where the state was the employer, he was able to apply his earlier suggestions to private industry for regular management–labor contacts. He was still convinced that better working conditions and access to management would win the workers over to the republican system.[6]

Electoral reform, a simmering issue for three years, moved to the forefront of parliamentary concerns in the autumn of 1909. Long an

5. Millerand, *Réalisations*, pp. xxvii–xxxviii; Persil, p. 66. A.N., C7349, Chamber, Budget Commission, audition of Millerand, 29 March 1910, discussed France's proposed cables along the African coast and an exchange of German rights in Brazil for French in Africa.

6. Millerand, *Réalisations*, pp. xxxix–xlii, 140–52; Millerand's speech to the *sous-agents* of the P.T.T., 6 November 1909.

advocate of proportional list-voting, Millerand battled the *scrutin d'arrondissement* from his ministerial post, and held to his position even at the expense of cabinet unity. The new premier, who initially supported the change, retreated when it threatened the cabinet's survival.

During the parliamentary recess, Briand gave his subsequently famous speech of 10 October 1909 at Perigueux castigating the single-member constituencies of the current voting system as stagnant, putrefying pools (*mares stagnantes, croupissantes*) whose bad odors and morbid germs the great purifying current (*un large courant purificateur*) of proportional representation must dissipate. Briand thus plunged into the long-standing electoral reform controversy that the Chamber had voted to debate while Clemenceau was still premier. The issue, which linked the Catholic Right of Albert de Mun and the Socialist Left of Jean Jaurès as supporters, was guaranteed a stormy response because of vehement Radical opposition. Opening on 21 October, the debate lasted over two weeks and menaced Briand's cabinet.[7]

Millerand's speech at the Gare de Lyon of 24 October 1909 denounced the *scrutin d'arrondissement*'s shabby, selfish preoccupation with private concerns. It permitted legislators to focus on local projects that aided only their regions and to neglect national problems. Millerand had told Briand when he joined the cabinet that the electoral system had to be modified. Although Briand's Perigueux speech briefly aligned him with Millerand, the pressures of parliamentary debate undermined that agreement.[8]

The Chamber discussion, which culminated in a series of votes on 8 November, ended by rejecting proportional representation. When Briand recognized his government's peril, he reversed his position and made rejection of electoral reform a question of confidence. The Chamber, which was not ready to overturn the cabinet, temporarily shelved the issue. In the preliminary votes, Millerand and other ministers abstained, but on the final vote of confidence, Millerand alone did not vote despite the fact that

7. Duroselle, *Belle Epoque*, pp. 343, 345; Goguel, pp. 135–6; G. Bonnefous, I, pp. 145–6; Brogan, II, p. 427. David E. Sumler, 'Polarization in French politics, 1909–1914,' unpublished Ph.D. dissertation, Princeton University, 1968, p. 253, argues that Briand's Perigueux speech initiated the conservative revival.

8. Millerand, 'Souvenirs,' pp. 55–6; Millerand, *Réalisations*, pp. 288–301, Millerand's speech of 24 October 1909 to his electors of the 12th *arrondissement*, 'Discours de la Gare de Lyon,' celebrating his twenty-fifth year in the Chamber and his twentieth as representative of his 12th *arrondissement* constituency.

cabinet unity generally took precedence over personal opinions. Although Millerand had told Briand from the beginning that he could not yield, his independence provoked a considerable reaction but did not eliminate him from the cabinet. A similar incident in 1889 provided a precedent. At that time, Goblet abstained from voting to reinstate the *scrutin d'arrondissement* which Charles Floquet's cabinet supported.[9]

The incident illustrated the character of both Millerand and Briand. The former's independence and ideological commitment often produced a rigidity that jeopardized relations with his political colleagues. For Briand, political success outweighed ideological consistency. The supreme political opportunist, once termed a 'serpent' attuned to the legislature, he lacked fixed ideas, but his subtlety and charm won him support from various groups. While Millerand's opposition did not cost him his cabinet position in 1909, it may have influenced Briand's decision the following year to reconstitute his cabinet without his inflexible colleague.

The old *scrutin d'arrondissement* system was used in the national legislative elections of 24 April and 8 May 1910. The results did not significantly alter the Chamber's composition or the position of Briand's cabinet. Millerand, who was reelected on the second round, had less difficulty than in 1902, but seemingly experienced more opposition when he ran as a cabinet minister than when out of office. The Socialists increased their representation; the Right declined slightly; the Moderates and Radicals remained approximately the same. The latter was still the largest group in Chamber and dominated French parliamentary life until the First World War.[10]

Millerand was an active minister, who travelled extensively to investigate local and general public works' projects. Advocating decentralization and economic modernization, he urged France to institute those practical reforms (*politique de résultats*) which would contribute to the national strength and prosperity on which social change depended. He visited the Atlantic and Mediterranean ports

9. G. Bonnefous, I, pp. 146–53: the vote was 291 to 225; Duroselle, *Belle Epoque*, p. 345; Persil, pp. 70–2; Millerand, 'Souvenirs,' pp. 55–7; Millerand, *Réalisations*, pp. lxxxviii–xc.

10. G. Bonnefous, I, pp. 184–7; Duroselle, *Belle Epoque*, pp. 345–6; A.N., F.M.8, Millerand's election summary of past achievements.

of Dieppe, Caen, Cherbourg, Rouen, Le Havre, Nantes, Saint-Nazaire, La Rochelle, Bordeaux, Cette, and Marseilles. Foreign examples convinced him that greater autonomy would make French ports more prosperous. Decentralization would, he believed, foster local and regional enterprises and thereby contribute to economic growth. He suggested an administrative council, including representatives from local chambers of commerce and the state, to run the ports. Millerand was convinced that this reform would reduce bureaucratic delays and facilitate local decision-making. He also examined specific problems like the navigability of the Seine, expansion of the port at La Rochelle, port improvements at Bordeaux and the maritime station at Dieppe, and connections between the Rhone canal and Marseilles.[11]

A nationalistic concern to develop fully France's resources led Millerand to promote tourism as it had to develop port autonomy. His travels throughout France prompted him to propose a National Tourist Office in October 1909, which could provide information on regional attractions and help tourists reach different parts of France. It was established on 5 March 1910. As he later recalled, tourism was a major French industry that should be encouraged. Millerand wanted the new organization to link and supplement existing groups like the Touring and Auto Clubs. The former, which had encouraged sports, had served as a school of endurance, initiative, and self-control that aided the physical and moral development of men and women. It had also helped the Ministry of Public Works to construct an Alpine route and buttresses at Mont-Saint-Michel, thereby helping to preserve France's national heritage and to publicize its charms.[12]

Millerand wanted to exploit fully the nation's natural resources. To this end, he urged the expansion of French communications networks. For example, he inspected construction of the Trans-pyrenean rail line at Cerdagne and later met his Italian counterpart Rubini to discuss a link between Nice and Vintimille. He also criticized the local forces which had delayed construction of French access routes to the Simplon Pass, open since 1906. Millerand thought the route would aid French production and export com-

---

11. Millerand, 'Souvenirs,' p. 59; Persil, p. 66; Millerand, *Réalisations*, pp. i–iii, xi–xix, 288–301, Millerand's 'Discours de la Gare de Lyon,' 24 October 1909.

12. Millerand, 'Souvenirs,' p. 62; Persil, p. 66; Millerand, *Réalisations*, pp. xxii–xxvi, 240–50, Millerand's speech to the General Assembly of the Touring Club, 5 December 1909.

merce because it reduced the distance between Paris and Milan. Granting an international status to towns like Pontarlier would offset any harm to their economic position.[13]

Millerand's desire to strengthen France's economy also led him to promote mineral development. Rich iron resources in the Meurthe-et-Moselle region, which had prompted the granting of concessions for exploitation, had expanded France's metallurgic industry. A scarcity of coal had, however, forced France to import, mainly from its Belgian and German competitors. When extensions to the German coal veins were discovered in the Lorraine basin, Millerand urged their exploitation so that imports could be reduced, even though the potential supplies were not enough for French needs. The government was, however, willing to grant concessions to the large mining companies only if they agreed to improve working conditions and allow the workers to benefit from the enterprise. Millerand noted that the government could not postpone exploitation of mining resources but wanted to exchange better labor laws for new concessions. While it wanted to increase natural wealth and improve mining conditions, it could not wait indefinitely for passage of the necessary labor legislation. Since the finance law that granted the concessions had been passed, it was illegal to suspend application until labor's demands were incorporated. Millerand thus urged parliament also to pass the requisite labor legislation.[14]

Millerand consistently linked economic wealth and social change. Prosperity and the development of economic resources were necessary to finance expensive social reforms. It was therefore to the advantage of all citizens to submerge their differences and strive for French prosperity and greatness. Demanding a focus on France (*La France avant tout*), his program has been described critically as a *union sacrée*, beneficial to large industry and banking. Millerand's extra-parliamentary legal activities as lawyer for Creusot clearly involved him with the Comité des forges and may have influenced his political stances, but his linkage of wealth and reform predated his ties to big business and private banking.[15]

13. Millerand, *Réalisations*, pp. xx–xxii; J.O., *Sénat*, 23 December 1909.

14. J.O., *Chambre*, 26 October 1909; also in Millerand, *Réalisations*, pp. 43–59; A.N., C7408, Chamber, Mines Commission, audition of Millerand, 10 March 1910; J.O.,*Chambre*, 4 July 1910; also in Millerand, *Réalisations*, pp. 55–9.

15. Millerand, *Réalisations*, pp. 288–301, 'Discours de la Gare de Lyon,' 24 October 1909; Georges Michon, *La Préparation à la guerre. La loi de trois ans (1910–1914)*

Millerand's pressures for French economic development extended beyond metropolitan France to its colonies. The issue of Algerian railroad concessions illustrated his belief that decentralization would promote the initiative and freedom necessary for economic health. In 1909–10, the Algerians wanted to construct a railroad between the iron mines at l'Ouenza and the port of Bône. Algeria, which had not asked for French subsidies, should be entitled, Millerand argued, to exploit its subsoil mineral resources. Although it did not need Algerian minerals, France would also profit from its colony's prosperity. The railroad would thereby aid colonization. The concession would not harm mine-workers, as the Socialists charged, because Algeria had adopted French legislation governing the exploitation of resources. Furthermore, the contract would protect French interests by setting percentages for French labor, management, and capital (between 70 and 80 percent). France also had to allow some foreign participation so that it did not suffer reprisals incurred by an exclusionary policy. Since French entrepreneurs had contributed significantly to foreign industrial expansion, it would damage national interests to invite future reprisals. Millerand also recognized that France's competitors relied on industrial trusts and cartels. To compete effectively, France needed combinations capable of equivalent production levels. For Millerand, therefore, the empire increased France's prestige and its economic wealth.[16]

Two catastrophes, one natural and one human, dominated Millerand's attention as Minister of Public Works: the floods of late January 1910 and the railroad strikes. As he later recalled, the inundation of the Seine basin was an unparalleled devastation of the city and suburbs, flooding entire streets and driving people from their homes. Deputies even had to use boats in the courtyard of the Palais Bourbon. Telephonic communications were interrupted; normal supply routes were unusable; railroad stations, quays, and bridges were threatened. Millerand inspected the most seriously

(Paris: Marcel Rivière, 1935), pp. 12, 33; Michel Rouffet, 'Frédéric François-Marsal,' unpublished doctoral thesis, University of Paris I, Panthéon-Sorbonne, 1982, p. 48.
    16. A.N., C7353, Chamber, Public Works Commission, audition of Millerand, 24 November and 1 December 1909; J.O., *Chambre*, 18 February 1910; also in Millerand, *Réalisations*, pp. 60–93.

endangered areas – the stations in the Place Saint-Michel, Quai d'Orsay, and Invalides and the quays at Bercy and Passy – to discuss emergency measures with engineers, to console disaster victims and to report on aid plans. After the cabinet meeting of 26 January, he set up a program for handling the catastrophe. The program partially restored postal and telephonic communications and maintained rail service on unflooded lines.

An inter-ministerial parliamentary commission assessed the damage and proposed a public works program to avert future flood damage. Millerand informed the Senate of temporary remedies, to be completed by late summer, and long-range programs. Reforestation or new reservoirs, helpful against normal flooding, would not control such high waters any more than dikes or barriers. Dredging the riverbeds was the most seductive solution, but its costs were astronomical, and execution often impossible because of bridges, quays, and locks along the banks. In fact, the flood had not seriously damaged existing bridges, embankments, or railroad lines. Millerand, as crisis coordinator, met daily with the directors of navigation, railroads, hydrometric and telephone services, the engineers in charge of navigation on the Seine, of the water and sanitary services, of lighting and roads, and with representatives of the war ministry, the department of the Seine, and the prefecture of police. Their task involved such pressing issues as the maintenance of transportation, nourishment of Paris, evacuation of the threatened population, sanitary precautions, and the checking of drains, bridges, critical points and communication lines. To Millerand, such catastrophes elicited from Frenchmen qualities of self-abnegation and a willingness to subordinate individual concerns to the common effort.[17]

The most serious problem Millerand confronted was the rail strikes of 1910. He took office shortly after the western railroad was re-nationalized, an event that provoked considerable unrest among railroad personnel. Unrealistic expectations and excessive apprehension led railroad employees to besiege the ministry, using parliamentarians as their advocates. Millerand, who believed that

17. Millerand, 'Souvenirs,' pp. 62–3; Persil, p. 67; G. Bonnefous, I, pp. 164–7; Suarez, II, p. 254; J.O., *Sénat*, 4 March 1910, response to Audiffred's interpellation; Millerand, *Réalisations*, pp. xliii–l, 191–225.

political involvement hindered the solution of personnel issues, decided to receive rail personnel and parliamentarians separately. Discipline had to be maintained until a statute set promotion scales and opened regular channels of representation. Millerand denied Jaurès' charge that nationalization had profited the former owners and hurt the small shareholders. The state, which had closely surveyed the transaction to guard the small investors against cheating, had studied the costs and benefits of the move.[18]

The state had a greater stake and closer connections to management and labor in the public works domain than in purely private enterprises. Millerand's decrees of 10 August 1899 had set wages and hours for employees in public enterprises, but the state intervened only after contracts were signed to insure obligations were fulfilled. Millerand wanted employers to apply contracts scrupulously and collaborate with their employees, who had a reciprocal responsibility to perform their jobs adequately. As employer, the state had similar obligations to its workers but also had to provide an example to private industry. The government had tried, he insisted, to increase the state railroad's safety and efficient operation and improve its personnel situation. Receptive to grievances, it expected workers to perform their tasks. The state employees should set an example for other railroad workers, halting unrest and concentrating on performing their jobs.[19]

Millerand tried to calm railroad workers' fears that they would suffer from the transfer to state control. He pointed to recent legislation which had improved their material situation. To equalize pay scales, Millerand sought the same daily minimum 5-franc salary for railroad workers that P.T.T. employees received, and blamed the discontent on inadequate information about the changes. The state had also, he noted, improved salary and working conditions on the private lines. For example, it had persuaded the Compagnie du Midi to raise railroad engineers' monthly salaries from 80 to 120 francs. New pay scales, including retroactive application of the minimum daily salary to 1 January 1910, did not,

18. Millerand, 'Souvenirs,' pp. 60–1, 63; J.O., *Chambre*, 10 December 1909; Millerand, *Réalisations*, pp. l–li, 97–124; A.N., C7353, Chamber, Public Works Commission, audition of Millerand, 23 February 1910, on the proposed convention with the Orléans line.
19. Millerand, *Réalisations*, pp. 251–63, speech to the Syndicat des entrepreneurs des travaux publics, 20 December 1909; *ibid.*, pp. 153–62, speech to the Association fraternelle des employés et ouvriers de chemin de fer français, 22 January 1910.

however, calm the fears triggered by nationalization.[20]

Millerand took several railroad trips to study progress on the new bridge at Rouen, improvements in the stations at Rouen and Dieppe, and the electrification of suburban lines. He also tried to reassure personnel that the state was concerned about them and wanted their support. Concrete improvements, like a guaranteed minimum wage, and evidence of government concern, did not reduce agitation among the railroad employees, which erupted into overt hostility in the strikes of late spring and only ended with the attempted general strike in October.[21]

The series of accidents that plagued the railroads during 1910 may have fueled the unrest. Lives were lost when trains derailed at Moulineaux, Villepreux and, most disastrously, at Bernay in September, or when they collided head-on at Sablé and Saujon. Seeking to determine whether the accidents were caused by excessive speed, poor lighting, or simple human negligence, Millerand also wanted management and labor delegates to discuss changes in operating procedures.[22]

In late May 1910, a strike erupted on the southern rail lines, with employees demanding higher wages and greater leisure. The government, which decided not to let the strike interrupt public services, replaced striking workers with soldiers from the engineering corps. The strike ended on 25 June with some company concessions, but Millerand had to respond to a Senate interpellation. He argued that, as a public service, the transportation system could not be interrupted to respect the workers' right to strike. Furthermore, the strike was declared before the workers had formulated their demands to the company. On 16 June, Millerand argued to the national railroad union that the railroad administration was not like a normal employer, because conventions set the conditions of exploitation. As a public service, on whose regular operation essential national interests depended, railroad transportation was not a free commercial enterprise. The government, which had a 'primordial obligation' to maintain the service, would have been derelict in its duty if it let a conflict of private interests jeopardize a vital public service. Concessions had essentially met

20. J.O., *Chambre*, 5 April 1910; also in Millerand, *Réalisations*, pp. 125–39, lii–lvii.

21. Millerand, 'Souvenirs,' p. 63; Persil, pp. 67–8; Millerand, *Réalisations*, pp. lvii–lx.

22. Millerand, *Réalisations*, pp. lxi–lxv.

the railroad personnel's salary and working-condition demands. Millerand pleaded with them to acknowledge the concessions and avoid a more extensive work stoppage.[23]

In June, the government discussed its concessions with railroad union representatives, but failed to satisfy them. A general rail strike was planned in the summer, but was actually launched in October, to secure a guaranteed minimum daily salary of 5 francs and forestall the government's plans to renege on its promises. In early October, Millerand told a crowd of railroad employees at Saintes of his plans for an arbitration law and urged them to accept their duties as well as to defend their rights. Still convinced that strikes harmed all parties, workers included, Millerand believed regular management–labor contacts could avert most overt conflicts, with arbitration, not strikes, left to resolve irreconcilable differences. Although welcomed by the railroad personnel at Saintes, Millerand did not appease the mounting agitation, which he attributed to a revolutionary minority. A delegation of workers, accompanied by Socialist deputy Jean Allemane, were shown pay sheets at the public works ministry that proved the inaccuracy of charges that some workers received less than the promised daily minimum, but the evidence did not end the agitation. The national railroad union was gradually drawn in as the strike spread from the northern line to a general rail strike by 12 October 1910.[24]

The government responded rapidly and firmly. The suggestion to mobilize railroad workers subject to military service apparently originated at a morning directors meeting in the Ministry of Public Works. Millerand, who discussed the idea with Briand, then won cabinet approval. He and the premier agreed to meet the strikers

23. G. Bonnefous, I, pp. 198–9; J.O., *Sénat*, 28 June 1910, response to Pélissier's interpellation.
24. Millerand, 'Souvenirs,' p. 63; Millerand, *Réalisations*, pp. 302–40, speech to the Ligue de l'enseignement, 'Les Conflits sociaux et l'arbitrage,' 22 February 1910; *ibid*, pp. lxv–lxxii; Persil, pp. 67–9; G. Bonnefous, I, p. 200; Duroselle, *Belle Epoque*, p. 348. Goldberg, p. 410, notes that French railroad workers' salaries had increased only slightly in the preceding thirty years despite mounting living costs. The companies had refused to negotiate with the unions over the demand for a minimum wage of 1,825 francs and a six-day week. Kimon A. Doukas, *The French Railroads and the State* (New York: Columbia University Press, 1945), pp. 75–7, argues that the situation deteriorated during the summer because of the 'extravagent' demands of some leaders of the railroad federation, incitement by outside agitators, and the uncompromising attitude of the large networks that refused general agreements for all employees. He attributes the strike decision to the extremists among the labor leaders and notes the diversion of the strike into acts of violence and sabotage.

with 'inflexible resistance.' Their statements after the cabinet meeting on 12 October termed the strike abrupt and abnormal, a criminal enterprise of revolutionary political dimensions, not a professional, industrial conflict. Mobilization of workers for twenty-one days made them subject to military legal sanctions if they disobeyed orders. To forestall sabotage, the army guarded the rail lines. Millerand met daily with the prefect of police and representatives of the Ministry of War and railroad personnel. Despite vociferous Socialist complaints, the government held firm. Within a week (by 18 October), the strike collapsed, although normal rail service took several months to resume. Although strikers showed their resentment by inadequate job performances, the strike neither halted railroad operations nor won public support for the workers. Furthermore, negotiations continued between Millerand and the rail companies to ratify a daily 5-franc minimum salary for workers in the Paris area as of 1 January 1911.[25]

A special parliamentary session of late October focused on the government's handling of the rail strike. In a stormy debate on 27 October 1910, Millerand reported on the negotiations between the railroad unions and the government. He refuted charges of dictatorial tendencies levelled against the premier. The regular salary increases during the preceding eighteen months buttressed Briand's description of the strike as an unjustified criminal enterprise. The national railroad union knew that the government wanted regular contacts between the rail companies and their employees, and Millerand had urged the private lines to copy the nationalized arrangements. The union was also aware that the government would use the army to maintain service as it had on the southern line. The government considered rail transports a public service, not a free commercial enterprise, whose regular operation affected vital national interests. Since the union's offices had distributed a manual outlining sabotage tactics, Millerand considered it valid to call the strike a 'criminal enterprise,' an 'insurrectionary move-

25. Millerand, 'Souvenirs,' p. 63; Millerand, *Réalisations*, pp. lxxxiv–lxxxix; Persil, p. 70; G. Bonnefous, I, pp. 200–1; Duroselle, *Belle Epoque*, p. 348. Goldberg, pp. 411–12, incorrectly states that Millerand was opposed to mobilization. Suarez, II, pp. 278–9, claims Millerand, Barthou, and Viviani hesitated to sign the mobilization decree. Millerand preferred to apply a Canadian arbitration scheme. Although Suarez attributes decisiveness in the affair to Briand, evidence from Millerand material does not support his interpretation of the public works minister's position. Doukas, pp. 75–7, argues that there was ample statutory authority for the device of mobilization. Sumler, 'Polarization', pp. 89–90.

ment.' Although salaries were their basic grievance, strikers had not even formulated their specific demands after the strike collapsed. The budgetary ramifications of the 5-franc minimum for the Paris area still had to be worked out, but the government sought its general acceptance and hoped it would be a model for the rest of the network. In fact, several lines agreed to adopt the minimum by 1 January 1911. The strike had, however, broken out on the northern and state-owned lines which had already adopted that wage. Millerand, who believed the workers should have remained on the job until the changes were instituted, considered the demands as simply a pretext for a revolutionary political movement. He did not, however, address the government's mobilization of the strikers, which made them liable to a military court martial if they resisted. This new, effective weapon against strikes provoked Socialist and labor censure of Millerand, and intensified the workers' alienation. The government easily won a vote of confidence on 30 October despite Socialist and some Radical opposition.[26]

Millerand, who in 1910 used the threat of drafting strikers into the army to end the rail strikes, had seemingly changed from the man who criticized the use of troops to repress the mine strikes in Decazeville and Vierzon in 1886, or in 1891 to repress the textile strike at Fourmies. Millerand's theoretical consistency, his insistence ever since the 1880s that social reforms be enacted by peaceful, legal means, paralleled a tactical alteration. Perhaps the change from opposition to endorsement of official repression reflected a disenchantment with reformism, but Millerand's own political development and France's situation may provide a more persuasive explanation. As Minister of Commerce, he had endorsed the repression of the strike at Chalon-sur-Saône in 1900, and throughout the decade had argued that the government could repress conflicts harmful to national interests. In 1910, he played a key role in ending the rail strike, but his actions simply implemented a policy he had endorsed since 1900. His acquisition of ministerial status in 1899 may have been crucial; as a government member, he shared

---

26. Duroselle, *Belle Epoque*, pp. 348, 350. G. Bonnefous, I, pp. 201–7, notes the Chamber endorsed the Briand government 384–170 on 30 October. J.O., *Chambre*, 27 October 1910; Millerand, *Réalisations*, pp. lxxxi–lxxxvii, 163–90; Persil, p. 70; Millerand, 'Souvenirs,' p. 64; Doukas, pp. 75–7: the courts upheld the government's position, which the majority of members of parliament had endorsed, that the state could suppress an 'unlawful' railroad strike on the grounds of national security and social exigency.

responsibility for the maintenance of public order which as the youthful opposition deputy he had not possessed. The national crisis of the Dreyfus Affair and the international tensions of the new century's first decade, which encouraged a nationalist revival in France, altered Millerand's priorities. Still anxious to improve the lot of the workers, as demonstrated by his constant pressures to enact the old-age pension bill, he considered strikes, particularly in the public services, to be an unacceptable threat to vital national interests.

Despite his victory on 30 October, Briand abruptly resigned on 2 November. He argued to the cabinet that the bitter parliamentary attacks required him to seek presidential approval to remain in office. Since the cabinet's survival depended on a parliamentary majority and not on executive endorsement, this argument fails to convince. Briand immediately accepted President Fallière's offer to form a new cabinet, but changed its composition to eliminate the two independent Socialists, Millerand and Viviani, and accentuate the ministry's Radical character. This ministerial shuffle provoked considerable controversy, then and later. Although Millerand and Briand had been mutually congratulatory earlier in the year, there were rumors of a disagreement between them concerning the steps to end the strike. The new cabinet's weaker vote of confidence compared to that of 30 October indicated parliamentary discomfort at Briand's maneuver. The new ministry lasted only four months – until 27 February 1911.[27]

Millerand believed that Briand wanted to eliminate an awkward colleague. His departure from the public works ministry gave him, he later claimed, a sense of deliverance from numerous intrigues. Jealousy of Millerand's greater national visibility due to his active role in the rail strike may have influenced the premier. In fact, several parliamentary colleagues (Augagneur, Violette, and Paul-Boncour) lauded his departure from the ministry. Hoping that Millerand would return to social reform, they probably disliked his involvement with an obviously manipulative premier.[28]

Millerand and Briand had disagreed on electoral reform the previous year. While that dispute may have left a legacy of distrust

27. Duroselle, *Belle Epoque*, p. 350; G. Bonnefous, I, pp. 207–13; Suarez, II, pp. 259–60, 294–5. Elwitt's thesis in *The Third Republic Defended* that liberal reformers promoted social reform as a defense against socialism and the demands of militant labor is not a persuasive analysis of Millerand's behavior.

28. Millerand, 'Souvenirs,' pp. 65–6; Persil, pp. 72–3.

with Briand, it is unlikely that the move of November 1910 was
entirely due to the earlier issue. Parliamentary opposition threatening to his ministry had, however, led Briand to change his stance
on electoral reform. Possibly the heated parliamentary reaction to
the government's policy in the rail strike made Briand uncomfortable even though he had defended official actions and easily won a
vote of confidence. While the government did not abandon its
program, Briand may have wanted to calm parliamentary spirits.
By eliminating the ministers identified with the repression, especially Millerand, Briand could somewhat separate himself from the
previous cabinet's actions. He may even have regretted his endorsement of Millerand's mobilization proposal. His cabinet reshuffle of
November 1910 therefore resembled his abandonment of his Perigueux position on electoral reform of November 1909. A subtle
manipulator atuned to parliamentary intrigues, Briand let neither
personal loyalty nor ideological consistency determine his political
behavior. Millerand's characteristics were exactly opposite. A dislike of corridor politics, a commitment to certain ideas and goals,
and a loyalty to individuals made Millerand a vulnerable target for
Briand in 1910, as in 1915 and 1924.

From November 1910 until January 1912, Millerand continued to
work for obligatory arbitration and electoral reform and supported
the government in the second Moroccan crisis. During 1911, he
worked in the Chamber's Labor Commission on a law for the
compulsory arbitration of labor disputes. To him, arbitration of
labor conflicts symbolized the Republican Socialist party's entire
program. Settlement of labor conflicts by arbitration took as its
premise the equation of strikes and wars, necessary evils that
should gradually be eliminated by legal, peaceful collaboration,
whether domestically or internationally. Arbitration was the tip of
the iceberg of a social reform program designed to enhance republican France's strength and vitality. Since all citizens had a stake in
both reform and prosperity, social solidarity had to replace class
struggles. For Millerand, arbitration arrangements were an important aspect of this larger social program. He first proposed regulations for the railroads, hoping to expand them later into a general
industrial law. For Millerand, arbitration remained a tactic of the
last resort, the use of an impartial arbiter after conciliation had
failed. He wanted to make submission of disputes to arbitration

obligatory, but recognized that it would be tricky also to require acceptance of the verdict. The project's primary goal was the substitution of regular communication for confrontation.[29]

Parliament again tackled electoral reform in 1911. Still supporting list-voting with proportional representation to protect minority interests, Millerand opposed separation of the two parts of the program. He primarily wanted, however, to enact a reform that would eliminate the 'frightful danger' of the existing discredited system. On this issue, Millerand and Jaurès were allies. Although the Chamber passed proportional representation in July 1911, electoral reform progressed no further that year.[30]

The year 1911 has been termed 'The year of Agadir'. This second Moroccan crisis, which placed foreign affairs in the forefront of governmental concerns, distracted attention from domestic issues. Use of French troops to quell local unrest led Germany to accuse France of expanding police and port rights into a full protectorate for which it demanded compensation. The arrival of the German gunboat *Panther* in the Moroccan port of Agadir on 1 July 1911 threatened France's Moroccan position, which the Algeciras conference had recognized five years before. Although Franco-German tension eased after a few weeks, probably because of Russian and especially British support for France, it took several months to negotiate the compromise whereby Germany recognized French rights in Morocco in exchange for French concessions in the Congo.[31]

In the Franco-German convention of 4 November 1911, Germany relinquished claims to Morocco, thereby enabling France to establish a protectorate. In return, it received approximately a third of the French Congo. Only the Congo settlement required French parliamentary endorsement, but the Chamber actually debated the whole convention. On 15 December, Millerand defended the proposed treaty on the ground that national interest required a united French front to the outside world. France must show that domestic

29. A.N., C7486, Chamber, Labor Commission, sessions of 22 March, 5 April, and 7 June 1911; A.N., F.M.8, Millerand's speech of 7 October 1911 to the conference of the Republican Socialist party, 'Les Socialistes dans la république et dans la patrie – les conflits sociaux pour la réalisation des réformes sociales.'

30. J.O., *Chambre*, 3 July 1911; A.N., F.M.8, Millerand's speech to the conference of the Republican Socialist party, 7 October 1911; G. Bonnefous, I, pp. 233–9, 246–8; Duroselle, *Belle Epoque*, pp. 356–7.

31. Duroselle, *Belle Epoque*, p. 355; Brogan, II, pp. 435–9; G. Bonnefous, I, pp. 253–68; Jean-Baptiste Duroselle, *La France et les français, 1914–1920*, vol. 2: *Histoire de la grande guerre* (Paris: Editions Richelieu, 1972), pp. 19–30.

instability did not weaken it or jeopardize continuity of its foreign policy. He considered the pact a crucial step in France's protectorate in Morocco. The accord was the only way that France could reform Morocco's administrative, judicial, economic, financial, and military systems, exercise police or military action, and serve as its intermediary with other nations. Only limitation of a rival's power in Morocco and Tunisia could shield France's Algerian possessions from unrest. France paid heavily for German disinterest by its Congo concessions; the peacetime loss of territories won by French blood and skill was a painful separation (*douloureux arrachement*), that deprived France of important ivory and rubber resources. The Chamber overwhelmingly ratified the pact five days later. Despite parliamentary cohesion on this crucial issue, Premier Joseph Caillaux was soon forced to resign because of rumors about his secret discussions with German governmental representatives without the knowledge of Foreign Minister Justin de Selves and French Ambassador to Germany Jules Cambon, who were officially responsible for the negotiations. Foreign affairs indirectly triggered this governmental collapse, a relatively rare phenomenon in Third Republic politics.[32]

The Franco–German agreement of 4 November 1911 was significant in settling the two nations' remaining colonial differences. However, the nationalist fever which the crisis intensified did not abate after the colonial problem was resolved. A similar *rapprochement* between France and Germany did not accompany the elimination of concrete divisive issues as it had when Franco-British colonial disagreements were settled in 1904. Caillaux, anxious for harmonious Franco-German relations, was therefore at odds with the nation's temper in early 1912. His replacement with the nationalist Lorrainer Raymond Poincaré was a logical ending to the Agadir crisis. Poincaré's choice of Millerand to head the war ministry opened up a new area of responsibility for the long-time social reformer, but one for which his nationalistic statements and actions had paved the way. Millerand in 1912 was a deputy with twenty-seven years of parliamentary experience, a successful electoral record, and tenure of two ministerial portfolios, all of which

32. J.O., *Chambre*, 15 December 1911; G. Bonnefous, I, pp. 263, 267–8: the vote was 393 to 36 with 140 abstentions; Michon, p. 78. For a different interpretation see Frederic Seager, 'Joseph Caillaux as premier, 1911–1912: the dilemma of a liberal reformer,' *French Historical Studies*, XI, No. 2 (Fall, 1979), who downplays foreign affairs in Caillaux's fall to stress domestic issues.

had won him considerable respect as a decisive, effective politician, known for his integrity, independence, and dedication to French national interests.

Part III
The War Minister

6
The War Minister's Contribution to the Nationalist Revival

Alexandre Millerand was Minister of War for more than two years at a crucial moment in French history. His first tenure, from 14 January 1912 to 12 January 1913, which followed the Agadir crisis, coincided with augmented French anxiety about and preparation for war. His second stay, from 26 August 1914 to 29 October 1915, placed him in a vital position during the first year and a half of the First World War. Despite a chronological separation of a year and a half and the vast difference between wartime and peacetime, Millerand's ministries reflected a surprising consistency of attitudes and policies.

Millerand's first period as war minister revealed personality traits and beliefs characteristic of his entire political career. Despite shifting political labels and varied responsibilities, Millerand was always scrupulously honest, tenacious, methodical, and industrious. Seeming calm and unshakable, he was a taciturn man who preferred to keep his own counsel and to act independently. Repelled by the corridor intrigues of the French parliamentary system, he did not let political calculations influence his decisions, but a logical, clear style made him an effective public speaker. A strong loyalty to France was matched by a personal devotion to individuals whom he respected. These traits, which characterized his war ministry as much as his earlier career, illuminate his activities in that department.[1]

1. Derfler, *Millerand*, pp. 25, 31, 46, 88, 93, 109, 113, 167–8, 230; Jacques Bompard, 'Un ministre de la guerre: M. Alexandre Millerand,' *Revue politique et parlementaire* (Paris, 10 January 1914), pp. 31–2; John F.V. Keiger, *France and the Origins of the First World War* (New York: St. Martin's Press, 1983), pp. 85, 99. Millerand's reaction to two French diplomats illustrated his loyalty to Premier

Millerand's public statements had a patriotic aspect for two decades prior to becoming war minister. Although his choice for that post provoked considerable surprise, since he had taken little part in parliamentary debates on military issues, it did not require a conversion to new ideas or a betrayal of his own past. His actions at the rue Saint-Dominique (location of the war ministry) in no way violated his Saint-Mandé program of 1896. As a Socialist, his demand for social solidarity reflected a concern for national interests. The Socialist party's acquisition of political power was always viewed within the context of a strong and prosperous France; only economic health and military security could pave the way for social reform. Millerand had always defended a strong army, whose prerequisites were military service and a large budget. In 1893, he told Socialists that national security required support for the Franco-Russian alliance, and at Saint-Mandé called them patriotic Frenchmen to whom the nation represented an incomparable force of material and moral progress. In 1898, he denied that nationalism was any party's monopoly, and in 1905, argued that only a formidable army and a powerful fleet would enable France to preserve its independence.[2]

A leader of the new nationalism, Millerand streamlined the war ministry and the command structure, de-politicized the army, increased its numerical strength, including more colonial troops, and harnessed scientific and industrial developments to military needs. In his opinion, wartime civil–military relations should permit great freedom of action for the military and a diminished civilian role. Most significantly, Millerand fostered the 'nationalist revival' by strengthening military discipline and morale and by instilling a martial spirit in the public at large.

Raymond Poincaré picked his old friend Millerand as war minister in 1912 because of his decisiveness as Minister of Public Works

Poincaré and to France. He claimed that French Ambassador to Vienna Philippe Crozier's Austrophile attitude made him a public danger and French Ambassador to Russia George Louis' inefficiency argued for his recall.

2. A.N., F.M.1, Millerand's speech to the banquet of the Grandes Carrières, 1 October 1893; *ibid.*, Saint-Mandé speech, 30 May 1896; J.O., *Chambre*, 13 June 1898; A.N., F.M.5, speech to the pilot's union of Dunkirk, 28 August 1905; Bompard, pp. 34–5. David B. Ralston, *The Army of the Republic. The Place of the Military in the Political Evolution of France, 1871–1914* (Cambridge, Mass.: M.I.T. Press, 1967), p. 324, argues that Millerand's evolution from socialism in the Waldeck-Rousseau ministry to Minister of War in 1912 proved the revived acceptability of military patriotism among some left-wing politicians.

in the railway workers' strike of 1910. He was also convinced that Millerand's organizational ability, methodical habits and industriousness would enable him to serve the nation well as war minister. Poincaré, who wanted to give his cabinet moral stature, included men of recognized authority. It has been described as a cabinet of 'luminaries' and as a 'national union of center groups' to promote a nationalist revival. By 1912, Millerand, with a ministerial record in the commerce and public works departments, belonged to that small group of *ministrables* from which potential premiers chose their cabinets.[3]

Prior to his tenure of the war ministry, military matters did not particularly interest Millerand, but he soon became fascinated with them. As he later observed, along with his year as High Commissioner in Strasbourg, the year (1912–13) that he spent at the rue Saint-Dominique was the 'most beautiful and productive' of his career. A 'thrilling task' awaited him there.[4]

Millerand's modifications in the war ministry's procedures reflected his efficiency and organizational ability. He streamlined its complex bureaucracy, met weekly with departmental directors, and created a form of war cabinet. These meetings with subordinates and directors showed his ability to understand issues and synthesize various viewpoints. A decree of 20 January 1912, which reorganized the ministry's general secretariat, established a hierarchic chain of command with the secretary-general in control of army administration. Although Millerand did not have technical military expertise when he became war minister, he viewed himself as a director of directors, an organizer, administrator, and instigator, whose administration would supply the necessary technical information. Indeed, his extraordinary powers of work, clear judgements, and decisiveness, which impressed his collaborators, made him an excellent head of the military bureaucracy. He also elicited a loyalty and industriousness from his subordinates, probably because they believed he would support them in adversity and judge their performance only on its merits.[5]

3. David Sumler, 'Domestic influences on the nationalist revival in France, 1909–1914,' *French Historical Studies*, VI, No. 4, (Fall 1970), pp. 523–7; Derfler, *Millerand*, p. 262; Millerand, 'Souvenirs,' p. 67; Raymond Poincaré, *Au service de la France* (Paris: Librairie Plon, 1926–33), I, pp. 17–18.

4. Millerand, 'Souvenirs,' p. 67; conversation with Jacques Millerand, 20 May 1978, Sèvres, France.

5. Millerand, 'Souvenirs,' p. 58; A.N., F.M.9, 'Historique chronologique du ministère de Monsieur Millerand'; Bompard, pp. 36–7; Alexandre Millerand, *Pour la*

A concern for efficiency also influenced Millerand's changes in the command structure. To Millerand, the leader responsible for preparing the army for war must be able to control directly all relevant developments. The decree of 20 January 1912 unified the army's command structure by combining the duties of the army chief of staff with those of the commander of the northwest armies. Its goal was to eliminate the numerous intermediary authorities that hampered the ability of the head of the general staff to make military decisions. The decree gave the head of the army general staff control over the entire military apparatus, including representatives in the war ministry. It thus completed the change in the command structure begun by the decree of 28 July 1911 which linked the general staff to the supreme war council. The general staff became the military policy-making organ, and its head the undisputed military chief, answerable to the government through the war minister. Millerand, who defended the decree as an organizational change, argued that a system which left the army with two chiefs was not viable in wartime. Centralization of military power and reinforcement of the organs responsible for national defense would smooth the transition from peacetime to wartime.[6]

A desire to de-politicize the top command echelons also contributed to the change in the command structure. For, as General Joseph Joffre told Millerand, politics had dictated the previous division of responsibilities whereby the chief of staff handled personnel questions directly with the war ministry. Joffre, who benefited from the reform to become head of the French army, commented that for the first time an individual possessed total military control.[7] Organizational streamlining increased efficiency, but also gave some men greater power. This change in the command structure, which permitted the near military dictatorship of the war's first year, also fostered the subsequent hostility between the high command and the civilian legislators whose functions had been curtailed.

défense nationale. Une année au ministère de la guerre (14 janvier 1912–12 janvier 1913) (Paris: Bibliothèque Charpentier, 1913), pp. xi–xii.

6. A.N., F.M.9, 'Historique chronologique,' 20 January 1912; Millerand, 'Souvenirs,' p. 68; Persil, p. 75; J.O., *Chambre*, 22 March 1912; G. Bonnefous, I, p. 309. Ralston, p. 340, notes that the reorganization, though ratified by parliament, was the result of executive decree.

7. Joseph J.C. Joffre, *Mémoires du Maréchal Joffre (1910–1917)* (Paris: Librairie Plon, 1932), I, p. 28; Porch, p. 171; Poincaré, *Au service*, II, p. 77.

A unified command structure permitted the close contact between the war ministry and the commanding general which would be vital in wartime. Millerand, who came to respect Joffre's imperturbability, tenacity, and dedication to duty, established cordial relations with the general, but encouraged thereby parliamentary charges of being his dupe and willing sycophant. Likewise, Joffre appreciated Millerand's goodwill, and later acknowledged his immense services to France as war minister.[8]

More efficient civilian and military war administrations with augmented powers for the army chief of staff and the war minister affected the whole issue of civil–military relations. To the Senate, Millerand indicated his attitude toward those relations which in fact guided him in 1914. He believed that 'the hour of battle . . . should not be that of speeches.' With military victory their sole objective, the responsible military authorities must have entire freedom of action. The government retained overall strategic control, but the military freely conducted the operations that implemented it. 'Before the necessities of the supreme hour, everything will give way . . . the single endeavor will be to strain for the safety of the nation and the success of our armies.'[9]

At issue was a parliamentary republic's adaptation to a state of war. While Millerand recognized that parliament would not accept such a passive role in peacetime, he somewhat naively expected the legislature to abdicate its policy-making role in wartime. As the army's political leader, Millerand defended it against attack and arbitrated controversies. Indeed, a contemporary critic accused him of blindly obeying general staff directives with the result that much experience and loss of life were required to reverse his lack of foresight. This assessment undoubtedly reflected a parliamentarian's resentment at Millerand's concession of substantial power to the High Command, but cannot be dismissed as simply a partisan attack. Millerand seemingly failed to recognize that the

8. Joffre, I, p. 27; conversation with Jacques Millerand, 20 May 1978; Millerand, 'Souvenirs,' p. 67[1]; Millerand, *Pour la défense*, p. 401, Millerand's speech of 14 September 1912 at the close of the first period of maneuvers in the West.

9. Pierre Renouvin, *Les Formes du gouvernement de guerre* (Paris: Presses Universitaires de France, 1925), p. 22; J.O., *Sénat*, 6 June 1912, interpellation Lecomte; Millerand, 'Souvenirs,' pp. 70–1; A.N., F.M.9, 'Historique chronologique,' 7 June 1912. Ralston, p. 339, argues that Millerand, though a man of some stature, followed High Command directives, thus relinquishing the minister of war's prerogatives as head of the command structure. Gerd Krumeich, *Armaments and Politics in France on the Eve of the First World War*, trans. by Stephen Conn (Dover, N.H.: Berg Publishers Ltd., 1984), p. 32.

conduct of operations had political as well as military implications.[10]

A basic goal of Millerand's in 1912 was preparation for war in both its material and moral aspects. A wartime victory was only possible if the nation and the army had a fully developed military apparatus that made them always ready for the transition from peace to war. During 1912, Millerand and Joffre prepared secret plans for wartime eventualities that the Chamber in fact adopted in 1914. For Millerand was convinced that peace could be best preserved if they behaved as if it could be momentarily ruptured.[11]

Millerand tried to expand the size of France's human and material resources. Since its shortage of manpower, due to a falling birthrate, meant that France would have fewer troops than Germany, the war minister urged the Chamber to vote a new staff law (*loi des cadres*) to organize the reserves more effectively and use the resources of its African colonies. The new law would establish an equal number of reserve and active regiments and incorporate the former into the infantry. Despite the problems of assimilating metropolitan and colonial troops, France could not neglect its colonial reserves. Although the staff plan would incorporate the supplementary human resources represented by the reserves and colonial troops, the new law did not alter the army's basic structure or the existing troop division. It tried to rationalize wartime troop organization by economically administering the human resources of the different branches.[12]

During the debates on the proposed staff law in the Chamber and the Senate, most speakers, with the notable exception of Jaurès, favored the law. Millerand, who reminded the Chamber of the disastrous consequences following from Marshal Niel's inability to organize supplementary reserves for Napoleon III's army, urged

10. J.O., *Sénat*, 6 June 1912; Millerand, 'Souvenirs,' p. 71; Millerand, *Pour la défense*, p. 137; Porch, pp. 173–5; Paul-Boncour, I, p. 228.

11. Poincaré, *Au service*, II, pp. 77–8, 80; Bompard, p. 39; John C. Cairns, 'International politics and the military mind: the case of the French Republic, 1911–1914,' *The Journal of Modern History*, XXV, No. 3 (September 1953), p. 281; Joffre, I, p. 86; A.N., F.M. 13, Millerand, *Le Parlement et l'opinion*, pp. 4–5; J.O., *Chambre*, 18 June 1912.

12. A.N., F.M. 9, 'Historique chronologique,' 19 June 1912; J.O., *Chambre*, 18 June 1912; A.N., C7421, Chamber, Army Commission, audition of Millerand, no specific date, between 18 January and 15 February; Archives de la Guerre, 5N4, Millerand to Henry Paté, deputy, 3 August 1912, hereafter cited as A.G..

his compatriots to profit from that historical lesson. Even Napoleon had perceived the importance of the staff as the regimental nucleus. The new law attenuated the effects of France's declining birthrate by increasing available manpower and streamlining company organization. Although it did not confront the tricky issue of advancement, it tried to plug the army's organizational gaps by incorporating the reserves. The vast discrepancy between France and Germany required the French to utilize their reserves and also prepare them for eventual service. To this end, societies of military preparation played a significant role. Convinced that the law would reinforce the army, Millerand considered its passage a matter of national interest.[13]

Millerand also investigated a staff law for the cavalry to remedy the lack of manpower and insufficient training. As he later observed, the cavalry's ' squalid' appearance at the artillery school at Fontainebleau persuaded him that two years was not long enough to train that service. Quality of performance influenced his pressures for special training camps and a new cavalry staff law which would eliminate improvisation and organize the transition from a peacetime to a wartime footing.[14]

Millerand, who considered two years to be insufficient for cavalry instruction, had not yet accepted a general three-year military service in 1912. A three-year law was not a real option at that time, even though a newspaper campaign to repeal the law of 1905 that set a two-year service began in the spring of 1912. Millerand resisted pressures for a return to a three-year term, but did have the issue studied. Not until the summer of 1913, after he had left the war ministry, did he urge the longer period to counteract the effects of a new German law.[15]

13. Millerand, *Pour la défense*, pp. viii, 3–5, 8–26, 29; J.O., *Chambre*, 3 December 1912; J.O., *Sénat*, 21 December 1912; A.N., C7426, Chamber, Budget Commission of 1913, audition of Millerand, 5 November 1912; G. Bonnefous, I, p. 314; the law was passed by the Chamber on 10 December and by the Senate on 23 December.

14. A.N., F.M. 13, Millerand, 'Le Parlement et l'opinion,' p. 8; Poincaré, *Au service*, II, p. 78. Duroselle, *Belle Epoque*, pp. 368–71, notes the journalistic campaign for the three-year law of May–June 1912 and Millerand's preference for using reserves, although he did study an eventual three-year service. Millerand, *Pour la défense*, pp. 5–6, 36; J.O., *Chambre*, 20 December 1912: the new law, extending cavalry service to three years, was passed by the Chamber on 20 December but not voted by the Senate until 27 March 1913; Alexandre Millerand, 'La loi de trois ans,' *Le Parlement et l'opinion*, 20 July 1913, speech to his 12th *arrondissement* constituents, 11 July 1913.

15. Poincaré, *Au service*, II, p. 76; Jacques Bariety and Raymond Poidevin, *Les Relations franco-allemandes (1815–1975)* (Paris: Armand Colin, 1977), p. 209.

Recognition that France must tap additional manpower resources to compensate for its inadequate birthrate also led Millerand to demand a greater use of colonial troops. He suggested using French recruits in domestic units and letting natives defend France's colonies. He tried to increase Algerian recruitment by extending the period of service beyond twelve years and by providing better pensions. France's native troops had proven, he maintained, their value and endurance in European and colonial campaigns for fifty years. Rapid Algerian economic development had, however, created a recruitment crisis because the French *colons'* need for manpower permitted natives to earn a living outside the military. Furthermore, those recruitment problems coincided with France's need for additional troops to occupy Morocco. Millerand preferred to secure necessary manpower by improving enlistment conditions rather than by conscription.[16]

Millerand also tried to reorganize native recruitment in French West Africa, where the Sudanese and Senegalese, especially, were superb soldiers. Their native customs and warrior traditions made military service particularly appealing. France should therefore, he argued, improve native recruitment to regularize the use of colonial resources and share the burden of military service.[17]

Millerand considered the watertight separation of colonial and metropolitan forces detrimental to French interests, since it precluded the most efficient use of manpower. He wanted to assimilate blacks into French regiments to give them the same instruction and military experience. While a permanent fusion of colonial and metropolitan troops was not desirable, temporary cross-assignments would enable the two groups to become acquainted. The will to fight and conquer, the true nerve of war, as well as initiative and responsibility, were as necessary for African success as for European. Notable generals like Joseph Gallieni, Louis Hubert Lyautey, and Joffre had proved the utility of colonial military experience.[18]

Millerand's concern with France's preparation for a European war did not, however, lead him to devalue its overseas military

---

16. Millerand, *Pour la défense*, pp. 45–7, 49–50, decrees of 31 January 1912; J.O., *Lois et décrets*, 3 February 1912, p. 1208.

17. Millerand, *Pour la défense*, pp. 45, 54, decree of 7 February 1912; J.O., *Lois et décrets*, p. 1347.

18. J.O., *Chambre*, 21 November 1912; also in Millerand, *Pour la défense*, pp. 45, 60, 62–8, and Millerand's instructions of 14 December 1912.

obligations. He often defended the military campaigns in Morocco, insisting that exaggerated reports of controversial incidents had provoked unjust accusations. He was confident that General Lyautey could handle the situation. Indeed, French troops had achieved considerable success in Morocco and had also instituted some precautionary health measures. The increased need for colonial troops had, however, made it difficult to relieve the officers. Their stays in France between colonial assignments had been progressively reduced. Millerand suggested giving reserve officers one-year assignments in Morocco to allow them contact with professional officers and active experience, and simultaneously ease the pressures on the regular army.[19]

The training of France's manpower was as important to the war minister as its quantitative strength. Maneuvers gave French troops practical exposure to combat conditions even though it was difficult to make fiction resemble reality. They gave the High Command the opportunity to demonstrate that initiative which would enable it to handle the unforeseen that was inherent in a true war situation. The maneuvers of 1912 had the further advantage of exposing soldiers to scientific and industrial developments of military use. Training camps also performed an important function in giving the officers and men the necessary technical and tactical instruction. The increased specialization of modern warfare required different training for artillery and engineering officers. Millerand designated Fontainebleau for the artillery and Versailles for the engineers, with provisions for communication between them. He considered it more rational to have two schools that offered specialized instruction rather than duplicating their functions. Finally, he streamlined the military power structure to let service chiefs handle administrative details and thereby relieve the general staff.[20]

19. J.O., *Chambre*, 21 June 1912; also in Millerand, *Pour la défense*, pp. 367–72; *ibid.*, pp. 83–6, circulars of 25 May and 5 June 1912 on the use of reserve officers in Morocco. Alan Scham, *Lyautey in Morocco. Protectorate Administration, 1912–1925* (Berkeley: University of California Press, 1970), p. 14, notes Lyautey's choice as resident-general of Morocco after the cabinet meeting of 27 April at Rambouillet and his meeting with Millerand on 8 May prior to his departure for Morocco.

20. J.O., *Chambre*, 18 June 1912; also in Millerand, *Pour la défense*, pp. 71–2, 401, Millerand's speech of 14 September 1912 at the close of the first period of maneuvers in the west; J.O., *Chambre*, 18 June 1912; Millerand, *Pour la défense*, p. 93, circulars of 24 January and 28 February 1912 on training camps; *ibid.*, p. 217, decree of 5 April 1912 on inspection of the artillery's technical expertise and study program; *ibid.*, p. 229, decree of 24 July 1912 giving the war ministry supervisory control over

Millerand, who considered it vital to supplement human resources
with technological preparation, urged that all scientific and industrial developments with military ramifications be fully applied.
Convinced that aviation had a potentially important wartime role,
Millerand wanted laws passed that would provide for the construction of planes, their operation, and pilot training. Although its
technical and organizational requirements were difficult to assess,
haphazard progress and a lack of definitive statutes had provoked
passionate attacks as much as excitement. The war minister argued
that this 'marvelous discovery' gave Frenchmen a chance to develop their native qualities of ingenuity, audacity, and composure.
Parliament had to set the framework so that expenditures could be
wisely, but flexibly, allocated. To Millerand, this new field must be
protected from inter-service rivalries; aviation belonged to the
whole army, the entire nation, not just the Engineer Corps. A
military aeronautic section within the Engineer Corps should
centralize aviation matters, but inform regional commanders about
the new machines' relevance for their needs.[21]

The law of 29 March 1912 and subsequent decrees provided the
charter of French military aviation. Its development, however, had
financial as well as organizational and human dimensions, since
equipment, research, and personnel training were expensive. Parliamentary and public opinion, however, was ready to establish and
finance an air fleet. France accepted the costs of training aviation
personnel, pilots as well as mechanical support staff. Three groups
of ten aeronautic sections were established, and yearly refresher
courses in flight training arranged for officers who had rejoined
their original regiments.[22]

Millerand's pressures for the production of explosives illustrated
a similar desire to use scientific progress. Problems of surveying

military schools and providing for annual inspections; *ibid.*, p. 236, decree of 23 July
1912 assigning future artillery officers to Fontainebleau and engineering officers to
Versailles; *ibid.*, p. 240, decree of 4 September 1912 establishing a liaison commission between the constabulary and the departments of war, justice, and interior;
ibid., p. 243, circular of 9 October 1912 on decentralization of the power structure.

21. Poincaré, *Au service*, II, p. 77; Joffre, I, p. 83; J.O., *Chambre*, 18 June 1912;
Millerand, *Pour la défense*, p. 4: telegraphic communication's increased importance
to military operations and its personnel's technical specialization necessitated special
service regulations which were adopted on 30 March 1912 with little parliamentary
discussion; J.O., *Sénat*, 13 February 1912.

22. Millerand, *Pour la défense*, pp. 142–4, decree of 12 May 1912, setting salaries
for military personnel; J.O., *Lois et décrets*, p. 4463; A.N., C7421, Chamber, Army
Commission, audition of Millerand, 7 March 1912; G. Bonnefous, I, p. 309.

private production dictated a governmental monopoly of explosive fabrication, but it had financial limitations. Fewer inspectors would be necessary to survey a government monopoly of gunpowder production than many private producers. Even so, the six-fold production increase over the preceding thirty years required more surveillance personnel, with their attendant costs. Developments which permitted a larger production of explosives meant that there were not enough chemists, engineers, or research staff. Although they had improved recruiting procedures to get more personnel, the engineers' better material status did not, Millerand argued, justify relaxing discipline within the gunpowder factories. To eliminate politics from the factories, he suggested militarizing the gunpowder engineers even though it might rigidify their hierarchy and stifle innovation, fostering a *fonctionnairisme* over promotion tied to ability, as applied in private industry. When war came, France, which would need private industry's resources, would have to define the relationship between the governmental monopoly and private production. If the government ordered explosives for the war ministry's account, it would expand production and give industry a peacetime apprenticeship. The war minister did, however, criticize private industry for offering the militarized civil servants higher salaries.[23]

Military preparation had a moral as well as a material dimension. Millerand, who for nearly thirty years had urged the application of professional rather than political criteria to military problems, sought to de-politicize the army. By 1912, the army's politicization, which had fostered distrust, had undermined the military spirit. Millerand decided, therefore, to remove politically involved officers from Paris and constant parliamentary contacts, to limit officers' assignments in Paris to six years, and to disqualify those who had been in the capital for four years from serving in the central administration. A provincial tour of duty thenceforth followed any Parisian assignment, with faster promotions and shorter assignments offered to attract officers to eastern garrisons. To break the capital's hold on promotions, he included generals from outside

23. A.N., C7421, Chamber, Army Commission, auditions of Millerand, 8 March and 20 November 1912; J.O., *Sénat*, 31 May 1912; also in Millerand, *Pour la défense*, pp. 160–73.

Paris on the promotion committees.[24]

To separate politics from the army, Millerand suppressed political information on officers; only professional considerations, he argued, should influence evaluations of their performance. His decree setting yearly promotion schedules outlined uniform procedures that linked promotion to ability. War minister Maurice Berteaux, General André's successor, had established a system of prefectoral reports which indicated those officers with 'incorrect' or disloyal attitudes. Considering that the prefects' political reports undermined the military command's authority, Millerand ended this surveillance system, and the following year ordered all political dossiers burned. The war minister also wanted to limit officers' participation in non-military groups. The war ministry had to approve adherence to any association, but officers were prohibited from joining the military leagues that appeared during the summer of 1912 or any societies with political or religious objectives.[25]

On the other hand, his constraints on the military's freedom of expression, which reflected his wish for solidarity and discipline, introduced a political control somewhat at odds with his criticism of André's system. Officers, who had to submit their publications to their superiors for approval with a copy to the war ministry, could not indicate their military function. Millerand's anxiety to suppress publications that might undermine the military spirit or national interests led him to introduce anti-democratic controls. Solidarity and discipline proved antithetical to de-politicization although the objective of a stronger army remained consistent.[26]

Millerand also streamlined the system of military justice to make it more rational and efficient. Since the court-martial system's overly severe penalties and inadequate protection for the accused violated the current legislature's liberal principles, he improved the rights of the accused and accelerated trial procedures to bring

24. J.O., *Chambre*, 28 June 1912; J.O., *Sénat*, 3 February 1912; also in Millerand, *Pour la défense*, pp. vi–viii, 263–4, 305–7, also circulars of 1 February and 25 June 1912; *ibid.*, pp. x, 317, decree of 12 June 1912; Porch, p. 179; Millerand, 'Souvenirs,' pp. 67–8; Persil, p. 74; Sumler, 'Domestic influences,' pp. 525–7.

25. Millerand, 'Souvenirs,' pp. 67–8; Persil, p. 74; Sumler, 'Domestic influences,' pp. 525–7; Millerand, *Pour la défense*, vi–ix, 253–5, circular of 25 January 1912 to the prefects; Porch, pp. 98, 170, 179; Ralston, p. 324; Millerand, *Pour la défense*, pp. ix–x, 256ff., circular of 4 September 1912; *ibid.*, pp. 262–3, circular of 9 September 1912.

26. Millerand, *Pour la défense*, pp. 273–6, circular of 15 May 1912; J.O., *Lois et décrets*, p. 4495.

violations of the penal code to the appropriate tribunal as rapidly as possible. If preparatory formalities were kept to a minimum and the commanding officer was responsible for assembling and transmitting the relevant material, Millerand believed discipline would be fostered.[27]

To restore military discipline and encourage a sense of comradeship in the army, Millerand issued regulations governing military clothing and dining arrangements. Since he considered the uniform an exterior mark of an hierarchical authority, its wear promoted discipline. Its correct usage bolstered the army's spirit and its prestige among civilians. Although he accepted the use of civilian garb in certain war ministry offices, he rejected it in the barracks except on holidays. In his opinion, costly clothing encouraged rivalry among officers prejudicial to corps unity, while a common uniform encouraged solidarity. Other regulations, like an obligatory dining requirement, were also designed to promote a sense of solidarity in the army. A general mess, Millerand argued, served as a 'school of comradeship and solidarity' as well as providing financial advantages and removing dangerous temptations from the junior officers who would otherwise be separated into groups based on school, wealth, or social position. His regulations on drinking cooperatives, which made them annexes to recreation halls that sold beverages, were designed to improve soldiers' leisure time by providing a place where they could relax when off duty and also give them a chance to develop their common bonds. He did, however, restrict their number and possible functions so that they would not compete with the military canteens or become simply business ventures. He also tried to enliven military life by reviving bugle calls to mark various points of the day.[28]

Moral force, as important to Millerand as material, required confidence between the nation and its army. To revive military popularity, he instituted colorful reviews, tattoos, and torchlight parades in Paris, notably the large military review of 12 March 1912 at Vincennes, which attracted crowds from all social groups. Remi-

27. Millerand, *Pour la défense*, pp. 180–6, 211–12, circular of 18 December 1912 relative to the preliminary investigation; J.O., *Sénat*, 21 November 1912; Porch, p. 185.
28. Millerand, *Pour la défense*, pp. 268–72, cites circular of 8 April 1912. Porch, p. 184, notes that Millerand did, however, hinder efforts to introduce camouflaged battle dress. Millerand, *Pour la défense*, pp. x, 283, decree of 23 July 1912; J.O., *Lois et décrets*, p. 6752; Porch, pp. 85, 128, 185; Millerand, *Pour la défense*, pp. x, 287, 314, circular of 18 June 1912 and decree of 30 October 1912.

niscent of Boulangism but without the personal demagogic
ingredient, these patriotic displays, which helped restore military
esprit and popular confidence in the army, also became anti-German
demonstrations and aroused the young to shout such *revanchiste*
slogans as 'Long live Alsace-Lorraine' and 'Down with Germany.'
Millerand, who had staunchly opposed such popular manifestations in the 1880s, had become the proponent of a military revival
by 1912. Still hostile to the individual dictatorship of someone like
Boulanger, he probably encouraged the military displays because
of increased anxiety about Germany.[29]

Always a supporter of military service, Millerand saw it as a link
between the army and the public that taught citizens to respect
discipline and encouraged sacrifice and self-denial. The army was
an essentially democratic institution and a school for patriotism
which assigned priority to service and merit but ultimately implied
the supreme individual sacrifice for the nation. Identifying with
Gambetta, who had played such a crucial role in France's earlier
material and moral revival, Millerand noted that Gambetta, who
wanted stronger ties between the nation and its army, considered it
above political quarrels and party intrigues. He would, Millerand
believed, have been proud of the army's soldiers of 1912.[30] Public
exposure to a military existence and martial pageantry helped to
militarize society and create the moral unity vital to war preparation, but Millerand never expressed any desire for war. Preparation
for war risks encouraging it, but it was never the sole national
preoccupation that would have made it inevitable.

France had gradually cut military service from five to three and
finally to two years, but this shorter period meant that the young
needed some military instruction before reaching the barracks.
Societies of military preparations contributed to the transformation
of draftees into capable soldiers. Up to 1912, preliminary instruc-

29. A.N., F.M. 13, Millerand, 'La guerre libératrice,' p. 6; Poincaré, *Au service*,
II, pp. 78–9; Eugen Weber, *Action Française* (Stanford: Stanford University Press,
1962), p. 85; Eugen Weber, *The Nationalist Revival in France, 1905–1914* (Berkeley:
University of California Press, 1968), pp. 101–2; Porch, p. 180; G. Bonnefous, I,
p. 314; Bariety and Poidevin, p. 198. Michon, p. 90, dates the spring review as 10
March. Cairns, 'International politics,' p. 281; Krumeich, p. 33. Sumler, 'Polarization,' pp. 144–7, argues that Millerand's reforms favored the conservative groups,
encouraged chauvinism, and discredited leftist opponents of militarism.

30. A.N., F.M. 13, Millerand, 'La guerre libératrice,' pp. 2–3; J.O., *Chambre*, 22
March 1912; Millerand, *Pour la défense*, p. 391, Millerand's speech of 31 March 1912
at the annual ceremony honoring Gambetta; *ibid.*, pp. 395–8, speech of 30 June 1912
to the banquet Hoche at Versailles.

tion prior to actual service had only reached a small percentage of French communes. By the end of that year, there were approximately 8,500 societies of military preparation in France, but only a seventh of all conscripts had been members. Insistent that the societies remain purely educational, rigorously excluding all politics, Millerand urged the expansion of this military education. To him, those in the schools best inculcated the necessary patriotism.

> The experience of the scholarly battles of old taught you . . . You want to form healthy bodies, well-balanced, capable of enduring the necessary fatigue and eager for the lessons which make the good soldier . . . You prepare their minds as well as their bodies with the patriotic duty to love France, to place it above all else, to be ready to sacrifice even their lives.

The divisive influences of the teacher and the priest in certain regions must, however, be eliminated. The 'army was France,' requiring all Frenchmen, regardless of belief or social status, to serve their nation.[31]

Although Millerand described the army as a reflection of democracy, he strengthened its discipline and organization. His reforms therefore have sometimes been viewed as the general staff's revenge for the army reforms after the Dreyfus Affair. He is accused of using press chauvinism to revive a nationalism that would restore the army to its previously invulnerable position.[32] While Millerand's reforms may well have revived the army's prestige, his goal was preparation for war, not satisfaction of the general staff's injured sensibilities.

Identification of the army with France inclined Millerand to discount its divisive elements and popular anti-militarism, although he did try to eliminate them. He viewed the C.G.T.'s plans for a general strike as an anti-war manifestation. In wartime, young

31. Millerand, *Pour la défense*, pp. 99–102, speech of 15 June 1912 to the yearly banquet of the National Federation of the Societies of Military Preparation attended, among others, by the presidents of the Senate and Chamber and the heads of their army commissions; *ibid.*, pp. 105–7, speeches of 26 October 1912 at the annual celebration of the Seine departmental federation of the societies of military preparation and of 24 November 1912 to the celebration of the union of French and colonial scholarly societies.

32. Michon, p. 90. Sumler, 'Polarization,' p. 169, cites an interview of Millerand by two German newspapers in which he argued that the function of discipline in the army was to neutralize the general anarchy resulting from democratic institutions.

Frenchmen would not let such a campaign deter them from their duty, but instructions for sabotaging mobilization constituted, in Millerand's opinion, the 'most abominable crime against the fatherland.' He reminded corps commanders that defense establishment personnel could not strike or join any concerted work stoppage. They should also prevent anti-militarist groups like the Anarchist Communist Federation distributing subversive tracts among the soldiers.[33]

From its earliest days, the Third Republic had excluded from the army those threatening to contaminate morally the young. Laws of 3 February and 30 March 1912 excluded systematic detractors, those encouraging disobedience or desertion, and imposed service in African battalions on those convicted of inflicting wounds on themselves or of rebellion. Millerand's critics, who feared the law would assimilate political and common-law convicts, saw it as a weapon against working–class syndicalism and anti-militarism. He responded, however, that no 1912 conscripts had been affected; the nine men sent to Africa were guilty of common-law violations, not political acts or strikes. Drafting anti-militarists risked spreading adverse propaganda, but the war minister hesitated to assimilate those charged with anti-militarist speeches or publications with those guilty of insubordination or evasion of duty. Since he preferred to shield the army from all dangerous propaganda, he thought all anti-militarists should be sent to African regiments. Along with ostracism to the colonial service, he suggested precautions so that the move would not damage France's colonial position.[34] While he did not deliberately try to undercut worker organizations, his restrictions on unionization in the army, though

33. Cairns, 'International politics,' p. 284; J.O., *Chambre*, 2 December 1912; also in Millerand, *Pour la défense*, pp. 356–8 and circular of 7 December 1912 prohibiting war department personnel from striking; A.G., 5N4, Millerand to the commanding-general, 8th Army Corps, Bourges, 14 January 1913, concerning the distribution of subversive literature; Porch, p. 184.

34. J.O., *Chambre*, 11 November 1912; also in Millerand, *Pour la défense*, pp. 333–7; A.N., C7421, Chamber, Army Commission, audition of Millerand, 29 June 1912; G. Bonnefous, I, p. 309; A.G., 5N8, Millerand to the governor-general of Algeria, 15 December 1912. Krumeich, p. 33, cites Millerand's law of 30 March 1912 which, he argues, was designed to curtail syndicalist action in the ranks. Jean-Jacques Becker, *Le Carnet B* (Paris: Editions Klincksieck, 1973), pp. 38–9, notes that the law Millerand–Berry which permitted the despatch of 'antimilitarists, strikers and demonstrators' to African battalions or forced labor sections was passed without opposition even from the Socialists, although it aroused the anger of the *congressistes* meeting at Le Havre.

motivated by a desire to control an anti-militarism harmful to war preparation, did attack those organizations he had long sought to strengthen.

Similar concerns led Millerand to survey workers in national defense factories and inscribe potentially disloyal ones in the Carnet B to prevent damage to the war effort. Established in 1857, the Carnet B was designed to observe foreigners and Frenchmen who might endanger national security during mobilization. To Millerand, it would be paradoxical to halt this vital precautionary measure at the gates of the national defense establishments. While the vast majority of workers were loyal Frenchmen, the few 'abominable fomenters' of anti-militarism and sabotage must be discreetly watched without infringing on a worker's rights of self-defense.[35] Defense-oriented factories became a very broad category in the reality of total war, but Millerand seemingly held the more restricted view common to the prewar period. He was perhaps naive not to recognize the extent to which industry would be drawn into wartime production and hence the police control over the industrial work-force which inscription in the Carnet B implied. Nor does he appear to have considered its practical implications – who and what constituted disloyalty. His objectives, to eliminate politics from the army and insure patriotic industrial workers, were not, however, totalitarian. His stance was indeed undemocratic and an alteration of his own earlier position, but he advocated measures that have since become common to modern warfare in all societies.

Millerand's reform program has received conflicting evaluations. It has generally been attacked by leftists hostile to moves to halt worker unrest within the military structure and praised by conservatives anxious for a strong French army in the event of war. To his critics, his goal was to forestall massive unionization and social unrest; to his supporters, he made an attempt to revive military prestige in an overheated international atmosphere. There is, however, general agreement that basic grievances existed that required solution. While his program clearly contained anti-democratic aspects, he significantly revived the army's prestige and efficiency, rendering it better prepared for war.[36]

35. A.N., F.M. 9, 'Historique chronologique,' 11 March 1912; J.O., *Chambre*, 11 March 1912; also in Millerand, *Pour la défense*, pp. 359–62.

36. Porch, pp. 184, 187, stresses the contemporary opposition to Millerand's reforms. Bompard, p. 30 notes his great popularity as war minister.

Despite Millerand's popularity and the general climate of anxiety, military preparation encountered delays and stumbling-blocks. Financial constraints limited the establishment of new training camps – less than half the requested funds were actually allocated. Diplomatic problems altered military planning. On 21 February 1912, Joffre, supported by Delcassé and Millerand, proposed a wartime offensive through neutral Belgium, if that nation and Britain agreed, but Poincaré opposed it and Belgian hostility forced Joffre to abandon the idea. Franco–British general staff talks in 1912 did, however, define collaboration in a possible Franco-German war. Finally, bureaucratic inertia in the war ministry delayed modernization of the artillery.[37]

The so-called du Paty de Clam affair, which abruptly ended Millerand's first war ministry in January 1913, revealed personality traits that illuminate his performance as war minister in 1912 and in 1914–15. Lieutenant-Colonel Mercier du Paty de Clam, of Dreyfus Affair notoriety, had requested reinstatement in the army from Millerand's predecessor, War Minister Adolphe Messimy. The Agadir crisis led Messimy to view the request favorably if du Paty de Clam would withdraw his complaint to the public prosecutor's office, but procedural delays postponed the reinstatement until the war scare had passed and Millerand was war minister. To Millerand, the matter was a simple administrative action to fulfill Messimy's formal promise and did not require cabinet ratification.

> In no affair should any consideration win out over concern for truth and justice . . . I was accused of striking in the back a friend of thirty years, the premier . . . [and] others said that I wanted by a *coup d'état* to bring him some rebellious voices . . . the truth is much more simple, I found

37. Millerand, 'Souvenirs,' p. 71; Joffre, I, pp. 83, 119–26; Samuel R. Williamson, Jr., *The Politics of Grand Strategy. Britain and France Prepare for War, 1904–1914* (Cambridge: Harvard University Press, 1969), p. 212; Charles Humbert, *Chacun son tour* (Paris: L'Ile de France, 1925), pp. 21, 28–9, 33. Cairns, 'International politics,' pp. 273–8, notes the malaise within the Triple Entente and the insecurity of France's ties to Britain and Russia. *Documents diplomatiques français (1871–1914)*, 3ᵉ série, vol. V (Paris: Imprimerie Nationale, 1933), p. 65, Millerand to Poincaré, 12 December 1912, described General Wilson's visit to Paris to work out with the French general staff measures for a Franco-German conflict and a hostile Belgium: hereafter cited as D.D.F. Guy Pedroncini, 'Stratégie et relations internationales: la séance du 9 janvier 1912 du Conseil Supérieur de la Défense Nationale,' *Revue d'histoire diplomatique*, 91ᵉ année, janvier–juin 1977, pp. 151, 153.

myself faced with an inevitable administrative decision . . . I asked advice of no one because I was tied by a commitment.

Premier Poincaré resented Millerand's failure to secure prior governmental approval for the decree of 10 January 1913 which legalized this move. He considered the war minister naive not to recognize that du Paty's name would revive the barely suppressed emotions of the Dreyfus Affair. Not surprisingly, the reinstatement outraged the Left but elicited praise from the Right, a curious situation for a strong Dreyfusard like Millerand. The war minister considered it a matter of honor, not choice, to fulfill his predecessor's commitment.[38] Millerand's approach to the reinstatement illustrated his legalism even at the cost of a political setback.

The standard interpretation of the du Paty de Clam affair has been Raymond Poincaré's. Poincaré and the cabinet, troubled by the uproar, wanted Millerand to resign. They did not want to accept responsibility for a move that had not been collectively ratified. Furthermore, the premier was reluctant, he said, to embarrass President Armand Fallières with a governmental crisis at the end of the latter's term of office. Millerand had been influential in persuading Poincaré to run for the presidency, but the excitement provoked by the du Paty affair strengthened the Left. The premier, however, strongly refuted charges that Millerand had provoked the crisis to destroy his friend's presidential chances, and acknowledged his persistent support. Poincaré faulted Millerand's independence and lack of political sensitivity, but praised his integrity, loyalty, and contribution to military preparation.[39] Poincaré's interpretation is understandable, since as premier he bore responsibility for his ministers' actions and resented not being informed of moves that affected him. Nor is it surprising that a name linked to the Dreyfus Affair would provoke a storm. Millerand should have

38. Millerand, 'Souvenirs,' pp. 72–3; Poincaré, *Au service*, III, pp. 40, 42–5; conversation with Jacques Millerand, 20 May 1978; J.O. *Chambre*, 31 January 1913; Persil, pp. 78–9; Millerand, *Pour la défense*, pp. 382–90; G. Bonnefous, I, pp. 317–8; Duroselle, *Belle Epoque*, p. 365; Derfler, *Président*, p. 72; Krumeich, pp. 42–3. Although Albert de Mun viewed Millerand's action as a demonstration of a new patriotic pact that eradicated the old division between 'Republic' and 'Reaction', there is no evidence to support Krumeich's claim that Millerand sought to offer a token of goodwill to the Right.

39. Poincaré, *Au service*, III, pp. 45–6, 48; Millerand, 'Souvenirs,' pp. 73–4; Suarez, II, pp. 399, 402. Evidence does not support Suarez's claim that Briand believed that Millerand wanted to harm Poincaré and that he was an ambitious social climber manipulated by the Right.

shown greater sensitivity to the political implications of his move.

On the other hand, Millerand's defense that the affair was a relatively minor issue that was exaggerated is valid. Perhaps Poincaré wanted Millerand to resign to protect his own presidential chances. Millerand was probably also correct in arguing that had Poincaré simply presented the facts and assumed governmental responsibility, his candidacy would not have been harmed. However, his verdict that Poincaré lacked civil courage and above all had a 'phobia of responsibility' appears overly harsh.[40] Millerand's own loyalty, shown by his continued support for Poincaré's presidential candidacy, led him to expect similar steadfastness from his friends. Poincaré's political calculations undoubtedly better reflected the realities of the situation. Millerand's training as a lawyer seemingly influenced this legalistic approach to all issues. Despite his quarter-century as a deputy, he remained surprisingly unpolitical, refusing to let corridor intrigues or even simple political calculations influence decisions. Lack of political sensitivity led him to arouse antagonism where calculation might have secured support; decisiveness and independence prompted him to act without consultation, to be rigid rather than compromising, so that extreme solutions like his resignation became unavoidable.

From January 1913 to August 1914, Millerand's principal concern was the reintroduction of a three-year military service to utilize

---

40. Persil, p. 77; Millerand, 'Souvenirs,' pp. 73–4; Gordon Wright, *Raymond Poincaré and the French Presidency* (Stanford: Stanford University Press, 1942), pp. 41–3. Benjamin F. Martin, *Count Albert de Mun. Paladin of the Third Republic* (Chapel Hill: University of North Carolina Press, 1978), pp. 262–3, describes Millerand's action as an amazing lapse of political sensitivity that Caillaux tried to exploit in the Chamber. Maurice Paléologue, *Au Quai d'Orsay à la veille de la tourmente. Journal, 1913–1914* (Paris: Plon, 1947), pp. 6–7, in describing the cabinet meeting at the Quai d'Orsay on 12 January, terms Poincaré's treatment of Millerand as an 'inexcusable weakness.' The following day he praised Millerand's behavior at a lunch for Russian War Minister Soukhomlinov and called Millerand's abrupt resignation 'deplorable.' Millerand told Paléologue that a little firmness would have enabled Poincaré to survive a parliamentary debate, but that their 'brilliant' friend was not courageous. Krumeich, p. 252. Paul Cambon, *Correspondance, 1870–1924*, (Paris: Grasset, 1946), III, pp. 29, 34, describes Poincaré as incapable of taking a stand; his fear of responsibility led him to hide behind collective decisions. He calls the resignation of Millerand 'distressing.' Poincaré's anxiety about his presidential candidacy led him to drop his war minister, but he tried to give the impression that he had yielded to his colleagues' pressures to avoid exposing France to a cabinet crisis at such a supposedly critical time.

fully France's human resources. As he later recalled, expectation of the cyclone dominated the period, with France resolved to make no further concessions after Agadir. Millerand confronted the connection between French national defense and the distressing social problem of depopulation. Germany's decision to increase substantially its army forced France, he claimed, to restore the ruptured equilibrium with a population two-thirds its neighbor's size. Still uncertain about a three-year service requirement in the spring of 1913, Millerand urged changes in the 1905 law that required a two-year obligation and expanded armaments production. However peaceful its intent, France could not justify the 'criminal' failure to adopt those vital national defense measures needed to increase its offensive strength.[41]

Parliament actively debated the issue of a three-year service in June 1913. Raised by the Barthou ministry, the Chamber passed the law on 19 July and the Senate ratified it on 9 August.[42] The Socialists and a majority of the Radicals opposed the change, although many Radicals, including Premier Barthou, supported it.

On 11 July, Millerand declared his official support for the proposed law, although he had been moving toward that position for several months. He noted that as war minister he had only endorsed the longer term for the cavalry to improve the quality of that branch, but that quantitative considerations persuaded him to back a three-year service for the entire army, specifically the German proposals of 1913 by which Germany would expand its army and military budget as much in two years as in the preceding thirty-seven. This change destroyed the approximate Franco-German equilibrium of five to six of 1910. 'We cannot have a power on our frontiers whose military force is so superior that the day she wants to use it, we will face either an overwhelming defeat or disgrace.' Germany's assertion of its pacific intents and claims that Balkan developments and not hostility to France motivated the military increases did not, Millerand insisted, outweigh the reality

---

41. Millerand, 'Souvenirs,' p. 75; A.N., F.M. 13, Millerand's speech to his constituents of the 12th *arrondissement*, 25 February 1913; A.N., F.M. 13, Millerand, 'La guerre libératrice: La France et son armée,' February 1913, published in *Le Gaulois*, 17 April 1913 and in *Les Lectures pour tous*, 15 April 1913; also in Millerand, *Pour la défense*, pp. 408–9. Krumeich, pp. 47–8, 254, notes that as of 25 February Poincaré and Millerand still considered a general extension of military service to three years as 'superfluous.'

42. G. Bonnefous, I, pp. 343–51, notes that the Chamber passed the law by more than a 3:2 majority. Duroselle, *Belle Epoque*, pp. 367–75.

of the ruptured equilibrium. Tapping additional categories of men, draft-dodgers or colonial reserves was not an adequate solution any more than better training or additional fortifications in the northeast. For France, the only viable option was a longer period of service that would give it an extra class. Millerand denied that the change would create a professional army any more than it had between 1889 and 1905. Clearly, the change had a financial dimension, since funds were necessary to support soldiers for an additional year, and their absence from normal occupations would reduce national production, but it would be less costly than an invasion. He urged Frenchmen not to make the same mistake they had in 1867–70 when they rejected War Minister Niel's request for additional troops. France's best hopes of peace lay in its military strength; weakness would simply fuel German hegemonic ambitions.[43]

Although the three-year law was passed in 1913, it remained controversial for the remaining year of peace, with Socialists and Radicals still in opposition. The leftist electoral victory of 1914 might have brought its repeal had war not broken out so quickly. Millerand, however, remained a consistent supporter, stressing the increase of German troops from 1911 to 1913 compared to the preceding thirty-seven years: in both eras, Germany had expanded its army by 180,000 men! Its financial implications led Interior Minister Louis Malvy to urge a gradual return to a two-year service, while Millerand suggested using direct taxation to tap French resources more effectively. He interpreted his electoral victory in 1914 as a national mandate for the three-year law. Although Millerand's stance on military service may have influenced his constituents, it is unlikely that it played a large role in his victory, and even less likely that it indicated a national verdict. He was particularly critical of the Socialists and Radicals for harboring men who advocated absence of discipline and desertion in the barracks. Unions were not, he argued, entitled to disseminate anti-patriotic propaganda.[44]

43. Millerand, 'Souvenirs,' p. 75; A.N., F.M. 13, Millerand, 'La loi de trois ans,' 11 July 1913, speech to his constituents of the 12th *arrondissement*; also in *Le Parlement et l'opinion*, 20 July 1913, pp. 3–9.
44. Millerand, 'Souvenirs,' p. 75; A.N., F.M. 8, speech by Millerand at Soissons, 22 March 1914, reported by Agence Havas; A.N., F.M. 33, Millerand's speech in Bordeaux, 15 April 1914, reported in *La Petite Gironde*, 17 April 1914, an electoral speech for Chaumet; A.N., F.M. 33, interview of Millerand by Louis Latzarus, 2 May 1914, published in *Figaro*; *ibid*., Millerand's speech at Juvisy, 3 May 1914, published in *Débats*, 5 May 1914. Krumeich, pp. 187–8, 283, comments that

During this period, Millerand also confronted domestic issues like electoral and financial reform. While a new electoral law was not enacted until 1919, it was much debated in 1913–14. Convinced that Frenchmen could no longer avoid the issue, Millerand portrayed continuation of the *scrutin d'arrondissement* system as a disaster for the republican majority, but considered pure list-voting equally iniquitous. The only viable option seemed to him a *scrutin de liste* with proportional representation to protect minority rights. To solve its economic and social problems, France needed an electoral system that eliminated entrenched interests. If deputies were drawn from a larger constituency, they might tackle national questions like tax reform, depopulation, or social legislation instead of narrow sectarian concerns.[45]

For the elections of 1914, Millerand helped found an electoral alliance, the Fédération des Gauches, to fight the Radicals. Mocked by Clemenceau, this group of moderate republicans, independent socialists, and some radicals included Millerand, Briand, Barthou, Dupuy, Pichon, Joseph Reinach, and Etienne. Its vague program for a general republican union sought social democracy, electoral and fiscal reform (without jeopardizing the creation of wealth), laicity, and maintenance of the three-year law. Without a national electoral base, the alliance only helped its members' election and complicated the electoral scene. Although twenty-three of its members were elected, the Socialists emerged the true victors with almost double their former representation (68 to 102 seats) and more than 10 percent of the popular vote.[46]

Millerand's fears that the staff law would not be passed before the elections led him to urge Poincaré to send a message to the Chambers. After the Chamber passed the law on 12 March, Poincaré expressed relief that he had not heeded Millerand's pessimism.

45. A.N., F.M. 13, Millerand's speech to his constituents of the 12th *arrondissement*, 25 February 1913; *ibid.*, Millerand's speech in Bordeaux, 15 April 1914, reported in *La Petite Gironde*, 17 April 1914; Alexandre Millerand, "La politique sociale d'un état moderne,' *Le Parlement et l'opinion*, 30 October 1913 (Paris), pp. 1–7, speech to a group of French merchants at the Ghent exposition; A.N., F.M. 33, speech to the banquet of the Chambre syndicale d'ameublement, 31 March 1914. Krumeich, pp. 160–1, Millerand joined other F.D.G. politicians in interpellating Caillaux on 27 February 1914 on the issue of tax reform. Although they preferred the 1.4 billion franc loan proposed by the Barthou government to Caillaux's proposed capital tax, the Chamber supported the government. G. Bonnefous, I, pp. 386–7.

46. Duroselle, *Belle Epoque*, p. 378; Watson, p. 247. Suarez, II, p. 457, notes Briand's leadership in founding the F.D.G. at the end of December 1913. Krumeich, p. 149, G. Bonnefous, I, pp. 374–5, 380–1, the Federation's liberal orientation was

Millerand was easily reelected to the Chamber in 1914. Only in 1902 and 1910, when he was a cabinet minister, did he experience electoral difficulties. He explained those problems by arguing that Paris supported the opposition. In 1914, he scarcely campaigned, only distributed a programatic circular, did not attend meetings or read his Socialist opponent's declarations, which he assumed called him a renegade. In his view, a campaign would simply have provoked unnecessary violence. His 'faithful' electors were familiar with him and his objectives since he had represented them for twenty-five years. While Millerand probably analyzed his constituents' wishes accurately, his behavior illustrated precisely the system's ratification of a sinecure that he denounced in demanding electoral reform.[47]

Despite his impressive electoral victory, Millerand continued to denounce the system that gave him its support. As a national figure, he would undoubtedly have fared as well with list-voting, but he saw the vote of 1914 as a popular mandate to reform the *régime de la clientèle* (the patronage system). He considered scandalous the system's plethora of petty tyrannies. Also desirous of fiscal reform, he understood popular reservations about opening businesses to the treasury's inquisition. Unemployment, sickness, and old-age insurance, however, required a sound financial base. On the eve of war, therefore, Millerand's focus on national military preparedness did not lead him to abandon those social, financial, and electoral reforms he had long espoused.[48]

reflected in its definition, 'La République, c'est la liberté.' In all, 126 senators and deputies attended its organizational meeting on 13 January 1914; *ibid.*, p. 406, notes the F.D.G.'s relative lack of electoral success.

47. A.N., F.M. 33, interview with Louis Latzarus, 2 May 1914, in *Figaro*.

48. A.N., F.M. 33, speech at Juvisy, 3 May 1914, published in *Débats*, 5 May 1914.

7
Politics Versus Patriotism: the Struggles of the Second War Ministry

During Millerand's second occupation of the rue Saint-Dominique from 26 August 1914 to 29 October 1915, he played a significant role in mobilizing the economy for war production. Along with Viviani, Poincaré, Briand, and Delcassé, he dominated the French political scene during the first year of the war. Millerand has generally been criticized for his devotion to General Joffre, which led him to give the general a free hand at the expense of civilian influence on military affairs.[1] His achievements in economic mobilization have also been questioned. A study of Millerand's policies contributes to an understanding of wartime civil–military relations. His relationship, as a civilian politician, with the High Command and other military personnel illuminates the interaction between the war ministry, a civilian bureaucracy, and the military leadership – the relative powers of each in military decision-making. As director of the department responsible for contacts with the army, Millerand represented that service in the domestic political process. He was the intermediary between the army hierarchy and the civilian political structure, most directly the parliament and the cabinet. His pivotal position permits a study of the role of a vital ministry in wartime and the degree to which it

1. General Adolphe Messimy, *Mes souvenirs* (Paris: Librairie Plon, 1937), p. 235, who calls Millerand the 'lawyer for the G.Q.G.,' and criticizes his passive submission to the commander-in-chief. George H. Cassar, *The French and the Dardanelles* (London: George Allen & Unwin, Ltd., 1971), pp. 14–15, claims Millerand's lack of strategic imagination and uncritical acceptance of information from the military made him a poor war leader. He permitted Joffre to usurp his authority over the military forces, making him a simple mouthpiece for the G.Q.G.

established autonomy from or was subordinate to parliamentary governance.

Millerand's personality and prior experience influenced his return to the war ministry in 1914. Although Premier René Viviani primarily wanted to expand the political base of his cabinet, he and President Poincaré chose Millerand for that difficult position because of his experience in 1912, his recognized composure in times of adversity, and his capacity for work. In their opinion, War Minister Messimy was too overwhelmed by the task and discouraged by the initial military setbacks to be a good wartime minister. Messimy, however, maintained he did not want to give up the war ministry but was forced to do so by Viviani for political reasons. He expected parliament to approve the choice of Millerand and his own elimination.[2] Messimy's departure for the front paved the way for Millerand to resume leadership of the war ministry.

Viviani's choice appeared vindicated, for Millerand's combination of calmness, dedication to work, and confidence in an eventual victory supplied the necessary tonic to the generalized panic of the early war period. He, in turn, believed that General Joffre's imperturbability and self-mastery would set an example for the army that would counterbalance the defeatism provoked by retreat and looming disaster. As war minister, his first act was a visit to the general's headquarters, where he stressed governmental and national confidence that Joffre and his army would eventually secure a French victory. As he said, to defend its territory and liberty, 'the entire nation . . . has resolutely accepted even the most cruel tests and has subjected itself to that rigid discipline which is the army's rule and strength.'[3] He demonstrated an admiration for and confidence in the army and its leadership that was essential to counterbalance the generalized anxiety.

The war minister's own firmness and composure matched the general's. With German forces nearing Paris, the atmosphere of anxiety reached even the Elysée, but Millerand carried on 'like a good work horse who plows his field,' untroubled by the general lack of serenity. His authority and composure calmed his subordinates and even impressed British War Minister Horatio Herbert Kitchener when they met in Paris on 3 September. British Prime

---

2. Millerand, 'Souvenirs,' pp. 76–7; Poincaré, *Au service*, V, pp. 174–6, 179–81, 183; Messimy, pp. 372–5.

3. Millerand, 'Souvenirs,' pp. 78–9; A.N., F.M. 33, Millerand to Joffre, 27 August 1914; Poincaré, *Au service*, V, p. 186.

Minister Herbert Henry Asquith, who knew Millerand before the war, considered him 'capable and level-headed.'[4]

Since 1912, Millerand had been convinced that the military authorities should be free to decide the conduct of military operations. The government could replace an inadequate commander, but should otherwise leave the development of strategy and tactics to the military. This view undoubtedly explains why it is virtually impossible to detect Millerand's influence on strategy. While his advocacy of military prerogatives was more extensive than that of many contemporaries, he did not want military power to eliminate civilian power. Although those prerogatives might have expanded into a military dictatorship, that development would never have received the endorsement of a war minister who was still a loyal parliamentary republican. Above all, he sought civil–military collaboration to permit wartime measures to be rapidly executed. For example, to avoid disputes Millerand instructed local civil and military authorities to submit to Paris any disagreement they could not settle locally, like precedence at ceremonial events. He suggested that the military governor take precedence at military ceremonies and the prefect at civil occasions.[5]

As in 1912, Millerand wanted an army that was as well organized and trained as possible. To reports of poor troop organization, instruction, and dress, he responded by demanding inspection visits by regional commanders. Retired officers should be reintegrated to fill staff gaps, distinctions between active troops, reserves, and territorials eliminated, and strict discipline imposed on all

4. Persil, p. 84; Colonel Emile Herbillon, *Souvenirs d'un officier de liaison pendant la guerre mondiale* (Paris: Editions Jules Tallandier, 1930), I, p. 13; Jere Clemens King, *Generals and Politicians* (Berkeley: University of California Press, 1951), p. 27; A.N., F.M. 32, General Edmond Buat, 'Souvenirs,' pp. 4–5: an extract from Buat's memoirs notes Millerand's calmness, punctuality, and clear comprehension of the state of affairs during the crisis of early September 1914 and Viviani's and Poincaré's total depression during the same period; Bibliothèque de l'Institut, General Edmond Buat, 'Souvenirs,' I, 1914–18; H.H. Asquith, *Letters to Venetia Stanley* (Oxford: Oxford University Press, 1982), p. 217.

5. Millerand, 'Souvenirs,' pp. 77–8; Joffre, II, p. 149, 26 June 1915. Joffre, who did not think responsibility could be divided in wartime, was determined to maintain his freedom of action *vis-à-vis* parliament. Charles Bugnet, *Rue St-Dominique et G.Q.G. ou les trois dictatures de la guerre* (Paris: Librairie Plon, 1937), pp. 78–9. A.N., F.M. 32, Buat, 'Souvenirs,' p. 1, notes Millerand's instructions to his staff of 29 August that their purpose was to serve (*servir*) the fighting army, not to subject it to an inquisitorial authority. A.G., 6N25, Millerand and the interior minister to the prefects and military governors (Bordeaux), 16 October 1914; *ibid.*, 6N22, Millerand to the commander of the 15th region (Marseilles), 23 July 1915.

troops, including sanctions for violations. The war minister was particularly dismayed by the sloppy dress and lack of supervision in many towns and garrisons, as well as by the inadequate combat instruction.[6] Millerand acted as an outside taskmaster, prodding the military to improve their services. While his specific complaints touched on the problems of transforming a nation from a peacetime to a wartime footing, they demonstrated an active rather than a passive relationship with the army.

The government's departure from Paris brought up the issue of the location of decision-making power. General Joffre feared the encirclement of Paris would isolate the government from the nation – a 'foolish' risk for the administrations on which the nation's existence depended. He also worried that the government's presence would limit his strategic plans. By 2 September, both Joffre and the military governor of Paris, General Joseph Gallieni, had decided that the government should leave Paris. Although Millerand described the military situation to the cabinet optimistically, he supported Joffre's argument about a governmental move. He called the capital's defense 'to the death' a top priority even at the cost of destroying historic monuments and buildings. The symbolic significance of Paris as the nation's capital meant that it could not be abandoned. The war, however, radically altered the 'fortress' concept, defined in the decrees of 1891 and 1909, that included Paris. Originally considered as a human and supply reservoir for defending armies, the fortress was vulnerable to capture unless it became part of a fortified region. In September 1914, Paris was saved not by its own resources but from outside. Individual strong points like Paris therefore had to be linked to regional planning. In fact, the battle of the Marne, which halted the German advance by 7 September, improved the French military situation shortly after the government moved to Bordeaux. Even Millerand's critics have recognized his contribution to the defense of Paris in September 1914, terming his 'audacity and cold resolution' irreproachable.[7]

---

6. *Ibid.*, 6N10, Millerand to the regional commanders, 5 September 1914.
7. Poincaré, *Au service*, V, pp. 186, 208–9, 220, 236, 261; Herbillon, I, p. 18; Persil, pp. 82–3; Joseph S. Gallieni, *Mémoires du Maréchal Gallieni* (Paris: Payot, 1920), p. 66; Louis Marcellin, *Politique et politiciens pendant la guerre* (Paris: La Renaissance du Livre, 1922–4), I, pp. 33–4. A.N., F.M. 32, Buat, 'Souvenirs,' p. 11, contrasts the ministers' pessimism throughout the autumn to the war ministry's optimism. Paul-Boncour, I, pp. 247–54; Archives du Sénat, Army Commission, File 158, auditions of Millerand, 6 and 26 August 1915, hereafter cited as *Sénat*.

The period from August to December 1914 has been called a 'military dictatorship,' since the Senate and Chamber of Deputies adjourned *sine die* after the session of 4 August 1914. Formal parliamentary control over the army was suspended, but political pressures and intrigues continued. The government's departure for Bordeaux freed War Minister Millerand from the daily interventions by parliamentarians and permitted his total concentration on national defense. Somewhat tartly, he reprimanded a deputy who reminded him that he represented Paris, saying 'I am not a deputy of Paris, I am the Minister of War.'[8] To him, national priorities had displaced partisan considerations. His reinforcement of the military's dominance further restricted civil powers.

A concern for efficient decision-making rather than a dislike of democratic procedures prompted Millerand to shield the military from political interference with strategic planning. He was reluctant to let Senator Paul Doumer join General Gallieni's staff until the general agreed to the move. He feared conflicts with the Parisian administration if a civilian politician were involved in the capital's defense. The same concern led him to oppose Poincaré's and the cabinet's request to return to Paris in mid-October. The government's proximity to the front lines might interfere with Joffre's strategic decisions. Although the war minister was the intermediary between the military and civilian political leaders, he was, Viviani and Poincaré believed, too secretive about military operations, failing to inform the cabinet about actions like the bombardment of the Camp des Romans (Meuse).[9] Millerand may have worried that news of a reverse would alienate governmental support from Joffre, but also viewed the issue as the war minister's concern.

The government's return to Paris from Bordeaux first tested the relative powers of the civilian leaders and the military hierarchy and indicated the gradual resumption of civilian control. Until November 1914, the French clung to their short war expectations. After his meeting with Poincaré, Millerand, Joffre, and Foch at Dunkirk on 1 November, Kitchener noted French optimism about an imminent German defeat. With the military stalemate making a long war

8. G. Bonnefous, II, pp. 32–3; King, p. 35; Renouvin, *Formes*, p. 78; Pierre Renouvin, *La Crise européene et la première guerre mondiale* (Paris: Presses Universitaires de France, 1934, 1962), p. 288; Millerand, 'Souvenirs,' p. 79; Marcellin, *Politique*, I, p. 42.

9. Poincaré, *Au service*, V, pp. 251–2, 328, 333, 380; Gallieni, pp. 132–6; King, p. 31.

increasingly likely by the end of the year, the Chambers wanted to resume their normal functions and the government to return to the capital. Joffre, however, feared proximity to general staff head-quarters in Chantilly would subject him to parliamentary visits, and Millerand was concerned that calm political deliberation would be impossible so close to the front. When Joffre finally yielded, Poincaré and the cabinet returned to Paris on 8 December, but the war minister stayed in Bordeaux until 7 January 1915, and only returned because of his colleagues' pressures. They feared Miller-and's presence in Bordeaux would convey a disdainful indifference to parliament and a concession of authority to the G.Q.G. (Grand Quartier Général) at the expense of the civilians.[10]

Civil–military relations also encompassed the interaction between military needs and economic realities. Although France's victory at the Marne insured a long war, the French had not stockpiled essential materials. Millerand immediately mobilized French in-dustry to meet the unexpectedly high wartime munitions require-ments, especially for field artillery shells, and the daily nourishment of the army. As Joffre noted, Millerand calmly confronted the enormous task by recalling factory workers from the front and meeting with factory directors.[11]

Millerand convened France's principal industrialists at the Faculté des Lettres in Bordeaux on 20 September 1914. They confronted France's desperate metal shortage and established an organization of war production. Their goal of increasing the daily shell produc-tion rate for the all-purpose field gun, the 75mm cannon, from 13,500 to 100,000 seemed unattainable, given the reduced produc-tion of metals because of the invasion of the northeast and the mobilization of factory labor. Millerand had to transform the industry from a virtual standstill to unforeseen production levels,

10. Herbillon, I, pp. 80, 89; Poincaré, *Au service*, V, pp. 479, 483–4, 531–2, VI, p. 10; King, p. 35; Marcellin, *Politique*, I, pp. 50–1; Jean Pédoya, *La Commission de l'armée pendant la grande guerre* (Paris: Ernest Flammarion Editeur, 1921), p. 8; Asquith, p. 302.

11. Joffre, II, p. 49; Renouvin, *Crise*, p. 270; Poincaré, *Au service*, V, p. 265; Persil, pp. 84–8; Herbillon, I, pp. 56–7; King, p. 34; Marjorie M. Farrar, *Conflict and Compromise: The Strategy, Politics and Diplomacy of the French Blockade, 1914–1918* (The Hague: Martinus Nijhoff, 1974), ch. 1. A.N., F.M. 32, Buat, 'Souvenirs,' p. 7, cites Joffre's telegram of 17 September 1914 about the munitions crisis for the 75mm cannon and Millerand's convocation of the industrialists on 20 September.

despite the scarcity of raw materials and manpower and the vast organizational problems. He abandoned the prewar monopoly of heavy artillery shell production held by the state arsenals, Creusot, and Saint-Chamond, and incorporated large-scale industry into war production. Millerand initially met weekly (later bi-weekly and eventually monthly) with the directors of large establishments, heads of war ministry services, group leaders, and representatives of the Comité des Forges and of trade unions.

Existing factories were enlarged, new ones created, and quotas allocated among regional groups to achieve production goals. To meet the initial metal shortage, Millerand borrowed from small artillery factories, put the steel mills in the non–invaded areas back to work, and bought abroad. The French did achieve the initial objective of 100,000 shells per day for the 75 by summer 1915, but the target was soon raised to 300,000. To resolve the manpower shortage, Millerand secured the release of workers from the front to the factories, but the expectation that the war would be quickly settled on the battlefield made it difficult to obtain factory manpower, even though they were needed to produce the artillery shells. By the end of 1915, approximately 500,000 men had returned to the armaments factories, a figure that remained relatively constant because the High Command refused to authorize more departures from the front.[12]

Even Joffre later acknowledged the awkwardness of Millerand's position. The war minister was caught between Joffre's incessant and growing demands for war material and the complaints of industrialists short of manpower, raw materials, and machines, but Millerand achieved results unmatched by any other nation.[13] Joffre's retrospective praise for Millerand may have been excessive: gratitude for the war minister's consistent support as much as an

---

12. Rials, pp. 75–7; A.N., F.M. 32, Buat, 'Souvenirs,' p. 7; Gerd Hardach, 'La mobilisation industrielle en 1914–1918: production, planification et idéologie,' in Patrick Fridenson (ed.), *1914–1918, l'autre front,* Cahiers du mouvement social, No. 2 (Paris: Les Editions Ouvrières, 1977), pp. 188–91; Robert Pinot, *Le Comité des forges de France au service de la nation (août 1914–novembre 1918)* (Paris: Librairie Armand Colin, 1919), pp. 78, 179–80. John F. Godfrey, *Capitalism at War. Industrial Policy and Bureaucracy in France, 1914–1918* (Leamington Spa: Berg Publishers, 1987), p. 48, notes that industrialists were divided into twelve regional groups whose leaders shared available steel, distributed military contracts and verified their execution, and established regional resources.

13. J.O., *Sénat,* 29 June 1915; A.N., F.M. 27, draft of Millerand's speech to the Senate of 29 June 1915; Joffre, II, pp. 49–50; Millerand, 'Souvenirs,' p. 80; Poincaré, *Au service,* V, p. 335.

accurate depiction of affairs in September 1914. Nonetheless, Millerand, as the intermediary who listened to the demands of both sides while insuring the satisfaction of basic wartime needs, did incorporate industrialists and workers into the military program.

The collaboration between the war ministry and private industry, subsequently termed a nascent military–industrial complex, altered techniques and reorganized the metallurgic industry to achieve seemingly impossible results. To Robert Pinot, Secretary-General of the Comité des Forges, who perceived few abuses, Millerand's role in the industrial mobilization was decisive. Millerand's program did, however, give Pinot and the Comité des Forges a virtual monopoly over metal imports, their distribution to private firms, and the allocation of armaments contracts. This preferential position, prejudicial to later state efforts to control heavy industry, probably influenced Pinot's praise for Millerand, but did not diminish the war minister's achievement.

In the autumn, Millerand delegated some of his responsibility for war production. In October, he persuaded Socialist deputy Albert Thomas to head the ministry's munitions service. Perhaps anxious for labor's cooperation, the war minister may also have wanted a trusted delegate to secure requisite manpower and raw materials and to stimulate enthusiasm for the overwhelming effort. To streamline the complex industrial mobilization process, technical officers were sent to production centers to help inexperienced suppliers and to supervise fabrication. Shortly afterwards, Millerand assigned General Baguet to inspect and centralize the production of shells for the 75mm field gun. In the beginning, Joffre was impatient at private industry's slowness in meeting its commitments. While Millerand was ready to punish those who failed to perform their assigned tasks or were behind on deliveries, he noted that many producers had been forced to adopt unfamiliar procedures and vastly to expand existing factories. He argued that the level of 75mm shell production had reached promised figures by mid-November, although other more complex production procedures had yielded less spectacular results because of sub-contracting and organizational difficulties. Although the results were less than Joffre expected, they were attributable, Millerand argued, to a production process that did not lend itself to improvisation rather than to unenthusiastic producers.[14]

14. Rials, pp. 77–8; Richard F. Kuisel, *Capitalism and the State in Modern France*

Civil–military relations also encompassed the more nebulous inter-action between military concerns and public attitudes. Millerand wanted to shield the public from excessive optimism and undue pessimism. To Joffre's dismay, he minimized German reverses at the Marne to avoid false optimism. On the other hand, he restricted freedom of the press to eliminate internal dissension. Millerand rejected the argument that the governmental distinction between political and military censorship permitted prefects to decide on newspaper articles. The military authorities would listen to the prefects' views on political censorship, but because of the state of siege had the sole right to suppress or suspend newspapers. Press controls operated internationally as well as domestically. A war ministry control section examined postal and telegraphic com-munication, foreign newspapers, and agent reports to deprive Germany of all external support. They used propaganda to impress the neutrals, stressing front-line heroism to prove French strength.[15] Designed to bolster national morale and reduce psychological malaise, press censorship distorted the information which the public received. A common governmental tactic in twentieth-century warfare, press censorship still increased military power relative to the population at large.

Elimination of dissent, whether within the army or between civilian and military authorities, was an important goal for Miller-and. He instructed regional commanders to stop some units spreading negative assessments of others. Since all soldiers had performed dedicated and heroic acts, unjust criticisms simply undermined the discipline and unity needed to confront the enemy and fomented a false rivalry.[16]

(Cambridge: Cambridge University Press, 1981), p. 35; Alain Hennebicque, 'Albert Thomas et le régime des usines de guerre, 1915–1917,' in Fridenson (ed.), *1914–1918, l'autre front*, p. 112. Godfrey, p. 50, argues that Millerand used the Comité des Forges to create a bureaucracy to deal with industrial problems con-nected with armaments production, but that the chemical industry was run by a new government office under the commerce ministry. A.G., 6N7, Millerand to Joffre, 1914, no exact date but in response to a despatch from Joffre of 16 November.

15. Joffre, I, pp. 426–7; A.N., F.M. 18, Millerand to the president of the press delegation, 17 October 1914; Renouvin, *Formes*, p. 42; A.G., 6N25, Millerand to the prefect of Saint-Etienne, 11 November 1914; Rouffet, p. 61: decree of 10 January 1915 setting up the control section; *ibid.*, p. 73: Millerand's demand to expand controls over the N.O.T.; *ibid.*, p. 84: Millerand to Delcassé, 27 August 1915, to deprive Germany of fodder for its cattle; A.N., C7488, Chamber, Foreign Affairs Commission, audition of Millerand, 11 March 1915.

16. A.G., 6N10, Millerand to the regional commanding generals, 27 June 1915.

Wartime controls also affected religious and political freedom. While determined to protect freedom of conscience, Millerand banned public religious demonstrations by mobilized troops, fearing that they would undermine the national consensus needed for victory. Religious representatives of all sects had access to the front and military hospitals and soldiers were free to practice their own religion, but group actions that invited protests were not permitted. Millerand refused to let the war compromise the state's neutrality in confessional matters or violate the laws separating church and state. It was illegal to reopen chapels in former religious establishments that had been converted into temporary hospitals; only military hospitals with regularly authorized chapels could legally hold religious services. The unauthorized use of premises must not, he insisted, exert pressure on military men of other persuasions. Millerand also forbade the distribution in military hospitals of religious articles, like Bibles and medals, except if individually requested. He did, however, portray reports of a clerical campaign in the army as exaggerated. Some regulations had been violated, but reported abuses had been corrected and efforts to disseminate religious propaganda at the front halted.[17]

Before 1914, many people feared that political opposition might harm the war effort. They had, therefore, provided for wartime scrutiny, including internment of politically unreliable Frenchmen, but ratification of war credits by all social classes and political parties initially shelved the issue. As Millerand commented, 'there is no longer anything but the war.' Workers' rights and social laws receded before national defense requirements. In fact, prefectoral powers under the state of siege effectively curtailed democratic rights, political opposition, and trade union activity, but the government may have suspended the scheduled arrest of potential dissidents under the Carnet B to avoid arousing working-class opposition to the war.[18]

17. *Ibid.*, Millerand to regional commanding generals, 26 September 1914; *ibid.*, Millerand to regional commanding generals, 14 October 1914; *Sénat*, Army Commission, File 158, audition of Millerand, 19 August 1915.

18. Annie Kriegel, *Aux origines du communisme français, 1914–1920* (Paris: Mouton et Co., 1964), I, p. 104, n. 2, refers to C.G.T. leader Merrheim's meeting with Millerand, 10 January 1915. Tom Kemp, *The French Economy 1913–39. The History of a Decline* (London: Longman, 1972), p. 37. Edouard Dolléans, *Histoire du mouvement ouvrier*, vol. 2, *1871–1936* (Paris: Librairie Armand Colin, 1948), pp. 206, 229, quotes Millerand's statement to delegates of the Fédération des metaux, 31 January 1915.

Relations between civilian political representatives and the war ministry between December 1914 and October 1915 were characterized by almost constant conflict. Although the Chambers officially reconvened on 22 December 1914, parliament's activities were concentrated in the Senate's and Chamber of Deputies' commissions in 1915. Millerand's difficulties with the parliamentary commissions began in Bordeaux. General Gustave Pédoya, head of the Chamber's army commission, found the war minister frank about current supply problems, but complained that Millerand's colleagues were less cooperative. Deputy Abel Ferry, however, faulted the war minister for blindly defending his subordinates instead of improving the operation of the health services. Senator Georges Clemenceau, a member of the Senate's army commission, criticized him for letting General Joffre and the war ministry bureaucracy become too powerful. Parliament gave Millerand a chilly reception in December; by January 1915, clans were forming for and against him and Joffre. As British Prime Minister Asquith noted on 21 January, the Socialists were intriguing against Millerand and Joffre, hoping to replace the latter with General Gallieni.[19]

Early in 1915, the army commission started pressuring and criticizing Millerand, and to a lesser extent Joffre. Described as the beginning of parliamentary control, their actions eventually forced Millerand's departure. To Pédoya, the war permitted parliament to expand its peacetime functions of advice and legislation to investigation and control. Commission inquiries replaced interpellations, which were used infrequently in 1915. They complained that Millerand's defense of Joffre's freedom of action shielded the general from civilian control. More vulnerable than the general, Millerand bore the brunt of commission attacks. To Ferry, the basic problem was Joffre's secretiveness. The general, on the other hand, expected Millerand to protect him from prying by the cabinet or parliament.[20] During 1915, this power struggle between parliamentarians seeking a system of control and Millerand and Joffre trying to preserve autonomy inevitably undermined domestic unity.

19. Pédoya, p. 8; Poincaré, *Au service*, V, pp. 517, 531–2; Millerand, 'Souvenirs,' pp. 83–4; Marcellin, *Politique*, I, pp. 53, 57–8. Persil, pp. 89, 91, 94, charged Briand and Louis Barthou with conniving with a group of leftists against Millerand. Asquith, p. 389; Abel Ferry, *Les Carnets secrets d'Abel Ferry 1914–1918* (Paris: Bernard Grasset, 1957), pp. 35, 38–9.

20. Renouvin, *Formes*, pp. 78, 144–5; Persil, p. 96; Pédoya, p. 9; King, p. 39; Ferry, pp. 39–40, 44, 51, Ferry, who was both soldier and a deputy, was invited by Viviani to attend cabinet meetings; Derfler, *President*, pp. 76–7.

Conflict between Millerand and the civilian politicians came to a head over specific issues, such as parliamentary rights to visit the war ministry, war-related factories, and the front lines. The parliamentarians maintained that their right to information about war-related issues justified free access to the war ministry, whereas Millerand considered the rue Saint-Dominique his own domain where entry required his permission. The crux of the problem was, however, less respective rights than their implications. The quantity and complexity of parliamentary queries (over 1,200 questions between January and March 1915), as well as visits from hundreds of deputies, overwhelmed the war ministry. His overburdened and short-staffed ministry could not, Millerand argued, perform its job in addition to answering the numerous demands from deputies. He preferred a general discussion of the most important issues instead of dry answers to each query. He insisted that his directors only respond to commission presidents, vice-presidents, and subcommission heads – the compromise eventually accepted.[21]

Visits by politicians to war industries posed the question of relative responsibility for war-related tasks. The army commissions argued their right to visit war industries to check on production, but feared that prior notice would invite a false impression. Millerand, however, wanted advance notice of impending visits for the factory directors. Visiting the front and factories with Millerand, Ferry described the war minister as insufficiently critical during their brief stops where everything was designed to impress favorably. Pédoya finally persuaded Millerand to authorize parliamentary inspection of the interior so that communications between the war minister and the Chamber did not totally break down.[22] This confrontation slightly increased civilian power relative to the war ministry, but throughout his ministerial tenure Millerand was accused of stalling on parliamentary visits to war industries.

Parliamentary visits to the front lines extended the conflict to the commander-in-chief. On this issue, Millerand was caught between

21. Marcellin, *Politique*, I, p. 67; J.O., *Sénat*, 10 August 1915; Pédoya, p. 12; Persil, pp. 90–1; King, pp. 48–9; Gabriel Terrail (Mermeix), *Au sein des commissions* (Paris: Librairie Ollendorff, 1924), pp. 64–5. A.N., F.M. 32, Buat, 'Souvenirs,' pp. 17–20, claims many commission reports were incomprehensibly superficial, trying to denigrate the war minister, or so specialized that they showed incomprehension of the relationship between specific problems. A.N., C7494, Chamber, Army Commission, auditions of Millerand, 9 February, 11 and 24 March 1915.

22. Poincaré, *Au service*, VI, pp. 196–7; King, pp. 50, 63; Ferry, pp. 92–3, 12 July 1915; Terrail, p. 63; Pédoya, pp. 13–14.

parliamentary demands and Joffre's resistance. In his opinion, the war ministry controlled the interior, whereas G.Q.G. regulations governed the front lines. Since Joffre found it awkward to grant special permission, he denied all individual requests, including those from members of parliament. To permit the parliamentary commissions to visit the front would enable them to influence the army's operation and its commanders' decisions. To Joffre, this interference was incompatible with his authority and the efficient conduct of the war. He also considered the visits disruptive of army morale and discipline, since they encouraged soldiers to air their grievances to visiting deputies. On a less official level, mobilized deputies, who travelled back and forth between the Chamber and the front, checked on front-line activities and passed on complaints from one zone to another. Ferry, a mobilized deputy, found, however, Millerand's demand that the deputies choose between the Chamber and the front 'irritating' and 'tactless.'[23]

Joffre consistently denied parliamentary requests to visit the front, and asserted his freedom from civilian control in the army zone. Millerand supported the general, but the parliamentary commissions maintained their right to survey the conduct of the war, a task which Millerand's obstruction made impossible. Millerand, as a dedicated parliamentarian, insisted on his respect for the Senate and Chamber army commissions, but felt he had no choice but to obey the commander-in-chief's decision to grant or withhold permission to visit the front. While he admitted the 'good' intentions of the commissions, he noted that regrettable incidents had allowed unauthorized individuals to reach the front lines. As the minister responsible to the army commission, Millerand bore the brunt of its 'tendentious' trial.[24]

A confrontation occurred in the summer of 1915, with Millerand requiring prior notification and permission for visits to the interior and the front and the Chamber's army commission asserting its

23. Terrail, p. 63; A.N., C7494, Chamber, Army Commission, audition of Millerand, 17 March 1915; Poincaré, *Au service*, VI, p. 33; Persil, p. 97; King, p. 51; Pédoya, p. 15; Bugnet, p. 78; Raymond Recouly, *Joffre* (Paris: Editions des Portiques, 1931), p. 218; A.N., F.M. 30, Joffre to Millerand, 18 January 1915; *ibid.*, Joffre to Millerand, 4 February 1915; *ibid.*, Joffre to Millerand, 20 February 1915; *ibid.*, Joffre to Millerand, 27 May 1915. Ferry, p. 247, cites Joffre's letter to Millerand which the latter read to the cabinet on 26 January 1915. Ferry, p. 53, 6 February 1915; Paul-Boncour, I, p. 256.
24. A.N., C7494, Chamber, Army Commission, audition of Millerand, 7 May 1915.

rights of inspection to guarantee effective control. A bitter stalemate continued on the whole question of parliamentary inspection rights, while the respective powers of the civilian and military authorities remained virtually unchanged.[25] Joffre's powers were not notably diminished, but his intransigence increased the hostility of the civilian politicians and their readiness to use more extreme measures to achieve civilian control.

Millerand's personality and his view of his prerogatives increased his problems with the civilian politicians. In general, they thought him too hermitic, evasive, and taciturn. For example, Ferry called Millerand's explanations to cabinet and the Senate commission vague and confused about a secondary line of defense and available manpower. Parliamentary pressures, he believed, forced Millerand's concession on supplies for divisions arriving in the Parisian fortified camp. Poincaré explained the war minister's reserve by the cabinet's need to cater to Joffre, but still thought Millerand might be more open. For example, his refusal to supply facts about arms production to the Senate's army commission gave the impression of hiding serious errors. To the president, Millerand's fear of possible indiscretions still did not justify total silence.[26]

Millerand's defenders argued that the deputies mainly disliked the war minister's lack of sociability and his repudiation of corridor gossip. In a 'regime of comradeship,' *tutoiement*, slackness, and sordid bargaining, this aloofness seemed an unpardonable crime. Parliamentary dislike of Millerand's persistent silence was as comprehensible as the war minister's hostility to corridor intrigues. When Millerand defended his activity to the Senate's army commission on 23 February 1915, his command of the details of production increases during his ministry was 'impressive.' Perhaps the crux of the problem was the need for a military victory.[27] As long as the military situation was unfavorable – February 1915 was

25. Poincaré, *Au service*, VI, p. 196; Pédoya, pp. 17–24; King, pp. 54–6, 60–3.
26. Ferry, pp. 58–61, 13 and 16 February 1915; Poincaré, *Au service*, VI, pp. 61–3, 71, 77: meeting on 13 February 1915 with commission members Freycinet, Bourgeois, Clemenceau, Doumer, and Boudenoot and cabinet members Viviani, Millerand, and President Poincaré; King, p. 52.
27. Persil, p. 107; Marcellin, *Politique*, I, pp. 80–1; G. Bonnefous, II, p. 81; Poincaré, *Au service*, VI, pp. 77–8; King, p. 53; Bugnet, pp. 80–1. A.N., F.M. 32, Buat, 'Souvenirs,' pp. 13–14, 20–1, calls Viviani an incompetent premier, emotional and irritable in cabinet meetings, and Poincaré, publicly so impeccable, was swayed

the period of the Champagne setbacks – the civilians wanted scapegoats. Military adversity and Joffre's invulnerability, which increased the civilians' frustration, perhaps tempted them to focus their opposition on Millerand.

Efficiency of decision-making partially dictated Millerand's desire to limit parliamentary activity. He preferred the government and the commissions to collaborate on appropriate wartime measures instead of legislative debates that postponed decisions. For example, a ministerial decree agreed on by the government and the commissions would allow them to modify rapidly the law assigning fathers of six children to the lowest reserve category. Such considerations had led Britain, Millerand claimed, to shelve parliamentary initiative for the duration.[28]

Parliamentarians, who faulted Millerand's independence toward them, considered him too lenient with his own services. To Ferry, he was simply a lawyer for the war ministry, slaving over his dossiers instead of leading, a plow pulled by his directors rather than a laboring ox, an obstinate, short-sighted bureaucrat with a paper rat's mentality hiding behind his administration, a good speaker but a poor administrator, in short, a 'mediocre' minister. To his claim that the Chamber was generally irritated with Millerand, Poincaré replied that his friend had always been a grumbler. The Senate's army commission argued that his inability to end departmental inertia and toleration of his subordinates' independence had led to internal chaos, even though it recognized that he was an indefatigable worker. General Buat, however, blamed the duplication of parliamentary commissions, budget, and army in both the Senate and the Chamber for forcing Millerand to answer all questions twice. Coping with parliamentary demands was so overwhelming that he could scarcely handle pressing ministerial affairs. For nine days in June 1915, for example, Millerand only had three half-days for departmental tasks, of which two were Sundays. Unless he had delegated responsibility to subordinates, ministerial business would have come to a standstill. To Buat, he was a 'giant' next to his critics, a man whose calm, upright personality enabled him to withstand such tests.[29]

by the last person he talked to. The parliamentary commissions were infatuated with their knowledge, and thought only of their postwar electoral success.

28. A.N., C7494, Chamber, Army Commission, audition of Millerand, 9 February 1915.

29. Ferry, pp. 41, 48, 53, 62–3 for 20 January and 2, 18 and 19 February 1915;

The confrontation between Millerand and the parliamentary commissions ended with a partial civilian victory. He had to drop his controversial artillery director, General Baguet, accept Albert Thomas as under-secretary for artillery and military equipment (on 18 May 1915), and three additional under-secretaries during the summer. Denying he had 'sacrificed' General Baguet, Millerand described the transfer of a military officer to a front-line division as simply a decision as to his most useful service. While his defense rings somewhat hollow, Millerand clearly considered the general a responsible war ministry official whose move to the front did not reflect inadequate performance. Thomas, who had served in the war ministry since the preceding October, had greater nominal power, but essentially the same tasks to perform and continued to defend Millerand's policy. Parliament did, however, successfully encroach on Millerand's prerogatives by eliminating an objectionable service director and assigning cabinet status to men charged with part of his former responsibility.[30]

Mounting criticism led Millerand to defend himself in the Chamber of Deputies on 1 April 1915. There he movingly portrayed governmental achievements and patriotically appealed to his fellow deputies to preserve their morale and unity. Since all Frenchmen had loyally accepted the sacrifices needed for a victory of civilization over barbarism, the only danger lay in their 'criminal' tendency to denigrate themselves. The government and parliament had a duty to sustain that essential confidence in victory. He appealed to parliament's national loyalty and patience, urging it to withhold criticism that might undermine confidence in the war effort.[31]

Civil–military relations also encompassed contacts between civilian War Minister Millerand and the military hierarchy, notably General Joffre. Although he granted the military full authority for strategic decisions, he tenaciously maintained his right to informa-

Poincaré, *Au service*, VI, pp. 110–12, 199, 204–5; Marcellin, *Politique*, I, pp. 79, 86; G. Bonnefous, II, p. 81; A.N., F.M. 32, Buat, 'Souvenirs,' pp. 30–5.

30. Poincaré, *Au service*, VI, pp. 207, 211; Joffre, II, p. 150; King, p. 64; Jolly, I, p. 69; A.N., F.M. 32, Buat, 'Souvenirs,' pp. 22, 36; A.N., C7558, Chamber, Army and Budget Commissions, audition of Millerand, 9 June 1915; Hennebicque, pp. 112, 118.

31. Poincaré, *Au service*, VI, p. 143; G. Bonnefous, II, p. 81; J.O., *Chambre*, 1 April 1915; A.N., C7494, Chamber, Army Commission, audition of Millerand, 18 May 1915.

tion about military developments. The numerous officers attached to the war ministry seemingly admired Millerand greatly. With Joffre, his relations were generally good but not entirely without conflict. Although accord with the commander-in-chief was important to Millerand, he carved out certain rights for the war ministry, particularly its right to informations about military events. An incident in January 1915 illustrated his problems with Joffre. After the setback at Soissons, Millerand noted that unsuccessful attacks, if due to inadequate preparation or liaison, were poor for national morale. Although this cautious rebuke infuriated the general, liaison officer Herbillon soothed Joffre by reminding him of Millerand's loyalty. While he good-humoredly tolerated Joffre's ill-temper, the war minister still insisted on information about military setbacks to answer cabinet questions.[32]

Millerand's attempt to visit the front lines also created tension. He disregarded the general's effort to exclude him from the battle area. Such tours, which were part of his duty, he claimed, allowed him to refute charges of being Joffre's dupe. Millerand apparently had good relations with military personnel. Accompanied from Paris by Buat, Pétain, and Humbert, he participated in a meeting at General Castelnau's headquarters in Pierry, near Epernay, in August 1915 just before the Champagne offensive. After the generals' speeches, Millerand succinctly summarized the arguments. At ease among the military, Millerand was termed a leader (*chef*) by Humbert, who argued that no other politician inspired such confidence.[33]

The magnitude of war production proved to be a bone of particular contention between Millerand and the civilian politicians. Visits to the armaments production plants convinced the politicians that they faced an unexpectedly serious crisis. Their studies showed, for example, that no new guns had been produced during the previous eight months – only a few old models transformed – and inadequate industrial mobilization had impeded an efficient organiza-

32. See, for example, Herbillon or A.N., F.M. 32, Buat, 'Souvenirs;' A.N., F.M. 15, Millerand to Joffre, 15 January 1915; Herbillon, I, p. 92; Poincaré, *Au service*, VI, p. 21. Ferry, p. 52, attributes Millerand's reprimand of Joffre to cabinet pressures. Since Ferry dates the session as 6 February, over three weeks after Millerand's letter of rebuke to Joffre, his account of the sequence of events is not convincing.

33. Herbillon, I, p. 152; King, p. 57; Raymond Recouly, 'Une visite au Président Millerand,' *La Revue de France*, 15 November 1923, pp. 225–6.

tion of manufacturing. Millerand, who categorically refuted charges of war ministry incompetence, faulted the commissions for such polemical complaints. The crisis required an end to political wrangling and collaboration between the ministry and parliament. Although mobilization plans had not envisaged any new weapons production, French industrialists had actually improvised a whole new industry with new procedures that had incredibly expanded production of explosives within six months, Millerand maintained. He blamed production problems on failure to prepare for a war of attrition. Pressures to push production had created some faulty explosives, but initial defects were later corrected. Since every projection was altered in execution, supplies promised in a month often arrived after six or eight weeks, but the war minister opposed sanctions, because inexperience and difficulties of accurate prediction, rather than bad faith, were responsible for the delays. President Poincaré, too, considered the commissions' evaluations overly pessimistic and defended the war minister's achievements. While understandable, their anxiety fostered dissension and complicated the government's task.[34]

Millerand feared the French press campaign for increased industrial production would encourage the mistaken belief abroad that France lacked artillery shells. Urging French military attachés to correct this error, he described the supply of munitions as sizeable and production as impressive. For example, on 9 May in the Nord Arras sector, the French had fired 50,000 heavy caliber shells and 200,000 of the 75mm, with comparable levels maintained there and elsewhere. High French production should therefore be publicized abroad and compared to Germany's less impressive achievements.[35]

Industrial rivalry partially explained parliamentary hostility to Millerand. François de Wendel, president of the Comité des Forges,

---

34. Poincaré, *Au service*, VI, pp. 110–12, 185–9, 196; A.N., F.M. 23, Senate subcommission report on guns, March 1915; *ibid.*, Millerand to Boodenoot, 30 March 1915, about subcommission report; *ibid.*, Clémentel to chairman of Budget Commission, 9 April 1915, about crisis in guns and Millerand's reply of 29 April 1915; *ibid.*, Naval Commission report of 30 July 1915 on armaments production. Ferry, p. 48, criticized Millerand on 2 February for his failure to increase gun production. A.N., F.M. 28, Millerand to Boodenoot, 31 March 1915; A.N., C7494, Chamber, Army Commission, audition of Millerand, 11 March 1915; *ibid.*, audition of Millerand, 18 May 1915; A.N., C7558, Chamber, Army and Budget Commissions, 8 June 1915, audition of Millerand, Viviani, and Albert Thomas.
35. A.G., 6N9, Millerand to French military attachés, 14 June 1915.

who in 1912 called Millerand France's best war minister in thirty years, closely observed his performance in Bordeaux and Paris during 1914–15. Admitting Millerand's meddling inclinations and rather prickly personality, de Wendel described him as an industrious worker, totally committed to his task. Since Millerand had been de Wendel's principal legal counsel since 1907, this positive evaluation may have been biased. The industrialist was, however, dismayed that he could not halt the 'conspiracy of daggers' (*conspiration des poignards*) in the Senate that rapidly exhausted his 'great man.' Naming Clemenceau and Briand the principal conspirators, the steel magnate's hostility to the latter dated from this period. The Senate committee's hostility to Millerand was reinforced by Schneider, of the Schneider–Creusot steel firm, who attacked the war minister and his delegate, General Baguet. Schneider's criticism, however, stemmed less from antipathy to the war minister than to de Wendel's legal adviser. De Wendel accused Creusot of inspiring Charles Humbert's and *Le Journal*'s attacks on Millerand. The increasingly acrimonious conflict between the war minister and the Senate's army commission at least partially resulted from the industrial rivalry between de Wendel and Schneider.[36]

Parliamentary control over war production complicated the war ministry's relations with producers. Millerand reprimanded the Schneider company for giving the parliamentary commission information from its correspondence with the war ministry that was not its exclusive property. Taken out of context, such communications, he argued, would be misleading. Demanding an immediate end to such procedures, Millerand required war ministry authorization for such communications.[37]

France's lack of industrial preparation necessitated wartime improvisation and expansion. By summer 1915, France faced the unforeseen danger of poison gas. Not only did it have to take such precautionary measures as glasses and masks, but it also needed its own supplies of this inhuman weapon. As with explosives, a failure to prepare before the war forced an intensive gas production to compete with other wartime needs. By July, Millerand claimed France had sufficient chlorine to produce poison gas and relatively effective masks. France had not only to expand production but

36. Jean-Noël Jeanneney, *François de Wendel en République. L'argent et le pouvoir 1914–1940* (Paris: Editions du Seuil, 1976), pp. 28–9, 50.
37. A.G., 6N18, Millerand to Schneider & Co., 20 April 1915.

avoid unnecessary effort. For this reason, Millerand defended existing quality of cloth and design for military uniforms. Limited resources precluded frequent alterations to the uniform even though France sought to improve the soldiers' food and clothing. Millerand constantly tried to streamline production and adapt competing financial demands to military priorities. For example, to move grenades to the front more rapidly, he by-passed intermediaries to deal directly with producers. Furthermore, even though the soldiers' pay was low, their basic expenses were covered. He rejected a pay raise because it would require a corresponding reduction elsewhere.[38]

War production, particularly of munitions, affected inter-Allied relations, because France expected Russia and Britain to export ammunition to France. It sent two missions (civil engineers and technical officers) to Russia to organize production, but the promised Russian supplies did not arrive on schedule. The British, too, were slow in exporting the 30–40,000 rifles per month that they had promised.[39] War production, including partial French reliance on Allied supplies, complicated inter-Allied as well as domestic civil–military relations.

The war ministry also participated in French blockade efforts to deprive the enemy of essential goods. Since a band of neutral states protected Germany's western boundaries, France operated its blockade through their intermediary. During 1915, it tried to persuade those border neutrals, particularly the Netherlands and Switzerland, to restrict exports to Germany. The French war and foreign ministries, however, took different approaches to those neutrals. The foreign ministry tended to trust the neutrals and approved the control organization, the Netherlands Overseas Trust (N.O.T.). Millerand, however, was skeptical about neutral commitments made by private organizations like the N.O.T. He thought a commitment by the government not to reexport war-related imports to the enemy would prove more effective, because the customs agents that enforced export prohibitions were not

38. A.N., C7558, Chamber, Army and Budget Commissions, audition of Millerand, 9 June 1915; A.N., C7494, Chamber, Army Commission, audition of Millerand, 22 July 1915; *ibid.*, audition of Millerand, 9 February and 11 March 1915; *ibid.*, audition of Millerand, 28 July and 12 August 1915.

39. A.N., C7558, Chamber, Army and Budget Commissions, audition of Millerand, 11 June 1915.

bound by N.O.T. promises. The war ministry's control commission, which scrutinized neutral–enemy trade, notified the French government of abnormally high neutral exports to Germany of militarily significant products such as industrial oils. The war minister believed that France had succeeded to a considerable degree in keeping the neutrals from acting as intermediaries for German overseas imports during 1915.[40]

The war of attrition used up men as well as material. France not only entered the war at a numerical disadvantage because of its smaller population and declining birthrate relative to Germany, but the decimation of its human resources in the stalemate defensive war made manpower a pressing problem. Millerand urged his compatriots to adopt a system that would allow rapid decisions and a rational allocation of manpower. He suggested expanding conscription to incorporate seventeen-year-olds and those beyond the normal service age. He divided available men into three categories: skilled workers, non-specialists with useful aptitudes, and those without a profession. To produce at the requisite levels, 20–40,000 skilled workers had to be found, at the front if necessary. While Millerand did not want draft-dodgers to hide in the factories, he sought to avoid restricting production because of a manpower scarcity. Refusing to let whole categories be returned to the front, he required individual examinations of factory workers so that essential personnel remained in the factories.[41] Throughout 1915, the front and the factories competed for available manpower.

While parliament was also concerned about manpower shortages, its response, the Dalbiez law, seemed to Millerand to make the situation more awkward. He endorsed the law's underlying principle of a rational division and use of men for the nation's defense, but feared it would not locate more soldiers but simply reduce production because of the impossibility of setting numerical limits for each category, such as mine, railroad, or postal workers. To Millerand, the Dalbiez law ignored essential exemptions for

40. Farrar, *Conflict*, pp. 63–4; *Sénat*, Army Commission, File 158, 27 October 1915, audition of Millerand and Viviani.

41. A.N., C7494, Chamber, Army Commission, audition of Millerand, 9 February 1915; Ferry, p. 43, 21 January 1915; A.N., C7494, Chamber, Army Commission, 17 March 1915; A.G., 6N25, Millerand to commanding general, 3rd region (Rouen), 5 June 1915.

industrial and agricultural work. It tried to make the system of evaluating exemptions from front-line service more flexible. Because of the initial difficulties of locating workers in the army, Millerand had allowed industrialists to search the depots so as to staff the empty workshops with capable workers. He had temporarily ignored likely abuses. With the factories again operating, those problems could be corrected, but the industrialists complained about the constant interrogation of their workers, their return to the front, and their replacement by less qualified men. The war minister wanted industrialists to have a veto over removal of men from their factories, but noted that measures to locate draft-dodgers had returned over 650,000 men to the army. Millerand's colleagues also disliked the Dalbiez law because it removed irreplacable men from the civil service and vital economic sectors.[42]

One reason for Millerand's objections to the Dalbiez law was its provision for greater parliamentary inspection in the war-related factories. The proposal permitted members of the army commissions to search for draft-dodgers in the factories. The war minister feared that a shuffling of personnel between industry and the front would hamper manufacturing. He also questioned whether the commissions could critically examine the quantity of relevant material. Also anxious to locate manpower and correct abuses, the war minister wanted to maintain war production levels that the Dalbiez law might jeopardize. On the other hand, he persuaded Joffre to let any worker required by industry for artillery, explosives, or aviation work be returned to the interior zone if the war ministry approved and if the worker was not already employed in the army as a specialist.[43]

The war of attrition stretched French human resources to the limit. The heavy death toll of approximately 50,000 killed and wounded in the October Champagne offensive, for example, made it difficult for France to supply the trenches and the factories. Only its achievement in the production of explosives had, Millerand argued, prevented greater losses. He attributed that relative success to a manpower policy that provided needed personnel to the factories. Manpower scarcity, however, remained as a pressing

42. A.N., C7494, Chamber, Army Commission, audition of Millerand, 7 May 1915; J.O., *Chambre*, 10 June 1915, Millerand's speech on the Dalbiez law.
43. A.N., C7494, Chamber, Army Commission, audition of Millerand, 22 June 1915; A.N., C7558, Chamber, Army and Budget Commissions, 8 June 1915, audition of Millerand, Viviani, and Albert Thomas.

French concern. In late October 1915, the war minister suggested the partial remedy of mobilizing and training the class of 1917 early so that they would be ready to serve by spring 1917. Tapping younger age groups was the only way, he believed, France could give the front the manpower it so desperately needed.[44] Clearly, this approach had limited utility, since the supply was not infinitely expandable.

An examination of Millerand's relations with the British further illuminates the issue of civil–military relations. Even in an inter-Allied context, he defended General Joffre. On 1 September 1914, a composed Millerand overcame Field-Marshal Sir John French's pessimism about the military situation by knowledge of Joffre's plans. In the interest of inter-Allied cooperation, Millerand suggested that Joffre consider French's scheme of a defensive line along the Marne to protect Paris, but left the final decision to the French commander. Refusing to restrict Joffre's prerogatives or choice of strategy, Millerand reluctantly backed the general when he rejected the British proposal.[45]

To British War Minister Kitchener, Millerand constantly urged military cooperation and unity of command. Throughout 1915, the Dardanelles campaign, which embittered Anglo-French relations, permitted him to outline France's view of a second front. Serbia's precarious situation faced the Allies with its possible collapse, but the French hesitated to shift troops from the western front to the Balkans. In London, 22–25 January 1915, Millerand demanded that all available British troops be sent to France, not to the Balkans. A stormy interview with strongly pro-Serb David Lloyd George led the latter to call Millerand a 'sturdy and aggressive exponent of the views of the French Commander-in-Chief' who refused to release a single battalion from his French command.[46]

In Paris, Millerand also presented Joffre's case against a Serbian

44. *Sénat*, Army Commission, File 158, audition of Millerand, 1 October 1915; A.N., C7494, Chamber, Army Commission, audition of Millerand, 22 October 1915.

45. Herbillon, I, p. 21; Joffre, I, p. 361; A.G., 6N7, Millerand to Joffre, 1 September 1914.

46. David Lloyd George, *War Memoirs* (Boston: Little Brown & Co., 1933), I, p. 352; Maurice Hankey, *Diplomacy by Conference. Studies in Public Affairs, 1920–1946* (London: Ernest Benn Ltd., 1946), p. 14; Asquith, pp. 391, 393. Keith Neilson, *Strategy and Supply. The Anglo-Russian Alliance, 1914–17* (London: George Allen & Unwin, 1984), pp. 64–5, notes Millerand's lack of success in securing more British

expedition to the cabinet. The general feared the initial small force would be expanded at the western front's expense. The cabinet, however, decided to send one French division to the Balkans. In late February, when Millerand asked Joffre about that division, the general refused to release any troops from the western front. The war minister then told his staff to pick men from French depots and North Africa that did not fall under Joffre's jurisdiction, and appointed General Albert d'Amade as corps leader.[47]

Millerand continued to demand additional British troops for France and protest the diversion of resources to the Dardanelles. Comparing the Dardanelles campaign to a colonial war, he emphasized its peripheral nature relative to combat on the western front. Despite his reservations, however, Millerand believed that France should participate in the Dardanelles campaign. Considerations of prestige, though secondary to national survival, dictated that they show the flag by participation. Finally, in response to persistent British requests, he agreed to despatch another division and replaced d'Amade with General Henri Gouraud.[48]

To Millerand, unity of command was essential to the war's successful prosecution. Attributing the delays and duplication of effort to divided leadership, whether in the Balkans or in France, he urged Joffre's appointment as commander-in-chief of the Allied, not simply the French, armies. He was even prepared to accept a British commander-in-chief in the Dardanelles. He also wanted British acceptance of the French position (or more accurately his view of the government's role) on the relations between the civilian government and the military command: the government chose the commander, set the goals, then gave the military chief complete control over the conduct of operations. To Millerand, the British government intervened too often in military decisions.[49]

troops for France. While Churchill, Grey, and Lloyd George wanted troops for the Mediterranean, Kitchener postponed immediate support for the Balkans but did not commit additional men for France.

47. Ferry, pp. 50–2; Cassar, pp. 77–8; A.N., C7488, Chamber, Foreign Affairs Commission, audition of Millerand, 11 March 1915.

48. Cassar, pp. 115, 121–3; A.N., C7494, Chamber, Army Commission, audition of Millerand, 18 May 1915; Neilson, p. 70.

49. A.N., C7488, Chamber, Foreign Affairs Commission, audition of Millerand, 11 March 1915; Poincaré, *Au service*, VI, pp. 29–31; A.N., F.M. 15, Millerand to Kitchener, 2 March 1915; *ibid.*, Kitchener to Millerand, 4 March 1915; *ibid.*, Millerand to Paul Cambon, 14 April 1915; *ibid.*, Millerand to Kitchener, 30 May 1915; Cassar, pp. 134–5.

Members of the French and British governments met on several occasions in the summer and autumn of 1915 (mostly at Calais) to discuss problems of the Dardanelles campaign. These important conferences illustrated Millerand's view of the secondary nature of the Balkan effort and his unswerving support for Joffre. Backing Joffre's request for additional British troops for France, he rejected British demands for the diversion of French troops to the Orient. On 22 July, he warned the cabinet that a possible Russian collapse would release German troops to the western front. Western strength must therefore not be diluted by reinforcing secondary operations like that of the Dardanelles. Only at Calais on 11 September 1915 did the British persuade the French to send additional forces to the east. By September, therefore, Millerand had shifted his position slightly, but he told Joffre the plan was preparatory and the four French divisions would not be required until October. To the commander-in-chief, he argued that a Dardanelles disaster would seriously harm France as well as Britain. Millerand continued to press the British to ratify Joffre's demand for a unified command instead of the 'unacceptable' British concept of independent commanders in close liaison.[50]

Millerand showed some independence of the military in the autumn of 1915 over withdrawal from the Dardanelles. Despite the campaign's secondary significance, he feared the public would view a retreat negatively after all the sacrifices incurred. He even visited London with Joffre on 19 October to discuss the disastrous eastern situation and agreed to send additional troops to aid Serbia and keep Germany out of Constantinople, without specifying a date or strategic objectives. A potential Dardanelles defeat weakened Viviani's cabinet, leading the French to move from reluctant supporters to active proponents of reinforcements for the Dardanelles. The Salonika expedition to guard Serbian communication routes and act as a barrier between Austro-German and Bulgarian forces

---

50. A.G., 6N7, Millerand to Joffre, 3 September 1915. Cassar, pp. 146, 171–2, 183, 192, 195, describes a meeting of Millerand, Augagneur, and Sarrail at the war ministry on 2 September 1915 to set the eastern army's program. Neilson, pp. 108–9; A.N., F.M. 15, minutes of the Calais conferences of 6 and 7 July, 11 September and 5 October 1915 and of the Chantilly conference, 8 October 1915; Maurice Sarrail, *Mon commandement en orient (1916–1918)* (Paris: Ernest Flammarion Editeur, 1920), p. xii. Hankey, pp. 14–15, describes the meeting of 6 July 1915 at Calais of Viviani, Delcassé, Millerand, Augagneur, and Albert Thomas with Asquith, Balfour, Crewe, and Kitchener as the beginning of diplomacy by conference, prompted by problems of coordinating policy through normal diplomatic channels.

was a sidelight to the Dardanelles operation.[51] In this instance, Millerand considered the larger implications of military questions, their effect on national morale and France's diplomatic relations, whereas Joffre and the British commanders considered only military utility.

France's wartime colonial policy affected inter-Allied relations and domestic unity. Struggling for survival at home, France could not divert forces to maintain order overseas. Urging civilian governors and military commanders to collaborate, Millerand set pacification as France's colonial goal. He suggested, for example, that lifting the state of siege in three Algerian departments might better preserve order. The government also sought to preserve colonial harmony by eliminating enemy influences. A Turkish proclamation to the Moslem world condemning to damnation those fighting for France, Britain, and Russia led Millerand to urge native religious leaders to repudiate Turkish claims of Entente responsibility for Islam's misfortunes. African Moslems would be less suspicious, he believed, of a counter-proclamation from religious dignitaries and influential native civil servants and officers than of an official French statement.[52]

The war changed France's policy on native citizenship rights. Millerand argued that Algerian loyalty and bravery in shedding blood for France justified granting naturalization to native combatants. He expected the move would encourage battle enthusiasm and allow France to reduce conscription. It would also strengthen Algerian ties to France, a necessary counter to German and Turkish propaganda in the Moslem world. The move was, however, primarily a propaganda device against Germany and Turkey, but was not numerically significant, since the few soldiers who came from the native ruling élite and qualified for naturalization would probably retain their native status.[53]

---

51. A.N., F.M. 17, Millerand to the Minister of Foreign Affairs, 9 October 1915; Lloyd George, I, p. 440; Alexander S. Mitrakos, *France in Greece during World War I. A Study in the Politics of Power*, East European Monographs No. 101 (New York: Columbia University Press, 1982), pp. 17–18; A.N., C7494, Chamber, Army Commission, 26 October 1915, audition of Millerand, Viviani, and Augagneur.

52. A.G., 5N9, Millerand to the commanding general, North Africa, 27 October 1914; A.G., 5N10, Millerand to the North African commander, Algiers, and resident commissioner, Rabat, 14 November 1914.

53. A.G., 6N28, Millerand to the Minister of the Interior, 16 November 1914.

Great Power considerations sometimes influenced the war minister's fundamental concern for colonial order. For example, he
urged protection for Italians fleeing from Tripoli into Algeria and
assistance in reaching Algerian or Tunisian ports even at the cost of
local unrest along the Tripoli border. Anxious for Italy to join the
Entente instead of the Central Powers, the French were overly
solicitous of Italians in colonial areas.[54]

Even with Britain and France allied in a life-or-death struggle on
the western front, France was still concerned about its prestige.
Never a strong colonialist, Millerand still assigned a high priority
to France's status. He thus supported the despatch of an Algerian
expeditionary force to Syria to join a possible offensive in 1915 after
the western front had stabilized. Joffre, he noted, would probably
release Moslem conscripts because of their poor adaptation to the
northern French climate and military conditions. Pierre Etienne
Flandin strongly backed participation in a Near Eastern action.
Meeting the newly appointed British High Commissioner to
Egypt, Sir Henry McMahon in Paris on 30–31 December 1914,
Millerand expressed anxiety that Britain might send an expedition
to Syria without French knowledge. Traditional Near Eastern
interests and its prestige required France's participation. Not anxious
to mingle in Arab religious disputes, he still wanted to promote
dissidence within Turkey, a stand contrary to Britain's. Although
Millerand's assumptions about British plans proved to be er-
roneous, his reactions to the Syrian issue illustrated continued
Franco-British rivalry for overseas influence.[55]

Criticism of the war ministry's achievements led Millerand to
speak in the Senate and Chamber of Deputies several times during
the summer of 1915. His themes were always the same: defense of
his accomplishments and appeal to patriotism. In the Senate on 29
June and 10 August, he described the six-fold increase in produc-

54. A.G., 5N10, Millerand to the commanding general, Algiers, 8 February 1915.
55. Ministère des Affaires Etrangères, Série Guerre 1914–1918, No. 867, Turquie–Syrie–Palestine, pp. 130–1, note on Syria by de Margerie, 30 December 1914,
hereafter cited as A.E.; *ibid.*, pp. 176–7, Millerand to the foreign minister, 5 January
1915; *ibid.*, p. 219, Millerand to the foreign minister, 20 January 1915, about a
proposed French military mission to the commander of British forces in Egypt;
Christopher M. Andrew and A.S. Kanya-Forstner, *France Overseas. The Great War
and the Climax of French Imperial Expansion* (London: Thames and Hudson, 1981),
pp. 69–70.

tion during the previous ten months, but pleaded that the inevitable errors and setbacks would not create that internal anxiety which would in turn undermine the credibility of national defense organizations. The war's inherent bureaucratization was responsible for the delays and errors of war ministry operations. Arguing that collaboration between the government and parliament was essential, he insisted that he could only keep his post if he retained the representatives' confidence. It was the complexity of the job, and not a lack of deference or sincerity, that had complicated the task of informing parliament. To him, open discussions in parliament were preferable to secret sessions where the cabinet gave confidential explanations, since the counterweight of public opinion made any concealed tyranny impossible.[56]

Bickering and intrigues characterized Millerand's relations with parliament during the summer of 1915. After his speech to the Senate of 29 June, pressures for his resignation intensified. Although the cabinet resisted his speech, the war minister insisted he must defend his collaborators. Described as a dramatic surprise (*coup de théâtre*), the Senate session proved to be a bitter struggle. Determined not to resign 'for the good of the nation,' Millerand seemed to Ferry increasingly worn, his face ashen, a 'tired beast' who finally accepted a reduction in his responsibilities by the addition of two more under-secretaries. Ferry portrayed him as in conflict with the other ministers and 'detested' by the Chamber and Senate, which considered him a public danger. When Viviani tried to eliminate him from the cabinet, he found Poincaré, Briand, and Théophile Delcassé reluctant to alienate the army and the public. The army, which backed the war minister, would have blamed his resignation on intrigues. Ferry charged him with using his popularity with the army to protect steadfastly his ministerial subordinates and fight his cabinet colleagues. By mid-July, every cabinet meeting produced a 'Millerand incident.' At odds with the war minister, Poincaré kept urging him to inform the cabinet and accelerate war ministry procedures. Buat also noted pressures for Millerand's resignation, but claimed Viviani and Poincaré hesitated to demand it openly. He argued that the Chamber sought complete information to establish 'parliamentary control,' and blamed it for attributing insufficient supplies to incurable ministerial negligence

56. J.O., *Sénat*, 29 June 1915; A.N., F.M. 27, draft of Millerand's speech to the Senate, 29 June 1915; Poincaré, *Au service*, VII, pp. 44–5; J.O., *Sénat*, 10 August 1915.

or High Command stupidity instead of acknowledging the substantial increases in production. Buat also faulted Joffre for his
behavior in the cabinet on 31 July, which gave the impression that
Millerand alone was responsible for resistance to parliament when
in fact Joffre had constantly stressed his abhorrence of parliamentary prying into military affairs. Millerand was, however, reluctant, Buat claimed, to refute the general because he would thereby
undermine the commander-in-chief's credibility. 'As long as the
government retains him in his position, it is essential that the
general-in-chief not display a flagrant weakness of character,' the
war minister argued. Buat, however, predicted that Joffre would
not long outlast Millerand's departure from the war ministry.[57]

In the Chamber on 20 August, Millerand gave an impassioned
defense against the whole range of charges levelled against him,
'the trial of the war ministry.' Refuting charges of negligence and
inertia within his department, he noted his replacement of two-
thirds of the ministry's personnel instead of the systematic protection of his colleagues. Not a determined foe of parliamentary
control, but, rather, a persistent opponent of personal power, he
had frequently reported on his activities to the Chambers and tried
to reconcile the exercise of parliamentary duties and military requirements. A war situation, however, required a freedom of
action for the military with the corollary of self-discipline by the
public authorities. He denied abdicating his prerogatives to the
High Command, but insisted that military considerations alone
could guide the military chiefs in wartime. He saw it as the war
minister's duty to preserve close contacts with the commanding
general so that the conduct of the war would operate smoothly.[58]
Although Millerand assigned the military considerable influence in
wartime, he did not advocate their monopoly of power but tilted
the balance in their favor for military decisions while defending his
own prerogatives as a civilian war minister and those of the elected
representatives. The picture of Millerand as the High Command's
tool is therefore exaggerated.

In mid-August, Socialists and Radical Socialists forcefully demanded Millerand's replacement by someone better able to control

---

57. Herbillon, I, p. 162; Poincaré, *Au service*, VI, pp. 298–301, 303, 316, 344–6;
Ferry, pp. 81–6, 89–91, 94–5; A.N., F.M. 32, Buat, 'Souvenirs,' pp. 35–6, 47–51.
    58. J.O., *Chambre*, 20 August 1915; A.N., F.M. 26, draft of Millerand's speech to
the Chamber of 20 August 1915; G. Bonnefous, II, pp. 85–6; A.N., F.M. 32, Buat,
'Souvenirs,' pp. 56, 58.

the High Command. Considering that Millerand's presence morally compromised the cabinet, Socialists Marcel Sembat and Jules Guesde wanted to resign so that they would be free to join their Socialist colleagues in opposition. Buat learned in mid-August that Briand and Sembat were plotting to provoke an incident over army contracts that would pit Viviani and Millerand against each other and force the latter to resign. He claimed that Briand wanted the war ministry, while Sembat obeyed his parliamentary colleagues' orders. After the war, Barthe also attributed the incident to Briand's war-ministerial ambitions. To Millerand, leftist opposition stemmed from a pacifist belief that he represented the *guerre à outrance*, instead of his conviction that national interest required a united cabinet and resistance to corridor intrigues.[59]

The parliamentary Left's increased hostility was affected by the abrupt dismissal of General Maurice Sarrail as head of the Third French Army on 22 July 1915. This republican general with parliamentary contacts was considered to be a threat by Joffre, who believed a command outside France would limit contacts between disgruntled parliamentarians and the popular general. To the Left, his dismissal was an additional sign of Millerand's subservience to Joffre. Although Millerand initially opposed the choice of Sarrail for a Dardanelles command (late July) because of the general's previous rejection of native troops which were the core of the Near Eastern army, he gave in to Joffre on this issue.[60]

The specific details of the Sarrail affair are less significant than their illustration of the civil–military conflict. The incident demonstrated Millerand's persistent belief that in all military matters the High Command should have the final decision. Through the summer of 1915, the balance of power remained with the military. Despite Sarrail's popularity with the politicians, Joffre could transfer him to the Dardanelles. To Sarrail, Millerand appeared harsh, hostile to his political contacts, and anxious for him to leave France even before setting the details of an eastern campaign. He finally departed on 7 October after two months of negotiation.[61] It was,

59. A.N., F.M. 32, Buat, 'Souvenirs,' pp. 53–5; A.N., F.M. 41, extract from *Journal Officiel*, session of 24 January 1919, p. 213. Pinot added that Briand's aspirations indicated a confidence in victory. Otherwise, he would not have sought the war ministry. Poincaré, *Au service*, VII, pp. 14–15, 25–6, 28, 31–4, 46–8; J.O., *Chambre*, 20 August 1915; also in A.N., F.M. 26; G. Bonnefous, II, p. 87; King, pp. 79–81; Paul-Boncour, I, p. 256; Ferry, p. 105.

60. A.N., F.M. 32, Buat, 'Souvenirs,' pp. 44–5.

61. Sarrail, pp. vii–xv; King, pp. 70–1, 76–7; Jan Karl Tanenbaum, *General*

however, a pyrrhic victory for the general and the war minister, because the hostility provoked by this episode paved the way for Millerand's fall in October 1915 and increased parliamentary determination to reassert civilian control.

Reactions to parliamentary criticisms of the war minister varied in the cabinet. Often sympathetic to the complaints, President Poincaré generally defended Millerand in the interest of the *union sacrée*. He did, however, fault Millerand's reluctance to give the cabinet and the commissions precise information, and also his independence in making controversial decisions without cabinet consultation, such as naming former artillery director General Baguet to the Legion of Honor. To Millerand, the latter move was a minor reward to a loyal assistant; to parliamentarians, it was a red flag. To Poincaré, the war minister's intense patriotism and hardworking perseverance were vitiated by this tendency to operate in isolation, although he acknowledged Millerand's ability to defend himself persuasively against the mounting pressures.[62]

By the summer of 1915, Viviani considered Millerand's presence in the cabinet a liability; subject to constant parliamentary criticism, the exhausted premier blamed Millerand's obstinacy and blindness for the cabinet's destruction. To Viviani, Millerand's indiscretions (such as his reference to the Sarrail affair in the Chamber on 20 August) confronted the cabinet with an irreparable situation. A Radical Socialist delegation pushed him to drop Millerand, which he would probably have done during the summer except for opposition from some cabinet members. Briand, who noted earlier Millerand's popularity with the army and the public, preferred the government to seek a vote of confidence and persuade the war minister to direct his services better instead of forcing his resignation. By August, however, Briand evidently wanted to replace Millerand as war minister. Poincaré, seeking to preserve ministerial unity, insisted the Chamber should refuse its confidence to the government if it wanted to dump a minister. He did, however, try to mediate by urging Millerand to be less secretive. Several ministers (Victor Augagneur, Gaston Doumergue, Alexandre Ribot) backed the president, and echoed Briand's argument that the army,

Maurice Sarrail 1856–1929: The French Army and Left-Wing Politics (Chapel Hill: University of North Carolina Press, 1974), pp. 56–65.

62. Wright, *Poincaré*, pp. 156–7; Poincaré, *Au service*, VI, pp. 275–8, 284, 292–3, 298; G. Bonnefous, II, p. 82; Ferry, p. 81; Derfler, *President*, p. 77.

the nation, and France's allies would oppose Millerand's forced resignation. Minister of Colonies Doumergue's suggestion of a total cabinet resignation and its members' refusal to join the subsequent government somewhat calmed the agitation. The Chamber feared the repercussions on public opinion. By late August, only the Socialists still demanded a secret session with its anti-parliamentary overtones, and the political scene temporarily calmed down.[63]

By October, the parliamentary atmosphere was again stormy, with increasingly violent attacks by the commissions against Millerand. His continued defense of Joffre, whom the Socialists blamed for failing to end the war, fueled their determination to get rid of the war minister. For them, pacifism was the principal motivation. The Senate's army commission, particularly Georges Clemenceau, constantly bickered with Viviani's cabinet over its right to information on military developments and participation in control over the conduct of the war. While he may have presented the military situation overly optimistically, Millerand often reported to the parliamentary commissions. For example, he described the progress of the Artois and Champagne campaigns of autumn 1915, and blamed the stalled offensive on inadequate artillery preparation rather than on insufficient munitions. Furthermore, factors outside their control like rainy weather, which hampered the preparatory artillery barrage and aerial reconnaissance, depressed troop morale.[64]

The climax came in October 1915 when Delcassé's resignation (on 13 October) triggered a general cabinet shuffle. Potential foreign ministers refused to serve in a cabinet with Millerand. Viviani tried to appease Millerand by offering him the Ministry of Justice. Poincaré also wanted to keep him in the cabinet, but in a less controversial position. He acknowledged that the war minister was often the scapegoat for earlier mistakes of the military administration that were not his fault. Cabinet negotiations produced a fundamental shake-up, with Briand replacing Viviani as premier and Gallieni assuming the war-ministerial portfolio. Millerand himself bitterly refused another cabinet post and accused Poincaré of abandoning him and facilitating Briand's and Viviani's elimination of him from the cabinet. Poincaré, who defended Millerand

63. See above, note 59; A.N., F.M. 32, Buat, 'Souvenirs,' pp. 57–9.

64. Watson, pp. 254–5; *Sénat*, Army Commission, File 158, audition of Millerand, 27 October 1915; A.N., F.M. 32, Buat, 'Souvenirs,' p. 63.

during most of 1915, probably hoped to preserve the *union sacrée*, but increasingly recognized the problems posed by Millerand's independence and silence.[65] In the final analysis, Poincaré supported the civilians in the civil–military struggle, whereas Millerand aligned himself with the military. Millerand's departure illustrated the shift in the balance of power toward the civilians by late 1915.

Contemporary evaluations of Millerand as war minister reflected the political and professional orientations of the critics. His strongest advocates were the military and the political Right, undoubtedly because he effectively defended their interests. Joffre praised Millerand's success in surmounting the overwhelming obstacles to armaments production and acknowledged the war minister's loyal defense of the general's freedom of action. Liaison officer Herbillon, who viewed this loyalty to Joffre as the key to the Chambers' persistent opposition to Millerand, noted the war minister's ability to elicit devotion from his colleagues, and his calm industriousness amidst general turmoil. General Edmond Buat, too, lauded Millerand's contribution to war production and his loyalty to Joffre, and faulted the parliamentarians for their constant criticism and burdensome requests. To him, Socialists and independents like Briand sought Millerand's resignation out of personal ambition, while Poincaré, Viviani, and even Joffre lacked the moral fiber to stand by Millerand. To Lieutenant-Colonel Bugnet, Millerand became the self-effacing lawyer for the general and provider for the army, not because he was unaware of his potential role or unable to perform it but because he believed the G.Q.G. required full power to repulse the invader successfully. Bugnet linked Millerand's demise as an industrious and tenacious minister to his extraordinary patriotism and sense of duty.[66]

65. Poincaré, *Au service*, VII, pp. 190, 192–3, 195–7, 212; Persil, pp. 104–5; Herbillon, I, p. 196; Millerand, 'Souvenirs,' annexes, Millerand to Poincaré, 31 October 1915, and Poincaré to Millerand, 30 and 31 October 1915; Wright, *Poincaré*, pp. 156–7.

66. Joffre, II, p. 141; Herbillon, I, pp. 196–7; A.N., F.M. 32, Buat, 'Souvenirs,' pp. 68–9: faulted Thomas for not resisting his fellow Socialists, Briand for seeking power, and Poincaré for not warning Millerand of opposition plots and for once again (previously in 1913) abandoning an old and loyal friend; J.O., *Chambre*, 24 January 1919, p. 213, postwar publication of secret wartime session: Deputy Edouard Barthe noted this interpretation of Briand's scheming to achieve greater ministerial power. King, p. 64, calls Buat a 'Young Turk,' and, pp. 43–4, describes him as a strong defender of the war ministry's achievements. Bugnet, pp. 79–84.

The political Right also saw Millerand as a strong minister victimized by parliamentary intrigues. Recognizing his fallibility, they still perceived him as laborious, dutiful, and intelligent, secure in the army's and the nation's confidence but the victim of parliamentary hostility because he refused to join corridor intrigues and courageously opposed popular figures like Sarrail.[67] The Right admired his loyalty to the military, his patriotism, and his refusal to play parliamentary games. Since the political Right was not part of the parliamentary majority and had long promoted a nationalism that considered a strong military force essential, its support for Millerand was not surprising. For him, however, its backing could not have been entirely welcome even though their interests coincided in some areas.

The cabinet and parliamentary commissions as well as the political Left assessed Millerand's performance less favorably. Cabinet and parliament resented his taciturn manner, his reluctance to provide information on military developments, and generally his resistance to restrictions on his ministerial prerogatives. Poincaré frequently chastized Millerand for his failure to inform the cabinet, and for a lack of political acumen that could not counterbalance his industriousness and patriotism.[68] The cabinet and parliamentary commissions, which were entitled to share in decision-making, resented Millerand's myopic concern with his task and resistance to 'parliamentary prying.' To the Left, Millerand's subservience to Joffre and his defense of the military's freedom of action jeopardized the principle of civilian control and raised the specter of military dictatorship. In view of earlier military involvement in anti-republican causes, their fears were comprehensible. In 1915, Millerand's loyalty to Joffre during the protracted military stalemate reinforced the old suspicions by the need for a scapegoat. Millerand's attribution of mounting leftist opposition to growing pacifism may have been partially correct since the Left, especially the Socialists, would revert to its prewar pacifism by 1916. The adverse military situation of 1915 paved the way for that development.

Millerand's own evaluation of his behavior and achievements, though obviously biased, adds another dimension. To him, war-

---

67. Marcellin, *Politique*, I, p. 116; Persil, p. 107.
68. Poincaré, *Au service*, V, pp. 328, 333, VI, pp. 62, 71, 277–8, VII, pp. 32–4, 192; Pédoya, p. 330.

time patriotism required a temporary, voluntary reduction of civilian powers relative to military. He blamed his own and Joffre's fall on parliamentary intrigues which he considered inappropriate in wartime. Reflecting on the war's outbreak and his own ministerial record, he noted that in peacetime parliament had the constitutional right to challenge ministerial views, but in wartime the Chambers had to back the decisions taken by the military ministers. Freedom of the press, fundamental to free government, yielded to press censorship; free citizens, who cherished the right to criticize civil servants and government members, had to exercise self-restraint so that denigration did not destroy confidence. 'Yesterday, each of us bore a Christian name which he hoisted ostentatiously and hurled with a crash on the public square: radical, moderate, socialist, royalist, plebiscitarian . . . Today we only have the right to remember our family name: Frenchmen, for whom nothing exists above and beyond France.' A few years later, Millerand looked back on his fifteen months as war minister to urge his compatriots to suspend their personal quarrels and assess the motives for the aggressive criticism of his actions: patriotic passion or political calculation? Despite his admiration of Joffre and belief that only 'iron discipline' could produce victory, he had not had blind confidence in the High Command or systematically mistrusted parliament. Always mindful of his primary obligation to defend the position he held in the nation's name, he had acted not in a spirit of defiance but in appreciation of the leaders' sacrifices and high moral value. His loyal support for the general did not preclude his recognition of the contributions made by the commissions and parliament generally.[69]

As French Minister of War, Millerand consistently assigned priority to patriotic considerations over political calculations, even at the expense of his own political career. His personality was both a strength and a liability: hard work, intense loyalty, scrupulous legality, and an independent taciturnity encouraged decisiveness but invited hostility. Not simply the dupe of the military, he did nonetheless accept and augment military power at the expense of civilian control. This relative increase of military power has be-

69. Millerand, 'Souvenirs,' pp. 83–4; conversation with Jacques Millerand, 20 May 1978; A.N., F.M. 34, Millerand, 'La guerre libératrice,' speech in Versailles, 22 October 1916 (Paris: Librairie Hachette, 1915), pp. 24–7; A.N., F.M. 34, undated handwritten draft of Millerand's speech in response to his critics, written after the Russian Revolution but prior to the war's end.

come a normal accompaniment of modern warfare, but no evidence proves that either Joffre or Millerand deliberately sought a military dictatorship or repudiated parliamentary prerogatives. While Millerand allowed the general to increase military efficiency, he was not the foe of democracy so often depicted.

As a deputy during the rest of the war, Millerand remained in the background. He occasionally participated in the Chamber's army commission or spoke outside parliament. These limited public and parliamentary statements still asserted the nation's priority, the military's freedom of action, unity of command, and governmental prerogatives over parliamentary ones. Near the end of the war, he suggested war aims, policy guidelines, and probable postwar problems. The period from 1915 to 1919 was a link between Millerand the war minister and Millerand the postwar premier.[70]

To Millerand, a wartime spirit of total sacrifice for the nation was dominant. The war, which had shaken normal values, gave priority to action over words, making discussion impossible with compatriots fighting and dying so heroically. 'Once again, civilization has faced the assault of barbarians; once again, faithful to its secular traditions, France has taken the lead against barbarians.'[71]

Millerand was dismayed by the corridor intrigues against Joffre, whom he still admired. To the Chamber's army commission, he strongly opposed a change of the High Command, which he termed a 'folly.' For parliament to encroach on the High Command during the Verdun battle was, in Millerand's opinion, an irresponsible invitation to disaster, a pernicious (*néfaste*) procedure. He agreed with Premier Briand that it was inopportune to examine the conduct of operations during a battle. The former war minister still defended the High Command's right to define military policy and conduct operations without legislative scrutiny. Battlefield success

70. Millerand, 'Souvenirs,' p. 85; A.N., C7735 (Merchant Marine) and A.N., C7771 (Economic Reorganization): Millerand was a member of the Chamber's merchant marine and economic reorganization commissions but their minutes do not reveal his participation. A.N., C7494–7501, Chamber, Army Commission, minutes of sessions from January 1916 to October 1919, collection of 24 dossiers, reveal that Millerand participated in less than a quarter of the sessions.
71. A.N., F.M. 33, Millerand's speech to the Visiting Nurses Association, 4 April 1916; A.N., F.M. 35, Millerand's speech at the Sorbonne, 23 November 1916, on the United States charitable effort for France; A.N., F.M. 34, Millerand, 'La guerre libératrice,' 22 October 1916.

also precluded the requirement of a daily accounting by the High Command or the government of operational decisions.[72] With France's position at Verdun near its nadir in May 1916, clamors mounted for a change of leadership. Joffre, who had survived two years of the disastrous war of attrition, did not emerge unscathed from the Verdun bloodbath. Increased civilian control gradually altered Millerand's conception of relative civil and military prerogatives.

Millerand, who as war minister had termed unity of command to be a precondition of victory, held to that view. Although the Allies had agreed in principle to act together, they kept postponing coordination of either the High Commands or the governments. As Millerand later recalled, he had pleaded for a unified command in his first speech to the Chamber after leaving the war ministry, but that vital precondition of victory was still not generally accepted. To the Chamber's army commission, he called Allied unity of command a matter of 'capital importance.' The premier should designate a military commander for all Allied operations instead of giving the different national leaders control over their separate forces.[73] He expected a unified command to eliminate the delays and contradictions of separate national policies and to reinforce the Allied position.

Millerand, who argued for governmental as well as military efficiency, defended wartime decree powers. To him, the government's request for such powers was not unconstitutional or dictatorial; dictatorship could not be at issue as long as the legislature, permanently in session, controlled the ministry's existence. Other proposals, such as a constitutional revision or regulatory arrangements to achieve the same objective, appeared to him overly slow and cumbersome.[74] Millerand endorsed the expanded executive prerogatives at the expense of legislative control for the war's duration. Although the change tilted the balance of power toward the executive, the legislative, with its ability to reverse the government, remained dominant. Nevertheless, decree laws opened a

72. Millerand, 'Souvenirs,' p. 85; A.N., C7495, Chamber, Army Commission, 12 and 17 May 1916. As premier in May 1916, Briand advocated the self-same military freedom of action for which he had criticized Millerand.
73. Millerand, 'Souvenirs,' p. 85; A.N., F.M. 34, Millerand, 'La guerre libératrice,' 22 October 1916; A.N., C7499, Chamber, Army Commission, 31 October 1917; A.N., F.M. 42, Millerand, 'Jusqu'à la victoire,' no specific date, probably autumn 1917.
74. A.N., F.M. 35, Millerand's statement in the Chamber, 19 December 1916.

194 Principled Pragmatist

wedge to greater executive power, which hinted at a future use
should legislative divisions immobilize governmental operation.
The limited resort to government by decree in France and elsewhere during the First World War was a premonition of later
French and European tactics, as well as of totalitarian procedures.
Perhaps a necessary wartime device, decree laws potentially
threatened democratic procedures in ways that Millerand seemingly
did not foresee in 1916.

Millerand's legalistic mentality affected such specific wartime
issues as the abolition of court martials or the utilization of manpower. A draft bill to abolish court martials, seemingly of humanitarian benefit, might jeopardize military discipline, Millerand
feared. He wondered whether the suppression of court martials
would lead to the reprieve of all condemned men. He urged that a
decision be postponed until the appropriate documents were
examined. Mobilization of seminary students led him to defend his,
as well as his predecessor's and successor's, former policy of
following the Council of State's interpretation of Article 23 of the
law of 1889. Specifically, Messimy, Millerand, and Gallieni applied
the Article's military exemptions to those seminary students who
had satisfied the requirements of the separation laws.[75]

The period from 1915 to 1919 not only linked Millerand to the
past, but served as a premonition of his future policies as high
commissioner in Alsace-Lorraine and as premier. Postwar France,
he argued, must be worthy of the nation whose spirit of renunciation and sacrifice had placed patriotic obligations above political
interests. The enormous debt and reconstruction costs would force
Frenchmen to work together and use all their resources to produce
agricultural and industrial goods. They must also promote scientific developments, mechanization, and capital concentration,
which alone could restore France to a postwar Great Power status.
For some industries, like chemicals, the war had acted as an
economic stimulus. Two specific problems endangered France's
human potential: alcoholism and depopulation. Its lower relative
birthrate required that motherhood be a high priority, but did not
preclude granting the suffrage to women, which he also endorsed.
He still argued for extensive electoral reform to enlarge constituencies and eliminate the hold of local interests. Furthermore, a strong,

75. A.N., C7496, Chamber, Army Commission, 23 June and 22 September
1916.

stable executive, similar to that of the United States, would provide France with the leadership needed to surmount the postwar crises. To him, Clemenceau, as much as the military hierarchy, was France's 'savior' because of his direction of national energy toward winning the war – a considerable shift of opinion since 1915 when the two men had been bitter opponents.[76]

Late in 1917, Millerand assessed the current situation and defined future goals. For him, the roots of 1914 lay in the Great Powers' disregard for the implications of Germany's victory in 1871. The 'rape' of Alsace-Lorraine disrupted Franco-German relations and altered the victor's position relative to other states. Consecrating the primacy of force over law, the Treaty of Frankfurt proved Germany's intent to base its hegemony on strength. Peace therefore required the destruction of Prussian militarism as much as the restitution of Alsace-Lorraine to France.[77] The return of Alsace-Lorraine, France's basic war aim, required Germany's defeat for its fulfillment. Not an outspoken prewar *revanchard*, Millerand, like most Frenchmen, refused to accept the loss of Alsace-Lorraine as permanent. His demand for its return reflected a common national sentiment.

The advent of peace confronted France with numerous important tasks. With its leadership fully occupied with drafting the peace treaties, by early 1919 mounting political opposition confronted Premier Clemenceau with hostility and isolation. Although there were rumors of a possible Millerand ministry, Millerand himself considered the transition to peace as central. He wanted to relax wartime regulations gradually to avoid the problems inherent in a too-rapid demobilization, and suggested pay raises for officers to forestall the formation of unions in the army.

On 19 March 1919, Clemenceau offered Millerand the post of commissioner-general of the Republic for Alsace-Lorraine. Although he first offered it to Charles Jonnart, the premier told President Poincaré that he considered Millerand a better choice. 'He

76. A.N., F.M. 37, Millerand, 'Le devoir de demain,' to the Ligue de l'enseigne-ment français, 30 March 1917; A.N., F.M. 42, Millerand, 'Les leçons de la guerre,' 19 January 1919 in Versailles, to the Ligue française et de l'union des grandes associations.
77. A.N., F.M. 42, Millerand, 'Jusqu'à la victoire,' undated, probably autumn 1917; *ibid.*, Alexandre Millerand, '1914–1918,' *Revue des deux mondes*, 1 August 1918.

might drive them into a rut but he would extricate them.' Miller-
and, who accepted on condition that he have full powers to run the
area from Strasbourg, later commented that his year in Strasbourg
was only equalled by his first war ministry (1912–13) as the most
'beautiful and fruitful' of his career. To Poincaré, Millerand lacked
subtlety but was orderly and industrious. 'Only he was a little
greedy; he wanted to control all appointments.' Millerand, who
considered it essential to be able to make decisions locally instead of
awaiting instructions from Paris, persuaded the cabinet to agree
that he report only to Clemenceau and have access to the cabinet for
matters affecting the provinces. The decrees of 21 March 1919 that
established a commissioner-general of the Republic in Strasbourg
and gave Millerand the title as a temporary mission, created a
ministry for Alsace-Lorraine.[78] Warmly received in Strasbourg on
24 March, Millerand, as a prominent politician, lent prestige to his
post.

In Strasbourg, Millerand had to solve several problems immediately. It was not simply necessary to substitute French control for
German, but to combine the best of both systems. Three matters
were particularly pressing: valorization of the mark, liquidation of
sequestered property, and the status of French personnel. The
return to France left Alsace-Lorraine with a depreciated currency
that could have triggered a serious financial crisis. To local bankers,

---

78. Millerand, 'Souvenirs,' p. 67; Poincaré, *Au service*, XI, pp. 92, 94, 165–6:
Reinach suggested a Millerand ministry to Poincaré. On a visit to Alsace-Lorraine
after the armistice, Poincaré had observed the region's enthusiasm for reunification
with France, but also hints of administrative problems and anxiety about local
interests. A.N., F.M. 92, Millerand, 'Souvenirs d'Alsace et de Lorraine,' 23 January
1925; Poincaré, *Au service*, XI, pp. 257–8, 260, 262, 270: Maginot told Poincaré that
Clemenceau, prompted by Mandel, had thought of Millerand because of the latter's
tearful visit to the premier the day he was shot. *Ibid.*, p. 329, noted that by 10 April,
many were disillusioned with Clemenceau and expected an eventual Millerand
ministry. *Ibid.*, p. 333; Millerand, 'Souvenirs,' p. 88; A.N., F.M. 44, interview with
Millerand, reported in the *Petit parisien*, 11 May 1919; A.N., F.M. 92, Millerand,
'Souvenirs d'Alsace et de Lorraine,' 23 January 1925. Initially, the French established
a general service in Paris to direct Alsace-Lorraine's affairs. They also appointed
three commissioners, similar to prefects, as well as delegates from different ministries. These civil servants received instructions from the capital. To general prewar
complaints about Parisian administrative congestion were added the problems of
dealing with the area's unfamiliar legislation. At a meeting of the Conseil Supérieur
on 25 February 1919, representatives of Alsace-Lorraine requested a high commissioner in Strasbourg with authority to act without reference to Paris. The decree
of 21 March 1919 satisfied both local wishes and Millerand's demand that the high
commissioner control matters affecting Alsace-Lorraine from his office in Strasbourg.

Millerand suggested allowing local residents a reasonable exchange rate for German currency and postponing the larger problem of replacing the local tax system with French fiscal laws. Secondly, he provided for transferring German property to French citizens, although large German industrial holdings in mining and metallurgy posed legal as well as economic questions. Finally, they tried to recruit local administrative personnel to replace German civil servants rather than bringing in Frenchmen from outside the area. For example, Lorraine railroad-strikers had demanded that they fill all positions instead of French civil servants replacing the German. Although the German monopoly of senior civil service posts had relegated the Lorrainers to subordinate positions, there were not enough qualified local candidates to fill all vacancies. Millerand, who had to import some French civil servants, tried to choose ones who spoke German.[79]

Beyond these specific initial problems, Millerand confronted the spectrum of issues provoked by the reintegration of the provinces into France. Local enthusiasm for the return to France could not eradicate nearly fifty years of German control. Furthermore, the local population clung to regional institutions, notably social and religious, in preference to comparable French arrangements. The French had to enforce the transition cautiously, amalgamating French and local institutions, and not simply imposing their own. Millerand suggested a ten-year transition period in which representatives from Alsace-Lorraine would participate. Insufficient information about local legislation meant that the area could not be administered from Paris like a normal department. To Millerand, a powerful high commissioner assisted by a local council was the best administrative solution. The decree of 21 March 1919, which made Strasbourg the administrative center of Alsace-Lorraine, initiated a decentralized system that permitted local decisions on most issues.[80]

An able administrator, Millerand radically altered the administrative system within three weeks of being named commissioner-

---

79. Millerand, 'Souvenirs,' p. 89; A.N., F.M. 44, interview with Millerand, reported in the *Petit parisien*, 11 May 1919; Alexandre Millerand, *Le Retour de l'Alsace-Lorraine à la France* (Paris: Bibliothèque Charpentier, 1923), pp. 6–9, 27–37, 70–80; A.N., F.M. XII, Millerand to Clemenceau, 15 September 1919.

80. Millerand, *L'Alsace-Lorraine*, pp. 16–17: the law of 17 October 1919 established a ten-year transition period; *ibid.*, pp. 130ff, Millerand's speech to the general assembly of the Caisses d'Epargne of Alsace-Lorraine, 17 May 1919; J.O., *Chambre*, 1 October 1919; A.N., F.M. 44, Millerand's speech in the Chamber, 1 October 1919; *ibid.*, Millerand's interview in the *Petit parisien*, 11 May 1919.

general. He established ten new subdivisions through which to channel his authority that eventually became virtual small ministries. He discussed major local issues with the consultative Conseil Supérieur d'Alsace-Lorraine, an appointed council of representatives from all political parties, religious factions, and union general secretaries. He hoped an elected regional council would eventually replace this appointed body.[81]

Millerand wanted Alsace-Lorraine to elect deputies to the French Chamber in 1919. Electoral participation would, he argued, promote reintegration, since the national legislature was morally bound not to alter local legislation or deal with Alsace-Lorraine's problems unless the area's elected representatives were present. To Clemenceau, Millerand urged that national elections take place before municipal ones, as the latter might encourage political divisions and separatism. Local divisiveness should not influence the choice of representatives dealing with Alsace-Lorraine's national reintegration.[82]

Millerand wanted Alsace-Lorraine to be a genuine region whose local authorities could settle all outstanding issues. Even after he left Strasbourg, he defended the commissioner-general's prerogatives and the region's special budget against Parisian centralism. On 22 January 1920, he proposed legislation giving Alsace-Lorraine a forty-member regional council with seven delegates named by decree, twelve elected by general councils, and twenty-one professional representatives. Violent criticism of the text came from both Left and Right. The Left, preferring regional councils elected by universal suffrage, opposed decentralization on anticlerical and educational grounds. Spokesman for the Right, Paul Reynaud, defended centralization and the rapid assimilation of Alsace-Lorraine. Even in Alsace-Lorraine, however, there were local pressures for the direct election of some delegates and for cultural and educational responsibilities, not simply financial, for the pro-

81. Persil, p. 116; J.O., *Chambre*, 1 October 1919; Millerand, *L'Alsace-Lorraine*, p. 19. François G. Dreyfus, 'Le malaise politique,' in P. Dollinger (ed.), *L'Alsace de 1900 à nos jours* (Toulouse: Privat, 1979), p. 102, lists the following departments: military affairs, interior, finance, justice, commerce, industry and mines, public instruction, fine arts, public works and communications, waters, forests and agriculture, work, worker legislation and social insurance, and P.T.T.

82. Millerand, *L'Alsace-Lorraine*, pp. 107–8, 137–42, Millerand's speech to the Conseil Supérieur d'Alsace-Lorraine, 2 June 1919; A.N., F.M. 44, Millerand interview in the *Petit parisien*, 11 May 1919; A.N., F.M. XII, Millerand to Clemenceau, 15 September 1919; J.O., *Chambre*, 1 October 1919; also in A.N., F.M. 44.

posed council. Millerand, who wanted Alsace-Lorraine to serve as a regional model, finally accepted the consultative committee of thirty-five members established by the decree of 9 September 1920.[83]

Alsace-Lorraine's adaptation to French ways had implications of an economic, social, linguistic, educational, and religious nature. Millerand basically wanted France to respect those local institutions, freedoms, customs, and beliefs that had enabled the region to preserve its character despite half a century of German pressure. Economically, he thought that Alsace-Lorraine's revival was tied to the reconstruction of France's devastated regions. Proposing a vast public works' program supported by national funds (development of the Rhine's hydro-electric resources and cutting a passage through the Vosges), he also wanted to restore the area's transportation facilities (railroad and river) and exploit its subsoil mineral resources (iron, coal, salt, oil, and potassium). To secure food and raw materials, he suggested a requisition and purchase program similar to the successful wheat arrangement. The area could export freely to Germany for five years and Germans in Alsace-Lorraine were given the right to choose French nationality. Millerand adopted an interventionist economic stance toward Alsace-Lorraine's revival whereby French representatives reinforced local initiative and industriousness.[84]

The transition to peace provoked social problems in Alsace-Lorraine, as elsewhere in France. Demobilization, which initially created substantial unemployment, fostered worker discontent which erupted in strikes. Millerand organized the work system to eliminate the dole and find jobs for returning workers. He also urged arbitration of strikes, noting the common interest of workers and employers in increased production. Since the local social insurance legislation was more complete than that of France, Millerand recognized that the provinces would oppose the substitution of French for local legislation. Indeed, Alsace-Lorraine could provide

83. François G. Dreyfus, *La Vie politique en Alsace, 1919–1936* (Paris: Armand Colin, 1969), p. 43; Dreyfus, 'Malaise,' p. 106: this committee included three senators, chosen by their colleagues, representing each department, two deputies similarly designated, twenty-one general councilors (6 designated by the Upper Rhine general council, 8 by that of the Lower Rhine, 7 by that of the Moselle), and five nominated by the government; Millerand, *L'Alsace-Lorraine*, pp. 109–13.

84. Millerand, *L'Alsace-Lorraine*, pp. 40–52, 118, Millerand's speech to the banquet of the Union des grandes associations françaises, 24 April 1919; A.N., F.M. 44, Millerand interview in the *Petit parisien*, 11 May 1919.

a model for the nation as a whole. Although he reassured local
workers that their social insurance system would be preserved,
such legislative discrepancies argued for the transitory integration
period.[85]

Education and religion were particularly awkward issues. Since
Alsace-Lorraine was removed from France before the separation of
church and state, the old Napoleonic Concordat was still in effect.
When French bishops were appointed to replace German in Strasbourg and Metz, Millerand reassured local church dignitaries that
the French regime would not encroach on their religious freedom.
He was also anxious to guard the area's artistic and historic wealth,
including the Strasbourg cathedral. Educational problems were
both linguistic and administrative. A considerable segment of the
population was unable to speak French. While anxious to preserve
the German language, Millerand argued, however, that French
must again become the primary language. Since many teachers did
not have an adequate knowledge of French, language instruction
for all age groups in the population was necessary, and not just for
children. The French secondary school system replaced the German, and at the University of Strasbourg imported French profes-
sors filled the initial gaps in personnel caused by the departure of
Germans after the armistice. In one area, however, Alsace-Lorraine
provided educational leadership: the Chambre des Métiers in Strasbourg had fostered a strong professional apprenticeship system. In
essence, Millerand's libertarianism guided his gradual reintegration
of Alsace-Lorraine. As he commented in Metz, the Republic was a
government of liberty and justice that respected all opinions. The
Republic wanted to hear local views, including those of Alsace-
Lorraine. A liberty, however, that acknowledged authority was
necessary if the ravages of four years of war were to be repaired and
the economy restored.[86]

The Chamber debate of 3 June 1920 revealed considerable opposition to the government's policy in Alsace-Lorraine, especially
to the region's administrative status. Should it retain a special status

85. Millerand, *L'Alsace-Lorraine*, pp. 142, 145–8, Millerand's speeches to the
Conseil Supérieur d'Alsace-Lorraine, 2 June 1919, and to the Chambre de Métiers
d'Alsace-Lorraine, 18 June 1919; J.O., *Chambre*, 1 October 1919; also in A.N., F.M.
44; *ibid.*, Millerand interview in the *Petit parisien*, 11 May 1919.

86. Millerand, *L'Alsace-Lorraine*, pp. 82–5, 88–102; *ibid.*, pp. 33–8, Millerand's
speech at the mairie of Metz, 22 May 1919; A.N., F.M. 92, Millerand, 'Souvenirs
d'Alsace et de Lorraine,' 23 January 1925, to the Société des conférences.

with different local legislation? Indeed, Alsace-Lorraine's integration into the French community remained problematic throughout the interwar period. Almost fifty years of separation had produced a clerical and autonomist Alsace-Lorraine that inevitably clashed with the secular, centralized nation it re-joined. A prestigious commissioner-general like Millerand, who was sufficiently powerful and perceptive to give local services a genuine function, temporarily averted the disputes. When a normal civil servant replaced him, the central administration in Paris again became dominant. During the Bloc National's legislative control (1920–4), the debate over regionalism continued, but when Edouard Herriot and the Cartel des Gauches took power, the Alsatian problem intensified; the Left was determined to reintegrate fully the region into France by eradicating all legislative differences.[87]

87. Dreyfus, *Vie politique*, p. 265; Dreyfus, 'Malaise,' p. 106.

Part IV
The Premier

8
'Work, Security and Freedom': Domestic Politics and Foreign Policy

In France, the overwhelming Bloc National victory of November 1919 gave the 'Blue Horizon' Chamber the largest Right majority since the early Third Republic. An electoral alliance of Right and Center-Right parties, the Bloc National won about two-thirds of the seats in the new legislature, primarily because its discipline and unity confronted leftist division, as had been the case in 1885. Other factors like the new electoral law, a desire for renewal, and an anti-Bolshevik atmosphere also influenced the verdict. The electoral law of 1919, which introduced departmental list-voting (*scrutin de liste*), combined proportional representation with a majority principle. The party or electoral group with a majority within a department received all the seats; proportional representation applied only when no group had a majority. This odd combination distorted public opinion to give the Bloc about sixty seats more than it would have won by genuine proportional representation, and to reduce Socialist representation by thirty-four seats, despite a slightly larger popular vote than in 1914. The vote also led to a change of personnel as veterans replaced many old parliamentarians, an anti-parliamentarian phenomenon that often followed wars. The 1919 victory of the nationalist, conservative Bloc National also reflected a fear of domestic disorder and anti-communism. The Right of 1919, marked by its republican dedication, was, however, significantly different from the monarchist or Bonapartist Right of the 1870s and 1880s, which partially explains its exclusion of the Action Française. More sympathetic to the church than the prewar leftist majorities, it still endorsed the laic laws. Its chauvinism, illustrated by severity toward Germany, fear of communism at home and abroad, and an economic and financial orthodoxy linked the Bloc National to the Right. The electoral alliance sought constitutional revisions that would restore the President of the Republic's powers, like the right of dissolution, stabilize the executive, and provide for professional representation and administrative decentralization.[1]

Millerand's famous Ba-Ta-Clan speech of 7 November 1919, often termed the charter of the Bloc National, outlined his foreign and domestic programs. Its fundamental theme was unity, the vital necessity for all Frenchmen to collaborate in France's postwar recovery:

> Such a river of blood and glory separates the spring of 1914 from the winter of 1919 . . . Frenchmen did not live four and a half years side by side, heart to heart, under the same dangers, struggling, suffering from morning to night . . . so that scarcely back home they suddenly forget that yesterday they lived in full confidence, helping each other like brothers. It is not possible that today, scarcely out of this frightening torment, they will return, as though nothing had happened, to their former divisions.

To him, the magnitude of wartime bloodshed had so transformed the political scene that the shabby divisions of 1914 could not revive in the political contest of 1919. The war had demonstrated those profound qualities that linked Frenchmen and the need for collaboration.

Millerand insisted that unity must be based on clearly defined ideas, specifically work, security, and freedom. Postwar France had to produce to survive. Its vast natural resources and its colonies had

---

1. E. Bonnefous, III, p. 69; Duroselle, *La Grande Guerre*, pp. 359–61: the Bloc held 380 seats, monarchists and unaffiliated right-wing deputies another 57, the Left 180; Goguel, pp. 215–18; Donald J. Harvey, *France Since the Revolution* (New York: The Free Press, 1968), pp. 219–20; Gagnon, pp. 339–41; David Thomson, *Democracy in France Since 1870* (New York: Oxford University Press, 1964, 4th edn), p. 186; René Rémond, *La Droite en France* (Paris: Aubier, Editions Montaigne, 1963), pp. 195, 202, 206, 209. J. Plumyène and R. Lasiera, *Les Fascismes français, 1923–1963* (Paris: Editions du Seuil, 1963), p. 23, note Millerand's refusal to link the Action Française to the Bloc National. Persil, pp. 116–17, notes that from July 1919 on, Millerand was involved in the election campaign even though he spent most of his time in Strasbourg. Seeking a republican, socialist union, he wanted prominent figures and not those with local ties. He balanced Barrès on the Right with Heppenheimer, a former Broussist, on the Left.

not been fully exploited economically. For example, if hydro-electric power were developed, it could supplement inadequate coal supplies. Wartime miracles like the production of explosives proved to Millerand that France was capable of comparable peace-time progress if the government and private industry cooperated and shared the nation's financial burdens. France's huge debts to its allies, its obligations to its veterans and devastated regions required that all citizens accept proportional taxation. He did, however, hope France's former allies would assist the nation that had suffered most to defend civilization's interests. Recognizing that production required collaboration, he urged that class solidarity replace class struggles. Successful wartime institutions like work councils, where employers and workers discussed common interests, and compulsory arbitration to avert strikes should be perpetuated.

In the French libertarian tradition that traced its roots to Montes-quieu, Millerand argued that 'the essential guarantee of liberty is the division of power . . . Tyranny . . . is the reunion of all powers on one head, man or assembly.' To him, 'the Republic is synonymous with liberty.' Dedicated to France's parliamentary regime, Millerand was convinced that the legislature had so en-croached on executive prerogatives that the necessary balance of powers had been undermined. The 'detestable' electoral system, the *scrutin d'arrondissement*, had given deputies dictatorial control over local appointments. To Millerand, France's excessive central-ization was a liability. His experience in Strasbourg persuaded him of the advantages of decentralization and led him to promote regional councils with genuine responsibilities. For example, Alsace-Lorraine could provide a model for a social insurance sys-tem. The President of the Republic should not, he believed, be the product solely of parliamentary deals but be chosen by a larger electoral college that included regional and professional representa-tives, a reform similar to de Gaulle's modification of 1958. Mem-ories of Napoleon, however, made men of Millerand's generation wary of a popularly elected president. His corporatist proposal to include professional representatives in the Senate resembled de Gaulle's 1969 proposal and interwar fascism.

His desire for liberty also led him to defend freedom of opinion, political and religious, and of association. To Millerand, separation of church and state promoted religious freedom by eliminating official involvement in matters of belief; likewise, church absten-tion from politics fostered political freedom. He pleaded with

Frenchmen not to revive their prewar religious battles any more
than their internecine political struggles. Indeed, the congregations'
wartime record had secured their recognition as patriots. Millerand
mentioned restoring relations with the Vatican should national
interests dictate it. To him, 'freedom of association was the necessary instrument of progress,' whether in the work-place, churches,
or elsewhere. Finally, he defended educational freedom; the state
must protect the neutrality of the schools so that they did not
degenerate into forums for political maneuver. To Maurice Barrès,
he argued that the public schools' neutral, laic character did not
prevent religious associations from setting up schools if they observed the separation laws:

The Ba-Ta-Clan speech's final theme was security. Despite its
postwar financial burdens and dislike for armaments, France must
maintain its means of defense, preserve its alliances, and insist on
strict execution of the Versailles Treaty; it could not rely on the
League of Nations. International unity was as essential as domestic
to consolidate the Allied victory, insure Treaty execution, and erect
a bulwark against revolutionary forces like the Russian Bolsheviks.[2]

Millerand has frequently been charged with political inconsistency, with abandoning his early socialist commitment for the conservatism of the Bloc National of 1919. Others have argued that a
surprising unity characterized his political career. Cornilleau termed
Millerand's 'Clemencisme' the unifying ingredient; Clemenceau's
patronage marked the beginning and ending of his career. Furthermore, a Jacobin patriotism and loyalty to democratic and socialist
ideals made him always a 'patriotic socialist.'[3]

The concept of Jacobin patriotism implied the mobilization of

2. Alexandre Millerand, *Union républicaine sociale et nationale* (Paris: Imprimerie
'Le Papier,' 1919), speech in Paris, 7 November 1919, commonly referred to as his
'Ba-Ta-Clan' speech; also in A.N., F.M. 43; A.N., F.M. 43, 'Appel aux electeurs,' 3
November 1919; *ibid.*, program of the *liste d'union républicaine*, 25 October 1919;
Persil, pp. 122–5; Adrien Dansette, *Histoire des présidents de la République* (Paris:
Amiot-Dumont, 1953), p. 199; Michel Soulié, *Le Cartel des gauches* (Paris: Jean
Dullis, 1974), p. 250. Maurice Barrès, *Mes cahiers*, vol. XII (*1919–1920*) (Paris:
Librairie Plon, 1949), p. 327, noted Millerand's conviction that church–state separa-
tion did not preclude the relations with the Vatican necessary to defend French
interests. The *associations culturelles* could respect the Catholic hierarchy without
jeopardizing the separation: Millerand to Barrès, 28 October 1919, from Strasbourg;
Wright, *France*, p. 425.

3. Robert Cornilleau, *Du Bloc national au front populaire* (Paris: Editions Spes,
1939), p. 63: Millerand began as an intransigent radical, a collaborator in
Clemenceau's paper *La Justice*, and finished as premier on Clemenceau's suggestion
when the latter resigned to campaign for the presidency.

the whole nation to defend the ideals of freedom and equality proclaimed by the Revolution in France against the threat posed by the conservative, monarchist regimes outside its borders. It also encompassed the expansionist, aggressive dissemination of revolutionary ideals outside France. During the first half of his political career, Millerand belonged to this patriotic Jacobin tradition, as did many French Socialists whose loyalty to France included a desire to institute the social and economic freedom and equality implied by the revolutionary ideals. The transformation of that patriotism into the conservative nationalism of the early twentieth century indicated a divorce of the two components, loyalty to the nation and the achievement of social and economic reform. The standard view is that the Boulanger and Dreyfus affairs transformed nationalism from a leftist to a rightist ideology. The Left abandoned its aggressive attachment to the nation in danger to move toward pacifism and the conviction that war would distract from necessary social reforms. The Right, on the other hand, relinquished its attachment to monarchism and accepted the Republic but made the nation's defense and grandeur its principal objective. It did not, however, seek those social and economic reforms that had been an essential component of revolutionary patriotism. By the end of the first decade of the twentieth century, Millerand was as dedicated to France as he had been in the 1880s. Although his speeches still defended social reforms, such as compulsory arbitration, his actions in repressing strikes and penalizing workers for disturbing social peace aligned him with the new conservative nationalism more than the earlier Jacobin patriotism. While Clemenceau did play a role at several points in Millerand's career, the young Millerand who wrote for *La Justice* was a different Millerand from the mature premier of 1920. While Millerand's public statements reveal remarkable consistency over the fifty-five years of his political career, that seeming consistency masked a considerable change in priorities and actions.

Largely responsible for defining the spirit of the Bloc National and its most important personality, Millerand was the logical successor to Clemenceau in January 1920. France needed a pilot who could restore order, an organized administrator and hard worker, a national rather than a party figure. As French premier and foreign minister from 20 January to 23 September 1920, Millerand held office just as the Versailles Treaty entered into effect. A study of his foreign policy illuminates not only Franco–German difficulties provoked by the Treaty but contrasting French and British views toward postwar Germany. Toward Russia and Eastern Europe, Millerand adopted a *cordon sanitaire* that led him to resist Russian military advances and encourage White Russians and the new Polish nation. Turkish treaty negotiations, establishment of a French mandate in Syria, and renewed ties to the Vatican required significant foreign policy decisions. While Millerand's primary concern was foreign affairs, serious domestic unrest also forced him to elaborate a social policy. His premiership illustrated the diversity of foreign and domestic pressures that postwar France confronted, and the government's response.[4]

Millerand's ministerial declaration of 22 January 1920 lauded a Republic that in fifty years had transformed a defeated, invaded France into a victorious nation. A parliamentary system based on freedom and legal equality precluded neither a strong executive nor an active regional life. 'The era of sacrifices and restrictions is far from over, the nation is ready to impose them on itself as it did in the war . . . the civic duty is summed up in four words: produce more, consume less.' To rebuild French national wealth required thriftiness, a renunciation of unnecessary expenditures to permit the replacement of destroyed stocks, and the acceptance of progressive taxation ('to pay the tax is to serve France'). France's need for its citizens' toil matched its wartime need for their blood. Committed to fiscal orthodoxy, Millerand sought a balanced budget and the collaboration of private enterprise in economic reconstruction. The immense task required social solidarity, cooperation between workers and employers, to avert conflicts or settle disputes by arbitrations. With security as France's principal foreign policy goal, the prevention of a comparable catastrophe in the future held priority. A reorganized military force was the necessary supplement to reparations. The keystone of French

---

4. Millerand, 'Souvenirs,' p. 92, attributed Clemenceau's 'incredible' defeat for the presidency to Briand's corridor intrigues. Duroselle, *Grande guerre*, p. 365, claims that Briand, bitter at his exclusion from the peace negotiations and over the Lancken incident, was at the heart of the plot. E. Bonnefous, III, p. 95, notes that Clemenceau clearly indicated he would keep Briand out of office as long as he was president. Recent publications have investigated specific aspects of postwar France, such as reparations or Rhineland separatism. While they have revised traditional views, a focus on Millerand permits the reintegration of monographic contributions.

foreign policy, execution of the Versailles Treaty, required that the wartime alliance be preserved and ties established with smaller nations.[5] Millerand's declaration illustrated his optimism and patriotism as well as a somewhat utopian vision of a French future in which domestic and international problems could be readily resolved. Most ministerial declarations are couched in idealistic, hopeful tones, but Millerand's showed little awareness of the difficulties his programs were likely to encounter.

Millerand's ministry reflected the prime minister's priorities as much as the election results. While his cabinet was conservative, it did not belong to the traditional Right. As he later observed, he wanted a 'republican union' of all groups (excluding socialists and monarchists) committed to national and social policies that transcended factional interests. He also noted that harmonious relations with his colleagues eased the burdens of the premiership. Moderates like Viviani, Doumergue, André Tardieu, and Raoul Peret declined cabinet posts and some ministers came from the Right, but it was not entirely a government of conservatives. Millerand chose Radical Senator Théodore Steeg as Minister of the Interior and Radical Deputy Albert Sarraut as Minister of Colonies. Steeg's nomination proved particularly controversial as the extreme Right, notably Léon Daudet, bitterly attacked Millerand for picking a key minister from outside the victorious Bloc National. Termed a *maladresse*, the choice proved politically prudent; it won the support of the Radicals (important in the Senate) for the government's foreign and domestic policies and proved the premier's intent to align all Frenchmen behind his national program. Insisting that his government was above parties, Millerand ignored the traditional political cadres, naming only three professional politicians, and filled key economic posts with bankers and businessmen. Frédéric François-Marsal, Director-General of the Banque de l'Union Parisienne, headed the Ministry of Finance. Using financiers to solve the nation's economic problems, Millerand was accused of by-passing parliament to open government ranks to economic power, even though he did not alter the existing administrative structure or eliminate the old governing groups.[6]

---

5. A.N., F.M. 54, Millerand's governmental declaration, 22 January 1920; J.O., *Chambre*, 22 January 1920.

6. Millerand, 'Souvenirs,' p. 93; Cornilleau, *Bloc national*, p. 68; Charles S. Maier, *Recasting Bourgeois Europe* (Princeton: Princeton University Press, 1975), pp. 108–9; Marc Trachtenberg, *Reparation in World Politics: France and European Economic*

To the Chamber on 30 January, Millerand argued that premiers had always been entitled to choose their collaborators. With France confronting enormous difficulties, it needed a ministry of all republican factions, a political *union sacrée* parallel to social collaboration and international cooperation, but his nominations did not imply a desire to abandon Clemenceau's policies. National interest, he believed, dictated an end to political wrangling and greater governmental authority. In fact, he advocated concentrating on work within the parliamentary commissions and shelving interpellations, since the overcharged atmosphere of the Chamber invited controversy – a considerable shift from his hostility to the commissions in 1915. To enable France to fulfill its primary obligation, execution of the Versailles Treaty, domestic peace was essential, particularly within the production process. Still a dedicated parliamentarian, Millerand, in his defense of his cabinet, indicated not only a persistent dislike of factionalism but also a more conservative, authoritarian inclination. Although he won a reluctant vote of confidence, large-scale abstentions indicated dissatisfaction with his cabinet choices.[7]

Described as a nationalist in foreign policy and a conservative in domestic policy, Millerand tried to satisfy the Right but govern in accordance with the Chamber's moderates. As premier, he reacted firmly to the social unrest that plagued France during 1920. The social laws of 1919 had not defused the agitation which spread from the railroads to other industries in 1920. Unrest in turn provoked harsh repression. Economic and social problems accompanied de-

Diplomacy 1916–1923 (New York: Columbia University Press, 1980), p. 119; E. Beau de Loménie, *Les Responsabilités des dynasties bourgeoises* (Paris: Editions Denöel, 1954), III, pp. 212–13; Michel Soulié, *La Vie politique d'Edouard Herriot* (Paris: Armand Colin, 1962), p. 83; Stephen H. Roberts, *The History of French Colonial Policy 1870–1925* (Hamden, Conn.: Archon Books, 1963), p. 612; Ragnar Simonsson, *Millerands Presidentur. En Studie över Presidentmakt och parlamentarism i Frankrike* (Upsala: Almquist & Wikells Boktryckeri-A.-B., 1938), pp. 72–6, privately translated by Mrs. Leslie Derfler; Maurice Baumont, *La Faillite de la paix (1918–1939)* (Paris: Presses Universitaires de France, 1967), pp. 142–3; Rouffet, p. 244, quotes François-Marsal, 'Nos amis les anglais,' pp. 1–2; Cambon, III, p. 373.
    7. J.O., *Chambre*, 30 January 1920; Beau de Loménie, III, pp. 225–6; E. Bonnefous, III, pp. 107–8; Simonsson, p. 76; Paul C. Helmreich, *From Paris to Sèvres. The Partition of the Ottoman Empire at the Peace Conference of 1919–1920* (Columbus: Ohio State University Press, 1974), pp. 221–2.

mobilization as a short, sharp world-wide depression followed the initial postwar boom. Real wages declined as prices increased; production had been distorted by wartime needs and manpower losses. Strikes became endemic, with almost daily notices of work stoppages. It is difficult to assess the role of sympathy or antipathy to Soviet Russia, but proceedings against the Confédération Générale du Travail (the C.G.T.) provoked a social hostility of prewar intensity. Fear of domestic disorder had contributed to the Bloc National's victory. To Millerand, who considered the reestablishment of order and social peace the most urgent domestic problem, responsibility lay with the C.G.T. which he considered as the tyrant of the work-force.[8]

The first concrete manifestation of worker discontent was a railroad-workers' strike on the Paris–Lyon–Méditerrannée (P.L.M.) line on 25 February. Prior to the strike, Millerand instructed the prefects to organize a voluntary work-force should a strike be declared. Wartime strains on men and material, which had undermined profitability, made the railroads particularly ripe for social conflict. Furthermore, increased unionization of railroad workers (approximately five-fold between 1917 and 1920) fostered politicization and promoted demands for higher wages and nationalization. In late February, a relatively minor incident escalated into a test of power. A carpenter was briefly suspended for attending a union meeting against orders. A stand-off occurred when the unions refused to negotiate until the worker was reinstated and Millerand rejected arbitration unless the union ordered work resumed.[9] Behind the seemingly minor incident, vital principles

8. Millerand, 'Souvenirs,' pp. 93–4; Soulié, *Herriot*, p. 83; Jacques Néré, *La Troisième République, 1914–1940* (Paris: Librairie Armand Colin, 1967), p. 30; Simonsson, pp. 72–3; Anne Hogenhuis-Seliverstoff, *Les Relations franco-soviétiques (1917–1924)* (Paris: Publications de la Sorbonne, 1981), pp. 159–60; Gagnon, p. 341.
9. Maier, p. 155; Kriegel, I, p. 384; Robert Wohl, *French Communism in the Making, 1914–1924* (Stanford: Stanford University Press, 1966), p. 161; Jacques Chastenet, *Histoire de la Troisième République* (Paris: Librairie Hachette, 1960), V, p. 66; Simonsson, pp. 78–80. Adrian Jones, 'The French railway strikes of January–May 1920: new syndicalist ideas and emergent communism,' *French Historical Studies*, XII, No. 4 (Fall 1982), p. 529: talks between National Railway Federation negotiators Toulouse and Boisnier and Le Trocquer on 25–26 February and with Millerand on 27 February failed to settle the dispute provoked by Campanaud's dismissal. The government refused to intervene on a question of 'internal company discipline.' Harvey J. Bresler, 'The French railway problem,' *Political Science Quarterly*, XXXVII, No. 2 (June 1922), p. 219, describes the National Railway Federation as a very radical organization whose leaders Monmousseau, Levêque, and Sarolle

were at stake: the rights of unions versus national social peace.

Millerand responded to the strike with a patriotic appeal, a plea for order, and governmental firmness. On 27 February, he defended Minister of Public Works Yves Le Trocquer for not shielding the laid-off worker from disciplinary action. Once work resumed, the government would instruct an arbitration commission to investigate regulations governing holidays for syndical workers. To Millerand, two days' suspension of work scarcely justified disrupting the nation's economic life, halting production, and threatening all workers' interests. France, he believed, confronted a revolutionary political movement, not simply a corporative or professional protest. Willing to settle the crisis by mobilizing sectors of the P.L.M. (as he had done in 1910), he appealed to the workers' patriotism, asking that national solidarity transcend professional. The Chamber authorized the government to requisition other forms of transport. A generally hostile public reaction and the failure of the unions' call for a general railroad strike led to the collapse of the movement. On 29 February, Millerand became the arbitrator between the union and the companies. An agreement of 1 March raised wages and prohibited sanctions. Although both sides soon claimed violations, work generally resumed by 3 March. On 2 March, Millerand noted to the Chamber that mobilization had proved unnecessary because most *cheminots* had obeyed the government's request to continue service. The union and the rail company had agreed on four points and had accepted Millerand's arbitral decision on the remaining obstacles. Furthermore, both sides agreed to abide by the Tissier Commission's proposals for a new statute for the railroads and salary levels. As a republic based on universal suffrage and the Declaration of the Rights of Man, France could not, Millerand insisted, permit a dictatorship of one class, the proletariat. While ready to revise the law of 1884 to give workers and unions greater responsibilities and rights of ownership, he would not permit them to substitute force for law or impose a minority's views on the nation:

> No social conception frightens us that is based on reason, but if we want the social policy to become a truth, everyone must understand that it can

---

were active in the anarchist federation. The huge operating deficits on the railroads (a six-fold increase between 1918 and 1920) and discontent among personnel fueled demands for nationalization.

only be in order, peace and respect for legality. The greatest service that you [members of the Socialist party] can render to those you defend is to tell them that the Republic puts at their disposition all the means of allowing their claims to triumph, but outside of legal means there is nothing that a republican government worthy of its name would ever allow to be used.[10]

Social unrest was not limited to the industrial sector. In February, Millerand received reports of complaints from landlords in the Landes along the Bay of Biscay about revolutionary workers stirring up sharecroppers. Fearful that the proposed concessions would eventually produce a rural emigration, the landlords considered the sharecropping syndicates a camouflage for an agrarian socialism seeking to reduce the French peasantry to the Russian level. Millerand rejected right-wing deputies' demand that the responsible unions be dissolved and their leaders barred from office for a decade, but still opposed efforts to revolutionize the working class, agricultural as much as industrial.[11]

Relatively unsympathetic to working-class demands, Millerand assigned national unity and peace priority over social reform. He particularly sought a formula for forestalling future strikes and providing for peaceful settlement. A draft bill of 9 March required that worker delegations notify employers of their demands and submit to obligatory conciliation before stopping work. Relatively rare before the war, general strikes that affected whole industries instead of individual enterprises had become more numerous and significant because of the shock of the war to national economic and social life, and because of postwar inflation, with its pressures on salaries. Such strikes, however, magnified the problem in Millerand's opinion, since they deprived workers of their salaries, promoted anxiety and instability, and paralyzed industrial reconstruction. Not intending to violate the law of 1864 by prohibiting all strikes, Millerand wanted to exhaust all possibilities of peaceful settlement before work ceased. To him, strikes were a duel in

10. J.O., *Chambre*, 27 February and 2 March 1920; E. Bonnefous, III, pp. 119–20; Maier, pp. 155–6; Wohl, p. 162; Kriegel, I, pp. 393, 451; Simonsson, pp. 78–80. Jones, p. 532: both sides reached agreement by 29 February and submitted the issue of dismissals to Millerand, who ruled that only those applied before the settlement could be maintained. The company agreed to respect union rights, institute the Federation's proposed pay scales and work regulations and consult the union on the future reorganization of the railroads.

11. Maier, p. 193.

which one side sought a definitive advantage but inflicted the greatest harm on an involuntary spectator, the public. When a work stoppage threatened national economic and social life, workers had to await an arbitration decision before acting or face a requisition of services and penalties.[12]

Millerand's opposition to strikes reiterated his reformist arguments of the 1890s, but with a nationalistic component. He always opposed strikes as a form of social warfare that substituted violence for the peaceful, legal route to social change. In 1920, however, he equated action with disloyalty to France; the objectives of one class were sought at the nation's expense. To the Senate, he reiterated his determination to repress revolutionary threats to law and order. In the case of the railroads, the government was determined to maintain service, but repression of the strike was only one option. The right of association, established in 1864, 1884, and 1901, allowed professional associations to study and defend their interests, but it was 'criminal' if those rights were used to establish a one-class tyranny over the nation. To him, regular meetings between employers and employees would foster the *rapprochement* needed for social peace. A law providing for compulsory arbitration was a necessary supplement to existing social legislation if strikes were not to become an intolerable form of war. Civil servants, on the other hand, did not have the right to strike, since they were not covered by the law of 1884 and worked for essential national services.[13]

Social tension, which mounted during March and April, also triggered financial difficulties. Beginning on 7 March in the Pas-de-Calais and 10 March in the Nord, miners' strikes were declared. The railway strike left both sides embittered. To the workers, management had violated the agreement when it imposed fines and suspensions; the companies resented labor gains. From San Remo, Millerand telegraphed on 23 April that he could not revise the previous agreement or suspend proceedings against those charged with inciting disobedience. Crisis again loomed on 24 April when a general railroad strike was set for 1 May. Furthermore, the strikes had led to a depreciation of the franc and spiralling prices.[14]

---

12. A.N., F.M. 52, Millerand's exposé des motifs, projet de loi of 9 March 1920, annex to procès verbal no. 489.

13. *Ibid.*, Millerand's speech in the Senate, 29 March 1920; *ibid.*, Millerand's exposé des motifs, projet de loi on status of fonctionnaires, undated; J.O., *Sénat*, 29 March 1920.

14. E. Bonnefous, III, p. 120; Maier, p. 156; Kriegel, I, p. 417; Wohl, p. 162;

A major confrontation seemed increasingly inevitable as both sides adopted more rigid stances that hampered compromise. The C.G.T. triggered the break on 29 April by its announcement of a general strike for 1 May. Seeking wage increases and railroad nationalization, the strike leaders hoped to force the government to capitulate by paralyzing the distribution of goods. Scattered violence erupted in Paris on 1 May. The strike, which began with railroad workers, miners, seamen, and dockers, spread on 7 May to metalworkers and on 10 May to builders, automobile, aviation, navigation, and transportation workers. Most workers, however, refused to strike, notably the railwaymen of the north and east. As Millerand noted, workers were ordered to cease work just as France confronted the burden of reconstruction. The strike, which accentuated the cost of living crisis, principally hurt the workers. Its true cause, he believed, was the desire to undermine public order in order to pave the way for revolution. Determined that work continue, he pleaded with labor to resist criminal attempts to incite them.[15]

Despite its pessimism about a successful strike, the C.G.T. still assumed leadership, probably to retain control of the movement. Timing, however, was poor; the continuous unrest during the preceding year had alienated the public from the working class. Furthermore, mass apathy and strikers' disagreement over goals (revolutionary change or improved conditions) undermined the movement. Finally, the strikers confronted a forceful government and a parliament resolved to respond energetically.[16]

Millerand's reaction consisted of mobilization of volunteers and sanctions against the union. He used students from the *grandes écoles*, volunteers from civic unions and soldiers on special duty to replace strikers. Numerous militants, railroad union leaders and important left-wing figures were arrested and more than 20,000 railroad workers were dismissed. Legal action was taken against the C.G.T. for declaring a strike that violated the law of 1884 by creating anarchy in the transport system. Charging the C.G.T. with exercising tyranny over the work-force, Millerand argued that such a forceful response was the only way to end the agitation.

Baumont, pp. 142–3.
   15. A.N., F.M. 54, Millerand's declaration to the press, 2 May 1920; E. Bonnefous, III, p. 120; Wohl, p. 164; Simonsson, p. 80; Jones, p. 539; Bresler, p. 219.
   16. Chastenet, *Histoire*, V, p. 67; Wohl, pp. 163–4.

Dissolution of the union was ordered in January 1921 but never implemented, as Millerand was reluctant to launch a social war. In fact, the strike was a dismal failure for the unions. On 21 May, the leaders called it off, and by the end of the month, work was generally back to normal, ending both the specific episode and the year-long wave of unrest.[17]

Millerand viewed the strikes as a revolutionary threat rather than a plea for reform. To the Chamber, he insisted the government could not timidly allow strikes to disrupt the nation's economic life at a time when full production was vital. He was convinced that Bolshevik agents had manipulated the strikes for revolutionary ends. Denying that the government wanted to attack syndicalism, he noted plans to extend social legislation by an eight-hour day, with rest periods for women, and a minimum-age requirement. It could not, however, tolerate such disruptions by a violent minority.[18] No evidence supports Millerand's charge of Bolshevik involvement in the strikes, but his analysis of their impact on the troubled economic and social situation was valid.

The failure of the strike movement, which was disastrous for the unions, significantly affected postwar France. In the short run, it secured industrial peace and weakened the C.G.T., which lost half its membership and eventually split. Millerand's actions seemingly surprised the C.G.T. leaders, who considered him irresolute, but strengthened the revolutionary minority, thereby facilitating the communist victory of December 1920 in the union and the Socialist party and the long-range division of the working class. Millerand, who had to prove to the Left and the Right that his socialist past had not made him sympathetic to Bolshevism, emerged as the defender of order against revolution. The employers' victory, however, did not ease their anxiety about workers' goals or the Bolshevik menace. Social antagonism therefore increased even as social unrest abated.[19]

Millerand combined his opposition to unrest with an appeal to patriotism. To the railroad workers, he conveyed his distress at the

17. Millerand, 'Souvenirs,' pp. 93–4; Chastenet, *Histoire*, V, p. 67; Wohl, p. 165; E. Bonnefous, III, p. 120: Millerand's statement following a cabinet meeting on 11 May 1920; Maier, pp. 156–7; Kriegel, I, pp. 458–9. Simonsson, p. 81, gives the figure of 35,000 strikers.

18. J.O., *Chambre*, 21 May 1920; also in A.N., F.M. 54; E. Bonnefous, III, p. 124; Chastenet, *Histoire*, V, p. 67; Kriegel, I, p. 488, no. 1; Wohl, p. 168.

19. Simonsson, pp. 81–3; Néré, p. 30; Baumont, pp. 142–3.

civil war among Frenchmen, but stressed that national solidarity superceded professional solidarity. With France's crucial need to produce after the war's enormous devastation, all Frenchmen had to restrain consumption, increase production, and cooperate with other states. No specific interests could jeopardize that national endeavor. To him, France's wartime victory at the Marne had proved its ability to lay aside internal wrangling and partisan concerns. He evoked that triumph to remind his countrymen of their ability to surmount seemingly overwhelming odds and to encourage them to apply similar qualities to postwar crises.[20]

Millerand's conviction that full production was crucial to France's postwar survival prompted him to promote foreign trade as a stimulant to internal production and a balance of payments asset. A restoration of normal commercial relations with France's former enemies would foster world prosperity, as long as France did not suffer economic discrimination. To Millerand, Germany's commercial regime violated Articles 264–267 of the Versailles Treaty by discriminating against France. The premier was indignant when he learned in April that Germany had answered French proposals for an economic *modus vivendi* by reinstating wartime import prohibitions. He finally persuaded the British to protest German violations of the Treaty with their commercial legislation. He urged an Allied protest through the Conference of Ambassadors. Britain's strong exchange position and control of vital raw materials gave it a strong bargaining position relative to Germany. In the Franco–German commercial negotiations, which opened on 17 March, France agreed to allow German goods free entry into France if Germany reciprocated. It recognized Germany's right to control imports and exports, and set prices and tariffs, but insisted on a common policy for all nations; Germany could not sell more cheaply to Austria, for example, than to France and Italy. The Allies did not plan to impede Germany's commercial revival, but, in return, it must treat all nations similarly. Too often, German businessmen proved hostile to their French counterparts. Millerand also wanted to

20. A.N., F.M. 54, Millerand's speech to the Fraternal banquet of railroad workers and employees, 5 June 1920; *ibid.*, Millerand's speech to the international parliamentary conference of commerce, 7 May 1920; *ibid.*, Millerand's speech to the International Chamber of Commerce, 28 June 1920; *ibid.*, Millerand's speech at Meaux, 5 September 1920.

restore rail links between France and Germany and work out a common plan to rebuild the devastated regions. To him, economic collaboration would promote French economic health.[21]

A similar concern for its financial situation led France to adopt restrictions of its own. Foreign tariffs hurt the French export market and exchange rate, whereas French import limitations kept foreign products from competing with domestic goods, thereby protecting national industries and improving the French trade balance. Protectionist tactics, which could elicit reprisals that hurt the instigator as much as the victim, were necessary if France were to establish a favorable balance of trade that would permit it to repay its debts to Britain and the United States and cover reconstruction and pension costs. A governmental decree of 23 April prohibiting hundreds of imports initiated a French import restriction policy, but provoked immediate protests from its trading partners. Although the prohibited articles represented only 3 percent of French imports, Millerand feared retaliation against French exports would counterbalance any gains. British bankers might hesitate to advance credit; other nations might not purchase French luxury exports, whereas France required vital resources like British coal. France could only exercise an economic control comparable to the United States and Britain if it exported substantial amounts of essential resources, like phosphates and iron ore. Finance Minister François-Marsal considered the exchange rate the real problem; France was not the only nation to use tariffs to buttress its currency. When the Belgians seconded British complaints in May, Millerand and François-Marsal agreed to study specific cases in a 'friendly' manner but to keep the decisions secret and avoid general concessions. At the same time, France planned to prohibit phosphate exports to Spain and Spanish imports into France. Claiming that its debts to its wartime allies took precedence, France maintained its resources were inadequate to cover all its obligations. Political consideration took precedence over financial policy; nations vital to French security or economic strength required satisfaction first. Millerand did, however, compromise by continuing financial negotiations and making a partial repayment on

---

21. A.E., z Europe 1918–29, no. 522, Millerand to de Marcilly, French chargé, Berlin, 27 March 1920; *ibid.*, Millerand to de Marcilly, 14 April 1920; Ministère des Affaires Etrangères, Archives Diplomatiques, Papiers Millerand 13, Millerand to the president of the German delegation, 22 June 1920, pp. 13–18, hereafter cited as A.E., P.M..

the Spanish loan. The import restriction policy was dropped in July when it became clear that the financial rewards did not compensate for the attendant hostility.[22]

Foreign policy was Millerand's principal concern in 1920. His assumption of the premiership coincided with the application of the Treaty of Versailles; his ministerial declaration of 22 January made the Treaty's execution French law, which would be sought without violence or weakness but with 'unshakable firmness.' French security and European peace required strict application of the Treaty, particularly of its military clauses. The year 1920 proved to be a test of German good faith. As premier, however, Millerand confronted pressures for a return to normal relations that conflicted with his electoral program of strict Treaty enforcement. He found little opportunity to innovate, and was mostly forced to plug the gaps in Clemenceau's construction. Caught in a current of British influence, he found the Quai d'Orsay committed to *détente* and stabilization that implied non-intervention in other nations' domestic affairs. To Millerand, German bad faith was responsible for the defaults in Treaty execution, rather than excessive French demands. Convinced, however, that a bitter peace would make another conflict inevitable, he wanted to associate vanquished Germany with the enforcement of the Treaty. He was ready to revive Franco-German economic cooperation if the Germans performed their Treaty commitments in good faith.[23]

Strict Treaty execution required, in Millerand's opinion, collaboration with France's wartime allies, notably Great Britain. Yet his ministry has been described as a high point of Franco-British tension. Referring to a crisis in the alliance, he told François-Marsal that the French must extract everything possible from the Treaty. From his experience in Strasbourg, he had learned that a devious

22. Dan P. Silverman, *Reconstructing Europe After the Great War* (Cambridge, Mass.: Harvard University Press, 1982), pp. 236–7, 240, attributes the proposed tariff restrictions for Spain to French Ambassador Count Auguste de Saint-Aulaire and notes François-Marsal's claim that the French treasury was unable to meet the June installment on the Spanish debt. Rouffet, pp. 183–4.

23. Hogenhuis, pp. 168–9; Millerand, 'Souvenirs,' pp. 95–6; Soulié, *Herriot*, p. 83; Marcellin, *Politique*, III, p. 210; André François-Poncet, *De Versailles à Potsdam* (Paris: Flammarion, 1948), p. 84; Walter A. McDougall, *France's Rhineland Diplomacy, 1914–1924: The Last Bid for a Balance of Power in Europe* (Princeton: Princeton University Press, 1978), p. 97; Persil, p. 132.

Germany would seek to evade its stipulations. Although British support was crucial, François-Marsal believed that France could not rely on Britain because of its fears of a strong French continental army. French disappointment at its failure to win the Rhine's left bank, the Saar, or abolition of the 1815 Treaty convinced Britain that a close scrutiny was necessary to keep France from extending its frontier to the Rhine. It therefore considered French financial problems, including expensive reconstruction, huge foreign debts, and a weak currency, as a blessing. Since the British hoped financial distress would curb French political aspirations, they did not want German payments to alleviate it.[24]

Millerand later recalled his desire to work with the British, along with his refusal to yield on essential questions. With the signature of the peace treaty, Britain had again adopted the policy of impeding France's establishment of a continental hegemony, a policy of which Lloyd George was a 'brilliant exponent.' By early 1920, Millerand had become suspicious of British moderation toward Germany, fearing a compromise of French Treaty rights if dependent on British support. The French asserted a right to act independently by occupying the German Maingau towns in April. British hostility, however, which nearly destroyed the alliance, forced Millerand to accept future concerted action.[25] Although Millerand met frequently with his British counterpart Prime Minister David Lloyd George, their divergent policies accentuated their hostility. Policy toward Russia, Poland, and the Near East, as well as Germany, elicited differing responses.

To the Chamber of Deputies and the parliamentary commissions, Millerand stressed the importance to France of its alliances. Forswearing secret diplomacy, he promised not to sign any treaties without parliament's knowledge, but argued that negotiations could not be publicly conducted. To the Chamber's foreign affairs commission, he argued the need for close Allied financial relations. On 6 February, he surveyed the spectrum of French foreign concerns to the Chamber of Deputies. Maintaining that a continuity transcending ministerial changes characterized Third Republic foreign policy, he claimed that fidelity to alliances had

---

24. Rouffet, pp. 244–5, quotes François-Marsal, 'Nos amis les anglais,' pp. 1–2.
   25. Millerand, 'Souvenirs,' pp. 97–8; Arnold Wolfers, *Britain and France Between Two Wars* (New York: W.W. Norton & Co., 1966), pp. 78, 88; W.M. Jordan, *Great Britain, France, and the German Problem, 1918–1939* (London: Oxford University Press, 1943), p. 74.

enabled France to defeat German aggression. France's defense of its national interests had not obliterated the struggle for ideals like freedom and justice as ingredients of its foreign policy. Inter-Allied cooperation to secure postwar French goals was essential to Millerand's policy along with a concern for security and international status. When the United States refused to ratify the Treaty of Versailles or the pact against German aggression and Great Britain proved reluctant to defend French interests, Millerand had to rely on strict Treaty application, including reparations, to guarantee French security.[26]

During the first half of 1920, Millerand attended numerous inter-Allied conferences: at London, San Remo, Hythe, Brussels, and Spa. As he later noted, 'first-rate' collaborators like Marshal Ferdinand Foch, François-Marsal, Yves Le Trocquer, and Camille Barrère accompanied him, and Maurice Paléologue, the new secretary-general of the Quai d'Orsay, was a great help. The first inter-Allied meeting in London on 12–13 February discussed relations with Germany and the treaty with Turkey. Millerand invited Finance Minister François-Marsal to accompany him to England to meet with Chancellor of the Exchequer Austen Chamberlain and Prime Minister Lloyd George. The latter, François-Marsal recalled, denying German military revival, refused to revive the guarantee to France that Clemenceau had given up during the Treaty negotiations. The calculation of reparations percentages provoked the first serious dispute. Millerand urged that Belgium and Italy be included, but Lloyd George held to Clemenceau's commitment of 15 December. A general disagreement over the applicable damages for calculating the percentages of reparations convinced François-Marsal that Franco-British mistrust was present from the beginning. The issue of heads of state attending frequent meetings provoked recriminations: the British, who stayed in Paris for seven months during the Versailles Treaty negotiations, resented Millerand's claim that domestic problems, specifically the looming railroad and mine strikes, required his

26. Chamber of Deputies Archives, Palais Bourbon, Foreign Affairs Commission, 4 February 1920, audition of Millerand, hereafter cited as C.D.A.; A.N., F.M. 51, Millerand's notes for speech of 6 February 1920; J.O., *Chambre*, 6 February 1920; also in A.N., F.M. 52; E. Bonnefous, III, pp. 127–31; Cambon, III, p. 374, notes the Chamber's approval of Millerand's commitment to apply the Versailles Treaty; Piotr S. Wandycz, *France and her Eastern Allies 1919–1925* (Minneapolis: University of Minnesota Press, 1962), p. 141; Cornilleau, *Bloc national*, p. 77; A.E., P.M. 95, Millerand's statement on French foreign policy, undated, but prior to March 1920.

presence in France. While they also disagreed about the site for the Turkish negotiations (Paris or London), policy toward Germany was the chief source of dispute, and especially the issue of German coal. Dependent on British coal and anxious to perpetuate Allied wartime solidarity, Millerand conceded on levelling sanctions against Germany for not meeting its coal commitments. He attributed British opposition to French proposals to traditional fears that a strong France needed the counterweight of a restored Germany. The French, however, who felt the British were more sympathetic to Germany, blamed them for obstructing French efforts to receive German coal.[27]

On his return from London, the premier referred to his heavy burdens (*mes très lourdes fonctions*) in describing the Allied conference where his double objective had been to defend France's interests while remembering that preservation of the alliance with Britain was an essential precondition. All questions had required negotiation and compromise to prevent a rupture of that pact. Guided by good faith and unshakable firmness, the French government had sought full German execution of the Treaty without exceeding its stipulations.[28]

In response to Louis Barthou's interpellation, Millerand gave a second major foreign policy speech in the Chamber on 26 March that discussed inter-Allied relations as well as French policy toward Germany and the East. Although France was especially vulnerable geographically to German militarism, Britain was not safe from danger. Allied solidarity, Millerand maintained, was as necessary to postwar peace as to a wartime victory. Denying a crisis in the alliance, he insisted that each state must watch out for its own interests as well as strive for the common good. Shared ideals and interests, economic, political, and military, reinforced France's need for British and American support, but it was, he insisted, a conservative nation, not bent on territorial aggrandizement. To Millerand, the emergence of new states and the defeat of German

27. Millerand, 'Souvenirs,' p. 98; A.N., F.M. 56, minutes of Allied Council meetings, London, 12–13 February 1920; *Documents on British Foreign Policy, 1919–1939*, edited by Rohan Butler and J.P.T. Bury, (London: Her Majesty's Stationery Office, 1958), 1st ser., vol. VII, pp. 1–40, hereafter cited as *D.B.F.P.*; Trachtenberg, p. 124; Maier, p. 202; Cornilleau, *Bloc national*, pp. 72–3; McDougall, p. 108; Helmreich, *Paris to Sèvres*, pp. 242–3; Jukka Nevakivi, *Britain, France and the Arab Middle East 1914–1920* (London: The Athlone Press, 1969), p. 233.

28. C.D.A., Foreign Affairs Commission, 20 February 1920; *Sénat*, Foreign Affairs Commission, 19 February 1920, audition of Millerand.

militarism consecrated the principle of freedom that France had long championed. Furthermore, its 'genius' for dissipating misunderstandings made France a force for peace and conciliation in international affairs.[29]

Inter-Allied relations included the United States, Belgium, and Italy as well as Britain. Millerand and Lloyd George often tried to win American support for Franco-British policies. In mid-February, they tried to prevent the United States from adopting a different stance on Fiume; later they attempted to persuade it to accept the mandate for Armenia. Franco-American tension emerged particularly over war debts. To Millerand, as to subsequent French governments, American demands for repayment were unrealistic. Although the money was expended in a common cause, the Americans expected France to repay but did not recognize that the current exchange rate would have more than doubled its obligation. As he poignantly observed, 'we have spent our blood and our money, can one now ask double the debt we contracted?' He insisted the French sought only the normal treatment of any debtor, not charity. The American suggestion of greater French exports to improve the exchange rate ignored the devastation of France's richest areas and the decimation of its manpower. The export of gold would have undermined French currency, and increased taxation was unrealistic, he argued.[30] Millerand was not entirely consistent on the issue of taxation; he rejected higher taxes to pay war debts, but urged them for domestic economic renewal.

Concern for French security in the north led Millerand to seek a military alliance with Belgium. At a decisive conference at Ypres on 28 January 1920, Millerand, President Poincaré, French Ambassador to Belgium de Margerie, and Marshal Ferdinand Foch discussed a possible Franco-Belgian military alliance with Belgian Prime Minister Delacroix, King Albert, Foreign Minister Hymans, and Belgian Ambassador to France Baron Edmond Gaiffier d'He-

29. A.N., F.M. 51, Millerand's draft of speech to the Chamber of 26 March 1920; J.O., *Chambre*, 26 and 27 March 1920; also in A.N., F.M. 52; Jacques Bariéty, *Les Relations franco-allemandes après la première guerre mondiale* (Paris: Editions Pedone, 1977), p. 66; Trachtenberg, p. 119; E. Bonnefous, III, pp. 137–41; Hogenhuis, p. 173; E. Malcolm Carroll, *Soviet Communism and Western Opinion, 1919–1921* (Chapel Hill: University of North Carolina Press, 1965), p. 46.
30. A.N., F.M. 54, Associated Press interview of Millerand, 15 March 1920.

stroy. Their military staffs were assigned the task of drafting an agreement, but control over the Guillaume–Luxembourg railroad line proved controversial. The Belgians wanted France to relinquish its economic control over Luxembourg, including the railroads, whereas the French considered the rail line to be an extension of the Alsace-Lorraine system. Hymans insisted that the Versailles Treaty had not settled the railroad issue, and demanded British participation in any Franco–Belgian pact.[31]

The railroad issue, which elicited continued Franco–Belgian recriminations, delayed progress on a military pact. To Millerand, the railroad and military conversations were connected. France would accept a Franco–Belgian agreement to exploit jointly the Guillaume–Luxembourg railroad only if the Belgian government fulfilled the commitment made at Ypres for Franco–Belgian military talks. France was prepared to let Belgium participate in the administrative council of the Alsace-Lorraine railroad along with France and Luxembourg if Belgium would re-open military discussions. In fact, the railroad issue forced a suspension in the military talks between Foch and Belgian General Gillain. Recognizing Millerand's refusal to compromise, de Margerie suggested some Belgian concessions. To the Belgians, control over the Luxembourg railroad was the counterpart for the military pact, whereas, to Millerand, the pact did not require French concessions. Foreign Minister Hymans' irritation about the railroad issue clearly matched Millerand's anxiety about the military negotiations. Insistent that the Versailles Treaty had restored the pre-1871 railroad situation, Millerand believed that the railroad could be operated in a way that would safeguard the interests of both nations. He suggested that experts should study the issue and that military negotiations open two weeks later.[32]

The turning-point came in early April after Belgium backed France in occupying the Maingau. Appreciative of its demonstration of friendship, Millerand noted that gratitude broke the deadlock. He again suggested that a commission of experts seek a

31. Jean-Baptiste Duroselle, *Histoire diplomatique de 1919 à nos jours* (Paris: Dalloz, 1978), p. 20; Jonathan Helmreich, 'The negotiation of the Franco–Belgian military accord of 1920,' *French Historical Studies*, Spring 1964, pp. 363–4.
32. A.E., z Europe 1918–29, ss Belgium no. 27, Millerand to Baron de Gaiffier, 19 February 1920; *ibid.*, Millerand to the French Ambassadors, London, Brussels, 18 February 1920; *ibid.*, Millerand to the French Ambassador, Brussels, 22 February and 7 March 1920; J. Helmreich, p. 364; A.E., z Europe 1918–29, ss Belgium no. 57, Millerand to de Margerie, 16 and 31 March 1920; J. Helmreich, p. 365.

solution to the Luxembourg railroad problem that would satisfy Belgium. He also supported Belgium's inclusion in the San Remo conference and on the commission handling the Ottoman debt. Millerand did, however, want Marshal Foch to assess the railroad's military importance to France. The negotiations finally opened on 23 April and a general agreement to partition the railroads was elaborated by May. France then urged Luxembourg to negotiate an economic *entente* with Belgium.[33]

The question of a military agreement was not finally settled until September. The Belgians finally recognized after Lloyd George's and Delacroix's meeting on 12 July at Spa that the British would not sign a Franco–Belgian pact. At Millerand's meeting on 16 July with Delacroix, Hymans, and Jaspar at Spa, the Belgians accepted in principle a secret military pact with France. They decided on a staff accord ratified by an exchange of governmental letters rather than a formal alliance. France's military accord of 15 September 1920 replaced Belgian neutrality with a Franco–Belgian pact. The governmental letters described the accord as purely defensive, applicable only against unprovoked aggression. Belgium's commitment to support France contributed to French security on the Rhine for the next fifteen years. The two premiers also discussed closer Franco–Belgian economic ties, Belgian representation on the Danube commission, support for Poland, and possible commercial exchanges with Russia.[34]

Millerand's conviction that national interests dictated an official presence in Rome led him to press for diplomatic relations with the Vatican. As he later commented, ever since the separation of church and state he had considered ties to the Vatican a necessary corollary, and in his Ba-Ta-Clan speech of 7 November 1919, he endorsed reopening relations with the Vatican on grounds of national interest, and noted the impossibility of expelling religious orders from France and the importance of freedom of association for religious groups as well as others. He repeated his support for

33. A.E., z Europe 1918–29, ss Belgium no. 57, Millerand to de Margerie, 9 and 13 April 1920; *ibid.*, Millerand to Foch, 16 April 1920; J. Helmreich, pp. 366–7, 371.

34. Duroselle, *Histoire diplomatique*, p. 20; J. Helmreich, p. 374; A.E., z Europe 1918–29, ss Belgium no. 58, Millerand to the French Ambassadors, London, Rome, Brussels, 5 September 1920; Duroselle, *Histoire diplomatique*, p. 20; J. Helmreich, p. 374.

ties to the Vatican in his address to the Chamber of 6 February. He clearly hoped to bury the bitter divisions provoked by the politics of clericalism by a compromise that linked acceptance of Vatican diplomatic ties to guarantees of a secular state.[35]

On 11 March 1920, Millerand requested funds to re-open a French embassy at the Vatican. Stressing that the separation of church and state was so rooted in French customs and law that the laicity of republican institutions was no longer an issue, he argued that diplomatic ties should be restored, since issues vital to France were under discussion at the Vatican. Frontier changes in the Near East and Eastern Europe, notably Syria, Palestine, and Constantinople, often provoked religious as well as national and linguistic conflicts. Millerand considered it important for French representatives to participate in defending the Allied position to the Roman Curia. Franco-Vatican negotiations were necessary to define the application of the Concordat in Alsace-Lorraine and the position of French missions in colonial areas like the Cameroons, Morocco, and Tunisia.[36]

Millerand reassured his compatriots that the Italian government did not object to a Franco–papal reconciliation. On 18 March, he named career diplomat Jean Doulcet as minister plenipotentiary to negotiate a renewal of diplomatic ties with the Vatican, and Louis Canet as technical adviser for religious affairs within the foreign ministry. Relations with the Vatican would not, however, alter French laic laws for schools, associations, or religious practice.[37]

The vote on credits was delayed until November 1920, partially because of Radical and Socialist opposition, but also because the

---

35. Millerand, 'Union républicaine sociale . . .' (Ba-Ta-Clan speech), 7 November 1919; E. Bonnefous, III, p. 130; J.O., *Chambre*, 6 February 1920; Harry W. Paul, *The Second Ralliement: The Rapprochement Between Church and State in France in the Twentieth Century* (Washington: Catholic University of America Press, 1967), pp. 34, 47. Derfler, *President*, pp. 90, 257 n.11, suggests that Deschanel may have persuaded a 'previously hostile' Millerand to support re-opening a Vatican Embassy. Since Millerand had already mentioned the possibility in his Ba-Ta-Clan speech of 7 November 1919, it is unlikely that Deschanel played a significant role in this decision. Louis Sonolet, *La Vie et l'œuvre de Paul Deschanel, 1855–1922* (Paris: Librairie Hachette, 1926), pp. 277–8, also attributes to Deschanel initiative for reestablishing a Vatican Embassy and for winning over the cabinet, including Millerand.

36. Millerand, 'Souvenirs,' p. 95; A.N., F.M. 53, 11 March 1920, Millerand's exposé des motifs; J.O., *Chambre*, 11 March 1920; Paul, pp. 51–3.

37. A.E., z Europe 1918–29, ss Saint-Siège no. 14, Millerand to Doulcet, 18 March 1920; Paul, p. 53; Jean du Sault, 'Les relations diplomatiques entre la France et le Saint-Siège,' *Revue des deux mondes*, October 1971, p. 117.

government wanted Doulcet to complete negotiations with the Vatican first. Millerand, who was interested only in the Vatican's views and not in the French episcopacy's, refused to consider any pact that did not accept the French laic laws and religious associations. His policy toward the Vatican finally materialized when the funds were voted and Jonnart was sent to the Vatican as ambassador in May 1921.[38]

In September 1920, Millerand met with the prime ministers of France's neighbors, Belgium, Italy, and Switzerland. The conferences permitted him to emphasize the need for Allied accord and to outline his attitude toward Germany and Russia. On 12–13 September, he met Italian Prime Minister Giolitti at Aix-les-Bains, where he argued that relations with the Soviet Union were more politically dangerous than commercially advantageous, a position he held as premier and for the next four years as president. Restoration of a general peace would, he believed, be fatal to the Bolshevik regime unless it simultaneously restored diplomatic ties to the Great Powers. Convinced that Soviet progress was antithetical to genuine peace, he maintained its activities were dangerous to the West. Not afraid of Soviet propaganda, Millerand was determined to limit it as much as possible. He sought a conclusion to the Russo-Polish conflict that respected the principle of nationalities and the independence of both nations. France and Italy agreed to defend Poland's independence within ethnographic frontiers and defined their basic goals as a general pacification respectful of people's independence and a restoration of normal economic relations. General peace, however, required an end to conflicts like the Russo-Polish, those among the Turkish nationalities, and Italo-Yugoslav differences in the Adriatic. France and Italy must work together to solve postwar problems, including the elimination of Franco-Italian economic frictions, by such devices as a tonnage agreement. The two premiers agreed to apply the Treaty of Versailles in a moderate way, but expected the defeated nations to execute it loyally.[39]

38. Paul, pp. 53, 71, 90; du Sault, 'Relations diplomatiques,' p. 117.
39. E. Bonnefous, III, p. 158; Marcellin, *Politique*, III, pp. 209–10; Jacques Bardoux, *De Paris à Spa* (Paris: Librairie Félix Alcan, 1921), pp. 380–1; A.E., y internationale no. 682, minutes of conference between Millerand and Giolitti, Aix-les-Bains, 12 and 13 September 1920; Carroll, p. 215.

On 15 September, Millerand met Swiss leaders Motta and Schulthess in Lausanne to discuss French policy toward Germany and Russia as well as Franco-Swiss relations. Anxious for better relations with Switzerland, he tried to mitigate problems stemming from the French establishment of an eight-hour day, control over the *zône franche*, and navigation on the Rhine. He was especially upset by the presence of an official Soviet representative in Berne who might serve as a focus of propaganda against France. Individuals, he agreed, could have business dealings in Russia, but a Soviet commercial delegate would really be a political representative, since it had proved impossible to establish commercial relations with the Soviet Union. The prospect of a harsh winter, however, convinced him that the Bolshevik government would try to use contacts with the West to bolster their prestige and authority. As to Germany, Millerand claimed that faithful execution of the Versailles Treaty was the essential prerequisite for genuine peace. France could not admit Germany to the community of nations, symbolized by entry into the League of Nations, unless that precondition was met.[40]

Contemporary French opinion viewed Millerand's foreign policy as effective by late summer 1920. France had helped Poland repulse the Bolshevik army; General Gouraud had entered Damascus; pacts with its neighbors protected France's borders; and Germany seemed willing to fulfill its commitments. Yet, retrospective assessments have been more critical. Except for Poland, his foreign policy has recently been termed a record of setbacks. Reparations did not arrive; disarmament was incomplete; British cooperation was bought at the expense of Treaty rights; independent policy like the occupation of Frankfurt proved unviable; federalist and separatist schemes came to nothing.[41]

Alexandre Millerand was forced to handle a mutiplicity of problems during his eight months as premier. On an international level, he had to enforce the Versailles Treaty despite German resistance and delays, particularly to its reparations and disarmament provisions. In theory, he held tenaciously to French rights, but in

40. A.E., y internationale no. 682, meeting in Lausanne between Millerand, Motta, and Schulthess, 15 September 1920.
41. E. Bonnefous, III, p. 158; McDougall, p. 137.

practice yielded to the necessity of German delays. Bolshevik Russia constituted a dual threat to republican France. Internally, Millerand opposed the diffusion of revolutionary propaganda that demanded a dictatorship of the proletariat. Internationally, he sought to contain the Bolshevik menace within Russia by refusing the government recognition, supporting White Russian opponents, and aiding threatened Poland. Definition of a policy toward Germany and Russia often brought Millerand into conflict with the British, who were more conciliatory toward both nations. He sometimes had to implement his decisions without British support or compromise them to win British acquiescence. Without recourse to arms, it is doubtful whether Millerand could have fully enforced his German or Russian policies, but war weariness made military pressure unviable in 1920. Possibly a closer Franco–British alignment might have won greater compliance from Russia and Germany, but it is unlikely. As defender of French national interests, Millerand was as effective a premier in 1920 as was realistically possible.

On the domestic level, his strong reaction temporarily quelled the social unrest. Greater concessions to the workers might have mitigated class bitterness and worker alienation, but wartime devastation made intensified production essential. The unrest hurt the working class as much as the producers. In domestic affairs, as in foreign, the war conditioned the policies of the postwar premiers.

Millerand's program was appropriate for the situation he faced in 1920 and its results were not insignificant. Had he been able to concentrate his attention on one problem, reparations for example, it is likely that his achievements would have been more impressive. The fact that so many thorny issues required solution limited his success in any one area. The year 1920 was difficult for France; the magnitude of its problems limited the effective role which any statesman could have played. Although nationalism had emerged triumphant at the polls in 1919, it was constantly on the defensive during 1920. Millerand, with his patriotic determination to protect French interests, was beleaguered but nonetheless reasonably successful. His premiership illustrates in microcosm the thorny dilemmas that postwar France confronted.

9
'Without Violence or Weakness but with Unshakable Firmness': Policy Toward Germany

With the execution of the Versailles Treaty as the keystone of his foreign policy, Millerand spent considerable time in 1920 on problems related to Germany. He had affirmed in his ministerial declaration of 22 January that application of the Treaty would be France's law, to be carried out without violence or weakness but with unshakable firmness (*inébranable fermeté*) – a position he reiterated in his major address of 6 February. To Millerand, postwar peace required German compliance with its stipulations, particularly the military aspects.

The issues of German disarmament and coal, which troubled Millerand's entire premiership, were already problematic in February. Determined to press for German disarmament and surrender of those guilty of violating the laws of war and humanity, Millerand noted that the Allies had been unable to achieve much on disarmament because they had postponed their inspections until Germany completed a questionnaire on its armaments. Disarmament was progressing satisfactorily in the occupied zone where, for example, an explosives factory near Cologne had obeyed the control commission's prescriptions, as had neighboring factories. In unoccupied Germany, however, Millerand claimed examples already existed of Germany's evasion of the Treaty, and he expected further German efforts to disguise armament levels. Coal deliveries were also a serious problem. To indemnify France for its devastated regions and destroyed mines, the Treaty set Germany's coal obligations at 27 million tons per year or 1,660,000 tons per month. In January 1920, however, Germany supplied less than one-fifth of that amount, only 300,000 tons. Millerand discounted Germany's claims of inadequate resources because information indicated its per capita supply exceeded that of France. Allied occupation rights were tied to German execution of obligations; if Germany met its commitments, the occupation could be gradually reduced. Voluntary German defections entailed financial and economic reprisals. France could, Millerand argued, legitimately apply those sanctions envisaged by the Treaty, like delayed reduction of the occupation, commercial prohibitions, or financial and economic reprisals.[1]

The primary concern of the inter-Allied meeting in London of 12–13 February was treatment of Germany, especially German surrender of the guilty, and coal deliveries. Millerand noted Germany's default on its coal obligations to the French while it continued to export to the Netherlands. It had delivered, he claimed, less than half its required contingent. He suggested a temporary occupation of the Ruhr by the French army to force compliance. Not only did the Ruhr possess the major deposits, but its industrialists were the backbone of German resistance to the Treaty. Although the French premier assured the British that France did not want to cripple Germany economically, he did not win their support for sanctions. Lloyd George was not convinced that bad faith motivated Germany's coal delinquencies. French dependence on British coal forced Millerand to yield on sanctions toward Germany.[2]

On his return from London, Millerand reported on the German coal problem, stressing the discrepancy between production and deliveries. German defaults were particularly harmful because France's damaged mines could not produce at normal levels. Since Germany had supplied only a quarter of its quota, France, he believed, was justified in delaying its evacuation of occupied territory or in applying economic and financial sanctions. A French despatch of 8 February to the German government threatened sanctions if the Germans continued to evade their coal obligations.

1. C.D.A., Foreign Affairs Commission, 4 February 1920, audition of Millerand; A.N., F.M. 51, Millerand's notes for speech of 6 February 1920; J.O., *Chambre*, 6 February 1920; also in A.N., F.M. 52; E. Bonnefous, III, pp. 127–31; Wandycz, p. 141; Cornilleau, *Bloc national*, p. 77; A.E., P.M. 95, Millerand's statement on foreign policy, undated, but prior to March 1920.
2. Millerand, 'Souvenirs,' p. 98; A.N., F.M. 56, minutes of Allied Council meetings, London, 12–13 February 1920; *D.B.F.P.*, VII, pp. 1–40; Trachtenberg, p. 124; Maier, p. 202; Cornilleau, *Bloc national*, pp. 72–3; McDougall, p. 108; P. Helmreich, pp. 242–3; Nevakivi, p. 233.

German claims of economic hardship were unpersuasive to the French premier, because Germany had reserved more coal for itself than it had sent to France. It was not entitled to a privileged situation *vis-à-vis* France, whose privations, he claimed, stemmed from the systematic devastation ordered by the German High Command to ruin French industry, rather than because military needs required it. Although France was ready to take reprisals if German delinquencies persisted, the French government did not view an occupation of the Ruhr as desirable in itself, or consistently advocate it after 1919. It was simply a threat intended to influence German actions on reparations.[3]

A few weeks later, Millerand discussed the relationship between Germany and other French interests. France was involved in many areas: North Africa, the Near East, as well as on the Rhine. Since its principal duty and interest, he argued, lay in Europe, it had to restrict its commitments elsewhere, and proportion its ambitions to its obligations. In particular, it had to maintain a large enough army in Europe to defend French interests on the Rhine. It could not rely solely on the Treaty's obligation for Germany to reduce its army to 100,000 men by 10 July 1920.[4]

The trial of German war criminals was a major concern for Millerand at the beginning of his premiership. Domestic pressures for firmness led him to argue that provisions for the surrender of the accused must be obeyed before the Allies allowed German tribunals in the occupied zone to hold trials. Although German representatives in Paris had evaded the issue of surrendering war criminals, France was determined to press the matter. Millerand did, however, indicate that a German violation of Articles 228–230 would permit the Allies to institute economic reprisals and postpone evacuating the occupied territory. Furthermore, Allied trials *in absentia* of accused Germans could have moral advantages.[5]

3. C.D.A., Foreign Affairs Commission, 20 February 1920; *Sénat*, Foreign Affairs Commission, 19 February 1920, audition of Millerand; Georges Soutou, 'Problèmes concernant le rétablissement des relations économiques franco-allemandes après la première guerre mondiale,' *Francia*, No. 2, 1974, p. 586.
4. C.D.A., Foreign Affairs Commission, 4 March 1920, audition of Millerand.
5. A.N., F.M. 51, Millerand's notes for speech of 6 February 1920; J.O., *Chambre*, 6 February 1920; also in A.N., F.M. 52; E. Bonnefous, III, pp. 127–31; Wandycz, p. 141; Cornilleau, *Bloc national*, p. 77; A.E., P.M. 95, Millerand's statement on French foreign policy, undated, but prior to March 1920; James F.

The inter-Allied conference in London of 12–13 February spent considerable time on the issue of war criminals. Millerand argued that it would not be compatible with Allied dignity and would create a negative impression in France's devastated departments if they deleted any names from the list of guilty Germans. Despite Lloyd George's opposition, he wanted to add the names of Hindenburg, Ludendorff, and Bethmann-Hollweg. Hindenburg's responsibility for devastating northern France constituted a violation of the laws of war and humanity. If the Germans refused to surrender the guilty individuals on the ground of undue hardship, they could be tried *in absentia* to show them that their crimes had offended world opinion. The British, however, hesitated to alter the Treaty's stipulations by including the political and military leaders. Although Millerand feared German trickery would entangle the Allies in interminable negotiations, he finally agreed to let the Germans, not the Allies, conduct the trials after an inter-Allied commission had defined the charges. The Kaiser's surrender posed different questions, since he had fled to the Netherlands. The Allies were critical of the Dutch government for not interning the former German emperor, but, as neutrals, the Dutch had not signed the Treaty. Although they had therefore not violated its stipulations, they were irresponsible, the Allies believed, to let the Kaiser remain at liberty so close to the German frontier. Millerand opposed the British suggestion of interning him outside Europe, possibly in the Dutch East Indies, and wanted to pressure the Dutch to surrender him. The conference drafted letters to the German and Dutch governments stressing their obligation to surrender the Kaiser and other guilty persons.[6] For Millerand, the moral censure conveyed by a trial was seemingly more important than the physical restraint of imprisonment or exile.

The second inter-Allied conference in London of 23–25 February

Willis, *Prologue to Nuremberg. The Politics and Diplomacy of Punishing War Criminals of the First World War* (Westport, Conn.: Greenwood Press, 1982), p. 120, cites Derby to Lloyd George, 31 January 1920. *Ibid.*, pp. 123–4, cites Conference of Ambassadors meeting of 7 February 1920 and Millerand to Gustav Bauer, 8 February 1920. C.D.A., Foreign Affairs Commission, 4 February 1920, audition of Millerand.

6. Willis, pp. 109, 123–4; Millerand, 'Souvenirs,' p. 98; A.N., F.M. 56, minutes of Allied Council meetings, London, 12–13 February 1920; *D.B.F.P.*, VII, pp. 1–40; Trachtenberg, p. 124; Maier, p. 202; Cornilleau, *Bloc national*, pp. 72–3; McDougall, p. 108; Nevakivi, p. 233; P. Helmreich, pp. 242–3; *Sénat*, Foreign Affairs Commission, 19 February 1920, audition of Millerand; C.D.A., Foreign Affairs Commission, 20 February 1920, audition of Millerand.

again discussed the Kaiser's extradition or internment. Millerand and Italian Premier Nitti disliked Lloyd George's idea of demanding that the Dutch intern the Kaiser in a distant location, although they eventually gave in. In March, when the British criticized the Dutch for interning the Kaiser at Doorn, only 25 miles from the German frontier, Millerand instructed French diplomats to take a passive position on pressuring the Dutch. He responded to the Kaiser's public internment on 16 March in the Utrecht province by terming the move timely and urgent and urged the British to moderate their criticism of the Dutch so as not to offend public opinion. On the other hand, Lloyd George called Millerand's idea that the Allies conduct proceedings in the Kaiser's absence a 'futile' move.[7]

Allied disagreement about participation in German war criminal trials in Leipzig meant a delay in sending a list of war criminals to Germany. Convinced that they could not rely on German justice, Millerand feared Allied witnesses would receive a hostile reception in Leipzig. He suggested the Germans be held responsible for any failure and the Allies set up their own trials by default (*par contumace*). In March, the French arrested Germans in the occupied zone and conducted prosecutions, despite German protests. However, as Millerand noted to the Chamber on 26 March, Germany had still not surrendered any accused individuals. Lloyd George believed that Millerand simply wanted an excuse to occupy the Ruhr, but the French premier insisted that Germany had consistently proven unreliable about executing the Treaty, as illustrated by its failure to punish the guilty. After the San Remo conference, Millerand finally accepted Allied observers at the German trials. Although by late April the issue of German criminals was no longer a major concern for him, it illustrated his belief in German bad faith toward applying the Treaty.[8]

7. A.N., F.M. 51, Lloyd George and Millerand to Wilson, 17 February 1920, in response to Wilson's of 14 February 1920; *D.B.F.P.*, VII, pp. 219–42. Willis, pp. 110–12, cites A.E., 71 Paix, Millerand to Prevost, 10, 14 March 1920 and Cambon to Millerand, 9 March 1920.

8. A.N., F.M. 51, draft of Millerand's speech of 26 March 1920; J.O., *Chambre*, 26 and 27 March 1920; also in A.N., F.M. 52; Bariéty, *Relations franco-allemandes*, p. 66; Trachtenberg, p. 119; E. Bonnefous, III, pp. 137–41; Hogenhuis, p. 173; Carroll, *Soviet Communism*, p. 46; A.N., F.M. 59, Millerand to Derby, 9 April 1920; *D.B.F.P.*, IX, pp. 361–2, Derby to Curzon, 9 April 1920; F.S. Northedge, *The Troubled Giant. Britain Among the Great Powers 1916–1939* (London: G. Bell & Sons, Ltd., 1966), p. 164.

Millerand's fundamental goals were the guarantee of French security and reception of reparations. Inaugurating the Commission of Reparations, he noted that it had not only to set a total figure for German obligations by 1 May 1921 but also to insure that the commitments were met despite the debtor's ruses. It had to secure justice for those whose 'resistance to barbarism' had entailed misery and devastation. Possible military sanctions for German defaults, however, prompted Allied and French opposition. The military leadership noted probable public opposition to a Ruhr occupation because reserves would have to be recalled. Military action would have alienated the British, as the occupation of the Maingau in April did.[9] French reparations policy always depended on German fulfillment of Reparations Commission prescriptions rather than military force.

In March 1920, the British government launched a campaign to set the German debt that seemed to undermine the role of the Reparations Commission and irritated its president, Poincaré. Millerand was surprised that the Supreme Council would consider revising the Versailles Treaty's provisions for the Commission to let Germany set its obligations. It was the Commission's responsibility, he asserted, to force Germany to repair its crimes. The Quai d'Orsay's commercial section did, however, warn Millerand not to set reparation levels above Germany's capacity.[10]

Since France needed not only raw materials, notably coal, but also currency to repay the United States, reparations were closely linked to war debts. Those debts were increasingly a source of Franco-American discord as Millerand adopted the finance ministry's position of 1918 whereby France repaid the United States as it received payment from Germany. The American Senate's rejection of the Versailles Treaty on 19 March 1920 was crucially important. French security was jeopardized by the loss of the Anglo-American guarantee, and the Allied settlement with Germany, specifically the war guilt and reparations aspects, did not bind the United States. The United States was therefore unresponsive to French claims that war debts and reparations were linked. Perhaps surprisingly,

9. A.N., F.M. 54, Millerand's speech of 24 January 1920 inaugurating the Reparations Commission, extract from the *Petit parisien*, 25 January 1920; McDougall, p. 108.

10. A.E., P.M. 15, Millerand's telegram in response to one from London of 2 March 1920, precise date illegible; *ibid.*, Seydoux note of 15 October 1920 on reparations.

France did not use the American move to reclaim freedom of action *vis-à-vis* Germany. Germany's preoccupation with domestic problems and France's own internal unity and strong army may have removed any urgency. This illusion of French strength had the opposite effect on Britain, increasing its opposition to the French use of force. Indeed, the French occupation of Frankfurt affected Franco-American relations also, since an already suspicious Wilson withheld official American representation from San Remo.[11]

Probably because of British pressures, Millerand, François-Marsal, Léon Bourgeois, and Poincaré contemplated setting a lump-sum figure (*forfait*) for Germany on 2 April, but Poincaré wanted to keep French rights intact. He rejected a single payment that might prejudice the final reparations settlement. Millerand's initial responsiveness to British pressures for a total reparations figure was probably a conciliatory move designed to repair relations in the wake of increased American isolation and British hostility after the occupation of Frankfurt. The French leaders agreed to inform the committee that would organize the later Brussels conference that the Reparations Commission alone could set reparations – a position that Millerand would defend through the Spa conference. He particularly wanted a Franco-British agreement on the level of German capital or annuity payments to France and on encouraging Germany's economic revival so that it could pay its debts.[12]

During the second half of March, the German government requested Allied permission for German troops to repress the leftist uprisings in the Ruhr. A rightist Kapp *putsch* (an abortive coup attempt that seized Berlin) had triggered a leftist Spartacist (communist-led 'red army') revolt in the Ruhr. The Bauer government, which abandoned Berlin for Dresden and then Stuttgart, defeated the right-wing challenge and averted a general strike. It asked the Allies if it could send troops into the neutral zone of the Ruhr to end the disturbances and restore order, even though the

11. Carroll, *Soviet Communism*, p. 46; Néré, p. 31; Denise Artaud, *La Question des dettes interalliées et la réconstruction de l'Europe (1917–1929)* (Lille: Atelier reproduction des thèses, 1978), p. 273.

12. Artaud, *Dettes interalliées*, p. 290; A.E., P.M. 15, Seydoux note, 15 October 1920, on reparations; Georges Soutou, 'Une autre politique? Les tentatives françaises d'entente economique avec l'allemagne, 1919–1921,' *Revue d'allemagne*, VIII, 1 (January–March 1976), p. 25.

move would violate the Treaty's stipulated demilitarization of the Rhineland. Millerand, who had suggested an Allied Ruhr occupation the previous month in London to guarantee German coal deliveries, may have used the disorders as a pretext for Allied involvement. In a lengthy, impassioned address to the Conference of Ambassadors in Paris, he urged a common Allied response through actions, not words. Although a supporter of Allied unity, British Ambassador Lord Derby did not want to act before the Treaty was actually violated. Millerand retorted that Treaty enforcement was at issue because of repeated German violations of its disarmament clauses. Occupation of additional German territory seemed to him an appropriate Allied response that would forestall a German Ruhr occupation. Marshal Foch maintained that the disorders were no more severe than elsewhere and that German troop levels in the Ruhr already exceeded Treaty figures. Since Germany had ignored disarmament stipulations, Foch opposed Allied permission for German troops to enter the Ruhr. The conference rejected the German request, but Derby informed London that Millerand wanted an Allied policy toward persistent German Treaty violations. The British, who opposed an Allied Ruhr occupation, demanded a precise list of German defaults rather than just vague charges.[13]

Allied opposition forced Millerand to yield on a Ruhr occupation. He then suggested a German occupation in exchange for an Allied movement elsewhere to punish Germany for Treaty lapses. To Derby, the French wanted to use the Ruhr disturbances as a pretext for an Allied occupation. On 21 March, Millerand again proposed a brief German military engagement in the Ruhr if the Allies could occupy other German territory, but the Supreme Council in London rejected an Allied occupation and accepted a limited German one. Two days later, Millerand proposed occupying Frankfurt and Darmstadt as hostages for German evacuation of the Ruhr while the Conference of Ambassadors investigated proposed German troop movements.[14] Franco-British negotiations

13. *D.B.F.P.*, IX, pp. 158–60, Derby to Curzon, 17 March 1920; *ibid.*, pp. 170–83, record of the Conference of Ambassadors meeting, Paris, 18 March 1920, transmitted by Derby to Curzon; Northedge, pp. 163–4.

14. *D.B.F.P.*, IX, pp. 203–6, Derby to Curzon, 20 March 1920, summary of the Conference of Ambassadors meeting; *ibid.*, pp. 214–15, Derby to Curzon, 21 March 1920; *ibid.*, pp. 221–2, Curzon to Derby, 22 March 1920; *ibid.*, pp. 238–40, Derby to Curzon, 23 March 1920; Northedge, p. 164. Derfler, *President*, pp. 90, 257 n. 12,

dragged on for three weeks, but the French failed to win British support for an official protest or an Allied occupation of the Ruhr or other German territory. Nor did independent Franco-German negotiations lead to any agreement by late March.

In his second major foreign policy speech to the Chamber on 26 March, Millerand discussed the current problems in the Ruhr as well as the state of all Franco-German issues. He faulted the German government for not reducing its army to the specified 100,000 figure, not surrendering war material for destruction, and not imposing sufficient punishment on German soldiers for the numerous attacks on Allied officers. The abortive military *coup d'état* of 13 March, Millerand argued, at least partially stemmed from Germany's failure to obey the Treaty's disarmament clauses, since one of the divisions backing the insurrectionary Kapp government had been scheduled for disarmament. The Allies had turned down the German request to send troops into the Ruhr to repress the leftist Spartacist uprising that had followed the Kapp *putsch*. To the French, the presence of the troops constituted an unacceptable threat to French security. Should Germany violate the Treaty, the French, Millerand maintained, had the right to defend that security and insure their reception of reparations by occupying the Rhine's left bank or by not evacuating the Rhineland.[15]

The ingredients for a Franco-British confrontation existed by early April. On 1 April, Millerand told Derby that he had notified German chargé d'affaires Goeppert that France would not permit German troops to enter the Ruhr because the situation did not require their presence; local working-class leaders apparently preferred to have the Allies restore order. He considered a German despatch of troops to be a violation of Articles 43 and 44 of the Versailles Treaty, in return for which the French would need an additional Allied occupation to guarantee their security. When

notes that Deschanel still urged a Ruhr occupation on 30 March but that Millerand and the cabinet had decided on the more limited occupation of the Maingau towns.

15. A.N., F.M. 51, Millerand's draft of speech of 26 March 1920; J.O., *Chambre*, 26 and 27 March 1920; also in A.N., F.M. 52; Bariéty, *Relations franco-allemandes*, p. 66; Trachtenberg, p. 119; E. Bonnefous, III, pp. 137–41; Hogenhuis, p. 173; Carroll, *Soviet Communism*, p. 46. Sonolet, p. 279, claims that on 30 March Deschanel pressed for a French occupation of the Ruhr, but that Millerand opposed it because of possible difficulties with Britain. In fact, Millerand had suggested a Ruhr occupation six weeks earlier in London and had only reluctantly settled on the more limited Maingau occupation when he failed to win over the British. Sonolet notes that all the cabinet backed Millerand except for War Minister Lefèvre.

Derby told him that reports of a possible independent French action had unfavorably impressed the British, Millerand denied any such plans.

Goeppert, who also met with Derby on 1 April, accused the French of a breach of faith. He claimed Millerand had telephoned him on 29 March to give the French government's permission for German troops to enter the Ruhr for two to three weeks. If they failed to withdraw on schedule, France would occupy five German towns. On 31 March, Goeppert charged, Millerand withdrew his permission, arguing an occupation was no longer necessary. The German chargé blamed Millerand's shift on pressure from the French military. To Derby, however, Millerand was in a vulnerable position domestically; he adopted a strong stance because he was not secure enough to resist. To give an impression of strength, Millerand, Derby believed, told the press that the French would act even without British support. Foreign ministry official Jules Cambon confirmed the British ambassador's impression. Despite Millerand's repeated assurances that he would not move without Allied support, he seemingly feared his government would be overturned if he yielded to British demands.[16]

Despite French opposition, the Germans sent troops into the Ruhr on 2 April. On 5 April, French troops occupied five German Maingau towns outside the Treaty's specified occupation zone (Frankfurt, Darmstadt, Hannau, Homburg, Dieburg). Although the French public reaction was generally favorable, independent French action provoked an angry response from the British. They suspended coal exports to France and told their ambassador to boycott the Conference of Ambassadors until the French promised to await Allied permission for such important decisions in the future. To Millerand, however, Germany's defiance of the French prohibition made French troop movements the only possible response. He considered Britain's threat to abandon a cooperative policy and withdraw from the occupied zone to be unjustified and contrary to its formal commitments. He even hoped Britain would change its position and support French sanctions. The premier's indication that Marshal Foch was examining further military measures confirmed British suspicions of the marshal's role in the French deci-

16. *D.B.F.P.*, IX, pp. 283–5, 287–90, Derby to Curzon, 1 April 1920; E. Bonnefous, III, p. 141; McDougall, pp. 110–11; Trachtenberg, pp. 125–7; Jordan, p. 71; Suarez, V, p. 78. Northedge, p. 164, notes that extremists in Paris had long demanded the occupation.

sion. Warnings of British hostility, however, failed to deter the French premier.[17]

Millerand consistently linked French action to illicit German troop movements into the Ruhr basin, not hostility toward Germany. Its goal was exclusively penalty and precaution. To the French, the German despatch of supplementary troops was unnecessary and hazardous to mining operations. If Germany had obeyed the Treaty's disarmament clauses, the revolting Kapp troops would already have been disbanded and the weapons used by the Spartacists would have been surrendered to the Allies. Although the French government, Millerand insisted, had repeatedly consulted its Allies before occupying the five German towns, this German violation of the Treaty so threatened French geographical security that a response was essential. Millerand claimed that on 29 March Goeppert had promised that the German government would wait for French authorization before sending in troops, but the German chargé told Derby that Millerand telephoned his authorization that very day. Although no written evidence supports Millerand's claim, Goeppert himself admitted on 31 March that the French government had refused to authorize the move. On 2 April, Millerand again told him that the French would accept German troop movements only if the French could occupy five German towns. The following day Goeppert requested *ex post facto* French authorization for German troops which already exceeded permissible limits in the Ruhr. Meanwhile, German undersecretary for foreign affairs de Hamiel informed General Barthelemy that the German government had authorized Imperial Commissioner Severing to use troops in the Ruhr. Millerand charged the Germans with violating Article 44 of the Versailles Treaty and creating a *casus belli*. He hoped France's allies would therefore join in military sanctions which were indispensable to French security and in conformity with the Treaty and general Allied interests. He promised the French would vacate the occupied towns as soon as the Germans left the neutral zone.[18]

Franco-British tension mounted in the wake of the French ac-

17. *D.B.F.P.*, IX, p. 317, Grahame to Curzon, 5 April 1920; Wolfers, p. 43; A.E., z Europe 1918–29, ss Grande Bretagne 44, Millerand to the French Ambassador, London, 5 April 1920.

18. A.N., F.M. 59, Millerand to the French ministers in London, Rome, Brussels, Berlin, 4 April 1920; A.N., F.M. 54 and 59, Millerand's speech to the Conference of Ambassadors, 7 April 1920.

tion. The British were angry that the French had acted without Allied assent; the French resented British compliance toward Germany and refusal to support French sanctions. Millerand denied that France's actions or its intentions merited British charges, since his government had repeatedly consulted its allies and requested collaboration in the planned occupation.

> What is at stake? It is a question of applying one of the most solemn clauses of the Treaty . . . How has France abandoned this policy [set by the Treaty]? I do not want to insist on the fact that the dignity of the French government is at stake in Germany's failure to keep its word given spontaneously . . . that the French government was justified in claiming a territorial stake [*gage*] for this violation of Article 44 of the Treaty.

To the French, the German promise to withdraw troops once order was restored was inadequate, since Germany had persistently ignored Treaty provisions for punishment of the guilty, delivery of coal, or disarmament. At what point, Millerand critically asked, would the British government admit the danger of these systematic violations and stop treating the Germans so compliantly? Promising to await Allied agreement on all Treaty-related issues, he side-stepped the real problem. The French had indeed repeatedly sought British support, but they had acted even though they knew the British were opposed. His commitment to consult in future therefore elicits some skepticism. Would the French actually subordinate policy to British support? This incident implied that they might act alone if vital French interests were at stake. In fact, subsequent premiers were increasingly reluctant to do so.[19]

The general view is that by 11 April Millerand gave in and promised to await Allied ratification in the future for questions affecting Treaty application. While Millerand argued that the misunderstanding had been dissipated, he still portrayed the occupation of the five towns as forced on the French. He promised Derby to withdraw when the Germans evacuated the Ruhr. He generally minimized Franco-British tension and defended the French decision. Geographical factors, he thought, explained a contrast in methods that disguised common principles. The English Channel shielded the British, while France shared a Rhine frontier with

19. A.N., F.M. 59, Millerand's memorandum to Derby, 9 April 1920; *D.B.F.P.*, IX, pp. 361–2, Derby to Curzon, 9 April 1920; Northedge, p. 164.

Germany. To Millerand, a Franco-British understanding was the prerequisite to resolve postwar problems. Common interests and years of shared sacrifice rendered that alignment invulnerable. He blamed continued German militarism for the war and postwar difficulties. Millerand has been criticized for following a confused line. Despite his repeated assertions that the French would act only with the British, he still moved alone. He was, however, caught in an impossible bind. French security required Treaty enforcement and maintenance of the alliance, but, in this situation, the two goals were mutually exclusive.[20]

Far from apologizing for the French actions, Millerand seemingly threatened not to join Lloyd George at San Remo unless the British approved the wording of his statement to the Chamber on 13 April. He charged the Germans with violating those Treaty stipulations which prohibited German fortifications on the Rhine's left bank, within 50 km of the right bank, and the gathering of armed forces or the exercise of maneuvers in that area. If the French accepted the infraction of the Treaty implied by the despatch of troops into the Ruhr, their only remaining weapon would have been destroyed. To Millerand, the French had behaved with great moderation. The Germans had been apprised of the French response to a German occupation. He therefore viewed the Ruhr occupation as an attempt by the Germans to establish military control over the area. His overwhelming concern for French security explains his policy of seeking both German disarmament and Allied collaboration. Destruction of the German fleet had given Britain security; elimination of German militarism would provide a similar guarantee for the French.[21]

Determined to win German compliance with the Treaty and blaming defaults on German faithlessness and not on French unreasonableness, Millerand still considered Franco-German cooperation as essential. As he noted on 26 March, France would collaborate economically with Germany if its neighbor loyally executed the

20. D.B.F.P., IX, pp. 379, 382, Derby to Curzon, 11 April 1920; Suarez, V, p. 78; Trachtenberg, p. 128; A.N., F.M. 54, interviews of Millerand by Agence Reuter, *Morning Post*, 13 April 1920; Trachtenberg, pp. 128–9.

21. J.O., *Chambre*, 13 April 1920; E. Bonnefous, III, p. 141; Wolfers, p. 43; Northedge, pp. 164–5; A.N., F.M. 54, interview of Millerand by the *Daily News*, 16 April 1920.

Treaty. He believed that France was more likely to receive reparations if Germany revived economically. Millerand therefore did not press the Germans on reparations, except for coal, hoping that moderation would encourage the collaboration. His frequent demands for a Ruhr occupation, however, obscured his leniency. Millerand's chief financial advisers, Finance Minister François-Marsal and foreign ministry official Jacques Seydoux, also sought German economic recovery and normal international economic relations. While pressures for closer contacts with Germany partly reflected disillusionment with the British, they also indicated Millerand's belief that France would benefit from its former enemy's economic revival.[22]

Although Millerand, like his predecessor Clemenceau, wanted France to extract the utmost from its victory over Germany, his policies were not the same. In economic affairs, the different orientation was clear from their instructions to French representatives in Germany. In January 1920, Clemenceau urged de Marcilly to survey closely Germany's commercial and industrial development to spot dumping or unacceptable practices. Uninterested in economic collaboration, Clemenceau primarily wanted to receive reparations for France's recovery and to undermine German economic competition. His directives conveyed a pessimistic, mistrustful attitude. The tone of Millerand's instructions to Ambassador-designate Charles Laurent in June was conciliatory, anxious not to augment the economic difficulties of those moderate forces that France supported. As has been stated, to Millerand, Germany's economic revival would benefit France. Proposing that pacts between French and German metallurgic industries be renewed, he wondered whether Russia might be a possible zone for industrial collaboration. Not the first to consider Franco-German economic cooperation, Millerand revived Loucheur's idea of 1919 which Seydoux, the Quai d'Orsay's director of commercial relations, also endorsed. Seydoux viewed collaboration as the best way to control France's former enemy. Millerand's choice of Laurent as ambassador illustrated the importance of economic collaboration. A novice to diplomacy, Laurent was the president of the Union of Metallurgic and Mining Industries with close ties to industrial circles.

22. J.O., *Chambre*, 26 and 27 March 1920; Bariéty, *Relations franco-allemandes*, pp. 65–6; Trachtenberg, pp. 118–21; E. Bonnefous, III, pp. 137–41; McDougall, p. 135; François-Poncet, *Versailles*, p. 84.

Essentially, Millerand hoped a Franco–German *rapprochement* would promote French economic development and make the Treaty more palatable to Germany.[23]

During the spring of 1920, Franco–German economic relations elicited three different responses. The army of the Rhine wanted a Ruhr occupation to secure German coal. French industrialists, supported by the commerce ministry, wanted direct contacts with their German counterparts so that they could purchase coal. Millerand took an intermediate position which advocated adherence to the Treaty along with economic collaboration; France hoped to resume normal Franco–German economic relations and would therefore react favorably to German initiatives. The precondition, however, was Germany's more loyal execution of the Treaty. Furthermore, he argued that Germany's economic revival would promote general prosperity. Convinced that a focus on common economic interests would foster peace, Millerand noted that any economic collaboration required Germany's renunciation of bellicosity. While all three policies sought to secure German coal for France, the means varied.[24]

During 1920, Millerand generally tried to orient French policy in a less anti-German direction and to foster economic solidarity between the two nations. His pressures for Franco–German industrial negotiations foundered, however, on German opposition. He hoped that direct negotiations between French and German industrialists might produce an *entente* that went beyond the problem of prohibitions. From late April until the Spa conference of July, two parallel sets of negotiations were conducted: strictly customs dis-

23. Soutou, 'Relations économiques,' pp. 581–3; Georges Soutou, 'L'impérialisme du pauvre: la politique économique du gouvernement français en Europe centrale et orientale de 1918 à 1929,' *Relations internationales*, No. 7, autumn 1976, p. 228; Artaud, *Dettes interalliées*, p. 295.

24. A.N., F.M. 59, Millerand to the French ministers in London, Rome, Brussels, Berlin, 4 April 1920; J.O., *Chambre*, 13 April 1920; E. Bonnefous, III, pp. 141, 146–7, 151–2, 155; Wolfers, p. 43; A.N., F.M. 54, interview of Millerand by the *Daily News*, 16 April 1920; J.O., *Chambre*, 28 May 1920; Trachtenberg, pp. 139, 152; C.D.A., Foreign Affairs Commission, 10 June 1920, audition of Millerand; *ibid.*, 27 July 1920, Millerand's defense of his Spa policies reported to the commission by Barthou; Raymond Poincaré, *La victoire et la paix* (Paris: H. Daragon, 1921), p. 15; A.N., F.M. 51, notes for Millerand's speech of 20 July 1920; *ibid.*, Millerand to the French ambassadors in London, Rome, Brussels, 20 July 1920, discussing coal agreement and financial details; J.O., *Chambre*, 20 July 1920; Bariéty, *Relations franco-allemandes*, p. 66; Maier, p. 207; McDougall, p. 112; Soutou, 'Une autre politique,' pp. 26–7, 33.

cussions and those between economic experts, both of which focused on the crucial French coal problem. Since coal occupied a central position in the concept of an economic weapon, Millerand wanted French industry to participate in the ownership of German coal firms. Delayed by the French occupation of Frankfurt, negotiations finally opened on 20 May. The absence of major German industrialists, however, indicated lack of German interest in economic collaboration, which was confirmed at Spa by German steel magnate Hugo Stinnes' negative response. Only if German heavy industry had responded positively could Millerand's hopes of a dynamic economic cooperation between the two nations have been fulfilled. France's desperate postwar fuel situation made coal a central issue in Silesia, as in the Ruhr, but direct French *ententes* with Silesian industrialists also met German resistance. Germany insisted that Silesia remain German, but France did not consider its nationality essential to an economic accord. To Millerand, Franco-German economic collaboration, especially among the metallurgic industries, would enable France to use and control Germany's eventual economic resurgence. While the advantages for France were clear, Germany's were less obvious and its opposition to a one-sided collaboration comprehensible.[25]

French policy toward German separatism was linked to security and economic revival. On becoming premier, Millerand instructed the Rhineland occupation army to show discreet sympathy to federalist pressures. A federal structure that undermined Prussian militarism and made Germany less powerful would promote French security. He encouraged federalist movements in Catholic Bavaria and the Rhineland. The Rhineland federalist movement's apparent strength influenced Millerand's decision to occupy Frankfurt, but the coal crisis made him waver between strict Treaty execution and encouragement of regional separatism. His Rhineland policy was also economically motivated: a special relationship between France and the Rhineland might let the former benefit from the area's economic prosperity and increase its political influ-

25. Soutou, 'Une autre politique,' pp. 26–7, 33; Soutou, 'Relations économiques,' pp. 584–5, 588–9, 595; Georges Soutou, 'Les mines de Silésie et la rivalité franco-allemande, 1920–1923,' *Relations internationales*, No. 1, 1974, pp. 136–8; Artaud, *Dettes interalliées*, pp. 289ff.

ence there. By May, however, it was clear that these hopes had little chance of success.[26]

When Germany's domestic problems seemed to favor separatist tendencies in the spring, Millerand sent Emile Dard to Munich as minister plenipotentiary. He did, however, differentiate between separatism, which should not be encouraged, and particularism or federalism, which should. He defended his assignment of a minister to Munich as the continuation of a long French tradition, rather than a desire to promote Bavarian separatism. Denying that France planned to intervene in German domestic affairs by encouraging separatist movements, he argued that it was legitimate to hope for a free development of diverse elements within Germany without the suffocation of Prussian hegemony. During the summer of 1920, Millerand's concentration on the struggle against Bolshevism reinforced this orientation. Activity in Poland, Hungary, Rumania, and the Crimea required calm along the Rhine. A strong Bavaria and Rhineland, friendly to France, would encourage German passivity. France's Bavarian negotiations were, however, no more successful than its Rhineland ones.[27]

The Allies met at San Remo on 18–26 April to discuss the Treaty with Germany as well as other international issues and to dissipate the tension of the preceding weeks. Abandoning his earlier support for France, Italian Premier Nitti adopted Britain's position toward Germany. To French Ambassador to Italy Barrère, the French occupation of the German towns had harmed Franco-Italian relations. The coolness between France on the one hand and Britain and Italy on the other made the San Remo conference, Barrère believed, an unpropitious setting for France. Millerand was surprised when Lloyd George suggested inviting the Germans to San Remo to discuss reparations. To him, the invitation would permit the Germans to expect possible Treaty revisions. Nitti supported British pressures for direct meetings with the Germans rather than

26. McDougall, pp. 97, 110–11, 118–20, 130–3.
27. A.N., F.M. 51, notes for Millerand's speech of 20 July 1920; *ibid.*, Millerand to French ambassadors in London, Rome, Brussels, 20 July 1920; J.O., *Chambre*, 20 July 1920; E. Bonnefous, III, pp. 151–2, 155; Bariéty, *Relations franco-allemandes*, p. 66; Trachtenberg, p. 152; Maier, p. 207; McDougall, p. 112; C.D.A., Foreign Affairs Commission, 27 July 1920, Millerand's explanation of Spa policies reported to commission by Barthou; Soutou, 'Une autre politique,' pp. 28–30; Jules Laroche, *Au Quai d'Orsay avec Briand et Poincaré* (Paris: Hachette, 1957), p. 130.

exchanges of notes and for a total reparations figure. Millerand, whose principal concern was an integral execution of the Treaty without revisions, agreed to meet German governmental representatives only to settle past difficulties. Above all, he insisted that the Allies decide in advance on their demands and sanctions for German defaults. To ask the government to explain its failure to execute the Treaty would allow the Germans to portray their difficult situation in such a way as to elicit compassion for their failures. Only the Reparations Commission, he maintained, had the right to set the total German indemnity or make reparations concessions. Since the commission was not yet ready to set that figure, the Allies could not arbitrarily make a decision which would violate the Treaty. To the French premier, therefore, contact with the Germans offered few advantages and many drawbacks. He risked disrupting the conference by firmly refusing to invite the Germans to San Remo, although, in the interest of Allied relations, he did agree to a future meeting if the Allies first set the conditions. Behind the heated discussion lay a fundamental difference which, Millerand believed, conditioned the contrasting Allied responses. Lloyd George and Nitti basically trusted the Germans, whereas Millerand did not. Until his two preconditions (Allied agreement on demands and sanctions for failures) were met, the French premier refused to meet the Germans. Since the Treaty outlined specific procedures for obtaining what Germany owed, Millerand was determined to abide by it. To Lloyd George, Millerand's conviction of German Treaty violations had led him to jeopardize their alliance. Only if they met with the Germans could they dispel the impression of Allied disunity.[28]

Millerand wanted a final Allied declaration that would reassure public opinion about a common stance toward Germany. He suggested that it deal with two matters vital to world peace: German disarmament and a financial and economic equilibrium. Not planning to annex German territory, the French would officially repudiate territorial ambitions, but the Germans must

28. A.N., F.M. 56, meeting between Millerand, Lloyd George, and Nitti, 18 April 1920, and minutes of conversation between Millerand and Lloyd George, 18 April 1920; *D.B.F.P.*, VIII, pp. 5–20; David Felix, *Walter Rathenau and the Weimar Republic: The Politics of Reparations* (Baltimore: The Johns Hopkins Press, 1971), p. 7; Laroche, *Quai d'Orsay* (Paris: Hachette, 1957), p. 113; Jordan, p. 71; McDougall, p. 133; Trachtenberg, pp. 130–5. Instead of a total figure, Millerand suggested the Avenol plan which proposed German payment of 3 billion gold marks in annuities until the total figure was set.

evacuate the neutral zone more quickly and make amends for the attacks on Allied officers in March. The French would withdraw their troops from the Maingau once German troop levels returned to the figure of the Protocol of 8 August 1919. He held fast to his preconditions for meeting the Germans, which Lloyd George finally accepted on 24 April.[29]

The Allied declaration of 26 April outlined a common policy toward Germany. The Allies rejected Goeppert's request of 20 April for a German army of 200,000 men instead of the 100,000 Treaty figure as long as the Germans violated the Treaty and did not disarm. Germany had failed to destroy war material, reduce troop levels, or provide coal, reparations, or occupation costs. Nor had they explained satisfactorily the attacks on Allied representatives. They had not met their obligation to study reparations so that a total figure could be reached or delinquencies remedied. The Allies unanimously refused to condone persistent Treaty infractions; to secure its execution they were even ready to contemplate occupation of additional German territory. Since a direct exchange of views might permit a better settlement of Treaty-related questions than written communications, they invited the German prime minister to meet Allied leaders. They instructed the Germans to provide the conference with explanations, which, if satisfactory, could pave the way for an investigation of German domestic order and economic well-being.[30] Lloyd George, who persuaded Millerand to accept a conference with the Germans, gave British acquiescence to sanctions if Germany did not execute the Treaty – precisely the tactic that had recently elicited British opposition in the Maingau.

Barrère attributed Lloyd George's reluctant acceptance of the French text of the final declaration to his need to take account of British concern over Franco-British tension. To him, the conference was a well-deserved victory for Millerand that enabled him to establish the bases for a truly national French policy. Poincaré also praised Millerand's decisiveness in recognizing the dangerous drift in Allied relations with Germany. Noting his support from the

---

29. A.N., F.M. 56, minutes of meetings between Millerand and Lloyd George, 18 and 24 April 1920; *D.B.F.P.*, VIII, pp. 222–5, 26 April 1920.

30. A.N., F.M. 54, Allied declaration of San Remo, 26 April 1920; *D.B.F.P.*, VIII, pp. 209–10; Jordan, p. 71; Suarez, V, p. 84; McDougall, p. 112; Lucien Petit, *Histoire des finances extérieures de la France. Le règlement des dettes interalliées (1919–1929)* (Paris: Berger-Levrault, 1932), pp. 31–2.

French public, Poincaré claimed the premier tried to stop that fatal progression, despite pressures from his British counterpart. Only Millerand's firmness had prevented a German invitation to San Remo. Like the British and Italians, however, the Americans also worried that Millerand's 'risky' tactics might push Germany into alignment with the Soviet Union.[31]

Responding to criticism of French concessions at San Remo, Millerand argued that the conference had promoted Allied rapport and settled several problems. To him, its principal achievement was a common Allied policy toward Germany whose basis was the exclusion of all Treaty revision. Before meeting the Germans, the Allies planned to set their demands, particularly for military and reparations questions, and decide on sanctions if Germany defaulted. The San Remo text, by proposing a meeting with the Germans, did not indicate an Allied willingness to revise the Versailles Treaty.[32] While Millerand had not made substantive concessions at San Remo, his relations with the French parliament and public thereafter assumed a defensive tone.

Millerand and Lloyd George met several times during May and June to elaborate an Allied position on reparations and disarmament prior to the Spa conference with the Germans in July. After San Remo, the French and British governments sent Germany a note outlining the Spa conference objectives and requesting proposals for a total debt figure. The first Franco-British conference of Hythe–Folkestone, 15–16 May, postponed the Spa conference until after the German elections. Although Lloyd George wanted the Spa conference to focus on disarmament, the Hythe discussions concentrated on finances. To his pressures for a total reparations figure, Millerand responded that experts should study the question and set a minimum debt that would be compatible with Germany's capacity to pay and acceptable to the Allies. Furthermore, he

31. Poincaré, *Victoire et paix*, pp. 6, 13, 15; Keith Nelson, *Victors Divided. America and the Allies in Germany, 1918–1923* (Berkeley: University of California Press, 1975), p. 142, quoting article in the *New Republic* of 28 April 1920; Camille Barrère, 'La conférence de San Remo,' *Revue des deux mondes*, 1 August 1938, pp. 510–13.

32. A.N., F.M. 54, Millerand's speech to the Chamber, 28 April 1920; J.O., *Chambre*, 28 April 1920; C.D.A., Foreign Affairs Commission, 30 April 1920, audition of Millerand; E. Bonnefous, III, pp. 141–3, 145: France withdrew its troops from the Maingau on 17 May when German troop levels accorded with the 1919 Protocol; Jordan, p. 71; Wolfers, p. 43.

considered British figures too low. The French and British, however, agreed to make Germany responsible for occupation costs, to
insist on rapid payment for war damage, and to elaborate a comprehensive arrangement that would encompass the war's international costs, thereby linking war debts and reparations. Millerand
capitalized on Lloyd George's wish to resolve the reparations issue
by linking it to war debts; he refused to cut German obligations
unless France's debts were also lowered and its reparations priority
recognized. When he steadfastly refused to accept a total reparations figure, the conference ended with both sides dissatisfied.[33]

The generally accepted view that Millerand yielded to Lloyd
George at Hythe on a lump-sum payment is inaccurate; he firmly
opposed the proposed British total of 120 billion French francs and
only agreed to have experts study the question. However, the
decision that the two governments should investigate a total figure,
acceptable to the Allies and reflecting German ability to pay, was a
shift in French reparations policy that reduced the role of the
Reparations Commission. An irritated Poincaré immediately resigned as commission president, arguing that an invitation to the
Germans to discuss their capacity to pay instead of simply demanding total reparation of damages constituted a dangerous innovation. The former president accused the Franco-British conference
of removing its principal function from the Reparations Commission. Clemenceau also criticized Millerand for his alleged concessions at Hythe. Claiming that Lloyd George had easily won Miller-
and over to a lump sum (*forfait*), the former premier termed it the
first abandonment of the Versailles Treaty – a policy that France's

33. A.E., Papiers Barrère, III, pp. 212–13, Millerand to Barrère, 8 May 1920,
hereafter cited as A.E., P.B.; A.E., P.M. 15, Seydoux note on reparations, 15
October 1920; A.N., F.M. 57, minutes of meetings, 15–16 May 1920, between Lloyd
George and Millerand at Hythe; *D.B.F.P.*, VIII, pp. 258–9, 267–72; Suarez, V, p. 84;
Jordan, pp. 116–17; Trachtenberg, pp. 136–8. McDougall, p. 133, reports in-
accurately that Millerand accepted a global sum of 120 milliard payable in
thirty-three annuities in return for immediate German payments. Artaud, *Dettes
interalliées*, p. 290, also notes incorrectly that Millerand accepted a *forfait* at Hythe.
The idea that Millerand accepted the principle of a *forfait* at Hythe has been generally
accepted in the literature on the subject but is inaccurate (see McDougall, Artaud).
The minutes of the meetings do not bear out this assessment. On the contrary, they
show Millerand firmly opposed to the idea. E. Bonnefous, III, p. 144, claims
Millerand's concessions led Poincaré to resign from the Reparations Commission.
Petit, p. 33. Baumont, p. 166, dates Poincaré's resignation 19 May 1920. A. Antonucci,
Le Bilan des réparations et la crise mondiale (Paris: Editions Berger-Levrault, 1935),
p. 32.

negotiators had resolutely opposed at the peace conference.[34]

The Hythe conference was, however, an advance toward Millerand's goals of establishing a priority for reconstruction of the devastated regions and persuading Lloyd George to link explicitly war debts and reparations. The British prime minister, who wanted the French to accept a *forfait*, persuaded Millerand to let experts study a total debt figure in exchange for an international debt settlement. This agreement constituted at least a superficial Franco-British reconciliation. Although the Hythe statement linked credits and debts, its validity depended on American acquiescence, which Wilson refused when he denied the connections between war debts and reparations in October.[35]

Millerand was caught in an awkward position. His allies considered him overly harsh toward Germany, while his compatriots thought him too conciliatory. Socialists and nationalists like Poincaré, Louis Loucheur, and André Tardieu were increasingly critical of insufficient reparations payments. Although Millerand noted that the reconvening of parliament had augmented his domestic problems, he won an overwhelming vote of confidence from the Chamber on 28 May. He did, however, maintain that interpellations on preliminary discussions such as his conference with Lloyd George at Hythe were counterproductive. He stressed that the Allies had not reached any final decisions at Hythe, but had discussed the German Treaty defaults and reparations situation. He noted particularly the Allies' anxiety to resolve the whole issue of debts so that a normal economic life could be resumed.[36]

Millerand and Lloyd George met again at Hythe and Boulogne on 20–22 June, and this time included the new Italian Premier Sforza in some of their discussions. At Boulogne, Millerand sought a common Franco-British stance on all issues and not just German reparations. He and Lloyd George again rejected a figure of 200,000 men for the German army and insisted on the surrender of German weapons, particularly 15,000 cannons, to the Allies for destruction.

---

34. Chastenet, *Poincaré*, p. 227, dates his resignation 18 May 1920; Artaud, *Dettes interalliées*, p. 290; Antonucci, p. 32; Georges Clemenceau, *Grandeurs et misères d'une victoire* (Paris: Librairie Plon, 1930), p. 263.

35. Petit, pp. 32–3; Artaud, *Dettes interalliées*, pp. 277–8, 291; Alfred Sauvy, *Histoire économique de la France entre les deux guerres (1918–1931)* (Paris: Fayard, 1965), p. 175.

36. A.E., P.B., III, p. 215, Millerand to Barrère, 21 May 1920; J.O., *Chambre*, 28 May 1920; E. Bonnefous, III, pp. 146–7; Trachtenberg, p. 139; C.D.A., 10 June 1920, audition of Millerand.

They agreed to hear German reparations proposals at Spa, but planned to present counterproposals. Millerand particularly wanted a common Franco-British policy to counteract the German view of French harshness and British conciliation. The Boulogne conference abandoned a 'fixed sum' in favor of the so-called 'Boulogne scheme' whereby Germany would pay, according to financial capacity, a series of annuities of three billion gold marks for forty-two years beginning in May 1921. Equivalent to a fixed sum of 100 billion gold marks for France, the plan would have given France less than half its original claim. France agreed to accept 35 billion immediately (Millerand's *forfait*) – approximately what John Maynard Keynes had originally proposed in *The Economic Consequences of the Peace*. To liquidate the entire German debt, the Allies proposed international loans. Until Boulogne, Millerand had held steadfastly to the Treaty, but, at this meeting, he reluctantly accepted the forfeit system, so repugnant to French public opinion, in the interest of Allied agreement. While the sums envisaged were still substantial, the system was innovative in shifting reparations matters from the juridical to the economic domain. By considering Germany's capacity to pay, it recognized its inability to repair completely all damage. The division of the German indemnity among the Allies, however, elicited a heated debate. To Millerand, it was repugnant to assign monetary values to the respective sacrifices of states that had fought together. If France received 55 percent of the indemnity, French sufferings would be acknowledged even though its heavy human and material losses would be only partially repaid. Millerand's primary goal of Allied unity was achieved at Boulogne by an agreement on German disarmament and a reparations scheme, but at the cost of some sacrifice of French Treaty rights.[37]

37. A.E., P.B., III, pp. 216–17, Millerand to Barrère, 18 June 1920; A.E., P.M. 15, Seydoux note on reparations, 15 October 1920; Soutou, 'Une autre politique,' p. 26; A.N., F.M. 56, minutes of meeting between Lloyd George and Millerand, 20 June 1920 at Hythe; A.E., P.M. 44, minutes of meetings between Lloyd George and Millerand at Boulogne, 21–22 June 1920; E. Bonnefous, III, p. 148; Trachtenberg, p. 141. McDougall, p. 133, seemingly confused the conference of Hythe of May and the Hythe and Boulogne meetings in June. Laroche, *Quai d'Orsay*, p. 114. Felix, p. 7, notes incorrectly that the Allies agreed to give 52 percent to France and 22 percent to Britain, which did not occur until Brussels; Suarez, V, p. 85, notes incorrectly that Millerand accepted a figure of 120 milliard at Boulogne of which France's share was 66 milliard; Bariéty, *Relations franco-allemandes*, p. 67, comments that Millerand's concessions prompted Poincaré to resign the chairmanship of the Reparations

In Brussels on 2–3 July, the Allies met for a final preparatory conference prior to meeting the Germans at Spa. There they accepted Millerand's suggestion of attributing 52 percent of the German indemnity to France and 22 percent to Britain. Still anxious for a united Allied front toward the Germans, he reiterated that the purpose of Spa was to hear German explanations of Treaty related problems. France, he insisted, vitally needed German coal which still had not arrived. Indeed, he even met secretly with Stinnes who, he hoped, might use his influence to facilitate coal deliveries to the Lorraine steel mills. A tone of Anglo-French recriminations again surfaced just on the eve of meeting the Germans. For Lloyd George, Millerand's stubborn combativeness was difficult to tolerate, whereas the French premier considered his British counterpart deliberately obstructive. Possibly the legacy of wartime camaraderie had enabled him to work better with Clemenceau. Differences in temperament as much as in doctrine may have conditioned their poor relations.[38]

The Allied conference with the Germans at Spa, 5–17 July, was the climax of this diplomatic phase. For the first time, the Germans were able to explain their position as equals. Pleading revolutionary conditions and generalized hardship, they won considerable concessions. The conference first discussed a disarmament schedule, since, as Millerand critically observed on 8 July, nothing had yet been done to limit the German army. The Germans asked for an additional fifteen months; British counterproposals seemed to Millerand too vague. He was convinced that the Germans neither wanted nor intended to apply a treaty that they considered unjust. The French premier acknowledged that the military requirements would have to be postponed, but suggested a precise response

---

Commission in June. Actually, it was the Hythe meeting in May which led to his resignation.

38. *D.B.F.P.*, VIII, pp. 400, 412, 417; E. Bonnefous, III, p. 149; Bariéty, *Relations franco-allemandes*, p. 66; Felix, pp. 7, 63; Laroche, *Quai d'Orsay*, pp. 117–18; Néré, p. 31. A.N. F.M. 69, Millerand to Jacques Bardoux, 24 November 1923, corrects Bardoux's assertion in *Lloyd George et la France* that Millerand reduced the French percentage from 55 to 52 to insure a share for Belgium. Millerand insisted that he had fought for a Belgian share to tighten the Franco-Belgian *entente*. He asserted that all nations' shares were set at Spa, whereas, in fact, the distribution was established at Brussels and confirmed at Spa. Belgium received 8 percent and Italy 10 percent.

should the Germans not meet their commitments, such as a Ruhr occupation. They drafted an Allied protocol that set the following conditions: if the Germans removed arms from the citizen guard and security police, demanded the surrender of all civilian arms, replaced conscription with a long-term army, surrendered excess arms for Allied destruction, enforced the Treaty's naval and aerial clauses, then the Allies would extend the period for the army's reduction to 150,000 to 1 October and 100,000 to 1 January 1921. If prior to those dates, however, Allied control commissions reported German lapses, then the Allies would occupy additional territory, such as the Ruhr. German signature of this protocol on 9 July temporarily resolved the disarmament question. Millerand secured Allied agreement to a possible Ruhr occupation and a precise disarmament schedule, but the Germans won a six-month delay in applying the Treaty's army reduction clauses.[39]

The coal question dominated the conference. The French were particularly worried about expected hardships during the coming winter unless German coal arrived. Reminding German delegate Carl Bergmann on 9 July that the Treaty set a German obligation of approximately 25 million tons of coal per year for France, Millerand complained that it had received only 51 percent of the Reparations Commission's lower figure and less since mid-June. Germany had lowered its exports to the Allies to compensate for Upper Silesian coal sent at their request to Poland, but Millerand denied that Germany had the right so to alter the Reparation Commission's program. Furthermore, he found unconvincing its pleas of coal scarcity, since it continued to export to the Netherlands and Switzerland. The Germans also blamed lower deliveries on the transport strike, but French sailors, Millerand noted, had replaced striking dock workers in Rotterdam. While the Germans had satisfied 79 percent of their own coal requirements, they had only met 59 percent of the French. He threatened economic reprisals unless the situation changed. The Reparations Commission's calculations, he noted, were continually adapted to reflect German domestic conditions, but the Germans had failed to provide even those 'reasonable' amounts. The Allies were convinced that Germany had 'deliberately' disregarded its obligations by supplying the neutrals at the expense of the Allies. Although the

---

39. *D.B.F.P.*, VIII, pp. 473–4, 480–1; E. Bonnefous, III, pp. 149–51; Trachtenberg, p. 147; Maier, p. 203.

Spa conference's objective was Treaty enforcement, Millerand privately informed German Foreign Minister Walter (von) Simons that it could still be applied in a 'liberal spirit.' Denying any secret commitments to the Germans, Millerand suggested a temporary solution whereby the Germans would supply 2 million tons per month for the next six months, leaving future levels for experts to set. German recalcitrance, which Millerand blamed on Stinnes, forced him to retreat to the Reparations Commission's higher figures. To encourage expanded coal production, he proposed that the Allies supply food to the German miners.[40]

Perceptions of Millerand varied. British Ambassador to Germany Viscount d'Abernon, describing him as dignified and moderate, termed Millerand's description of Germany as a necessary and useful member of the European community a turning-point in European history and thought it significant that the German delegation joined the Allies for tea. While Millerand did not use the precise phrase attributed to him, he did argue that Germany's revival was important to world prosperity. On the other hand, German delegate Bergmann portrayed Millerand as emotional, claiming that he attacked Germany's whole attitude on coal because of reduced deliveries from the Ruhr, without considering German economic difficulties or the substantial deliveries already made. To Bergmann, Millerand was unreasonably harsh to expect Germany to grant priority to reparations coal over its own needs.[41]

Millerand demanded Allied firmness because moderation had seemingly yielded little reward. He also feared Allied weakness might create a dangerous situation *vis-à-vis* Germany and Bolshevik Russia. On 14 July, Franco–British tension erupted over coal prices, the world versus the internal German one. Meanwhile, Millerand steadfastly insisted that France receive all coal promised by the Treaty, both compensation for the destroyed mines' production and reparations payments. They finally drafted a protocol by 16 July whereby Germany would send the Allies 2 million tons of coal per month for six months (Millerand's original suggestion) to be credited against the reparations account at the internal German

---

40. A.N., F.M. 58, Millerand's speech to the conference, 9 July 1920; *D.B.F.P.*, VIII, pp. 534–8, 566–9, 571, 577, 580–1. Soutou, 'Relations économiques,' p. 589, notes Stinnes' negative attitude.
41. Felix, p. 63; Viscount d'Abernon, *Diary of an Ambassador* (New York: Doubleday, Doran & Co., Inc., 1929), I, p. 69; Carl Bergmann, *The History of Reparations* (Boston: Houghton Mifflin Co., 1927), p. 40.

price plus a premium of 5 gold marks per ton payable in cash and applicable for food purchases for miners. The difference between the German and world prices represented an Allied loan that Germany was expected to repay but never did. If by 15 November the Germans were in arrears, additional territory, such as the Ruhr, might be occupied. Millerand and Lloyd George particularly blamed Stinnes for German resistance to Allied demands and the difficult negotiations that resulted. Millerand, however, was pleased that the German delegation abandoned Stinnes' position. To him, a possible Ruhr occupation was decisive in securing a German signature to the Spa protocols. Millerand indeed made substantial concessions: the coal protocol eliminated the competition between German and British coal, but the French received less coal at a higher price. Lloyd George persuaded Millerand to reduce Allied demands from 2.4 to 2 million tons per month. Millerand's 'capital concession' of inscribing German coal on the reparations account at the internal price was the condition for winning British agreement to an eventual occupation.[42]

Although the Spa coal settlement temporarily eased international pressures, the French strongly criticized Millerand's commitments. The public and parliament particularly disliked giving money to Germany. Spa was seen as a defeat for French coal policy and a victory for Britain by eliminating competition from German coal. As the premier later commented, his critics faulted him for letting the British win out on higher prices for German coal, but they ignored the counterpart of support for sanctions for German defaults. Probably Millerand overrated the importance of a possible Ruhr occupation as a penalty for German disarmament and reparations defaults, but, considering British hostility after the Maingau occupation in April, it is not surprising that he viewed British theoretical acquiescence as significant.[43]

42. *D.B.F.P.*, VIII, pp. 582–4, 608, 643–4; Trachtenberg, p. 151; Soutou, 'Relations économiques,' pp. 590–4. Recouly, 'Une visite,' p. 226, describes a lunch on 14 July during the Spa conference attended, among others, by Foch, Weygand, François-Marsal, Le Troquer, and Berthelot, as well as Millerand. Recouly briefly noted the common feeling that Millerand, who had strongly defended French interests, finally compromised with the British to avert a breach in relations. His critics failed to recognize Lloyd George's dominant position at that time; Trachtenberg, pp. 149–52; Bariéty, *Relations franco-allemandes*, p. 66; Maier, pp. 204–7; McDougall, p. 112; Laroche, *Quai d'Orsay*, pp. 121–2; Jordan, p. 71; Soutou, 'Relations économiques,' p. 595.
43. Millerand, 'Souvenirs,' pp. 98bis–99; Felix, pp. 73, 120; Trachtenberg, p. 152; Soutou, 'Relations économiques,' pp. 590–4; Soutou, 'Mines de Silésie,' p. 137.

The premier defended his actions at Spa on 20 July. He stressed that his primary goal had been to protect France's interests by having Germany execute the Treaty. With disarmament a priority, he described the protocol of 9 July as a reasonable solution to current problems. Furthermore, the settlement of the shares which each nation would receive of German reparations had eased inter-Allied relations. General interest dictated that they set German annuities and a global figure for German obligations. German coal defaults were a particularly worrisome issue in view of French needs for the coming winter. Millerand, who optimistically claimed that reparations promises would finally become reality, maintained that the final arrangement would give France double the coal it had thus far received. Called overly sanguine by Socialists and dissatisfied nationalists like Poincaré and Tardieu, Millerand still won a strong parliamentary vote of confidence.[44]

Millerand's victory was, however, short-lived. On 30 and 31 July, he again defended the Spa protocols to the foreign affairs and finance commissions of the Chamber and Senate, which disliked advancing money to feed German miners extracting coal for France. Unless the Chamber ratified the protocols, Millerand feared France would not receive its coal. The Spa agreement would provide 80 percent of French coal requirements at less than one-fifth the current price, Millerand argued, but the Allies faced the problem of feeding the miners. His choice of an international loan proportional to coal deliveries maintained a German financial subordination to the Allies. An arrangement of 27 July regularized payments under Reparations Commission supervision and set proportionate shares of the advances whereby France's contribution of 61 percent would be repaid with 6 percent interest by 1 May 1921. If France rejected the financial arrangement, it would lose the coal agreement that obliged Germany to send the Allies 2 million tons per month and be left with the Treaty commitments and German defaults of the preceding six months. The Spa protocols, he stressed, did not alter Germany's total obligations under the Versailles Treaty or under-

Marcellin, *Politique*, 3, p. 210, describes Millerand as a diplomat '*à courtes vues*' who grasped temporary benefits, unaware of sacrificing fundamental gains. Although he considered the Versailles Treaty and subsequent accords essential to European peace, he did not realize that those accords (such as Spa) seriously undermined the Treaty. Nor did he recognize that British policy sought French concessions for Germany's benefit.

44. See above, note 27.

mine the role of the Reparations Commission. They were, rather, a temporary *modus vivendi*. Although he was determined to maintain the Treaty, he hoped to interpret it as liberally and generously as Allied needs permitted so that they might receive a reasonable sum from Germany in reparations.[45]

Millerand again won parliamentary ratification, but did not eliminate growing uneasiness. Perhaps his achievements were realistic in the context of 1920, but difficult negotiations were required to preserve an ever-less satisfactory situation for France. Within six months of the Treaty's application, serious defaults existed. Germany's bargaining position *vis-à-vis* the Allies had strengthened, while the Franco-British alliance showed signs of severe stress.

45. J.O., *Chambre*, 30 July 1920; J.O. *Sénat*, 31 July 1920; E. Bonnefous, III, pp. 156–7; *Sénat*, Foreign Affairs Commission, 31 July 1920.

10
'Cordon Sanitaire' and Aid for 'An Especially Dear Ally': Policy Toward Russia and Eastern Europe

Millerand's policy toward Eastern Europe was characterized by hostility toward Bolshevik Russia and sympathy for Poland and the other small nations. To term his stance an anti-Bolshevik crusade may be too dramatic, since he did little actually to overthrow the Russian government, but he clearly wanted minimal contacts between it and the West. He refused to re-open diplomatic relations until the Russians recognized tsarist obligations and ceased their propaganda for an international proletarian revolution. He was prepared to consider commercial exchanges, but was less interested than were the British. His ministry has been described as a break with Clemenceau's policy. In January 1920, the former premier was prepared to open negotiations with the Bolshevik government, while Millerand was more responsive to Marshal Foch's anti-Bolshevik plans. Millerand's arrival in power did not, however, reflect a reversal of French policy. He, like Clemenceau, wanted to contain Bolshevism by strengthening the border states but seemed more willing to help anti-Bolshevik groups within Russia like the Volunteer Army in the Don region.

French domestic considerations may have conditioned Millerand's greater support for non-Bolshevik forces; as a former socialist, he had to prove his opposition to Bolshevism. His ministry's conservative character may also have influenced him, since its large business supporters expected an uncompromising policy toward communism in France and Europe generally. The new secretary-general at the Quai d'Orsay, Millerand's old school friend Maurice Paléologue, could have changed the emphasis. This former French ambassador to Russia, who became Millerand's chief foreign policy adviser, was considered intensely anti-Bolshevik.[1]

This change in orientation prompted Millerand's support for Wrangel, Denikin, and Poland's anti-Bolshevik struggle. Had Clemenceau remained in office throughout 1920, it is impossible to predict what his policy would have been. He might not have recognized Wrangel's government or sent a military mission to Warsaw, as Millerand did. Toward Franco-Russian economic relations, however, Millerand followed his predecessor. It is not accurate that Millerand steadfastly denied that the economic contacts would benefit France. He only gradually adopted that line toward the end of his premiership. He was, however, always suspicious of Bolshevik propaganda and determined to bar it from France.[2]

Initially, Millerand tried to slow down efforts to re-open contacts with Russia. In mid-January, Clemenceau apparently agreed to adopt a conciliatory position by lifting the blockade as a first step toward renewing diplomatic relations. Millerand, however, preferred to replace the blockade with a gold embargo so that Russia could not use gold to pay for foreign purchases. Arguing that this specie belonged to private individuals or guaranteed Russia's debt, Millerand irritated the British by prolonging the blockade with an embargo. He instructed French agents not to support British moves for peace with the Soviet Union or for revived commercial relations. He backed Foch's and Weygand's plan of 14 January for a Polish advance into Russia to overthrow the Bolshevik regime. On 5 February, he rejected Lloyd George's suggestion of a Polish–Soviet peace.[3]

In early February, Millerand explained his government's policy toward Russia and Eastern Europe to the Chamber of Deputies. France's guiding principle was the remembrance of Russia's aid in 1914 and its wartime sacrifices and the hope that it would return to the community of nations. Until that time, he urged the application of a *cordon sanitaire*. France would not, he insisted, restore diplomatic relations with a state that rejected basic international law, but

---

1. Carroll, *Soviet Communism*, p. 72; John Bradley, *Allied Intervention in Russia* (London: Weidenfeld & Nicolson, 1968), pp. 165–8; Andrew and Kanya-Forstner, p. 213. Although Berthelot soon won Millerand's confidence to retain his influence on foreign policy, he did not replace Paléologue until Millerand became President in September 1920. Nonetheless, Berthelot, who has been described as Millerand's second-in-command, came to supplant Paléologue during Millerand's premiership.

2. Watson, p. 379; Marcellin, *Politique*, 3, p. 210; Wandycz, p. 141.

3. Bradley, p. 173; Hogenhuis, pp. 173–5; Carroll, *Soviet Communism*, pp. 43–4.

it might revive economic contacts through Russian cooperatives. Economic exchanges, however, created problems of transportation and security; Allied exports must not help the Bolshevik government. He noted the Supreme Council's decision to withhold military support from all White Russian forces because of their weak position. He nonetheless encouraged Denikin and the Volunteers, despite their setbacks. To France, however, Poland was 'an especially dear ally' that required all possible assistance, as did Rumania. Asked why France had excommunicated a revolutionary government, Millerand answered that the Third Republic incarnated the French Revolution's Declaration of the Rights of Man and Citizen, and not its Terror. The Russian movement, founded in blood, was a hateful class dictatorship. Furthermore, the Soviet government, seeking to spread its views abroad, was a menace to civilization. Despite the Russian threat, however, France refused to intervene in any nation's domestic politics. While determined to prevent the spread of Russian propaganda, France did not believe it could dictate domestic policy to the Russian government.[4]

Millerand's policy toward Russia seemingly differed from Lloyd George's in its sympathy for anti-Bolshevik forces, but Franco-British differences were more apparent than real. Millerand's strong statements were probably designed for internal consumption. As the Volunteers soon discovered, no concrete assistance was provided. The French, who froze Russian funds in France, kept the Volunteers from using them to buy weapons. Volunteer plenipotentiary in Paris Sazonov's concern that Millerand would follow Lloyd George's Russian policy proved unfounded. If he had recognized the Bolshevik regime, Millerand would have been vulnerable to charges of pro-communism that would have doomed his premiership. Indeed, France's reluctance to re-open trade illustrated its stiffer attitude in the Supreme Economic Council.[5]

When he returned from London after the conference of 12–13 February, Millerand told the French parliament that Russo-European contacts would probably be revived through the in-

---

4. C.D.A., Foreign Affairs Commission, 4 February 1920, audition of Millerand; A.N., F.M. 51, notes for Millerand's speech of 6 February 1920; J.O., *Chambre*, 6 February 1920; also in A.N., F.M. 52; E. Bonnefous, III, pp. 127–31; Wandycz, p. 141; Cornilleau, *Bloc national*, p. 77; A.E., P.M. 95, Millerand's statement on French foreign policy, undated, but prior to March 1920; Hogenhuis, p. 172; Carroll, *Soviet Communism*, p. 44; Bradley, p. 168.

5. Bradley, p. 169.

termediary of Russian cooperatives. Given Russian instability, he refused to alter official French policy. He even hoped that the apparent victory of Denikin's army might lead to a collapse of Bolshevik forces. In the meantime, France faced a government that used its agents to foment disorder abroad and spread its revolutionary doctrines. Although he was anxious about a possible Russo-Polish peace, he did not want to encourage anti-Bolshevik behavior by the Poles. Urging Poland to follow a non-aggressive policy, Millerand promised that France would help it to repel a Russian attack. France's interventionist policy was simply preventive, he argued, designed to forestall a Bolshevik attack on Eastern Europe. While France was ready to aid Poland, Rumania, the Baltic states, or the Volunteers, Britain preferred a passive alliance and eventual peace with the Russians. Britain's wish for commercial exchanges with Russia, which ran counter to French anti-Bolshevism, also jeopardized the Franco-British *rapprochement.*[6]

Allied policy toward the East dominated the inter-Allied conference in London of 23–25 February. Praising the Supreme Council's decision not to renew diplomatic ties with Soviet Russia, Millerand urged his allies to resist Italian pressures to change it. Since Russia represented instability, he considered it irrational to expect more moderate behavior if the Bolshevik government signed a peace with the Allies. A change in Allied policy would, he argued, simply bolster the power and prestige of the current government at the expense of the West. To the French premier, recognition of the regime would threaten Western civilization, since the Bolsheviks wanted to institute a dictatorship of the proletariat in all nations. He managed to persuade his colleagues to endorse a stronger statement against official recognition. Although French businessmen wanted peace, they had little effect on official policy in this instance. Millerand merely agreed to consider commercial exchanges after a technical commission of the International Labor Bureau had investigated Russian economic conditions. He was also prepared to negotiate particular problems with the Russians, such as the repatriation of Frenchmen detained in Russia. To this end, he authorized the French chargé in Copenhagen to negotiate with Litvinov.[7]

6. C.D.A., Foreign Affairs Commission, 20 February 1920; *Sénat,* Foreign Affairs Commission, 19 February 1920; Bradley, p. 173; Artaud, *Dettes interalliées,* pp. 279–80.

7. *D.B.F.P.,* VII, pp. 197–209; A.N., F.M. 64, Millerand to the French minister

By early March, Millerand had delineated the French government's position toward the Bolsheviks which he subsequently altered little. France adopted a policy of containment – it refused to establish diplomatic relations with the Soviet Union until it accepted the principle of national sovereignty, even though it agreed not to intervene in Russian domestic affairs. A Russian nation with certain rights apart from the Soviet government existed in French eyes. Indeed, France had recognized certain *de facto* states on Russia's borders. They decided to send a League commission of inquiry to Russia to secure authoritative but impartial information on local conditions. To enable Western Europe to exchange manufactured goods for Russian raw materials, France was ready to open economic contacts via Russian cooperatives. There was, however, no question of accepting the wealth of the Russian state. To Russia's neighbors, the Allies agreed to counsel against an aggressive policy, but to promise assistance against a Russian attack. Although the Franco-British conference of late February had ended on a note of concord, Millerand feared the Soviet problem would endanger the *entente*. It was increasingly clear that financial rather than ideological concerns guided Millerand's policy toward the Bolshevik regime. To him, the indispensable precondition for economic negotiations became Russia's acceptance of the private and governmental debts of the tsarist regime, so that French firms with investments in Russia could be indemnified.[8]

Millerand considered Poland's territorial integrity essential to a definitive peace. Like Clemenceau, he supported cooperation between Poland and Czechoslovakia, even if Poland had to relinquish claims to Teschen. A Polish–Czech territorial dispute would undermine East European stability to the benefit of Germany and Russia. France's sentimental attachment to the Poles undoubtedly increased tension with the British. To France, it would be dishonorable to re-bury Poland; from Protestant England, Catholic Poland elicited

in Copenhagen, 11 March 1920; Carroll, *Soviet Communism*, p. 45.

    8. A.E., P.M. 69, Millerand to the French ambassadors, 1 March 1920; Richard H. Ullman, *Anglo-Soviet Relations, 1917–1921*, vol. 3, *The Anglo-Soviet Accord* (Princeton: Princeton University Press, 1972), pp. 29–30; C.D.A., Foreign Affairs Commission, 4 March 1920, audition of Millerand; Artaud, *Dettes interalliées*, pp. 279–80; Hogenhuis, pp. 175–6; J.O., *Chambre*, 26 March 1920; also in A.N., F.M. 52; E. Bonnefous, III, pp. 137–41; Hogenhuis, p. 173; Carroll, *Soviet Communism*, p. 46.

only lukewarm support. Although Millerand warned Polish Minister in Paris Count Maurycy Zamoyski to view Soviet promises skeptically and promised French aid against Russian aggression, the Allied Council only agreed to help Poland if it was attacked within its frontiers. Although Foch favored Polish offensive plans, no evidence exists of Millerand's or the Council's support for a Polish attack on Russia. During the spring, Millerand became increasingly concerned about Polish expansionism. On 10 March, he informed Warsaw that the Great Powers would set Poland's eastern frontiers.[9] Not until Russia seemed likely to defeat Poland in the summer did the French premier alter his verbal reassurances to concrete actions.

In early March, Millerand confidently predicted considerable French influence over the new Polish nation to French Minister to Poland, de Panafieu. Given its pivotal geographical position as a neighbor of Germany and Russia, Poland was vulnerable to German propaganda against Allied influence in Poland and to Russian military moves; its political inexperience invited outside intervention. To Millerand, the creation of a political, economic and moral climate favorable to France was vital. He was convinced that Poland would benefit if a final peace set its eastern boundaries. The Allies were prepared to help Poland repel a Bolshevik attack, but counselled it to restrain its territorial ambitions; the frontiers of 1772 were not only unrealistic but violated the Treaty's principle of national self-determination. Lithuanian pressures for autonomy proved the changes in the population's character since the first partition. Its problems over Teschen should not preclude cordial Polish–Czech relations or invite a Hungarian–Polish conspiracy against Czechoslovakia. Millerand recognized that the nation's spiritual unity could revive only gradually after a hundred and fifty years of division. Since Poland's foreign policy would be vulnerable to hidden pressures, France, because of historic ties and support for Polish independence, seemed to him to be its logical adviser.[10]

Economic collaboration was often an ingredient of French policy in 1920. France seemingly hoped that an economic restructuring of Central and Eastern Europe might promote reconstruction. While

---

    9. Millerand, 'Souvenirs,' p. 98; Wandycz, pp. 136–8, 141–3, 147.
    10. A.E., z Europe 1918–1929, ss Poland 130, Millerand to de Panafieu, 4 March 1920.

Berthelot supported aid only to France's allies, Millerand wanted some economic cooperation with the Austro-Hungarian successor states. The premier argued that economic assistance to Austria would foster its economic recovery so that it could repay its debts to France. International prosperity, on which France's economic revival depended, was more conducive to peace than economic hardship.[11] The French government, which favored economic penetration into Eastern Europe, did not, however, convince major bankers and industrialists. Without the necessary means, French economic expansion became an *impérialisme du pauvre*. At its height in early 1920, France's economic offensive did not stem simply from Millerand's personal ties to de Wendel and Schneider, but major industrialists often attended Quai d'Orsay meetings and participated in foreign policy decisions. Despite diverse French investments in Eastern Europe, commercial exchanges did not fulfill initial hopes. Contradictory political and economic objectives, except in Czechoslovakia, explained the hesitant economic policy toward Eastern Europe.

Millerand and Paléologue favored a revision of Hungary's frontiers at the expense of Czechoslovakia and Rumania. Semi-official Franco-Hungarian negotiations during the spring of 1920 investigated border changes in exchange for granting France financial and industrial influence in Hungarian railroads and the General Credit Bank. Although Millerand and Paléologue were ready to accept frontier changes that would create ethnic or economic injustices, they yielded when Czech Foreign Minister Eduard Benes protested. There were also reasonable grounds for the Quai d'Orsay's suspicion that the Hungarian government was in secret contact with German military milieus. As a result, French diplomats withdrew from the negotiations. In July, Millerand admitted the time was not propitious to encourage Hungary to re-arm to aid Poland. Anxiety about Hungary's intentions, however, may have influenced the Little Entente's formation. Since Paléologue was blamed for several risky endeavors, notably the Hungarian, his replacement by Berthelot in September 1920 has been seen as a new

11. J.O., *Sénat*, 30 June 1920. M. Adam, 'Confédération danubienne ou petit entente,' *Acta Historica*, XXV, 1979, pp. 67–8, comments that Millerand and Paléologue favored an economically-focused Danubian Confederation led by Hungary. They preferred the more conservative, counter-revolutionary Hungary with its better strategic site for aiding Poland to an anarchic Austria currently under leftist control.

orientation.[12] Millerand's readiness to abandon the principle of national self-determination for economic advantages illustrated the priority he assigned to national interests over ideological commitments.

The possibility of resuming commercial relations with Russia led Millerand to define the conditions for such trade. He refused to remove all commercial restrictions or let the Soviet Union pay for foreign imports with illegal securities. His concern about the Soviet government's acknowledgement of the tsarist debt and Russia's domestic chaos made him wary about commercial negotiations. In view of Russia's devastated transportation network and general disarray, he questioned its ability to export; its immense needs would probably drain world resources and increase current hardship. Its lack of other assets might, Millerand feared, lead Russia to grant monopolies on its public domain. That domain, however, represented the common pledge of those state creditors, notably subscribers to prewar loans, whose property had been nationalized without indemnity. Until that pledge was guaranteed, Millerand refused to lift commercial restrictions. He considered it paradoxical to sign new agreements with a government that ignored its former obligations. He suggested ways for Russia to fulfill the obligations it had inherited from the former regime.[13]

Despite his firm stance on Russia's debt, Millerand still hesitated to break with Lloyd George over Russia. At San Remo, therefore, he reluctantly encouraged the British prime minister to open negotiations with a Soviet trade delegation. His cautious endorsement of trade negotiations did not, however, imply acceptance of the Soviet regime to which he still refused official recognition. He also insisted

12. Hogenhuis, pp. 161–3; Carroll, *Soviet Communism*, pp. 72, 101, 107; Pierre Renouvin, *Histoire des relations internationales*, VII, *Les Crises du XXe siècle, I, de 1914 à 1929* (Paris: Librairie Hachette, 1957), pp. 281–2; Duroselle, *Histoire diplomatique*, p. 30; Soutou, 'L'impérialisme,' pp. 223, 236. Adam, pp. 71–6, 111: the negotiations of a Franco-Hungarian economic agreement came to nothing because France would not revise the Treaty which was the basis for Hungary's interest in a *rapprochement*. Millerand preferred a large Danubian confederation to the Little Entente because the latter divided victors and vanquished and pushed Austria and Hungary toward Germany.

13. *Papers Relating to the Foreign Relations of the United States* (Washington, D.C.: United States Government Printing Office, 1936), 1920, III, pp. 709–10, note from Millerand of 9 April 1920, transmitted by American Ambassador Wallace to the secretary of state, hereafter cited as *Foreign Relations*.

that if a fact-finding labor delegation visited Russia, it should do so without direct Allied–Soviet negotiations. The delegation could receive visas for Estonia and Finland, but not official permits to enter Russia. Meanwhile, he remained interested in anti-Bolshevik forces like the Volunteers, who might provide a useful link in his military, and eventually political, plans for a *cordon sanitaire*. Paléologue's indication on 7 May that the French might aid Wrangel in the Crimea also illustrated Millerand's hope for an eventual Soviet collapse.[14]

The Krasin delegation's arrival in London finally forced a French decision on commercial relations with Russia. On 1 June, Millerand defined the principles which should guide the Allies in their conversations with the Russians. In the interest of restoring Europe to a condition of economic normalcy, France was ready to renew private commercial relations with Russia if that nation demonstrated it had the facilities to carry on such exchanges. Millerand refused, however, to sign any agreements equivalent to treaties of commerce that implied recognition of the Bolshevik regime. The Soviet government must not dispose of Russia's wealth, which constituted its creditors' stake. He threatened therefore to confiscate or immobilize any gold exports. Above all, he argued, commercial credits must not be diverted to political ends; Soviet agents should not use their economic function to conceal the political dissemination of dangerous propaganda. Commercial transactions should be restricted to individuals, with no direct contracts signed with a government that the Allies had not recognized. Given the importance of restoring economic life, revival of traffic could not be subordinated to Russia's recognition of its debts. The French government did, however, investigate ways of regularizing the debt so that precise proposals would be ready once a regular Russian government existed that acknowledged its international commitments.[15]

During the following week, Millerand became increasingly cautious about commercial negotiations with Russia and added conditions to his acquiescence. France, he stressed, was not at war with Russia, nor did its commercial interdictions constitute a blockade.

14. A.N., F.M. 56, minutes of the meeting between Lloyd George and Millerand, 18 April 1920; *D.B.F.P.*, VIII, pp. 27–8, 172–7; Suarez, V, p. 79; Carroll, *Soviet Communism*, pp. 46, 68, 76; Bradley, p. 177.
15. A.E., P.M. 69, Millerand to the French ambassadors in London, Washington, Rome *et al.*, 1 June 1920.

The French government, which did not oppose individual dealings or private commercial correspondence with normal codes, was ready to discuss purely commercial matters with Russian agents. To Millerand, it seemed expedient to recognize the *de facto* existence of a private technical Russian agency rather than a representative of the Soviet government. He demanded that barter arrangements rather than gold be used to pay for merchandise. Export prohibitions were removed, except for war contraband, and Allied ports were opened to Russian ships. On 10 June, however, Millerand commented that he had instructed the French ambassador to London not to attend the British discussions with Krasin.[16] The premier evidently considered Krasin to be an official Soviet representative and not the private negotiator he had accepted. It is unclear whether Millerand altered his position, as the British charged, or whether the British assumed greater willingness to negotiate with the Russians than Millerand had actually demonstrated.

Serious differences over Eastern Europe surfaced between Millerand and Lloyd George at the Hythe–Boulogne meetings of 20–22 June. Millerand continued to oppose strongly political relations with the Soviet government before it accepted the preceding government's commitments, notably the tsarist debt to France. Although he was ready to consider commercial exchanges, he was determined to prevent the spread of Soviet propaganda, either through aggression in Persia or semi-pacific tactics, like tracts and money in France.[17]

By June, France and Britain were moving in different directions on East European policy. To the French premier, Lloyd George's suggestion that cabinet ministers negotiate with Krasin transformed the commercial conversations he had authorized in San Remo into political discussions. While he was ready to send technical experts to London and trade and manufacturing representatives to Russia, he resolutely rejected any political negotiations with the Soviet government until it accepted tsarist debts. Lloyd George, however, was willing to hold specific negotiations with a Russian government that possessed *de facto* control over the nation. The

---

16. A.E., P.M. 69, Millerand to French ambassador in London, 7 June 1920; C.D.A., Foreign Affairs Commission, 10 June 1920, audition of Millerand.

17. A.N., F.M. 56, minutes of meeting between Lloyd George and Millerand at Hythe, 20 June 1920; A.E., P.M. 44, minutes of meetings between Lloyd George and Millerand at Boulogne, 21–22 June 1920; E. Bonnefous, III, p. 148.

crux of the difference lay in their evaluation of Krasin's mission. Was it a purely technical delegation or a disguised official group? Simultaneously, Millerand urged Allied support for White Russian General Wrangel, whom he considered important for negotiations with the Reds and for the Polish struggle. While the British wanted peace with the Bolshevik government, the French sought not only to halt the Polish retreat but even to launch an offensive that would defeat the Red Army.[18]

Anti-Bolshevism characterized Millerand's policy toward Russia and Poland during the summer of 1920. At Spa, he and Lloyd George briefly discussed East European affairs. Denying that the reestablishment of political relations with the Soviet government was inevitable, Millerand again insisted that France could not deal with the Bolsheviks until they acted like a government, accepted the previous regime's commitments, and ceased revolutionary propaganda. Although the French clearly disliked the idea of contact with Soviet representatives, they did not want to alienate the British. By July, the Polish situation had become particularly pressing. Anxiety for British support on disarmament and reparations led the French to adopt a relatively passive position toward Poland at Spa even though the Polish prime minister pleaded for Allied aid. Millerand agreed with Foch that the French could not send in troops, a stance that Lloyd George also took after initially contemplating the despatch of British forces. In principle, the Allies agreed to assist Poland. The British wanted a Polish–Russian conference in London to draft an armistice, whereas Millerand encouraged Polish resistance. To pacify the British, the French reluctantly agreed to a conference, but reserved the right to help Poland if the Russians rejected an armistice. Millerand was convinced that the British would provide military assistance to Poland if a peaceful solution miscarried. Although he never permitted a debate on France's policy toward the Russo-Polish conflict in the Chamber, Millerand clearly sided with Poland from the outset.[19]

18. Ullman, pp. 111–13; Bradley, p. 178.
19. A.N., F.M. 51, notes for Millerand's speech of 20 July 1920; J.O., *Chambre*, 20 and 24 July 1920; E. Bonnefous, III, pp. 151–2, 155; *D.B.F.P.*, VIII, pp. 502–6, 518, 530; Laroche, *Quai d'Orsay*, pp. 123–7; Trachtenberg, p. 153; Wandycz, pp. 154–6; Carroll, *Soviet Communism*, pp. 100, 128; Néré, p. 32; Ullman, pp. 142, 145, 149, 152, 159.

Meanwhile, Millerand and Lloyd George agreed to despatch an Extraordinary Allied mission to Poland whose French contingent included General Maxime Weygand, Ambassador to Washington Jules Jusserand, Millerand's assistant Vignon, as well as munitions and war materials. Viscount d'Abernon, a British member of the mission, commented on his reception by Millerand in Paris and the premier's wholehearted support for the mission. Weygand later noted that Millerand had telephoned on 21 July about Franco-British plans for an Allied mission to Warsaw. He described the head of the French delegation, Jusserand, as irritated at the interruption to his vacation in the Jura and always bad-tempered. The mission, which arrived in Warsaw on 24 July, sought information about Poland's military and political situation in the hopes of ending the hostilities.[20]

As the Red Army approached Warsaw in late July, the Russo-Polish conflict assumed an urgency that temporarily distracted attention from Germany. Describing the Polish question as the most 'urgent,' Millerand noted the compromise which had been elaborated on the relationship between Poland and the free city of Danzig. Considering the desperate Polish situation, he was prepared to accept an armistice based on ethnographic frontiers, but wanted the Allies to support Poland if the Red Army disregarded those boundaries. He characterized the objective of the Allied mission as full support for Poland and information about its needs. He denied, however, that he had made any commitments to Poland at Spa, except to back the Anglo-French mission. He also commented on Foch's opposition to an Allied military involvement.[21]

Poland's precarious situation led Millerand and Lloyd George to elaborate a common policy at Boulogne on 27–28 July. Again, contrasting French and British views provoked tension, although Millerand won greater flexibility about Wrangel and rigidity toward the Soviet government from the British prime minister. The Russians wanted the Allies to back a conference that would compel the Poles to accept an armistice. The British were receptive; Millerand reacted negatively. The French premier argued that the

20. Ullman, p. 161; Edgar Vincent, Viscount d'Abernon, *The Eighteenth Decisive Battle of the World. Warsaw, 1920* (Westport, Conn.: Hyperion Press, Inc., 1977), p. 17; Maxime Weygand, *Mémoires* (Paris: Flammarion, 1957), II, pp. 93–7.
    21. See above, note 19; Carroll, *Soviet Communism*, pp. 110, 120; C.D.A., Foreign Affairs Commission, 27 July 1920, Barthou's report of Millerand's responses to Commission questions.

conference would sacrifice Poland, increase Soviet prestige, and further endanger all nations by exposing them to Bolshevik propaganda. He was also increasingly worried about a Russo-German understanding. To him, the Soviet objective of disseminating propaganda made Russia a formidable internal and external threat. Millerand refused to participate in a conference with the Russians before they freed all Entente prisoners, accepted the previous government's obligations, and called a constituent assembly, including General Wrangel, to draft a constitution. Since such conditions were clearly unacceptable to the Russians, French participation in any talks was precluded.[22]

Millerand was also troubled by reports that the United States as well as Britain might abandon the Allied stand on commercial restrictions toward Russia. Since Russia was unable to export, he feared its public domain would be used to pay for necessary imports. As a general guarantee for its foreign creditors, that stake (*gage*) required Allied protection before commercial exchanges were revived. Millerand maintained that France and the United States both viewed the Soviet leadership as representative of the wishes of a small minority and not the majority. The current government had denied those fundamental conventions and principles that guided relations between nations or individuals; it signed agreements without planning to observe them and repudiated ones concluded by non-Bolshevik governments. To the French government, relations were impossible with a regime that conspired against French institutions, whose diplomats promoted revolution and signed contracts that they did not plan to observe. France's anxiety for a Polish–Russian armistice did not outweigh its determination to insure that the negotiations did not result in Russia's recognition or Poland's dismemberment.[23]

The Russo-Polish situation dominated the third conference at Hythe of 8–9 August. Although Millerand later insisted that a close *entente* with the British was the best guarantee of European order, tension again characterized the meeting. Lloyd George still sup-

22. *D.B.F.P.*, VIII, pp. 653, 655–6, 658, 2nd conference of Boulogne, 27–28 July 1920; E. Bonnefous, III, p. 157; Wandycz, p. 166; Ullman, pp. 189–90. Hogenhuis, p. 274, notes that Millerand's basic policy was respect for Russia's creditors. Bradley, p. 179; Carroll, *Soviet Communism*, pp. 126–8.
23. A.E., P.M. 69, Millerand to French ambassadors in Rome, London, Washington, 8 August 1920; *Foreign Relations*, 1920, III, pp. 469–70, French chargé to secretary of state, 14 August 1920, transmitting statement from Millerand.

ported a conference with the Russians, while Millerand opposed it and was irritated that Britain had not expelled Krasin and Kamenev from London. To Millerand, a Russian conquest of Poland would be an unmitigated disaster for the postwar settlement. He therefore faulted the British for negotiating directly with the Russians instead of joining the French in guaranteeing Polish independence. Convinced that the untrustworthy Soviet government would use negotiations to win Allied recognition of its military gains and to establish Bolshevik propaganda agents in Allied capitals, he argued that they faced a 'redoubtable danger.' Since Poland was created in part as a buffer between Russia and Germany, the latter must not be able to exploit Poland's danger to reclaim Posen and Upper Silesia. Millerand suggested an Allied threat of reprisals on the Rhine's right bank if Germany assisted Russia. He admitted that French public opinion would oppose the despatch of troops to Poland, but still rejected Britain's demand for negotiations with the Russians. The Allies had, he insisted, to adopt a policy to ward off the 'international peril.' The French premier considered Poland's danger to be part of a larger threat from anarchic forces of world domination. Pilsudski he termed a megalomaniac whose desire for power prompted deals with the Russians. Polish independence represented in Millerand's eyes a defense of world peace against the forces determined to overthrow the Versailles Treaty. Allied support for Poland had considerably broader ramifications than simply the defense of a new nation.[24]

The Allied declaration of Hythe supported Polish independence and contemplated military aid but not troops. Supporting that freedom within ethnographic frontiers, the Allies agreed not to intervene in Russian domestic affairs provided that nation also stayed out of the domestic politics of other states. Urging Poland to seek an armistice that guaranteed its independence, they promised to support it if Soviet terms violated Polish territorial integrity. The Allies decided to suspend contact with Russian representatives

---

24. *D.B.F.P.*, VIII, pp. 711–12, 715–16, 734–5, 737, 3rd conference at Hythe, 8 and 9 August 1920; Wandycz, pp. 161–2; Alexandre Millerand, 'Au secours de la Pologne (août 1920),' *La Revue de France*, 12ᵉ année, IV (15 August 1932), p. 580; Ullman, pp. 211, 216; Carroll, *Soviet Communism*, p. 164; A.E., P.M. 69, Millerand to French ambassadors generally, 11 August 1920. A.N., F.M. 72, article from *Le Temps*, 12 August 1920, reported on cabinet's discussion of foreign situation, especially Poland. D'Abernon, *Eighteenth Battle*, p. 72, noted on 11 August his certainty that Millerand would reject German offers of military aid against the Soviets.

in England until a satisfactory Russo-Polish accord was achieved. They also agreed to send Poland armaments and military advisers, to maintain communications between Poland and the Allies, possibly through a blockade of Russia's Baltic coast, and to support General Wrangel's forces. In return, Poland had to appoint a commander who would accept Allied counsel, maintain an army of twenty-two divisions, and hold the Vistula line.[25]

Although Millerand strongly backed Weygand's military mission and sent arms, tanks, and munitions, he wanted the aid to remain inter-Allied. As he had commented on 3 August, the French must draw the British into a 'material collaboration' and 'moral solidarity,' a consensus which he believed the Hythe declaration represented. His satisfaction with that vague statement ended abruptly when he learned of the Soviet peace terms which would have eliminated Poland's capacity for self-defense. Russia demanded that Poland's army be reduced to 50,000 men, its war industry demobilized, and the neutral zone evacuated. To Millerand, Lloyd George's favorable response to those terms destroyed their recent agreement. Infuriated with the British, Millerand instructed Ambassador Jusserand on 13 August to promise Polish Foreign Minister Sapieha full French support for peace conditions guaranteeing independence and ethnic integrity. He urged them to heed General Weygand's military advice. Lord Derby's mediation eased the tension, which Pilsudski's victory settled. Millerand has been faulted for treating Poland as a pawn in France's anti-Bolshevik political game, but the premier insisted his goal was Polish independence and preservation of the new nation-state as the incarnation of national self-determination. Undoubtedly, hostility to communism contributed to Millerand's loyal defense of Poland, but was probably not its sole motivation.[26]

British support for Bolshevik pressures on Poland outraged Millerand, but French action toward the White Russian General Wrangel similarly irritated Lloyd George. After Spa, despite explicit British opposition, Millerand apparently told Wrangel's representative in

25. *D.B.F.P.*, VIII, pp. 754–5, Allied declaration at Hythe, 9 August 1920; A.N., F.M. 63, Allied declaration of 9 August 1920, 'secret'; Wandycz, pp. 168–70.
26. Millerand, 'Souvenirs,' p. 98; Millerand, 'Pologne,' pp. 580, 582–6, 590–1; Wandycz, pp. 169–71; Suarez, V, p. 88; Duroselle, *Histoire diplomatique*, p. 45.

Paris that he intended to recognize South Russia as a *de facto* government and send a high commissioner to the Crimea. Wrangel's military success and his seemingly significant popular support influenced the French premier, as did the hope that recognition would harm the Bolshevik cause. France's precondition for recognition remained Wrangel's acceptance of the tsarist debts. Officially recognizing Wrangel's government on 11 August, Millerand later portrayed the move as a response to Soviet conditions for Poland and to Wrangel's acceptance of the previous Russian government's obligations. His reliance on the general's promise is questionable, however, since Wrangel lost little by a commitment that required a Bolshevik defeat for its fulfillment. French recognition not only strengthened the general's position, but also, Millerand believed, contributed to the Polish victory at Warsaw a few days later by reviving Polish morale. In fact, the recognition was an empty gesture that only involved greater shipments of arms, but not enough to save the White general. A despatch of French troops was never at issue.[27]

British hostility prompted a forceful defense from Millerand. On 14 August, he charged the British with violating the Hythe agreement by sending the Russian conditions to Warsaw without informing the French. At Hythe, the Allies had encouraged Poland to defend itself, but Russian demands would have left it defenseless. France's recognition of Wrangel had not, he maintained, triggered Poland's rejection of the Russian conditions, since it had predated Polish knowledge of the French move. As Millerand reminded the British, he had told the French Chamber on 20 July that Wrangel had established a *de facto* government and noted France's prerequisites for recognition. Portraying that move as the logical development to a well-considered policy, he denied that it implied any French desire to alter the Hythe agreement. Determined to avoid any permanent misunderstanding, he still noted that the British had often met with the Soviet representatives without informing the French in advance. On 16 August, he emphatically denied that the French government was unconcerned about the break with Britain that recognition of Wrangel had caused. Again, he insisted that the move did not alter the Hythe agreement, involve any French troops, or relate to Soviet demands on Poland. To reestablish the

---

27. Millerand, 'Pologne,' pp. 586–8; E. Bonnefous, III, p. 158; Suarez, V, p. 88; Carroll, *Soviet Communism*, p. 184; Bradley, pp. 178–9.

entente, the French accepted in principle d'Abernon's proposed settlement of the Russo-Polish conflict. France would urge Poland to accept any peace conditions that respected its political independence and ethnic integrity. After a Russo-Polish peace was concluded, France would counsel Wrangel to seek a similar arrangement. Until then, the French would give him military support against Red attacks.[28]

Despite British opposition, Millerand continued his support for Wrangel. On 23 August, he told Foch to give the general rapid and full assistance before payment arrangements had been clarified. As he later noted, even Lenin connected Russia's defeat in Poland to its simultaneous fight against Wrangel, who had French recognition. By implication, recognition by France strengthened Wrangel sufficiently to make him a more formidable opponent for the Red Army.[29]

Like Poland and Rumania, Wrangel provided another link in the *cordon sanitaire* that Millerand wanted to erect against Russia. He was, however, also anxious to have Russia's debt to Frenchmen holding tsarist bonds recognized. The move was financial as much as ideological. Economic problems influenced diplomatic decisions, as they had earlier in the French refusal to participate in the trade negotiations with the Krasin delegation. At Aix-les-Bains in mid-September, Millerand confirmed the French decision that relations with the Soviet Union were more politically dangerous than economically beneficial. The French premier ultimately had to accept the White Russian armies' defeat. His initial willingness to aid Wrangel has been termed a triumph for Volunteer diplomacy, but the failure of the general's Kuban offensive made the French premier increasingly cautious. In September, he refused to meet Wrangel in Paris, and reduced his moral and material support to the Volunteers. Although he encouraged the Poles to delay signing an armistice with the Russians to occupy Red troops in Poland, his counsel did not avert a deterioration of Wrangel's situation as Poland's improved.[30]

28. *D.B.F.P.*, XI, pp. 491–4, Millerand to de Fleuriau, London, 14 August 1920; *ibid.*, pp. 496–7, Millerand to de Fleuriau, London, 16 August 1920; *ibid.*, pp. 500–1, Derby to London, transmitting letter from Millerand, 17 August 1920.

29. A.N., F.M. 63, Millerand to Foch, President of the Allied military commission, 23 August 1920; Millerand, 'Pologne,' p. 591.

30. Hogenhuis, pp. 161, 177; Maier, p. 193; Bradley, pp. 181–2; A.E., y internationale no. 682, conference between Millerand and Giolitti at Aix-les-Bains, 12–13 September 1920.

By mid-August, the military balance had shifted dramatically in Poland's favor. Its brilliant defeat of a Red Army too far from its base pushed the eastern boundary into Ruthenia. The Polish struggle not only influenced future French policy toward Eastern Europe, but led the British to blame persistent European political and economic disorders on French militarism. Poland's victory at Warsaw led to the Soviet defeat and withdrawal, which the armistice of Riga confirmed in October. Weygand and d'Abernon attributed a significant role in the victory to the Allied military mission's material and moral support. Millerand and Weygand emerged as heroes. The French viewed the Warsaw victory as the culmination of Millerand's foreign policy. A few weeks later, it proved a tremendous asset in making him the obvious candidate to replace ailing President Paul Deschanel.[31]

31. E. Bonnefous, III, p. 158; Persil, pp. 132–3; McDougall, p. 137; Wandycz, pp. 174–5; Néré, p. 32; Weygand, II, p. 97. D'Abernon, *Eighteenth Battle*, p. 115, noted the mission's cordial reception in Paris on 1 September and by Millerand at Versailles.

11
Prestige and Resources:
France's Colonial Policy in 1920

The colonial policy of Millerand's ministry represented a shift of emphasis from self-sufficiency to colonial specialization. He tried to substitute a program of specialization and division of labor for the earlier discontinuous and desultory schemes, believing that the general structure would be strengthened if each colony exploited its assets. His fundamental policy toward France's colonial possessions remained as outlined in his Ba-Ta-Clan speech of 7 November 1919: gratitude for their wartime contribution to France and insistence on a greater exploitation of their resources – an illustration of his nationalistic concern for France's international position.

In Berthelot, Millerand found an ardent colonialist, anxious to defend French interests throughout the subject areas. The decision to hold the Turkish treaty negotiations in London, with only the final signature in Paris, made Berthelot the principal French negotiator. Millerand's instructions to him to stand firm on the Mosul oil rights, the Palestinian frontier, and Tangiers met opposition from the British and Near Eastern nationalists. Shortly after he became premier, Millerand confronted British complaints about a disadvantageous position in Morocco. Insisting that possession of Tangiers was vital to the nation responsible for Morocco's security and economic development, he opposed British demands for an international regime. None of the earlier pacts had given Tangiers an 'international' status. If the British pressed the point, the French could legitimately demand a similar arrangement for the Suez Canal.[1]

1. Millerand, *Union républicaine sociale et nationale*, 'Ba-Ta-Clan' speech, 7 November 1919; A.E., z Europe 1918–29, ss Grande Bretagne 44, Millerand to Derby, 26 January 1920; Andrew and Kanya-Forstner, pp. 213–14, 216; Roberts, p. 162.

As premier, Millerand's principal colonial interest was Syria. To him, French status and prestige in the Middle East were paramount considerations. An Anglo-French agreement (Sykes–Picot) of 16 May 1916 had assigned Syria and Lebanon to France. On 6 January 1920, Clemenceau had worked out a provisional accord with local leader Feisal that gave France a mandate for Syria and Lebanon, including control over foreign and financial policies through technical advisers. In exchange, Syria remained a unitary state with some rights of self-determination. Initially willing to ratify Clemenceau's agreement, Millerand refused to evacuate French troops until the peace conference had finally settled the Syrian question. The area's unsettled conditions forced him to maintain almost daily contact with French High Commissioner in Beirut General Henri Gouraud. He instructed Gouraud to station troops in the areas and quantities necessary to preserve France's status *vis-à-vis* the local population or its ability to negotiate effectively with Feisal. He counselled the high commissioner to urge patience on the Arab leader, suggested payment of a subsidy of 2,850,000 francs, and insisted he guard France's prestige until order was restored.[2]

France's position in Syria was closely connected to a settlement of the whole Turkish problem. Nationalist movements in Syria, as elsewhere in the Turkish Empire, created problems for Britain and France. Millerand was convinced that Turkish nationalist groups, spurred on by Kemal, would exploit the uncertain and disorderly situation to intimidate the Allies into granting a more liberal peace settlement that preserved Turkey's territorial integrity. He did not expect the Turks to adopt an overtly hostile attitude before the status of Constantinople and Turkey generally was resolved, but still urged Gouraud to take defensive repressive precautions so that Arab or Turkish nationalist groups did not defeat French forces. Until the treaty was signed, the army had to protect France's Middle Eastern position. French national interests therefore took precedence over any ideological commitment to national self-determination.[3]

Millerand's concern to defend French interests eventually led him to reject Clemenceau's agreement with Feisal. To Gouraud, he claimed that France's prerequisites for an accord with Feisal were

2. A.E., E Levant 1918–29, ss Syrie–Liban–Cilicie 22, telegrams, Millerand to Gouraud, 31 January and 1 February 1920.
    3. *Ibid.*, Millerand to Gouraud, 1 February 1920.

not only the Arab leader's willingness to collaborate with France, but also his ability to compel Arab obedience. His goodwill and authority were equally essential, but he had proven unable to halt hostile acts toward the French. It was therefore necessary for France to protect its troops and maintain local order. The French occupation was an asset, he believed, to the Allies and local population, since it preserved order in the face of nationalist unrest and local brigandage fostered by uncertainty and delays in working out a final settlement of the Eastern Question.[4]

Millerand outlined French policy toward Syria to its parliamentary representatives. A program of justice and liberation, not conquest or oppression, would still permit France to defend its historic interests. A French occupation sought to safeguard those rights, but also to provide necessary justice and orderly administration. A series of British telegrams since 1912, which delineated French and British spheres of influence, had indicated a lack of British interest in Syria and a recognition of French predominance. The 1916 Sykes–Picot agreement formalized this position. Syria and Cilicia were assigned to a French sphere of influence and Mesopotamia and Bagdad to a British. Following the Franco-British decision of September 1919 for French troops to replace British troops in Syria, Gouraud was sent there as high commissioner. The replacement of British by French military authorities was not, however, without its attendant frictions. While France did not intend to expand troop levels in Syria beyond the 30,000 men already there, it still, Millerand argued, required sufficient military force to protect its interests and established rights. French control was likely to be formalized as a mandate from the League of Nations. In the meantime, Millerand instructed Gouraud to organize the administrative and judicial system in the coastal region that France already controlled; the French must gradually teach the local population self-government, but protect the sentimental and cultural ties to France. Anxious that French influence and administration not be oppressive, he was convinced that it had already brought greater regularity to Syrian administration, justice, and taxation. Gouraud, however, had not yet been able to expand French influence into the

4. Jan Karl Tanenbaum, *France and the Arab Middle East 1914–1920* (Philadelphia: American Philosophical Society, 1978), Transactions, vol. 68, part 7, p. 37; A.E., E Levant 1918–29, ss Syrie–Liban–Cilicie 23, Millerand to French ambassador in Washington, 7 February 1920; *ibid.*, Millerand to Gouraud, 10 February 1920.

Arab areas, despite his wish to unify the divided country. Syria, Millerand argued, was not yet a true nation but a collection of small groups in need of assistance and protection and incapable of self-government. France's world-wide obligations prevented it from following a policy that overly committed its resources.[5]

Millerand's despatches to Gouraud increasingly focused on Feisal's position. He instructed the high commissioner to reject Feisal's demands for greater political control. Local nationalists wanted Feisal to proclaim Syrian independence, but Millerand thought it would be easier for France to control Syria if it were divided into traditional ethnic and religious units. Information about a Syrian congress in Damascus called to proclaim Feisal as king led the French premier to insist that only the peace conference could define Syria's eventual regime. If Gouraud could not prevent an inopportune Syrian congress, he should at least keep Feisal from being proclaimed king of Syria. That step would hamper France's policy of autonomy. Millerand also demanded that the British not accord any authority to the Syrian congress. An unconsidered act could, he argued, seriously compromise Syria's future if it created public hostility to France and Britain. The premier instructed Gouraud to warn Feisal of the risks incurred if the Syrian congress took a stand which France opposed. The Turkish treaty, including Syria's status, was currently being negotiated in London. While ready to listen to Feisal's views, the Allies refused to let the Syrian congress take a position that could prejudge the outcome. Millerand even questioned whether the Franco-British subvention to Feisal should be reduced.[6]

Despite French warnings, the Congress of Damascus proclaimed Feisal king of an independent Syria. Millerand pressed for a joint Franco-British notification to Feisal that the proclamation lacked international validity. The French government refused to recognize the Congress of Damascus, whose composition and authority were unknown, and denied it was competent to settle the fate of Syria, Palestine, and Mesopotamia. Only the Allies could reach such decisions, not a self-appointed organization in Damascus. Not

5. J.O., *Chambre*, 6 February 1920; C.D.A., Foreign Affairs Commission, 10 and 20 February 1920, auditions of Millerand; *Sénat*, Foreign Affairs Commission, 19 February 1920, audition of Millerand.

6. Tanenbaum, *Arab Middle East*, pp. 38–9; A.E., E Levant 1918–29, ss Syrie–Liban–Cilicie 24, Millerand to Gouraud, 7, 9, and 10 March 1920, and Millerand to French ambassador in London, 9 March 1920.

certain that Feisal had received the Allied warning, Millerand invited him to Europe to discuss Syrian affairs.[7]

During March, French efforts to establish control in Syria increased Franco-British tension. Millerand wanted the Allies to repudiate local independence moves; Lloyd George thought the French were imposing themselves against local wishes. Millerand attributed British irritation at France's denial of royal status to Feisal to concern for British Near Eastern supremacy. The Congress' proclamation of Feisal as king had so unsettled northern Syria that he feared French troops would not be numerous enough to preserve order. Only the peace conference, he argued, could decide the area's regime. Although the French and British did not want to recognize Feisal as king, the French premier still hoped he would attend the forthcoming San Remo conference. France promised to permit the free development of national aspirations even though Syria's boundaries and the links between the different populations remained to be clarified. The only condition Feisal had placed on a trip to France was the recognition of the Arab states stipulated in the 6 January accord, not recognition of his royal status. That possibility had to wait until Syria's internal and external situation was settled. France was prepared to accord Arab populations of whatever religious persuasion the right to govern themselves as an independent nation. It would protect Syrian ethnic, linguistic, and ethnographic independence against foreign aggression. The French government's stated intent to accord Arabs of all confessions the right to self-government indicated a policy of divide and rule and opposition to the national unity Feisal had proclaimed.[8] Although Millerand promised independence to Syria, he viewed self-government within the context of a French mandate, a goal toward which Syria would move with French assistance, rather than an immediate achievement.

At San Remo, France officially received the League of Nations' mandate for Syria and Lebanon. Although Millerand tried to

7. A.E., E Levant 1918–29, ss Syrie–Liban–Cilicie 25, Millerand to Gouraud, 11 and 13 March 1920.
8. Tanenbaum, *Arab Middle East*, pp. 38–9; A.E., E Levant 1918–29, ss Syrie–Liban–Cilicie 25, Millerand to London, 31 March 1920; A.E., E Levant 1918–29, ss Syrie–Liban–Cilicie 26, Millerand to French ambassador in London, 5 April 1920; Nevakivi, p. 252.

persuade Curzon to issue a Franco-British invitation to Feisal to attend a conference on the Arab states' organization, the British minister first wanted to hear Feisal's plans. In Millerand's opinion, Feisal wanted to be recognized as king but to leave vague whether Syria's future frontiers would include Palestine, Mesopotamia, or the Mosul. France, in accepting the mandate, was ready to advise the Arabs on how to fulfill their legitimate hopes and organize themselves into a nation. Warfare and oppression had, however, so devastated the country that French aid was vital. France planned to guarantee Syrian ethnic, linguistic, and geographic independence against aggression within the frontiers set by the peace conference. Millerand was also ready to inform Feisal privately that France would observe the 6 January accord which permitted him to reassure his compatriots about French intentions. He reissued his invitation for Feisal to come to Europe to explain the Arab position, but insisted that official acknowledgement of him as king had to wait until the Syrian population could decide on the Damascus Congress' decision.[9]

French reception of the mandate for Syria and British for Mesopotamia and Palestine did not settle the details of implementation, which first required consultation with the League of Nations to protect Allied interests, prior agreements, and local wishes. Millerand wanted comparable rights for France in Syria as Britain had in its mandates, while the British, facing other colonial difficulties, yielded on Syria to avoid problems over Palestine. The Supreme Council invited Feisal to discussions scheduled for Paris in late May, but the Allies felt they had the sole right to organize the Arab states, after they consulted local wishes, since their military victories had freed the area from Turkish control. In fact, it took considerable time after San Remo to settle the frontiers between Syria–Lebanon and Palestine. Although the San Remo decision simply ratified the wartime agreements, it was significant in recognizing equal French and British status in the Near East.[10]

Despite considerable French involvement in Syria, policy there was always linked to French commitments elsewhere. Throughout

9. A.E., E Levant 1918–29, ss Syrie–Liban–Cilicie 26, Millerand telegrams from San Remo, 24 April 1920; Andrew and Kanya-Forstner, p. 218.

10. *D.B.F.P.*, VIII, pp. 172–7; A.N., F.M. 54, Millerand's speech in the Chamber, 28 April 1920; J.O., *Chambre*, 28 April 1920; Tanenbaum, *Arab Middle East*, pp. 38–9; A.E., E Levant 1918–29, ss Syrie–Liban–Cilicie 27, Millerand's telegram from San Remo, 26 April 1920; Andrew and Kanya-Forstner, p. 218.

the winter, Millerand tried to persuade the war minister to despatch additional troops to Syria to control unrest, but was also aware that France could not expand its military commitment indefinitely. He urged General Gouraud to adapt his strategic goals to available means. As he commented, his principal objective was to establish a balance in Syria between French objectives and means. Although Millerand had urged a Turkish treaty that neither aroused Turkish nationalism against the Allies nor assisted the Arabs or the Bolsheviks, he confronted British opposition to the 1916 Franco-British arrangement for Syria. The British argued that Russia's wartime collapse and American intervention, as well as their own human and financial sacrifices incurred in defeating Turkey and conquering the Arab regions, altered prior agreements. To Millerand, the impossibility of localizing effort and sacrifice invalidated such reasoning. Anxiety for agreement with Lloyd George even led Clemenceau to alter the 1916 accord by assigning the Mosul and Palestine to the British. In his provisional accord of 6 January with Feisal, the Syrian populations had received the right to unite and govern themselves with French assistance. In exchange for a French guarantee of Syrian independence, Feisal would use French advisers, instructors, and technical agents in Syria's civil and military administration and its diplomats would represent Syria abroad. To Millerand, the San Remo conference's attribution of the Syrian mandate to France was a direct response to the effort of the Damascus Congress to influence the peace settlement by proclaiming Feisal king.[11]

During May, France confronted increasing difficulties with Feisal and tension with the British. Even though Millerand had invited Feisal to Europe, he criticized British High Commissioner in Palestine General Edmund Allenby for a similar invitation, arguing that the Arab leader would view it as an indication of British support for Syrian independence. Insisting that only the peace conference could bestow the crown on Feisal, he charged Allenby with offering the Arab leader greater assurances than had Gouraud. In Millerand's opinion, Allenby's stand represented British intervention in Syrian affairs after France's reception of the mandate. It caused France considerable inconvenience, he maintained, if Feisal was indirectly encouraged to pursue a line hostile to France.

11. A.E., E Levant 1918–29, ss Syrie–Liban–Cilicie 27, Millerand to Gouraud, 4 May 1920.

British involvement permitted Feisal to play off the British and the French for his own benefit.[12] Although Millerand had frequently invited Feisal to Europe and recognized him as provisional leader of Syria, he disliked independent British contacts with an Arab leader in a French zone of influence.

During May, it was increasingly clear that Millerand and Feisal were headed for a collision. Viewing Feisal as personally ambitious, Millerand believed French patience had been pushed to the limit. He refused to tolerate further the daily violations of the accord with Feisal. Turkish Arab bands, based outside the French zone, had, he claimed, massacred French soldiers and then used Feisal to shield them. Disloyal or impotent Cherifien authorities had created a dangerous and intolerable situation for France. French concessions had, he believed, simply strengthened France's adversaries. Anxious for Franco-British collaboration in the Near East, Millerand argued that the assignment of mandates implied French non-intervention in Mesopotamia and Palestine and a comparable restraint by Allenby in Syria. Feisal should not represent interests in both French and British mandates or capitalize on contrasting Franco-British statements. Indeed, the Arab leader's equivocal attitude had led the French to suspend their subsidy since February.[13]

The crux of the problem was contrasting Franco-Arab goals for Syria. Feisal wanted a unitary state without French involvement; Millerand sought to preserve and if possible strengthen France's position. Recognition of local traditions and autonomy would, the premier believed, encourage appreciation of French services and thereby promote French influence. Described as one of the Quai d'Orsay's colonialists, Millerand had overly optimistic plans for a Syria without Feisal that failed to take sufficient account of local opposition to French rule. By 22 May, Millerand, who found the situation increasingly intolerable, decided, despite Gouraud's reluctance, to resolve the Syrian impasse by military means. The choice of a firm policy, and if necessary a showdown, came therefore from Paris rather than from Beirut.[14]

Toward Syria, Millerand pursued a two-fold policy. He wanted British support for French decisions about Feisal, but, at the same

---

12. *Ibid.*, Millerand to French ambassador in London, 6 May 1920.
13. *Ibid.*, Millerand to Gouraud and French ambassador in London, 11 May 1920.
14. Tanenbaum, *Arab Middle East*, pp. 39–40; Andrew and Kanya-Forstner, p. 218.

time, he mobilized French strength to compel the Arab leader to respect the French mandate. A draft Franco-British declaration to Feisal reiterated the Allied commitment on Syrian, Mesopotamian, and Palestinian independence within the context of the Franco-British mandates. This common recognition of France's duty to halt intrigues that threatened its occupation of Syria and Cilicia kept Feisal from using British concessions to strengthen his negotiating position with the French. Millerand denounced Feisal's hypocrisy in giving the French verbal reassurances and using their troops while he armed hostile bands and retained contact with Turkish nationalists. Although France was the mandatory power which Feisal directly menaced, Gouraud, Millerand argued, should deal with him in the name of France and Britain to demonstrate their common policy.[15]

Millerand feared a complete French military defeat in Syria, because French troops were so dispersed that they were vulnerable to attack. He counselled Gouraud to group his forces so that he could compel Feisal to respect his own commitments and the French mandate. Military measures might, he postulated, include a French occupation of Damascus, control over the railroad, and disarmament and demobilization of the population. The resort to force did not, however, interfere with French plans to issue a proclamation promising to respect local freedom. The mandate, he insisted, would be applied in a liberal fashion if those freed from Turkish oppression did not treat the French as enemies and appreciated the administrative and organizational methods, advisers, and capital.[16]

Millerand blamed the decision to use military force on Feisal's attitude. In June, the French government approved reinforcements and agreed with Gouraud's suggestion that they tighten their control over the northern railroad, since it was the only way to transport French troops. Would Feisal, Millerand asked, yield or would French troops have to occupy the Rayak–Alep line? He also wondered whether Feisal's rejection of his commitments would compel a direct French operation against Damascus. A measure of last resort, Millerand wanted Gouraud to assess it and reassure the local population about French intents. French military measures, he

---

15. A.E., E Levant 1918–29, ss Syrie–Liban–Cilicie 28, Millerand to Gouraud, 27 May 1920.
16. *Ibid.*

argued, were designed solely to maintain order and foster prosperity. Unless the French controlled the railroads, Syrian people and goods could not circulate freely. The local population would therefore benefit by withholding any support from the Damascan extremists. France was strong enough to insure execution of the Turkish treaty and maintenance of order in Syria. An Arab army lacked further justification; recruitment must therefore end and native civilian organizations replace the military administration.[17]

Millerand summarized relations with Syria to the French parliament in early June. The French position in Syria was sufficiently important to France's prestige for the premier to endorse whatever military commitments proved necessary. Willing to use diplomatic as well as military means, he hoped France's military strength could be reduced once its position was secure. The principle which Lyautey and Gallieni had established elsewhere guided French policy, namely to demonstrate strength in order not to use it. To demonstrate the pointlessness of native resistance, the French had assembled a powerful force. Many small and isolated actions, dictated by local conditions, instead of a significant manifestation had, however, compromised French prestige. Noting that the proclamation of Syrian independence had coincided with the attribution of the mandate to France, Millerand commented that British petroleum interests in the Mosul had posed a knotty problem. To compensate for its concessions, France finally accepted a petroleum arrangement at San Remo whereby it received 25 percent of Mesopotamian petroleum, the former German share, and 25 percent of Persian petroleum. The French had eventually won out on the southern frontier between Syria and Palestine, but in Cilicia had only received a zone of economic influence.[18]

During June, the impact of British behavior became as pressing a concern as French relations with Feisal. The Arab leader's continued hostility had forced France to protect its troops and make him respect French rights. On 18 May, Curzon had agreed that France must stop the intrigues which jeopardized execution of the Turkish treaty and menaced the safety of French troops. In response, Millerand proposed a joint declaration threatening to withdraw recognition of Feisal as the Hedjaz delegate unless he attended

17. A.E., E Levant 1918–29, ss Syrie–Liban–Cilicie 29, Millerand to Gouraud, 1 June 1920.
18. *Sénat*, Foreign Affairs Commission, 3 June 1920, audition of Millerand; C.D.A., Foreign Affairs Commission, 10 June 1920, audition of Millerand.

the next conference. Although he sent the draft declaration to London on 26 May, Millerand had not received a reply by mid-June. Meanwhile, Feisal continued to threaten French troops and solicit British support against France. In fact, Allenby had even recommended that Britain resume its subsidy to Feisal – a direct contravention of the Franco-British decision to suspend it, because Feisal was using it for military and propaganda purposes against France. Millerand termed Feisal's government simply a source of political agitation and recruitment for an anti-French army. Feisal continually intrigued against the French, organizing bands to attack their forces, proclaiming himself king of Syria, and ignoring the authority of the peace conference. French patience had been exhausted in dealing with a leader who consistently undermined French authority and prestige and encouraged hostile nationalist forces. Since France did not interfere with British decisions in its mandates, Millerand expected comparable British restraint in Syria. Feisal must not rely on British support to secure his claims to a Syrian kingdom. Determined to protect French rights in Syria, Millerand resented Britain's involvement there.[19]

Millerand not only had to deal with the Arabs and the British government in London but also with local British commanders. He strongly protested the continued meddling in Syrian affairs by local British officials. A specific example was the British decoration of Emir Zeid, called by Millerand the most notorious Arab extremist combating French influence in Syria. For the British to reward natives within the French mandate area caused France considerable embarrassment, as it surely would Britain if the situation were reversed. Allenby seemingly still considered himself the director of the Syrian military occupation and hence superior to the French authorities. His continued interest in Feisal and Syrian affairs prompted his suggestion that the Arab leader send a delegate to Europe, which proved to Millerand the British general's disregard for France's mandate position.[20]

France's attempt to organize its Syrian mandate continually encountered Feisal's efforts to arouse local nationalism. Millerand

19. A.E., E Levant 1918–29, ss Syrie–Liban–Cilicie 30, Millerand to French ambassador in London, 11 June 1920.
20. *Ibid.*, Millerand to French ambassador in London, 12 June 1920.

perceived the Arab leader as a resolute opponent of France whose artificial stimulation of a xenophobic nationalism contradicted the conciliatory position he had taken in signing the accord of 6 January. If Feisal attended the peace negotiations, he would probably use the occasion for further intrigues, Millerand believed. Despite the attitude of the Cherifien authorities, France wanted to fulfill the mandate's spirit by choosing native leaders capable of governing the country. Millerand expected councils of notables to reinforce the republicanism that France sought and to end the currently untenable situation of large financial outlays that failed to provide viable solutions.[21]

French concessions failed to halt the hostility of both Feisal and the Cherifien government. Indeed, Syrian resistance to the French mandate had required, Millerand maintained, the resort to force. While France did not plan to leave Syria, it preferred to limit its military involvement, cut back troop levels, and use diplomacy to secure its objectives. Linking Turkish and Syrian policy, he suggested signing an armistice with Kemal that would end hostilities in one area and free France to deal with the Cherifien problem. They must prevent Feisal from sending troops into the areas disputed by France and Turkey; such action would simply increase the level of violence and encourage a Turkish–Arab *rapprochement*. Since Feisal's behavior had invalidated the 6 January accord, Millerand urged Gouraud to find local authorities willing to work with France. He also considered French control of the railroad to be the only option. To Millerand, the French role was a civilizing one, helping the Syrians to develop their economic potential and to learn to govern themselves. The historic cultural ties with France made it the logical choice to reform the Syrian administration rather than to conquer the country.[22]

At Spa, the French stressed to the British the new situation which the French mandate had created in Syria. It implied a British lack of involvement in Syria in exchange for the free hand Britain had in Mesopotamia. Each ally had the right to organize its own mandate without external pressures. The British should, therefore, discourage movements which helped them and hurt French interests in Syria. Millerand emphatically refuted Britain's claim that certain

---

21. *Ibid.*, Millerand to Gouraud, 13 June 1920.
22. *Ibid.*, Millerand to Gouraud, 15 and 18 June 1920; J.O., *Chambre*, 24 and 26 June 1920.

towns, including Damascus, fell within the zone of French influence, but not its mandate. The peace conference had, he claimed, eliminated any distinction between zones of influence and direct administration by assigning France the mandate for all of Syria. Feisal's hostile intriguing had become intolerable to the French, who viewed his claim to the Syrian crown as a violation of his own commitment to France and contrary to the conference's permission for France to establish Syria's organization. France intended, the premier claimed, to occupy Syria militarily only on a temporary basis until native autonomous administrations were established to which France could provide advice.[23]

The approaching showdown between France and Feisal introduced a critical note into Millerand's communications with Gouraud. To the premier, the high commissioner seemed overly conciliatory to the devious emir. Millerand, who was determined to execute fully the mandate, seemingly favored a military solution more than Gouraud. The French sent two ultimatums to Feisal (on 14 and 22 July) that demanded he acknowledge the mandate, including French control over Syrian military, political, administrative, financial, educational, and judicial systems. Feisal accepted the first ultimatum but rejected the total control implicit in the second. Millerand insisted that Gouraud should not treat Feisal as an equal, but exploit the current French military superiority and strictly interpret the conditions of the ultimatum so that Feisal was rendered impotent. He suggested a French seizure of the railroad and Alep, application of precautionary military tactics elsewhere, and abolition of Syrian conscription. Rebuking Gouraud for seeming to recognize Feisal as head of state, the premier reserved the right for France to designate the local authority. With the pseudo-Cherifien government no longer a valid organization, Gouraud should, he instructed, cease any further contacts with Feisal. Should Feisal resist these conditions, Gouraud would regain the freedom of action that the ultimatum had restricted.[24] Millerand

23. J.O., *Chambre*, 20 July 1920; A.N., F.M. 51, Millerand memorandum, nd; A.E., E Levant 1918–29, ss Syrie–Liban–Cilicie 31, Millerand to French ambassador in London, 20 July 1920; also in A.E., P.M. 10.
24. Tanenbaum, *Arab Middle East*, pp. 41–3; William I. Shorrock, *French Imperialism in the Middle East. The Failure of Policy in Syria and Lebanon, 1900–1914.* (Madison: University of Wisconsin Press, 1976), p. 5; A.E., E Levant 1918–29, ss Syrie–Liban–Cilicie 31, Millerand to Gouraud, 21 July 1920; *ibid.*, Millerand to Gouraud, 23 July 1920; also in A.E., P.M. 10.

was clearly more anxious for Feisal's capitulation than was Gouraud. Perhaps the local commander recognized local complexities more fully than the premier, whose primary consideration was execution of France's rights.

Millerand criticized Gouraud for halting his military advance just short of Damascus. The general's hesitation would, he feared, strengthen Feisal's position and permit further intrigues. Gouraud should use his military advantage to resolve the Syrian situation by giving local posts to those dependent on France. He should not allow the partisan views of foreign consuls in Damascus, scruples prompted by Feisal's opposition to France, or Damascan crowds egged on by Cherifien agitators to influence his policy. Domestic peace required a French military presence; otherwise, the Cherifien army would not disband or the population disarm. When Feisal rejected the second ultimatum, Gouraud's troops conquered Damascus without strong resistance on 25 July.[25]

With Damascus secure, the French government was finally able to deal with Syria's future. Millerand favored decentralization as the most effective way for France to control the area. For months, he had hinted at France's future program. In June, he commented to Gouraud that the provisional agreement of 6 January had used the singular 'independent nation' for Syria, implying a unification of Syrian territories under the French mandate. France, however, envisaged this unity as a federation of local autonomies respecting ethnic diversity and popular wishes. Instructing Gouraud to eliminate all traces of Feisal's Cherifien pseudo-government, Millerand argued that France could not allow any Arab government to represent all Syria. The government in Damascus was only entitled to a provisional and limited recognition as a local authority. The only connection between the different parts of Syria should be the high commissioner as representative of the mandatory nation.[26]

In early August, the premier sent Gouraud some general guidelines for French policy until a formal program was established. In his opinion, Gouraud's complex and costly regime in Damascus

25. A.E., E Levant 1918–29, ss Syrie–Liban–Cilicie 31, Millerand to Gouraud, 24 July 1920; also in A.E., P.M. 10; Tanenbaum, *Arab Middle East* pp. 41–3; Shorrock, p. 5.

26. A.E., E Levant 1918–29, ss Syrie–Liban–Cilicie 29, Millerand to Gouraud, 5 June 1920; A.E., E Levant 1918–29, ss Syrie–Liban–Cilicie 31, Millerand to Gouraud, 29 July 1920.

gave that 'eccentric' city an excessive importance in a Syrian confederation that included autonomous groups in the four interior cities and surroundings, the maritime cities, and the mountain cantons. The French did not plan to model Syria on Morocco. No sovereign would rule a unified Moslem Syria, but the division between the east zone and the rest of the country would be eliminated. An Arab leader provided a center of opposition to the French and attracted dissidents from neighboring areas. Millerand suggested political and administrative autonomy for each group within Syria, with a local council of notables and a government nominated and controlled by a French high commission delegate. That delegate would gradually share power with a native Syrian federal council.[27]

Millerand viewed Syria as an asset to France's prestige. His despatch to Gouraud of 6 August set the pattern for France's interwar role. Rather than a new colony, France sought a guarantee of its Mediterranean position. It therefore wanted its influence recognized with minimal intervention and in as liberal a manner as possible. The chimera of a Cherifien government under French control had proven unworkable, since a nationalistic, militaristic monarchy violated France's democratic traditions as well as local desires and historic divisions. To Millerand, French and Syrian interests would best be served by a federation of autonomous republican groups that permitted racial, religious, and cultural diversity but were linked by the high commission's supreme authority. Preservation of ethnic divisions would pacify the population, he believed, by acknowledging traditional ethnic and religious distinctions; it would also create a divided nation that France could more readily control. Millerand envisaged the unity provided by the French administration as primarily economic, notably monetary and customs control.

France planned to treat the various parts of the mandate differently. The northern Turkish areas, without national ties to Syria, would serve as a market. Political pacification might require force but not military control; a local pasha could rule under French supervision. In the desert areas controlled by Bedouin tribes, France sought only tax receipts and open trade routes. Lebanon, outside the Syrian confederation, was a fertile area for commercial

27. A.E., E Levant 1918–29, ss Syrie–Liban–Cilicie 32, Millerand to Gouraud, 2 August 1920.

expansion; there, France had to protect small businessmen from clan abuses and expand the rights of the Christian population. In Syria proper, a confederation of eight autonomous groups could be formed around the main cities and linked to the high commission as its executive organ. The governments of the local groups should nominate a consultative Syrian council of state to aid the high commission in matters of common economic interest. While the League of Nations assigned the mandatory responsibility for instructing the natives in self-government, Millerand did not consider the Arabs ready to share in political decision-making. Representatives of the high commission and French technical advisers were responsible for general concerns like the railroads, ports, customs, and justice, but local groups shared in the operation of regional budgets, taxes, and police forces.

In essence, Millerand wanted Syria to share in the benefits of French civilization: higher living standards, a more equitable legal system, police maintenance of order, school and hospital facilities, and minority protection – a type of paternal authoritarianism. The French goals of economic development, improved morality, a unified judicial system, and protection of minorities were designed to insure the safety of Syria's population and property. In exchange for the benefits of French civilization, Syria had to supply the customary economic services of any colony: manpower, raw materials, markets, and financial outlets. While Millerand successfully used French military strength to curb the rising Arab nationalist movement, he underestimated Arab resentment of French domination.[28]

The mandate's organization continued to elicit differing responses from Paris and Beirut. To Millerand, Gouraud was too ready to accord excessive power to local Syrian groups. He feared it would encourage Syrian opposition that would hamper efficient administration and delay the population's political education. He proposed cantonal and municipal divisions within a large federation which could later be consolidated if desirable. The federal system would be compromised if the number of states were limited to two or three instead of municipal or cantonal groups. France planned, he commented, a system of French delegates to municipal councils rather than a complete French administration.[29]

28. *Ibid.*, Millerand to Gouraud, 6 August 1920; Tanenbaum, *Arab Middle East*, pp. 42–3.
    29. A.E., E Levant 1918–29, ss Syrie–Liban–Cilicie 32, Millerand to Gouraud, 7 August 1920; *ibid.*, Millerand to Gouraud, 23 August 1920.

France's conquest of Damascus had permitted it to focus on organizing the Syrian mandate, but Feisal remained as a continued source of Franco-British tension. Millerand reacted furiously to information about British plans to offer Feisal the throne of Mesopotamia (Iraq). As the incarnation of Pan-Arabism, Feisal seriously threatened France's mandate in Syria. His occupation of a neighboring throne would, Millerand argued, menace Britain's position as much as France's. Only a solid European front could contain such dangerous forces. The Arabs must recognize that Britain would never install France's enemy in Mesopotamia any more than France would reward Britain's in Syria. Despite French protests, however, the British installed Feisal as king of Mesopotamia in June 1921.[30]

Millerand's Syrian policy is comprehensible in the context of 1920, when a war-buffeted France needed tangible evidence of its world position. In the long run, his Syrian policy, like other French premiers' colonial programs, intensified pressures for independence. Perhaps Clemenceau's greater recognition of Feisal and Arab nationalism might have defused those demands, but Millerand's policy reflected the nationalistic character of the parliament he represented. The dominant Bloc National wanted a forceful defense of France's world-wide interests. Full exercise of a French mandate in Syria reflected this concern. With the wisdom of hindsight, it is tempting to fault Millerand for not recognizing the inevitable victory of Arab nationalism. His allies, notably the British, were, however, no more prescient. In 1920, establishment of a mandate in Syria offered potential benefits that far outweighed the difficulty of subduing opponents.

Although the Allies devoted considerable time in 1920 to drafting a treaty with Turkey, Millerand himself took a relatively small part. His Turkish policy, however, reflected a nationalistic concern for Franco-British Near Eastern equality and France's world power position at the expense of ethnic justice or national self-determination.

Decisions about Turkey's future frequently provoked differing Franco-British responses. The site of the Turkish treaty nego-

---

30. *Ibid.*, Millerand to de Fleuriau, London, 27 August 1920; Andrew and Kanya-Forstner, p. 222.

tiations created an initial problem; it was invested with symbolic implications considerably broader than the simple choice of a French or a British city. Millerand wanted them to be held in Paris because of France's heavy wartime losses, but urged that experts rather than prime ministers conduct the negotiations. The British, however, preferred London in recognition of Britain's dominant Near Eastern position and to compensate for negotiating the other treaties in Paris. Although Millerand finally agreed to London, the site remained as an irritant.[31]

The issue of control over Constantinople and the Straits pitted the French and British against each other. Millerand's principal concern in Turkey was France's substantial financial and economic involvement in the Turkish railroads and the Ottoman debt. He was therefore determined to have the French participate in any control arrangements, even if a conflict with their allies ensued. He countered Curzon's demand that Turkey give up Constantinople by arguing that the preceding fifteen months had so transformed Turkey's situation that expulsion of the sultan would jeopardize peace in the Moslem world. He finally won over Lloyd George. France's considerable needs and limited means forced it, he argued, to proportion the one to the other; the elimination of the Turks from Constantinople was likely to exceed French means. A military and naval commission presided over by Foch dealt with the crucial strategic issue of the freedom and neutralization of the Straits. Since few troops would remain in the future demilitarized Turkey, the Straits' fortifications would have to be destroyed.[32]

National self-determination and treaty commitments were often in conflict, as in Smyrna. While Turkey opposed the presence of the Greeks, the Allies had made commitments to Greece. The least bad situation, Millerand argued, would be to maintain Turkish suzerainty with guarantees for the Greek Christians. Nationalities were so intermingled in the area that it was virtually impossible to align boundaries with ethnic divisions. Montenegro also needed its rights

31. C.D.A., Foreign Affairs Commission, 4 and 20 February 1920, auditions of Millerand; *Sénat*, Foreign Affairs Commission, 19 February 1920; Millerand, 'Souvenirs,' p. 98; A.N., F.M. 56, minutes of Allied Council meetings, London, 12–13 February 1920; *D.B.F.P.*, VII, pp. 1–40; P. Helmreich, pp. 242–3; Nevakivi, p. 233.

32. C.D.A., Foreign Affairs Commission, 10 February 1920, audition of Millerand; A.E., E Levant 1918–29, ss Syrie–Liban–Cilicie 23, Millerand to Gouraud, 10 February 1920; P. Helmreich, pp. 242–3; *Sénat*, Foreign Affairs Commission, 19 February 1920; C.D.A., Foreign Affairs Commission, 20 February 1920.

protected if it were to be incorporated into Yugoslavia. In the case of Fiume, Millerand opted for treaty commitments to Italy over the nationalistic claims of Yugoslavia, thereby pitting Britain and France against the United States. American pressures for a free state of Fiume confused Millerand and Lloyd George. The absence of the United States from important conferences created difficulties, they argued, since it expressed views, but did not attend the relevant discussions. Without an Italo-Yugoslav agreement, the French and British had to follow the Treaty of London with its promises of future territorial adjustments for Italy. Reconciliation of ethnographic considerations in the Adriatic was, they claimed, no more complex than elsewhere. They reminded Wilson that the nationality principle had been violated for the Germans in Czechoslovakia. Clearly, the principle of national self-determination was not the sole guide to postwar treaty decisions. To placate the American president, however, they promised to take American views into account in settling the question. Only if Italy and Yugoslavia remained deadlocked would France and Britain retreat to the Treaty of London.[33]

Rumors of Armenian massacres in Cilicia reached Millerand in late February, but confirmation of the reports was difficult to obtain. Indeed, a reported massacre at Marash proved completely fictitious; Armenians, along with French troops, had suffered battle casualties. The premier insisted France must maintain order in Syria and Cilicia, but if the Allies detached areas like Thrace, Smyrna, and Cilicia from Turkey they must be prepared militarily to counter the attendant hostility. Confirmation in early March that 7,000 Armenians had indeed been massacred led Millerand to demand that General Gouraud refute charges that France had tricked the Christian populations and abandoned them to Turkish barbarity.[34]

By early March, Millerand was particularly concerned about

33. A.N., F.M. 51, memorandum from Lloyd George and Millerand to Wilson, 17 February 1920, in response to Wilson's of 14 February; *D.B.F.P.*, VII, pp. 219–41, conference in London, 23–25 February 1920; *Sénat*, Foreign Affairs Commission, 19 February 1920; C.D.A., Foreign Affairs Commission, 20 February 1920; Nevakivi, p. 235; P. Helmreich, pp. 266–8. Although Lloyd George wanted Greece to annex Smyrna, Millerand reluctantly accepted a Greek evacuation; A.E., P.M. 54, Franco-British memorandum to Wilson, 17 February 1920; *ibid.*, Millerand and Lloyd George to Wilson, 26 February 1920.
34. A.E., E. Levant 1918–29, ss Syrie–Liban–Cilicie 24, Millerand to Gouraud, 29 February, 6 and 8 March 1920; *ibid.*, Millerand to French ambassador in London, 7 March 1920.

Turkey's situation. Although the arrival of Greek troops made a conflict in Smyrna likely, he insisted France must concentrate its limited forces in Syria, Cilicia, and Constantinople. Lloyd George wanted the Allies to prevent further Armenian massacres, but Millerand feared the British preferred to occupy Constantinople alone so that they could dominate the Straits. Pressing for a joint Franco-British action, he argued that the Turks should receive an impression of Allied accord. Inter-Allied control of Constantinople raised the problem of command. Millerand believed that its military operations in Thrace, Cilicia, and the Levant entitled France to share military control. The two nations jointly controlled the Turkish navy, but General Milne wanted the British to possess exclusive influence over the Turkish army.[35]

Millerand was concerned that the American absence from the Turkish treaty negotiations indicated a lack of interest in Eastern affairs and feared that the United States would let the Allies make all the decisions, but then question the resolution of tricky issues like the Adriatic. To him, a solution to Eastern problems was of fundamental importance to the Great Powers, the United States included. Since continued anarchy seriously threatened the Christian populations, it was vital to restore order in Turkey. Millerand was therefore anxious to know the American president's decision on participating in the negotiations with Turkey. To him, the Allied task would be incomplete unless the United States shared in the general peace settlement.[36]

During March and April, Millerand's policy toward Turkey consisted of a defense of French interests. The Allies wanted to preserve a viable Turkish state, he noted to the Chamber on 26 March, but also to satisfy the principle of national self-determination by recognizing ethnic rights and independent nationalities. The Ottoman Empire's new boundaries, therefore, excluded the Arab states. While the sultan was permitted to retain his position, he must institute economic reforms and insure freedom of navigation in the Straits. Determined to guard French interests, Millerand insisted on Allied equality on the Constantinople control commissions and an equilibrium between French and British troop

35. A.E., E Levant 1918–29, ss Turquie 162, Millerand to French high commissioner in Constantinople, 5, 6, 10 and 11 March 1920 and Millerand to French ambassador in London, 17 March 1920.
36. A.E., Amerique, ss Etats-Unis 39, Millerand to French ambassador in Washington, 7 March 1920.

levels. At San Remo, the Allies settled such Near Eastern issues as France's share of the Mosul oil rights, long a thorn in inter-Allied relations. Facing a potentially catastrophic oil shortage, France wanted 50 percent of Mosul oil. Since the Mosul belonged to British Mesopotamia, Millerand reluctantly accepted 25 percent of any private Mesopotamian oil company's stock. Existing or proposed French concessions to exploit Heraclea's coal reserves at the time of the Mudros armistice were also recognized. Once Italian production reached that of other foreign concessionaires, France would receive a quarter of the remaining concessions. A Tripartite Pact of 11 May 1920 confirmed the arrangements. Armenia's status and frontiers were also settled. Millerand and Lloyd George hoped the United States would expel the Turks and assume the mandate for Armenia. In Smyrna, the Allies granted Turkey nominal suzerainty and reduced the area of Cilicia and Armenia. Millerand did, however, worry about the treaty's repercussions on the various nationalities, particularly the effects of aggressive Turkish nationalism on Syria. To satisfy his clerical supporters, Millerand tried to preserve France's religious protectorate in Palestine. Indeed, Jonnart's nomination to an extraordinary mission to the Vatican just before the San Remo conference may have stemmed from this policy. Combined British and Italian opposition, however, forced Millerand to yield. After Britain received the mandate for Palestine, France had to accept the end of its religious protectorate. Like Clemenceau, Millerand viewed the Near East as a secondary front, where he fought tenaciously for specific issues, but focused on Syria. After France won Syria, he used other concessions to buy British cooperation on more important European matters.[37]

By June, the premier had altered his Turkish policy to give greater weight to the nationalists. Perhaps increasing difficulties with Feisal led him to seek a settlement with the Turkish nationalist leader Kemal. To Gouraud, he suggested that the situation might

37. A.N., F.M. 51, draft of Millerand's speech of 26 March 1920; J.O., *Chambre*, 26 March and 28 April 1920; E. Bonnefous, III, pp. 137–43, 145; A.E., E Levant 1918–29, ss Syrie–Liban–Cilicie 26, Millerand telegram from San Remo, 24 April 1920; A.E., E Levant 1918–29, ss Syrie–Liban–Cilicie 27, Millerand's telegram from San Remo, 26 April 1920; A.N., F.M. 56, minutes of meeting between Millerand and Lloyd George, 18 April 1920; *D.B.F.P.*, VIII, pp. 27–8, 172–7; Andrew and Kanya-Forstner, p. 218; C.D.A., Foreign Affairs Commission, 30 April 1920; Nevakivi, p. 244; P. Helmreich, pp. 292, 297–8, 303–4, 329; Andrew and Kanya-Forstner, pp. 217–18; A.E., E Levant 1918–29, ss Syrie–Liban–Cilicie 27, Millerand to Gouraud, 4 May 1920.

improve if Kemal knew that France planned to preserve Ottoman sovereignty in Cilicia. An agreement with the nationalists might limit France's role in Cilicia and still protect its treaty rights.[38]

Millerand's summary of relations with Turkey in early June noted the Allied decision to retain the sultan in Constantinople provided he observed the treaty's stipulations for minorities. To insure free access to the strategically important Straits, the Allies would be represented on a Straits Commission that was independent of local authorities, and would maintain occupation troops in a demilitarized zone bordering the Straits. Greece received Thrace, but on the tricky issue of Smyrna the Allies compromised by granting sovereignty to Turkey and administration to Greece. Armenia's independence was recognized, but the attribution of its mandate remained unresolved. Since France held 65 percent of the Turkish debt before the war, it assigned the financial question particular significance. The French overruled the British effort to suppress the international committee on the Ottoman public debt and retained their special hold on Turkish revenues. Control over Turkish finances would continue, with a priority accorded to repayment to bearers of shares in the Ottoman public debt.[39]

Even after the Turkish treaty was negotiated, Turkey resisted its terms, and problems remained between Britain and France. A concern for Franco-British equality led Millerand to seek compensation for Britain's domination of the Turkish military situation. While unity of command for Constantinople aided effective military operations, Millerand insisted that the French should control the sea if the British controlled the land. If a British general had supreme authority, a French general should command the city of Constantinople. Turkish recalcitrance about applying the treaty, however, led the Allies to bury their own differences. In July, they reminded Turkey that its wartime alliance with Germany was a betrayal of the Great Powers which had defended it for fifty years. Furthermore, massacres that were revolting to the human conscience made it morally impossible to leave large non-Turkish populations under Ottoman domination. They were willing to have a Turkish representative on the Straits Commission, but

---

38. A.E., E Levant 1918–29, ss Syrie–Liban–Cilicie 29, Millerand to Gouraud, 1 June 1920.

39. *Sénat*, Foreign Affairs Commission, 3 June 1920; C.D.A., Foreign Affairs Commission, 10 June 1920.

otherwise rejected Turkish objections to the treaty. Indeed, to Millerand, a treaty that preserved a Turkish nation with a large and fertile territory showed considerable Allied moderation. Clearly, French policy toward Turkey concealed a steel hand within the silk glove.[40]

40. *D.B.F.P.*, XIII, pp. 96–7, Derby to Curzon, 27 June 1920, transmitting Millerand's response; J.O., *Chambre*, 20 July 1920.

Part V
The President

12
Bloc National Leader as President of the Republic

As President of the French Republic from September 1920 to June 1924, Alexandre Millerand tried to give this normally titular post an active interpretation. His presidency illuminates not only his approach to significant foreign policy issues but also his attempt to use the president's executive powers to counteract the parliamentary dominance which he had long criticized. His constitutional proposals for a stronger executive, suggested in vain in the 1920s, bore a remarkable resemblance to de Gaulle's modifications of 1958. Perhaps Millerand was a visionary whose views were in advance of his times, or perhaps internal disintegration and paralysis did not sufficiently threaten the nation in 1924 for entrenched interests to yield their power. Had Millerand confronted an external crisis comparable to the Algerian war, the all-powerful Chamber of Deputies might have accepted greater presidential powers, but the lingering economic malaise and international uncertainty of the early 1920s were not sufficient to dispel traditional republican fears of personal power.

Millerand's election to the presidency of the French Republic on 23 September 1920 recognized his dominant political position and hinted at the crisis which prematurely ended his tenure in 1924. As premier and undisputed leader of the dominant Bloc National, Millerand was the key political figure in France in September 1920 and the obvious replacement for ailing President Paul Deschanel. Since the crisis of 16 May 1877, when President Maurice de Mac-Mahon failed to impose a ministry without a parliamentary majority on the Chamber of Deputies, the presidency of the Republic had been a largely ceremonial position filled by elder statesmen or political mediocrities. Millerand was, therefore, reluctant to exchange the premier's real authority for the president's illusory power.

In the summer of 1920, Deschanel's precarious health led Millerand to speculate about a possible replacement for the sick president. During a lunch at Versailles in June, he sounded out Charles Célestin Jonnart about running for the presidency if his concern about Deschanel materialized; before turning to him, Millerand had evidently considered Léon Bourgeois. As Deschanel's condition deteriorated, Millerand again pressured Jonnart in mid-September and informed the cabinet of his overtures. Jonnart, who was willing to run only if unopposed, withdrew when it was clear he would face opposition. Unsuccessfully soliciting Aristide Briand and René Viviani, Millerand simultaneously came under considerable pressure to accept the nomination himself. His prestige as leader of the Bloc National had been bolstered by his forceful response to the strike movement in May and his support for Weygand's mission to Poland which had contributed to its military victory in August. A stream of politicians, including Briand, as well as the press urged Millerand to run. After much hesitation, he reluctantly agreed.[1]

From the start, Millerand clearly indicated his determination to pursue as president the policies he had defined as spokesman for the Bloc National and implemented as premier. His famous Ba-Ta-Clan speech of 7 November 1919 had outlined his view of the relationship between the executive and legislative branches, and clearly indicated his desire to augment presidential powers. His important statement to the press of 20 September 1920 explicitly linked the Bloc National program of 1919 to his goals as president. For eight months as premier, he had applied a program of social progress, work, and union, characterized abroad by an integral application of the Versailles Treaty along with France's allies, and at home by maintenance of the Republic's organic laws, restoration and development of the economy, decentralization and constitutional modifications. If the majority of the parliament preferred

1. Millerand, 'Souvenirs,' pp. 100–1; Persil, pp. 135–7; E. Bonnefous, III, pp. 163–5; Derfler, *President*, p. 93; Jean du Sault, *La Vie et l'œuvre de Charles Jonnart* (Paris: Imprimerie Moderne, s.d.), pp. 41–2; Robert David, 'Une grande carrière politique: M. Jonnart,' *La Revue hebdomadaire*, 22 October 1927, pp. 473–4; Néré, p. 30. Rouffet, p. 164, claims that only Millerand was in contact with Deschanel during the summer and the cabinet met only once (around 14 July). Dansette, pp. 197–8.

that he defend that policy from the Elysée, if it accepted his view that the President of the Republic, while not a party figure, could and should represent a policy closely worked out with his ministers, then Millerand agreed to accept the appeal of the nation's representatives. This program declaration, described as 'unprecedented' in the history of presidential elections, clearly linked Millerand's acceptance of the presidency to an interpretation of that position which would permit him to represent the Bloc National's policies. His stand clearly threatened the fundamental republican tradition of presidential neutrality. The president's only way to exert pressure on the deputies was his constitutional right to dissolve parliament, but no president since MacMahon had used it. Understandably, some deputies viewed Millerand as a threat to parliamentary democracy.[2]

Contemporaries recognized the sensational nature of Millerand's statement. If his views were applied, he would have been the most active president since Grévy. Although conservatives applauded the declaration, the Left feared Millerand wanted to increase his personal power. The latter rejected the substitution of presidential for parliamentary power. Premonitions of his difficulties in 1924 were already discernible. On 21 September, several parliamentary Radicals, including Gaston Doumergue, opposed Millerand's statement, arguing that the president already had sufficient power. A president with a personal political program might infringe on the premier's prerogatives or encounter problems if the legislative majority changed – a prophetic warning of Millerand's later difficulties. The group of parliamentary Radicals voted against presidential power (*pouvoir de l'Elysée*), but did not take an official stand on Millerand's candidacy, except to suggest that a preliminary electoral meeting nominate a 'republican' opponent. To reduce the concern prompted by his statement, Millerand stressed to a Senate delegation that current economic and financial problems took precedence over constitutional revisions. Furthermore, the existing constitution permitted the continuity of foreign policy, his princi-

---

2. Millerand, 'Souvenirs,' p. 100; Jacques Barty, *L'Affaire Millerand* (Paris: Longin, 1924), p. 73; A.N., F.M. 48, Millerand's statement of 20 September 1920; E. Bonnefous, III, p. 165; Gaston Jèze, 'Chronique constitutionelle de France: la présidence de la République,' *Revue du droit public*, October–December 1920, p. 575; Dansette, pp. 198–9; Soulié, *Cartel*, p. 251; Jean-Noël Jeanneney, *Leçon d'histoire pour une gauche au pouvoir. La faillite du Cartel 1924–1926* (Paris: Editions du Seuil, 1977), p. 19; Simonsson, pp. 87–8; Derfler, *President*, pp. 93–4.

pal concern. The president's right to negotiate treaties already permitted him to share in foreign policy formulation. He hedged when he claimed that his constitutional revisions would simply permit the president to serve the government more effectively. On 22 September, Millerand again noted that constitutional revision was a future concern. With Doumergue presiding, the Chamber and Senate Radicals met again on the 22nd prior to the preliminary election meeting which would settle on a republican candidate to present to the National Assembly. While Doumergue did not oppose Millerand personally, he still preferred the traditional concept of presidential power. However, when Millerand received an absolute majority at the preliminary meeting (also on the 22nd), he was declared to be the official republican candidate. Millerand's supporters, like Briand, tried to calm Radical fears by giving Millerand's statements a restricted interpretation, but his adversaries accused him of contradictions. Some noted ironically that they would have a Socialist president with increased powers (although he had not been a member of the Socialist party for seventeen years); others cited his bitter attack on President Casimir-Périer in July 1894 when Millerand asserted that a president with a personal policy could be criticized by parliament and the press. To the Left, Millerand's interpretation of the presidency implemented precisely that personal policy he had so bitterly denounced twenty-five years before. In the election of 23 September, he had a Socialist opponent, but his vote of 695 to 69 had been surpassed only once in the history of presidential elections.[3]

The choice of a successor to Deschanel pointed up two different conceptions of the head of state's role. The Republic's first president, Adolphe Thiers, exemplified the interpretation of the president as a prominent statesman. As the early presidents' authoritarian characteristics triggered conflicts with the legislature, a second conception took over. Less a preeminent citizen than a compromise figure who could reconcile conflicting tendencies, the president became a ceremonial figure without genuine executive functions. A president like Casimir-Périer, who tried to reinstitute the original conception, came into conflict with parliament. After the war, however, pressures mounted for a more active presidency.

---

3. *La Petite République*, articles by Millerand, 5 July, 8 November 1894, 18 January 1895; Jèze, 1920, pp. 575–81; Simonsson, pp. 89–92: in the preliminary election, Millerand received 528 votes, Péret 157, and Bourgeois 113.

To many Frenchmen, Millerand was a politician with a brilliant political past and a spokesman for policies that yielded results. While he would have preferred to remain premier, he was ready to accept the presidency if the original conception were applied. A respect for presidential prerogatives, he believed, would allow the head of state to exercise the authority appropriate to his functions and character within the governmental councils.[4]

The similarities between Millerand's election and those of Poincaré and Casimir-Périer were striking. They were all chosen because of their reputation for energy and willpower, with the resultant expectation of more than normal achievements from them. Poincaré and Millerand were both premiers when elected to the presidency, and their success in that post influenced their nomination. Both times, public opinion played a role; their national prestige outweighed considerations of domestic policy. All three had defended public order amidst social tension: Casimir-Périer against the revolutionary threats after Carnot's assassination; Poincaré during a foreign crisis; Millerand after repressing domestic social unrest. These considerations operated in favor of Millerand. Anxiety for authority inclined opinion to a stronger executive power, and few Frenchmen recognized the implications of removing from the parliamentary majority its most effective and prominent figure. The choice of a prominent figure for the presidency, however, raised the question of the president's role. If the traditionally passive view held, then it was inappropriate to select an outstanding statesman who would be more effective as premier and would fret at an impotent presidential role. The old fear of personal power also surfaced. Like Casimir-Périer and Poincaré, Millerand was chosen despite the reservations of many Radicals, who would later term the election a party victory. In fact, the only issue which divided the Bloc National and the Radicals was the reestablishment of a Vatican embassy which the Chamber had not yet debated. Nonetheless, Millerand's program statement of 20 September, with its explicit link to his Ba-Ta-Clan speech, implied that his election to the presidency was an endorsement of his program, as well as his view of his new role. It is, however, inaccurate to view his election simply as a party victory, since his massive support indicated a more general backing than that of his Bloc National supporters. He was chosen as a national statesman

4. *Le Temps*, 21 September 1920; Jèze, 1920, pp. 580–1.

above parties rather than as a partisan figure. Pressures for Miller-
and's acceptance essentially enabled him to set his own conditions,
making his election an implicit contract which permitted him to
believe that his electors had ratified his interpretation of his prerogatives.[5]

Millerand's acceptance speech, with its clearly nationalistic overtones, summarized his fundamental positions. It was, he argued,
his duty to represent the national interest amid partisan struggles.
Since a separation of powers offered the supreme guarantee of
liberty, the president must safeguard the rights of each branch.
While the form of republican government was beyond debate,
experience had shown the need for some constitutional changes.
Freedom still required authority; a free executive under parliamentary control and an independent judiciary were as essential to
applying universal suffrage as parliamentary debates. 'The confusion of powers is the seed of all tyranny.' 'Freedom under law' was
the French Republic's motto and its rule. Frenchmen must prolong
their wartime unity to handle the postwar problems of reconstruction and Treaty enforcement. Along with the ministers responsible
for governmental policy, the president must insure the continuity
of a foreign policy worthy of France's victory and of its dead. He
was, therefore, inclined to exercise his presidential prerogatives
primarily in the sphere of foreign policy. 'The republican that the
national assembly has just designated will use all his strength,
intelligence, and energy to show himself worthy of the confidence
of the representatives of the people.' His presidential message,
which Leygues read to parliament on 25 September, recapitulated
the themes of his Ba-Ta-Clan address and his statements of 20 and
23 September.[6]

Millerand clearly feared a parliamentary system that intermingled all powers. It was therefore important to establish an
equilibrium between the executive and legislative branches that
restrained legislative infringement on executive prerogatives. Millerand, however, never spelled out precisely how these ideas should
be implemented. What were the criteria for deciding between

5. Simonsson, pp. 92–8.
6. A.N., F.M. 48, Millerand's acceptance speech, 23 September 1920, extract
from the J.O., 24 September 1920, p. 14050; Jolly, p. 2467; Dansette, p. 201;
Derfler, *President*, pp. 94, 96; A.N., F.M. 48, Millerand's message to parliament,
25 September 1920; J.O., *Chambre*, 26 September 1920; E. Bonnefous, III, pp.
166–7.

legitimate legislative power and infringement? Millerand's 'compromise' system posed the problem of genuine power-sharing between the legislative and executive branches. Nor did he elucidate the relationship between the president and premier. What guidelines would resolve a conflict between them? If the president had the right to represent a policy, was he not vulnerable to changes in the national will and obliged to resign if a majority repudiated his policy? Neither he nor his critics in 1920 fully explored the implications of Millerand's views.[7]

The day after his election, Millerand designated his old friend and supporter, Georges Leygues, as premier. Briand's active support for Millerand's presidential candidacy led many people to expect a Briand ministry; Poincaré and Viviani were also mentioned. Instead, Millerand turned to Navy Minister Leygues, who retained intact the Millerand cabinet; only the person of the premier changed. No precedent existed in Third Republic history for perpetuating a former ministry with a new head, and it seemed to proclaim that Millerand was still the true governmental leader. Indeed, in his Chamber interpellation of the government's foreign policy, the Socialist Alexandre Bracke affirmed that the president and not the premier had formed the government. Leygues answered that it was logical to keep the ministers who had defined the policy supported by the Chamber's majority. The constitution in no way prohibited Leygues's procedure. Although the premier claimed he had been free to select his own ministry, it is questionable whether a prominent statesman like Briand or Poincaré would have accepted a similar arrangement. Indeed, for several months (until January 1921), Millerand governed by intermediary. Was he actually attempting to institute a presidential government or did he view the ministry as a caretaker regime that would fill in until a 'great' ministry could be formed to resolve the postwar crisis? In any event, Leygues's rather 'pale' personality and lack of real authority contributed to his brief tenure.[8]

Millerand's election prompted numerous assessments of his character, views, and political achievements. Former President of the Republic Raymond Poincaré was concerned about Millerand's conception of presidential powers, notably the president's right

7. Simonsson, pp. 99–121.

8. Millerand, 'Souvenirs,' p. 101; E. Bonnefous, III, p. 166; Jèze, 1920, p. 585; Dansette, p. 201; Néré, p. 30; Jeanneney, *Leçon d'histoire*, p. 20; Simonsson, pp. 124–6; Derfler, *President*, p. 96.

under Article 8 of the 1875 constitutional laws to negotiate treaties. The president did indeed, noted Poincaré, have enormous theoretical power: the right to initiate laws, to nominate to civil and military posts, to control the armed forces. These prerogatives were, however, more apparent than real, since they required the countersignature of a minister who was responsible only to the Chambers; the president was only responsible for high treason. Poincaré was noticeably wary about tampering with constitutional arrangements, and hoped Millerand would limit himself to supporting ministerial decisions as his predecessors had done.[9]

For his old friend and frequent political collaborator, René Viviani, Millerand's great achievement was his social legislation, particularly old-age insurance, enacted before the war. To Viviani, Millerand's election was a moral manifestation. An appeal to serve France was one that his friend could not reject. Described as a cannonball with no time to spare, Millerand headed for his goal, moving head bent and unspeaking through the political corridors. Conscientious and hard-working, he used his strong will to confront and resolve problems, but had only recently won public esteem. His contemporaries often thought him disdainful, unaware, Viviani claimed, that myopia and timidity lay behind his reserve. It seemed impossible that such an eloquent speaker could be personally shy. Yet Millerand was, Viviani asserted, an amiable man, whose loyalty to friends made him always ready to help the sick or defeated. His ability to perceive the essence of a problem made him an effective speaker, but one who preferred to convince rather than to impress.[10]

Millerand's character elicited mixed reactions. To journalist Jean Melia, a persistent coolness and combativeness concealed sincere warmth and loyalty to friends. A hard worker and eloquent orator, Millerand provoked apprehension among his adversaries by his fearlessness and tightly argued, clear expositions. His lack of a facile political manner and refusal to make unrealistic electoral promises had often prompted predictions of electoral defeat, but he had the unique record of consistent reelection by his Paris *arrondissement* for thirty-five years. His honesty even led him to jeopardize

9. *Le Temps*, 27 September 1920, article by Poincaré; Jèze, 1920, p. 585; Derfler, *President*, p. 96.
10. René Viviani, 'M. Alexandre Millerand,' *Revue des deux mondes*, 1 November 1920, pp. 84–95.

his political career for his beliefs, as in the Du Paty affair of 1913. Although Millerand always maintained a legal practice and retreated to it during political adversity, he had rejected Clemenceau's offer of the justice ministry in 1906, because an independent magistrature was so important to him. Melia portrayed his character as orderly and well balanced, a combination of realism and idealism, as illustrated by his choice of reformist over revolutionary tactics as a Socialist. He argued that Millerand's career reflected a continuity that others refused to acknowledge.[11]

To Charles Lavigne, Millerand was a 'great statesman,' whose ideas, despite shifting political labels, had remained remarkably consistent. An ardent patriot, he always refused to implement change by force. A true democrat, he defended universal suffrage but wanted to revise the constitution to avert a dictatorship; collective domination was as pernicious to him as individual. Lavigne praised his accomplishments as Minister of Commerce and Public Works as significant contributions to France's social legislation, notably his laws on the length of the work day, weekly rest periods, salary levels for civil servants, encouragement for unions, reorganization of the railroads, and autonomy of the ports.[12]

Contemporary assessments of Millerand's character and achievements reiterated the same themes, notably his patriotism and leadership qualities. As de la Rocca commented, he was a 'man of authority,' an upper-middle-class individual for whom the cult of the fatherland took precedence. To David, Millerand's elevation to the presidency was a tragedy for the Bloc National, since it removed its only true leader from the Chamber of Deputies, thereby facilitating the later victory for the Cartel des Gauches.[13] Millerand's dedication to duty, attachment to his beliefs, and serious confrontation of political issues clearly inspired respect, but his reserved manner and repugnance for facile *camaraderie* alienated political colleagues. Although France was aware of its new president's programs, Millerand's dominant characteristics of action and achievement were ones which the Elysée normally constrained. His

11. *Le Parlement et l'opinion*, 23 September 1920, special issue on Alexandre Millerand, article by Jean Melia on Millerand's character and personality, pp. 1653–64.
12. *Le Parlement et l'opinion*, 1920, article by Charles Lavigne on 'l'homme politique,' pp. 1679–85.
13. Comte de Peretti de la Rocca, 'Briand et Poincaré,' *Revue de Paris*, 15 December 1936, p. 776; David, pp. 473–4.

new situation was, therefore, destined to provoke either personal frustration or a crisis unless the constitution was revised or interpreted in ways that would permit the president to play a more than usually active role.

Not only in his choice of premier but by his whole behavior, Millerand tried to implement his view of presidential powers. 'With him, something changed at the Elysée.' Beginning in October 1920, he summoned all the prefects to the Elysée, which some people perceived as an infringement on the prerogatives of the premier and interior minister. He also consulted individual ministers, later claiming that he saw himself as a collaborator who observed and discussed his ministers' projects with them. Relations with his ministers, however, altered after his election; Finance Minister Frédéric François-Marsal described him as a *patron* rather than a colleague. François-Marsal noted that he sent copies to the president of all memos addressed to the premier and discussed economic issues with him. Millerand also discussed their departmental issues with ministerial directors, but emphatically denied by-passing the relevant ministers to do so. He insisted that he always informed the ministers in advance.[14]

Specific incidents create a picture of an active president who, if he did not set government policy, still tried to influence official personnel and procedures. In October 1920, Millerand, who was apparently asked to arbitrate a budget dispute between the war and finance ministers, declined. On a pardon for the striking railroad workers arrested in May, he did, however, answer the workers' lawyer directly rather than through a minister. Millerand, using his secretary-general, Alfred Vignon, preserved his contacts with the Quai d'Orsay, and required that he immediately receive copies of important despatches. The Comte de Saint-Aulaire attributed his nomination as French ambassador to Great Britain to Millerand. Terming Millerand's intervention as an extraordinary innovation, Saint-Aulaire claimed the president forced him on the cabinet in hopes that he would stand up to Lloyd George. To augment presidential prestige, Millerand reduced the ceremonial aspects of

14. Dansette, p. 201; Barty, p. 83; Millerand, 'Souvenirs,' pp. 102–3; Soulié, *Cartel*, p. 253; A.N., F.M. 87, Millerand to Léon Duguit, letter published in *Le Parlement et l'opinion*, August 1924; Rouffet, pp. 164–5; Laroche, *Quai d'Orsay*, p. 129.

his position by minimizing the common practice of conferring presidential patronage on insignificant association meetings.[15]

The episodes which most clearly illustrated Millerand's conception of the presidential role were generally linked to foreign policy. Convinced that Germany would always attempt to avoid executing the Treaty of Versailles, he believed that France must support those states that had benefited from the new order. Powerless as isolated small states, they would compel German attention if united and backed by the Great Powers. To the Czechoslovakian leaders Masaryk and Benes, Millerand portrayed France's military mission to Prague as a demonstration of French sincerity. Responsible for inviting Poland's Marshal Pilsudski to France, Millerand privately hammered out the basic political and military points of the Franco-Polish treaty of 19 February 1921 with the Polish leader after a dinner at the Elysée on 5 February. To Millerand, the alliance was important to the eastern barrier between Germany and Russia. On the other hand, he criticized the British Ambassador to Berlin, Lord d'Abernon, for pro-German positions that were detrimental to France.[16]

Two possible routes to Treaty execution existed for France: coercion and cooperation. Millerand's policies as premier and later as president inclined toward the first tactic, but he also hoped Franco-German economic cooperation would encourage a German recovery that would foster fulfillment of postwar commitments. Meeting with his economic experts (Seydoux, François-Marsal, and Louis Dubois, French representative on the Reparations Commission) on 23 October 1920, Millerand termed literal German Treaty execution to be a chimera; to force German compliance risked a breach with Great Britain. He endorsed the Seydoux Plan, a comprehensive solution of reparations by a settlement in kind. Until early 1921, Millerand believed that a Franco-German *rapprochement* was possible, which encouraged him to press for economic solidarity and a less anti-German orientation to French policy. His repeated conciliatory efforts were, however, rebuffed by German industrialists and by the British, who feared any Franco-German accommodation. When the Brussels conference repudiated the Seydoux Plan, it was virtually certain the French would revert to

15. Jèze, 1920, pp. 585–6; Millerand, 'Souvenirs,' p. 103; Soulié, *Cartel*, p. 250; Laroche, *Quai d'Orsay*, p. 129; Derfler, *President*, pp. 87, 96; Comte de Saint-Aulaire, *Confession d'un vieux diplomate* (Paris: Flammarion, 1953), pp. 534–5.
16. Millerand, 'Souvenirs,' pp. 105–7; Wandycz, pp. 214–16.

coercion. Only after conciliation moves had been rebuffed did Millerand become consistently hostile and skeptical.[17]

Toward the Roman Catholic Church, Millerand backed the policy of reestablishing a French embassy to the Vatican that he had inaugurated as premier. Negotiations with the papacy were re-opened when Jonnart was sent to Rome as ambassador to the Vatican in May 1921. Afraid of reviving old anticlerical passions, Millerand dealt semi-officially with the pope to avoid a debate in the Chamber of Deputies. The president's guarantees about treat-ment of diocesan associations in France eventually secured papal approval for the associations in January 1925 (after Millerand's resignation from the presidency). That issue and the French em-bassy to the Vatican owed much to Millerand's intervention.[18]

Although Millerand tried to preserve presidential prestige by avoiding frequent ceremonial appearances, he still had some formal obligations. Common themes, notably patriotic praise for his nation, recurred. On 9 November 1920, he stressed France's great-ness, most recently demonstrated in its wartime heroism, which had fostered French moral unity. An aspect of that unity, however, concerned the president: excessive centralization jeopardized that regional distinctiveness, which, far from undermining national loyalties, enriched the nation as a whole. A few days later, lauding republican achievements since 1870 and stressing the unity between Frenchmen of the past and the present that was cemented by wartime experiences, he attributed republican greatness to heroic individuals like Gambetta, Jules Ferry, and Waldeck-Rousseau as well as to scientists, artists, and writers and to institutions like the army, the schools, and the social insurance system.[19]

During 1921, Millerand's speeches reiterated a dedication to France, the war's importance, Treaty enforcement, and the need for unity and work for France's spiritual and economic revival. A wartime tenacity, self-sacrifice, and dedication to duty were also

17. McDougall, p. 135; Artaud, *Dettes interalliées*, pp. 297, 300, 302; Soutou, 'Une autre politique,' pp. 27, 30–3.

18. Dansette, pp. 201–2; Persil, pp. 154–7; du Sault, 'Les relations diplo-matiques,' p. 117; Paul, pp. 53, 90.

19. A.N., F.M. 48, Millerand's speech at a reception at the Hôtel de Ville, 9 November 1920; also in J.O., *Lois et décrets*, p. 18017; A.N., F.M. 48, speech celebrating the 50th anniversary of the Republic, given at the Pantheon, 13 Novem-ber 1920; also in J.O., *Lois et décrets*, pp. 18195–7.

vital, he argued, in postwar France, as was the fraternity which bound its citizens. Solidarity had linked the men in the trenches but also across time to past, present, and future Frenchmen – an organic view of the nation reminiscent of Edmund Burke's conservative philosophy of the early nineteenth century. Virtues that enabled France to triumph over aggression would, he believed, guarantee it received the fruits of victory. Work and union remained paramount. 'Peace has returned, to work.' As president, Millerand argued that neither the constitution's letter nor its spirit imprisoned him in a passive, decorative isolation. Indeed, he had collaborated closely with the cabinet and wanted to retain contact with the representatives of public opinion, particularly members of parliament and departmental delegates. He hoped the presidency's electoral base could be broadened to permit representatives of general councils to vote for the President of the Republic, as Adolphe Thiers had suggested in 1873. Stressing the intimate connection between social reform and public prosperity, he urged the collaboration of all productive forces as well as a decentralization of the French administrative structure to give local authorities expanded powers of decision. France must avoid its former internal divisions and remain united as it faced its postwar challenges.[20] Millerand's presidential position offered him a podium from which to proclaim his fundamental themes of national glory, wartime lessons in unity, postwar rehabilitation, and international treaty commitment.

When Leygues's ministry fell in January 1921, Millerand asked Briand to form the new cabinet. By late December, the Leygues ministry was clearly in a precarious position. Its collapse on 12 January 1921 was triggered by the Chamber's apprehension about the forthcoming Allied reparations conference scheduled to open in Paris on 19 January. The Chamber seemingly wanted a prominent statesman to lead the government in the tricky international negotiations. There were pressures on Millerand to nominate Poincaré because of his forceful stand on reparations, but the president

20. A.N., F.M. 74, Millerand's speech at St-Germain-en-Laye, 6 February 1921, at the granting of a legacy from an Alsatian to five French soldiers; *ibid.*, speech to the Chamber of Commerce of Lyon, 13 March 1921; *ibid.*, speech to the banquet of the Conseil General du Rhône, 13 March 1921; *ibid.*, speeches in Lille, 15 and 16 May 1921; also in J.O., *Lois et décrets*, 18 May 1921, pp. 5869–74; A.N., F.M. 74, speech at the Lycée Henri IV, 5 June 1921, inaugurating a monument; *ibid.*, speech at the Lycée Michelet, 22 June 1921.

recognized that the premier must be able to negotiate with the British, and Poincaré had strongly opposed the British position. Millerand vetoed Poincaré as foreign minister, his preferred post had he been chosen premier. Millerand first asked President of the Chamber Raoul Péret to form a ministry, but Péret gave up his attempt to create a national ministry when Poincaré declined the finance ministry. Millerand then appealed to Briand, a man for whom he had little sympathy but who seemed to reflect the current political climate. Worried about Briand's inclination to intrigue, of which he had several times been the victim, Millerand wanted to tie him to the Bloc National so that he would not be free to exercise his destructive, denigrating talents in the parliamentary corridors. Millerand's son has portrayed the Briand of the early 1920s as an amusing, prankish, slightly facile man, perhaps a blackguard but a good raconteur, the true skeptic who did not pay too much attention to state matters or changes of opinion: in sum, a rather lightweight, slightly disreputable figure with considerable charm. Millerand, who clearly did not consider Briand able or willing to pursue a firm policy domestically or internationally, continually pressed him to defend strongly French interests. For example, he succeeded in winning Briand's support for the alliance with Poland over Berthelot's and Foch's opposition.[21]

During 1921, Millerand supported policies which reinforced France's international position, as, for example, the episode of the Banque Industrielle de Chine. In January 1921, Millerand, aware of the bank's precarious situation, was informed about rescue efforts. On 22 January, he personally asked Stanislas Simon of the Bank of Indochina for his support. Millerand insisted that the Banque Industrielle's collapse would seriously damage French Far Eastern interests. In July, he asked businessman François Carnot to play a pivotal role in the bank's reconstruction, but Carnot was deterred by a cool reception from André Berthelot and the Banque de Paris. To Berthelot, the moves to rescue the bank since January had been slow, fragmentary, and controversial. Seemingly the 'Clemencistes' wanted to use the bank episode as a weapon against Briand, but Tardieu's campaign in the *Echo National* during February and March also cited Millerand's role. Efforts to link Millerand's interest

---

21. Simonsson, pp. 128–30; Derfler, *President*, pp. 96–7; Persil, pp. 139–40; Laroche, *Quai d'Orsay*, p. 138; Dansette, p. 202; Jolly, p. 2467; J. Millerand, p. 114; E. Bonnefous, III, pp. 205–7.

in the bank to his ties to André Berthelot during the 1919 elections did not, however, succeed.[22]

During 1921, Millerand played his most active role in policy toward Germany. That realm, therefore, proved to be a testing-ground for the relationship between the president and the premier. In early March, the Supreme Council in London decided on an Allied occupation of three key Ruhr towns on the Rhine's right bank, Düsseldorf, Duisbourg, and Ruhrort, as security for Allied receipt of reparations. The operation, which lasted six months (until 30 September 1921), increased the payment of reparations. Primarily a customs and financial effort, the move illustrated the thinness of Allied, and especially French, patience. Millerand, too, abandoned the conciliatory policy of the previous autumn. A mood of hostility to Germany influenced French support for a Ruhr occupation.[23]

Millerand's conviction that France must hold firm on reparations guided his telegrams to Briand in London. The premier was attending a conference there on reparations and the Ruhr occupation in May. Millerand thought German payment methods had received too much attention. To him, the crucial issue was Germany's acceptance of a total figure. It had rejected both the Reparations Commission's figure and the lower one of 132 billion gold marks set by the Accord of Paris. The president reminded Briand that French public opinion would view a withdrawal from the Ruhr before results were achieved as a German victory and a French setback. To satisfy opinion, therefore, the premier must win German concessions that produced immediate results and future French security. To Briand's query about limiting the Ruhr occupation to secure Allied agreement, the president answered that

22. Jean-Noël Jeanneney, *L'Argent caché* (Paris: Fayard, 1981), pp. 145, 147, 162, 176, 185, 190; Mermeix, p. 149. *Écho National*, 10 February 1922, article by 'Ignace', stressed the misinformation supplied by bank president André Berthelot about its prosperity. He noted the connection to the Quai d'Orsay where Berthelot's brother was secretary-general and the dissemination of false information to French diplomats abroad. Several consortiums were formed to bail out the bank with a total expenditure of about 250 million francs. Criticizing Millerand for dragging the presidency into the financial morass, the author noted the president's approval of the plan to save the bank and his permission for several meetings with bankers to be held in his cabinet.

23. Trachtenberg, p. 206; Denise Artaud, 'A propos de l'occupation de la Ruhr,' *Revue d'histoire moderne et contemporaine*, XVII, January–March 1970, p. 1; Paul Tirard, *La France sur le Rhin. Douze années d'occupation rhénane* (Paris: Librairie Plon, 1930), pp. 334–5, 341.

France had reached the limit of its concessions. The conference's ultimatum to Germany threatened an inter-Allied occupation of the entire Ruhr unless the reparations plan was accepted.[24]

Millerand's telegrams convey the impression of a firm president shoring up a wavering premier. His determination to exact reparations and his general suspicion of German good faith, reminiscent of his stance in the inter-Allied conferences of 1920, emerge clearly. Furthermore, he assumed the larger mandate of spokesman for French public opinion, possibly to legitimize his active participation in foreign policy decisions. There is no indication that Millerand imposed his views on a reluctant cabinet, but he clearly shared responsibility with the premier for foreign policy. Increasingly during 1921, Millerand's interpretation won out. By the end of the year, Briand, who was considered too conciliatory, was ever more isolated within his own government. The most important figures dealing with reparations, Millerand, Seydoux, and Loucheur moved toward a more forceful stance.[25] While the president never supplanted the premier, he did play a significant part in foreign policy decisions which somewhat altered the relationship between the two positions.

Millerand's suspicions of Germany led him to oppose its admission to the League of Nations. To John Fischer-Williams (British legal representative on the Reparations Commission), he claimed the move would place Germany on an equal footing with France. Although the Wirth cabinet had demonstrated a willingness to observe international commitments as required by the League's statutes, its position was precarious. Millerand was also convinced that Germany was secretly building the core of an army in Upper Silesia that threatened all nations, but especially France. German admission to the League should await a solution to the Upper Silesian issue and the successful implementation of Wirth's policy of fulfillment.[26]

During the autumn of 1921, Millerand's suspicions of German good faith increased. To Charles Laurent, French ambassador to Berlin, he verbalized his increasing skepticism, since Wirth's policy had not been continued. Furthermore, the good faith of the large

24. Jacques Chastenet, 'Une occasion manquée: l'affaire de la Ruhr,' *La Revue de Paris*, July 1959, pp. 5–6; A.E., P.M. 48, telegrams Millerand to Briand, London, 1, 2 and 4 May 1921; also in A.N., F.M. 69; McDougall, p. 155; Derfler, *President*, p. 98.

25. Trachtenberg, p. 219.

26. A.N., F.M. 70, meeting between Millerand and Fischer-Williams, 16 July 1921.

German industrialists, notably Stinnes, was suspect, which made comprehensible the negative attitude of their French counterparts. To Millerand, d'Abernon's refusal to recognize the dangers to Britain of a German bankruptcy was amazing. Clearly, Germany's allocation of 3 billion marks to navigation companies instead of to debt settlement hurt France. Would, he asked, the payments agreements be fulfilled or not? The French must demonstrate their determination to receive everything promised them. He expected Belgium to support France, although British aid was questionable.[27] Millerand's precise influence on French foreign policy is difficult to determine, but he was actively interested in the major issues.

By late 1921, the position of Briand's cabinet was precarious. Although the premier received a vote of confidence after his return from the Washington Disarmament Conference of November, the French feared that negotiations between Lloyd George and Briand, first in London and then at Cannes, would cut German reparations. Briand's policy resembled that of Britain in trying to internationalize questions of reparations and security. He also considered significant Britain's offer of a Franco-British security pact in exchange for French reparations concessions. Millerand mentioned to Saint-Aulaire in December that he was seeking a new premier, claiming he had originally chosen Briand as less dangerous and easier to control in power than in the opposition. By December, however, Millerand had recognized his mistake. Briand's parliamentary interpellations in the Chamber and Senate after his trip to London clearly reflected anxiety about his possibly excessive concessions.[28]

Although Millerand and Briand had moved in different directions during the second half of 1921, the final rupture occurred in January 1922 during the conference of Cannes, the subsequently notorious *coup de Cannes*. Briand and Lloyd George after their meeting in London travelled to Cannes, where the Supreme Council planned to set the agenda for the forthcoming economic conference in Genoa. Before his departure, Briand and the French cabinet agreed on the guidelines for French policy. The two fundamental prob-

27. A.N., F.M. 69, Millerand to Charles Laurent, 8, 11 and 22 November 1921 and 13 March 1922.
28. Saint-Aulaire, p. 576; Maier, pp. 276–7; Simonsson, pp. 131–4; Derfler, *President*, p. 98.

lems at Cannes, Franco-Russian relations and German reparations, triggered a confrontation between Millerand and Briand which culminated in the premier's resignation. On 8 January 1922, Millerand cited his letter to Lloyd George of 21 December 1921 which reiterated the president's position that it would be a dangerous mistake to accord any recognition to the Russian government. The British prime minister had summarized to Briand Millerand's policy at Lympne and Boulogne of June 1920 which subsequent French cabinets had followed. That policy, reaffirmed by Millerand to Giolitti at Aix-les-Bains on 12 September 1920, viewed relations with the Soviet Union as more politically dangerous than commercially advantageous. Since the cabinet had again endorsed that position prior to Briand's departure, Millerand wanted the premier to defend it at Cannes. British desires to include the Russians in the forthcoming economic conference led Lloyd George, Millerand maintained, to propose a British guarantee of French frontiers against German aggression in exchange for French acquiescence to the Russian presence. Millerand, however, rejected any contract that might imply official recognition. Although Poland's victory had temporarily freed Europe from the Russian menace, the president wanted it permanently eradicated. Should the Soviet government therefore be admitted to the Genoa conference, and under what conditions? In Millerand's opinion, the British were not interested in Eastern European security but were anxious to re-open a potentially profitable Russian market. He was also determined that the Allies hold firm on German reparations obligations and constraints if they were not fulfilled.[29]

The Cannes conference, which began on 6 January 1922, set the general guidelines for the later economic conference. The precondition for Soviet admission was recognition of tsarist debts and an end to revolutionary propaganda abroad – precisely the conditions that Millerand himself had demanded as premier in 1920. Although the Russians accepted the invitation on 8 January they did not mention these principles. Briand's report of this initial meeting prompted Millerand to telegraph his 'regret' and 'anxiety' about the conference's resolution. He feared the text would require Russian acceptance of the preconditions only if the Soviet government wanted official recognition. Lenin and Trotsky could, he feared,

29. Millerand, 'Souvenirs,' pp. 108–9; A.N., F.M. 71, note by Millerand, 8 January 1922; Persil, pp. 141–2; Laroche, *Quai d'Orsay*, p. 153; Derfler, *President*, p. 98.

participate without accepting the above principles if they decided that Russian commercial development did not require official recognition. Millerand again demanded that the Cannes conference not invite Russia to Genoa before that nation accepted the preconditions. He was also anxious about the British position on reparations. Even though Germany continually delayed its payments, Britain was reluctant to use force, as it had always been. Paragraph 6 of the Cannes conference's resolution might allow Germany to interpret the commitment to abstain from all aggression as an obligation for the Allies also to renounce future constraints. Millerand feared a general non-aggression pact would preclude French sanctions against Germany. If Germany received an invitation to the economic conference, considerable concessions might ensue.[30]

Between 7 and 11 January, Millerand's almost daily telegrams urged Briand to resist concessions. On 8 January, he expressed satisfaction that Russian representatives would be invited only if they accepted the Allied preconditions. He continued to maintain the Allied right of constraint if Germany defaulted on reparations. Following the cabinet meeting on 10 January, Millerand telegraphed to Briand the cabinet view that a Russian invitation to the economic conference must be subordinated to acceptance of Allied preconditions. Toward Germany, France reserved the right of constraint if Germany defaulted, and the French did not favor a moratorium. After the cabinet meeting of 11 January, Millerand again warned Briand that France would consider a moratorium only if it could apply sanctions should Germany not meet its commitments. Unless Briand could have the above conditions approved, the cabinet was ready to urge him to break off negotiations. The president and the cabinet also considered ambiguous the Supreme Council's position on reparations. Millerand's subsequent defense of his frequent correspondence with Briand stressed the gravity of the subjects under discussion at Cannes, which required close monitoring by the cabinet. The exchange of telegrams informed Paris about the conference proceedings and transmitted the cabinet's, not just the president's, views to the premier. Although Millerand acknowledged the premier's services and affirmed his confidence in his actions, Briand abruptly left Cannes on 12 January and returned to Paris to defend his behavior to the

---

30. Millerand, 'Souvenirs,' p. 109; A.N., F.M. 71, note by Millerand, 8 January 1922; A.N., F.M. 81, telegram from Millerand to Briand, 7 January 1922; E. Bonnefous, III, p. 277; Jolly, p. 2467; Trachtenberg, p. 235.

cabinet and the Chamber of Deputies. Even though he still enjoyed the support of his fellow ministers and was not repudiated by a vote in the legislature, Briand abruptly submitted his resignation the same day.[31]

This episode sparked both contemporary and subsequent controversy. Millerand, who later argued that Briand's abrupt resignation completely surprised him, denied that he had forced the premier to quit. He portrayed the foreign policy directives to the premier in Cannes as unanimous cabinet decisions supported by the President of the Republic. Briand, who returned to Paris on his own initiative, had implied to the cabinet that he planned to defend its unanimous opinion in the Chamber where he retained a legislative majority. Millerand's supporters have blamed Briand for the *Coup de Cannes* incident, charging that he sought to lay responsibility on the president for the divergent views culminating in his resignation. Briand spread the story, they claim, that Millerand's disavowal robbed him of any further ability to direct foreign policy, even though the cabinet had agreed on the guidelines before Briand left for London and Cannes. Millerand's telegrams merely reiterated those principles. When Briand altered the cabinet's directives, he used the *Coup de Cannes* as a pretext to escape the consequences of his commitments. Millerand's telegram of 11 January suggesting that Briand sever negotiations unless France's preconditions were met was hardly a *coup*, they argue, since it recognized the premier's contribution and accorded him cabinet and presidential confidence.[32]

Briand and his adherents viewed the episode quite differently. To the Chamber, Briand claimed that the difficult negotiations required a moral backing and sense of confidence which he did not feel. The policy directives from Paris undermined his negotiating authority. He argued that he could not continue as foreign minister after the president had disavowed him. For Briand's supporters, blame rested squarely on Millerand, whose telegram of 7 January

31. Millerand, 'Souvenirs,' pp. 110–11; A.N., F.M. 81, telegrams from Millerand to Briand, 8, 10 and 11 January 1922; Suarez, V, pp. 371, 389–91, 396–7; Trachtenberg, pp. 235–6; E. Bonnefous, III, pp. 278–9; Laroche, *Quai d'Orsay*, p. 154; Maier, pp. 278–9; Dansette, p. 203; Derfler, *President*, pp. 98–9.

32. Millerand, 'Souvenirs,' p. 112; conversation with Jacques Millerand, 20 May 1978, in which he, too, insisted that Briand's charge of being abandoned was inaccurate; E. Bonnefous, III, p. 282; Dansette, p. 203; Persil, pp. 140–1; A.N., F.M. 87, letter from Millerand to Léon Duguit, published in *Le Parlement et l'opinion*, August 1924.

launched a conflict with incalculable consequences. Described as a 'pathetic' duel between unequal opponents, a constitutionally irresponsible president was pitted against a premier who, as head of the government, was responsible to the Chamber. Custom and legal texts protected the president from partisan attacks even when he abused his power by following a personal policy. He sat in his Elyséean serenity far from the diplomatic battleground and despatched critical telegrams which paralyzed the premier's negotiations. Since Millerand considered the British pact of guarantee to be of little value, he viewed its counterparts, reparations concessions and the Russian invitation, as significant. A stubbornly patient Briand therefore faced an arbitrarily obstinate Millerand. Had the premier not confronted presidential intransigence and public disapprobation, his supporters maintain, a basic agreement might have been achieved. As Briand and Lloyd George gradually reconciled their differences, the conflict between the premier and Millerand intensified to the point where the former found the situation untenable. Fighting on two fronts, he felt he was negotiating above a trap-door which might open momentarily. Millerand's telegram of 11 January rendered Briand incapable of representing France and left him no option but to leave Cannes. Their heated interview in Paris on 12 January simply confirmed their differences. To his supporters, his untenable position prompted Briand's resignation. Although Millerand denied informing the newspapers of the controversy, Briand's supporters insisted that the president called cabinet meetings in the premier's absence to win over the government. They also insisted, however, that Briand did not take his revenge in 1924 by backing Millerand's opponents. Evaluations of the presidential crisis of 1924 often cited Millerand's treatment of Briand at Cannes as contributing to pressures for the president's resignation. A desire to protect a future cabinet position with the Left should the Chamber majority alter may also have influenced Briand's abrupt resignation. The affair marked not only Briand but also leftist opinion which already saw Millerand as overstepping the head of state's traditionally neutral role.[33]

The case is less clear-cut than Millerand's or Briand's partisans believed. Throughout the Cannes negotiations, a tense atmosphere reigned in Paris. The photograph of Briand being given a golf lesson by Lloyd George created an uproar. The premier's perceived

33. Dansette, pp. 203–4; E. Bonnefous, III, pp. 280–1; Suarez, V, pp. 364, 376–7,

subservience on the golf course was interpreted as a symbolic acknowledgement of British primacy. While leftist newspapers accused Millerand of systematically denigrating Briand, the Right worried about Briand's unacceptable concessions. Poincaré, chairman of the Senate's Foreign Affairs Commission, also strongly criticized Briand's concessions, and the Chamber accepted a demand to interpellate the premier. Millerand certainly exerted pressures on Briand which noticeably altered presidential tradition. His success, which was due to ministerial, parliamentary, and public support, was exceptional in the annals of political conflicts between France's presidents and premiers. The president's convocation of the cabinet in the premier's absence has been termed a constitutional innovation. To claim that Millerand 'badgered' and 'bombarded' Briand with telegrams implied that the president intruded excessively in the negotiations. By January 1922, a cabinet majority was clearly apprehensive about further French concessions. If the telegrams despatched under Millerand's signature reflected cabinet opinion, then they were a legitimate means of conveying governmental wishes to France's negotiators. If, however, Millerand transformed sympathetic opinion into criticism, then clearly his action was unprecedented, but no evidence exists that he overruled ministerial views instead of simply acting as a cabinet spokesman.

Briand's resignation not only destroyed the Cannes conference but created some disarray in European politics, provoking several cabinet changes. Although Briand's critics were no more successful in achieving their German and Russian objectives, it is not clear that Briand's policies would have been preferable. Millerand later recalled his stupefaction at learning shortly after Briand's resignation (on 19 January 1922) that the premier had sent instructions from Cannes to Jules Laroche (political director at the Quai d'Orsay) to draft an alliance between France, Britain, Italy, and Germany. Since Laroche's memoirs do not mention this communication, it is impossible to test the accuracy of Millerand's memory on this point. Laroche did, however, consider the Cannes conference a turning-point that had significant consequences for Anglo-French relations. It has also been suggested that industrial pressures on Millerand, notably by Secretary-General Robert Pinot of the Comité des Forges, contributed to Briand's resignation. Chronology, how-

389–91, 396–7, 400, 414; Barty, pp. 28, 81; E. Bonnefous, III, pp. 280–1; Soulié, *Cartel*, p. 252; Jeanneney, *Leçon d'histoire*, p. 20.

ever, makes it impossible that Comité intervention was solely responsible for the conference's collapse.[34]

Although Briand was not obliged to defend his foreign policy to the parliament, a vote of confidence might have dissipated the general climate of distrust. Considerable debate had focused on his motives for resigning. While discussion in the Chamber might have resulted in a negative vote, it was unlikely. Briand would probably have retained at least a fragile majority, since the Chamber would have been reluctant to overturn a ministry during international negotiations. It was also a general axiom that ministries did not fall on foreign policy issues. Increased opposition would, however, have made it difficult for Briand to remain long in power. His dramatic exit offered the political benefit of opening future contacts to the Left. In 1910 also, Briand had abruptly resigned while he still had a majority in the Chamber. For him, a resignation was apparently preferable to a confrontation which might reduce his strength or make him vulnerable to criticism. While Millerand clearly disapproved of the premier's conduct, he did not force Briand to resign. Implementing his conception of the president as representative of the nation's interest, Millerand applied Article 8 of the law of 16 July 1875 that permitted the president to negotiate and ratify treaties. His active involvement in cabinet directives to Briand corresponded to his extended interpretation of his presidential prerogatives. If his action remained within constitutional bounds, it was nonetheless contrary to presidential tradition. It failed to provoke a storm in the Chamber (not even from the Socialists) probably because Millerand reflected the general concern about French concessions to the British and because the relative prerogatives of the president and the premier were never subjected to parliamentary debate.[35]

34. Millerand, 'Souvenirs,' p. 113; Dansette, p. 204; E. Bonnefous, III, pp. 278–82; Maier, pp. 278–80; Néré, pp. 35–6; Mermeix, p. 149; Laroche, *Quai d'Orsay*, pp. 153–4; Jules Laroche, 'La Grande déception de Cannes (Souvenirs de 1922),' *Revue de Paris*, June 1957, pp. 39, 48; Jeanneney, *De Wendel*, p. 147 n.; Trachtenberg, pp. 235–6.

35. Simonsson, pp. 138–44; Derfler, *President*, pp. 99–100; François Albert, 'Chronique politique,' *Revue politique et parlementaire*, 10 February 1922, pp. 279–80. Joseph Barthélemy, 'Chronique de politique extérieure,' *Revue politique et parlementaire*, 10 February 1922, pp. 289–90, argues that Millerand adopted Guizot's conception of the head of state as elaborated in a famous debate with Thiers. Guizot maintained that as a human being the president had the right to have ideas, a program, and a policy, but could only implement them if he found a minister who would accept responsibility for them before parliament.

13
Firmness Toward Germany: the Dominant Presidential Concern

After Briand's abrupt resignation, Millerand had to find a premier who could command a Chamber majority, preferably someone of undisputed authority. His choice of Poincaré signified a stiffening of French policy toward Germany, but, as he later commented, the new premier inherited a difficult situation. Since leaving the presidency in 1920, Poincaré had persistently demanded strict application of the Versailles Treaty, particularly its financial clauses, and had denounced the inter-Allied conferences in which the British had won French concessions. After the conference of Hythe (May 1920), he had resigned as president of the Reparations Commission and had attacked the Committee of Experts' evaluations of German payment capacities. As president of the Senate's Commission on Foreign Affairs, he had telegraphed to Briand in Cannes his support for Millerand's stance. Millerand's selection also reflected parliamentary desires; the presidents of both chambers had urged him to nominate Poincaré. Poincaré's basic goals of German payment of reparations and Allied accord initially seemed feasible, but often proved incompatible.[1]

Poincaré, like Péret in 1921, would have liked to create a broad ministry, spanning much of the political spectrum, but Radicals like Edouard Herriot and Nationalists like Tardieu refused his offer. The keynote of his program was application of the Treaty settlement. That foreign policy had triggered two governmental crises within a year testified to its dominant position. Furthermore, foreign rather than domestic considerations had influenced the

---

1. Millerand, 'Souvenirs,' p. 113; E. Bonnefous, III, pp. 282, 284; Jolly, p. 2467; Dansette, p. 204; Persil, p. 147.

choice of premiers. Neither Briand nor Poincaré was an appropriate leader for the Bloc National majority. Briand was closer to the opposition than the majority, which became clear when he joined the leftist Cartel in February 1924. Poincaré, as former president, preferred to remain above parties. He would have liked to form a national rather than a party government, seeking throughout his ministry to create a republican coalition of center groups backed by the Radicals.[2]

Since the summer of 1920, the Radicals had increasingly distanced themselves from the Bloc National. Their initial reservations focused on religious issues, specifically the reestablishment of an embassy to the Vatican. Only a few Radicals voted to renew diplomatic ties on 30 November 1920. They considered the embassy, established by decree on 18 May 1921, as a threat to the Republic's laic laws, even though Ambassador Jonnart argued that it would not alter French domestic policy. The issue crystallized Radical opposition to the Bloc National. Although the Radicals loyally supported Briand's foreign and domestic policy throughout 1921, including occupation of the Ruhr towns, rumors of a possible leftist block had already surfaced, and Briand's resignation increased the gap between the Radicals and the Bloc National. They refused representation in Poincaré's ministry. While they generally supported the government's foreign policy, even occupation of the Ruhr, their reservations about domestic policy, particularly economic, augmented during 1922 and 1923 to the point where they openly favored a leftist alliance by the autumn of 1923.[3]

Millerand's presidential voyages generally provided an opportunity to outline his views of fundamental French problems. An almost month-long tour of France's North African colonies, Algeria, Morocco, and Tunisia, in April–May 1922 gave him first-hand information about North Africa as well as frequent chances to address France's concerns. The trip demonstrated his dominant characteristics of energy, tenacity, and realism, particularly his *'politique de réalisation'*. In 1920, he had described the growth of the French colonies as proof of the Republic's genius and tenacity. His

2. Simonsson, pp. 145–8, 161–8.
3. *Ibid.*, pp. 145–59. Plumyène and Lasierra, p. 23, note that as he lost support on the Left, Poincaré picked it up on the extreme Right. The Action Française supported his premiership in 1922 and the Ruhr occupation of 1923.

voyage was an expression of French gratitude for the colonies' wartime contribution and a mission of propaganda to demonstrate France's civilizing achievements in North Africa. Frenchmen, Millerand believed, were often ready to denigrate their accomplishments. A demonstration of the significance and success of their colonial policy in North Africa could counteract that tendency. Examining public works' projects and possible improvements, his trip also celebrated French colonial achievements and reinforced the links between France and its empire.[4]

Governor-General Lyautey viewed Millerand's visit to Morocco as an encouragement to the efforts of the colonial administration; his presence consecrated the protectorate. Anxious to preserve local traditions and institutions, Millerand felt that association with France had eliminated insecurity, developed communications networks, fostered industrial and agricultural progress, and promoted mass education, all of which illustrated, the president maintained, French greatness.[5]

Governor-General Steeg of Algeria considered Millerand to be a principal architect of France's deliverance, a positive, hard-working *'réalisateur'* responsible for France's reconstruction, who had tried to create a national union transcending partisan divisions. To him, Millerand's patriotism was paramount. In Oran, Millerand urged that the republican ideals of liberty and justice should guide colonial policy, but again noted that freedom also required a respect for authority. Acknowledging Algeria's contribution to the French war effort, he also stressed French assistance to the colony. In favor of economic modernization and a degree of decentralization, he was cautious about the too-rapid expansion of native political rights. Although Algerians should eventually participate in local government, they needed gradual preparation for political responsibility – the same position he had defended in Syria in 1920.[6]

In Tunisia, too, Millerand expressed gratitude for the colony's wartime aid and stressed France's role in Tunisian development. The French protectorate had fostered agriculture and commerce as well as political and administrative reforms. To unburden the central administration, France wanted to use natives in public

4. H. Pellier, *Le Président Millerand dans le nord africain* (Paris: Librairie Hachette, 1922), preface pp. v–vii; Derfler, *President*, p. 97.
5. Pellier, pp. 1–9, 52, Millerand's speech in Casablanca, 5 April 1922; Scham, pp. 40–2.
6. Pellier, pp. 56–65, 81–91, 137–9.

administration to the degree that they proved themselves capable. Natives would, he believed, more readily accept sacrifices if they could see how they directly benefited from them. While he did not believe the Tunisians were ready for direct suffrage, they could choose representatives to a consultative assembly in which they could discuss matters of interest to France and Tunisia with the colons. France had played an important educating role in North Africa, but progress required close cooperation between French and native populations. Since, he argued, France urgently needed all possible resources for reconstruction, its colonial potential must be fully developed.[7]

Gratitude for the colonial contribution to the French war effort and a definition of the postwar relationship with France's colonies were constant themes of Millerand's speeches to colonial audiences. France, he claimed to the emperor of Annan, intended to respect native customs and religions, but to promote moral and material progress: in other words, economic development and inculcation of French civilization. Colonial development would, he believed, benefit both the protected peoples and the protecting nation.[8] Millerand's nationalism emerged in his belief that the colonies promoted French prestige, but his statements also reflected a paternalistic concern for colonial welfare. The colonies were symbols of and reinforcements to French greatness, but France's civilizing influence and material contributions benefited the dependent populations. His plea that France respect native traditions introduced a libertarian concern for native freedom. Liberalism therefore tempered his paternalism and nationalism.

Economic prosperity and social peace were frequent themes of Millerand's presidential speeches. In La Rochelle, he defended commercial freedom and a gradual removal of wartime restrictions. Although French social legislation restricted freedom of work, prewar guarantees to workers had to be maintained. A contradiction existed, he claimed, between the need for a total

7. *Ibid.*, pp. 143, 156–62, 174. Scham, pp. 42, 44, notes that one result of Millerand's North African visit was the establishment of a permanent liaison between the administrators in Morocco, Tunisia, and Algeria for French action in the Maghreb. The first annual Conférence Nord-Africaine was held in Algeria, 6 February 1923.

8. A.N., F.M. 76, Millerand's speech to the emperor of Annan, 26 June 1922.

effort to repair France's devastated regions and a reduction of the work day by one-fifth, to eight hours. Anxious for legislation to promote social peace and national prosperity, he pleaded for workers and employers to preserve their wartime collaboration in the confrontation of peacetime tasks. The president particularly disliked threats to that social peace such as strikes, which he had long viewed as a form of social warfare, and questioned their legitimacy in the public sector.[9]

To Millerand, prosperity was an essential ingredient of national greatness. In Corsica, for example, he argued that transportation was the basic problem. To develop its natural wealth, it needed an internal network of railroads and external links to the continent, both of which he advocated. Since an island's needs differed from a continent's, Corsica would benefit, he believed, from a degree of administrative autonomy. In Toulon, he insisted a prosperous navy was vital to link the colonies and the mother country. Clearly addressing his audience's specific concerns, he linked concrete economic projects like the provision of drinkable water to cities and rural communes, reinforcement of local industries like shipbuilding, and development of new sources of power to the enhancement of France's grandeur. In Marseilles, he stressed that economic isolation was no longer possible. Europe's economic reconstruction was vital for France's prosperity.[10]

During his presidency, Millerand occasionally addressed peripheral foreign policy issues, notably France's relations with the new nations, the League of Nations, and other European states. As a strong supporter of the postwar Treaty settlement, Millerand wanted France to assist the new nations and to back the League. That policy would promote French security and thwart potential aggression in Eastern Europe.

The rather troubled course of postwar Franco-Italian relations prompted Millerand to seek more cordial contacts, but to assign

9. J.O., *Lois et décrets*, 6 April 1922, pp. 3787–8, Millerand's speech of 31 March 1922 to the Chamber of Commerce of La Rochelle; A.N., F.M. 86, Millerand's response to a speech by Hebrard de Villeneuve on strikes and the public services, 27 February 1923, at the Academy of Moral and Political Sciences of the Institut de France.

10. J.O., *Lois et décrets*, pp. 4736–7, speech in Ajaccio, Corsica, 4 May 1922; *ibid.*, p. 4871, speech in Toulon, 6 May 1922; *ibid.*, pp. 4872–3, speech in Marseilles, 6 May 1922.

priority to a defense of French interests. To Italian Ambassador Bonin, he argued that criticism of France in the Italian press jeopardized harmonious relations. Despite potential advantages, he was skeptical about French industrial or financial involvement in Italy. Mussolini's seizure of power in Italy and Italian involvement in several Mediterranean border disputes led Millerand to defend the new states' rights and the League of Nations. On the tricky Corfu issue, he suggested that the Conference of Ambassadors should settle the question of Corfu's occupation and reparations in exchange for a promise not to force the Italians to leave the island until the issues were clarified. Italy was, however, reluctant to delegate authority to the League or to the Conference of Ambassadors. It did not want to evacuate the island before Greece accepted Italian conditions, which the Conference of Ambassadors could not guarantee. If, by a given date, Greece had not fulfilled all prerequisites, Millerand suggested that an English, French, Italian, and possibly Japanese, occupation could replace the Italian one. Millerand refused to sacrifice the interests of minor Mediterranean states or international organizations for good relations with Italy. Advocating as cordial relations with France's southeastern neighbor as possible, the president acknowledged Mussolini's improvements, but expressed reserve about Italian behavior which tended to discredit the League of Nations. He feared that Mussolini was using demands for international compensation to distract attention from domestic hardships. In the case of Fiume, Millerand rejected French pressures on Yugoslavia to accept Italian proposals that hurt its interests.[11]

Despite his frequent defense of small states, Millerand never assigned them priority over French interests. For example, he argued that Swiss wartime support to France's enemies should weigh in deciding the fate of the *zones franches* area between France and Switzerland. It was unjust, in his opinion, to perpetuate the 'amputation of sovereignty' against the victorious France of 1918 that was exacted from the vanquished France of 1815. This statement brings him perilously close to an assertion of 'might makes right;' France's victory legitimized reclaiming territory lost by defeat a hundred years earlier. Or Switzerland's departure from

11. A.N., F.M. 70, interview between Millerand and Bonin, 5 October 1921; A.N., F.M. 69, Millerand's notes on the Corfu problem, 7 and 13 September 1923; A.E., P.B., III, p. 223, Millerand to Barrère, 13 October and 26 December 1923.

strict wartime neutrality permitted France to reclaim a disputed border region. Neither argument accorded with his oft-proclaimed respect for treaties or the legal settlement of disputes, but reflected his overriding preoccupation with French national interests.[12]

With Central and Eastern Europe, Millerand advocated economic collaboration, support for the new nations, and especially respect for the Treaty settlement. In Austria, he noted the economic crisis and French attempts to locate private sources of aid, but rejected French official responsibility for the meager results. Clearly, Millerand's support for the new nations reflected strategic concerns; they served as potential buffers against a hostile Germany or Russia. Toward the Baltic states, he suggested mutual support until Russia returned to normalcy; the former Russian territories should unite to defend themselves. To Czech Foreign Minister Eduard Benes, Millerand strongly defended the treaties that established the new Europe, including the new nation states. He favored stronger Franco-Czech ties, convinced that both nations were equally attached to the peace settlement. If Britain recognized the Bolshevik regime, as Benes feared might happen if Labor came to power, France would, Millerand argued, have to strengthen its anti-Bolshevik bulwark by tighter links to Russia's small neighbors.[13]

Millerand persistently advocated Allied agreement, although it came second to a defense of French rights, especially *vis-à-vis* Germany. To Curzon, he pleaded for a common Franco-British policy toward Turkey. To Camille Barrère, he argued that a close union with Britain was vital to France, not only during the current Lausanne conference, but in general. France must energetically defend its interests in Turkey, but the British appeared more interested in the East than in the Rhine. Upset when the Lausanne conference ended abruptly, Millerand assured Barrère on 4 February 1923 that he would still try to preserve close contacts with Britain.[14]

Millerand's trip to North Africa illustrated the significance he assigned Franco-colonial issues, but his primary concern was still

12. *Ibid.*, p. 222, Millerand to Barrère, 24 October 1923.
13. A.N., F.M. 69, Millerand's statement to the president of the Austrian Republic, 26 January 1922; A.N., F.M. 71, conversation with Pusta, 9 March 1923; *ibid.*, conversation with Benes, 18 December 1923.
14. A.N., F.M. 71, conversation between Millerand and Lord Curzon, 18 November 1922; A.N., F.M. 69, Millerand to Barrère, 7 and 12 December 1922, 2 January, 4 February 1923; McDougall, p. 253.

Europe, particularly Franco–German relations. After his return to Paris, he resumed his active involvement in shaping France's policy toward its former enemy, especially on reparations questions. With Germany increasingly likely to default on its obligations by May 1922, Millerand was anxious about the French response. To Belgian Ambassador Baron de Gaiffier, he expressed his conviction that France and Belgium would adopt a common position, even though Belgian parliamentary Socialists opposed a firm stand on Germany. The French refused to tolerate Germany's rejection of increased taxes or control measures designed to provide reparations. Millerand did not definitively answer de Gaiffier's query about a Ruhr occupation, but suggested Franco–Belgian discussions about an appropriate response. In June, when Belgium joined the majority in the Reparations Commission against France, Millerand bitterly criticized it for a stance that allowed the common man to believe that Belgium had abandoned France. He found it incomprehensible that the Belgians preferred the British to the French position. The president personally favored an international loan, for which he urged Belgian support. He had not yet settled on a Ruhr occupation as the only response to a German default.[15]

Millerand clearly wavered on a Ruhr occupation. As premier, he had considered the tactic several times (in March, when German troops moved into the Rhineland; in July, as a potential sanction for violation of the Spa protocols). As president, he returned to the idea because of German defaults. He apparently contemplated it in late 1921, when de Wendel suggested French action in the Rhineland as a demonstration of French action in an area other than the Ruhr. During the summer of 1922, the president apparently contemplated expanding French influence in the Rhineland, but by late autumn he again supported a Ruhr occupation. Only a firm policy, he was convinced, would put France in a position to collect something of what it was owed.[16]

During the summer of 1922, German defaults and demands for a moratorium required an Allied decision. While Premier Poincaré was in London in early August, Millerand again actively shaped

---

15. *Ibid.*, conversations between Millerand and de Gaiffier, 17 May and 13 June 1922.

16. Jeanneney, *De Wendel*, p. 157, reports on two interviews between Millerand and de Wendel, the first on 22 December 1921, the second (no specific date) a year later. *Ibid.*, p. 159, reports that Camille Cavalier saw Millerand on 11 December 1922.

French policy. Before agreeing to a moratorium or an international loan, the French wanted productive guarantees (*gages*), but the British feared pressures would tilt the European equilibrium in France's favor and against Germany. Millerand's telegrams to Poincaré in London urged firmness. On 8 August, portraying the resistance Poincaré was encountering as predictable, he argued that France should stand by its position regardless of the Belgian attitude. On 9 August, the president proposed a French concession on customs control in exchange for control over German crown forests, dye manufactures, and aviation factories. After a cabinet meeting on 10 August, he transmitted the government's continued opposition to a moratorium unless France was granted effective control rights in exchange. The French also refused to accept the agreements on customs and German exports previously signed by the German government to fulfill Article 7 of the state of payments as counterparts for a moratorium. The French cabinet demanded additional guarantees, such as products from the state-owned Ruhr mines and forests, the transfer to the Reparations Commission of 60 percent of the dye and aviation industries' capital stock for later distribution to the Allies, and the erection of customs barriers around the Ruhr and along the Rhine. The cabinet agreed with Poincaré that it would be disastrous for the French to relinquish too rapidly the position which the government had taken and parliament and public opinion had endorsed. The British counterproposals, which Poincaré transmitted, were viewed by Millerand as a setback that would substantially reduce German payments. Rejection of the moratorium, a temporary solution, appeared to him as the only viable response. Should the British remain adamant, the French would have to investigate measures that they could institute alone.[17]

Since the 'coup of Rapallo' (16 April 1922), pressures for a Ruhr occupation had mounted in Paris. Foch and Millerand seemingly favored this response, but Poincaré was hesitant. To Foch, only an occupation of the Rhine's left bank could insure French security.

17. A.E., P.M. 50, pp. 159, 170, telegrams from Millerand to Poincaré, 8 and 9 August 1922; A.E., P.M. 51, pp. 26–8, 117–19, 127, Millerand to Poincaré, 10, 12 and 13 August 1922; Millerand, 'Souvenirs,' p. 113; E. Bonnefous, III, pp. 330–1; Maier, pp. 290–1; Bariéty, *Relations franco-allemandes*, pp. 101–4; Persil, p. 148. McDougall, pp. 223–4, argues that Millerand considered a break with Britain necessary for France to regain its freedom of action toward Germany. Millerand was less willing than Seydoux and Laroche to accept concessions like the customs barrier. He was pleased by the failure of the conference, while Poincaré was upset by the Franco-British impasse.

Millerand also wanted territorial guarantees that would foster French security and assure French industry a permanent dominance. He advocated an occupation of the Ruhr unless Germany met its commitments. Although Poincaré had agreed with Millerand and opposed Briand earlier in the year, he refused to yield his prerogatives or accept any control but that of parliament. By summer 1922, the same gap between president and premier that had divided Millerand and Briand had opened between Millerand and Poincaré. Millerand continued to demand full German Treaty execution, but the premier was reluctant to jeopardize the *entente* with Britain. Perhaps a less dramatic assertion of presidential influence than the Cannes incident, Millerand's actions as cabinet spokesman while Poincaré was in London again illustrated his active interpretation of the presidency and a slight shift in the relative power of the two positions. The president's and Chambers' insistence on results, even at the cost of a Ruhr occupation, increased during the autumn, but Poincaré, like Briand, sought first to exhaust all other remedies.[18]

By autumn 1922, Millerand was convinced that a Ruhr occupation had become necessary and inevitable. The problem, however, remained to convince a reluctant Poincaré. As Millerand later argued, occupation of the Ruhr illustrated Poincaré's 'phobia of responsibility,' his inability to reach a decision in the face of conflicting pressures. The decisive cabinet meeting evidently took place on 27 November 1922 at the Elysée, with Millerand presiding. It included Foch, Tirard, Louis Barthou (the new French delegate to the Reparations Commission), and representatives of the coal office, in addition to the members of the government. This conference decided on French policy in the event that the Brussels conference did not satisfy French objectives, specifically, full control over the occupied Rhineland and expulsion of all German bureaucrats, and occupation of two-thirds of the Ruhr, including Essen and Bochum, to provide France with its reparations coal and metallurgical coke. Although Poincaré feared the potential dangers of the operation, Millerand maintained it would provoke neither disaster nor bankruptcy. When Poincaré threatened to resign, other cabinet members intervened to end the incident, and press reports noted that a decision had been reached on the Ruhr.[19]

18. McDougall, p. 214; Bariéty and Poidevin, p. 250; Chastenet, 'Ruhr,' pp. 7–9.
19. Millerand, 'Souvenirs,' p. 114; *Le Matin*, 28 November 1922; *Le Temps*, 29

Although there is no corroboration for Millerand's presentation of the session, considerable evidence exists of Poincaré's hesitation. André François-Poncet (French economic observer in Dusseldorf) later claimed that Poincaré told him that he did not favor the occupation even though history assigned him the responsibility. Although François-Poncet portrayed Poincaré and Foch as hostile to the move because of possible passive resistance and difficulties for France, other sources clearly show Foch as a strong supporter but Finance Minister Charles de Lasteyrie as reserved. Poincaré was unable, he claimed, to resist the insistent pressures of Millerand and other ministers, notably War Minister André Maginot. Laroche confirmed Poincaré's hesitation and his capitulation to Millerand. To the president, an occupation was the only way to counteract Germany's refusal to meet the Treaty's stipulations. After Poincaré failed to win British support in August 1922, the parliamentary majority also endorsed a forceful solution even without British support. The president's supporters refute the premier's claim that he made the serious decision to occupy the Ruhr simply to avoid conflict in the cabinet. Clearly, the premier was torn by contradictory inclinations. He leaned toward a forceful treatment of Germany, but was scared of weakening the *entente* with Britain, an indispensable protection against the German menace. He was also determined not to violate the Versailles Treaty's legal prescriptions. Without Millerand's pressures, he would probably have avoided the risky operation, but the president refused to let the intricacies of juridical discussions paralyze action. The advantages of the Anglo-French *entente* did not outweigh for Millerand the disadvantages of infinite concessions to Germany. While France must operate within its recognized rights, it still had to behave forcefully. The French decided to occupy the Ruhr, Germany's arsenal and its principal source of wealth, as soon as a German default was declared. By late December, pressures from Millerand, the cabinet, the parliamentary majority, and public opinion left Poincaré little option but sanctions. Millerand's motives, like those of the cabinet and Foch, were primarily political: a desire for France to regain its dominance of 1918 and definitively to insure its security. Poincaré, anxious for Germany to resume reparations payments, had largely financial motives.[20]

November 1922; Hermann J. Rupieper, *The Cuno Government and Reparations 1922–1923* (The Hague: Martinus Nijhoff, 1979), p. 55.

20. Jules Laroche, 'Quelques aspects de l'affaire de la Ruhr,' *Revue d'histoire*

Poincaré made a final attempt in London in December 1922 to win British support for a common policy toward Germany, but the trip was *pro forma*, since the French had already decided to occupy the Ruhr. In the currently tense atmosphere, the conference proved unable to reconcile conflicting Franco-British responses to Germany's request for a four-year moratorium. The French refused any moratorium without guarantees, and would only accept a reduction in Germany's debt if France's obligations to Britain were correspondingly reduced. The British were willing to grant the Germans a moratorium without restrictions. On 11 December 1922, Millerand telegraphed Poincaré in London to reject Bonar Law's proposals. The president was convinced that the British sought to buy time by postponing a Ruhr occupation until a decision was reached on a moratorium and inter-Allied debts. Millerand, supported by Maginot and Justice Minister Maurice Colrat, believed a delay would allow Germany to organize its resistance and would create an impression of French uncertainty. When the British rejected any constraints, the conference reached a deadlock. By the time Poincaré returned to Paris, he found the majority's political milieus favored forceful action, but he still hesitated to act without the British. Again pleading for British support at a conference in Paris on 3 January 1923, he was unable to sway his allies. When the Reparations Commission officially declared a German default, French divisions escorted a mission of French, Belgian, and Italian engineers to occupy the Ruhr mines and factories on 11 January 1923, and the French parliament ratified the government's decision.[21]

While the French preferred to have British support, they chose to occupy the Ruhr without their ally instead of accepting further delays. When Millerand pleaded with British Ambassador Lord Derby for British support, Derby claimed that the move would overturn the British cabinet, a domestic reason for its foreign

diplomatique, 1949, pp. 180–1; Chastenet, *Poincaré*, pp. 239–41; Persil, pp. 149–51; conversation with Jacques Millerand, 20 May 1978; Dansette, pp. 204–5; Jolly, p. 2467; Maier, pp. 292–3, 303; McDougall, pp. 238–9; Bariéty and Poidevin, p. 250; Bariéty, *Relations franco-allemandes*, pp. 107–8; Jacques Bariéty, 'Les réparations allemandes, 1919–1924: objet ou prétexte à une politique rhénane de la France,' *Bulletin de la société d'histoire moderne*, 15ᵉ série, no. 6, 1973, p. 25; François-Poncet; Chastenet, 'Ruhr,' pp. 11–12; Rupieper, p. 91.
21. Chastenet, 'Ruhr,' pp. 8–11; A.E., P.M. 51, pp. 159–60, Millerand to Poincaré, 11 December 1922; E. Bonnefous, III, pp. 343–4; McDougall, p. 239; Bariéty, 'Réparations allemandes,' p. 25; Persil, pp. 147–8; Derfler, *President*, p. 100.

policy decision. The British Labor Party's electoral campaign had attacked French militarism, blaming Foch for the Ruhr move. Millerand was, however, convinced that Germany did not plan to pay, as demonstrated by its campaign to prove its innocence; as an innocent victim, Germany would not owe reparations. To the president, it was therefore essential to seize guarantees (*prendre des gages*) so that the debtor could not evade its obligations. To Derby's query about Poincaré's motives in sending engineers and customs agents into the Ruhr, Millerand answered that it reflected France's desire to develop the Rhineland which depended on coal from the Ruhr, thereby hinting at a broader motive for the French occupation than simply German payment of reparations.[22]

Although Poincaré gave in to presidential, cabinet, and parliamentary pressures to send French troops and engineers into the Ruhr, he was still uncomfortable about the lack of British support. Millerand, who found the premier's hesitations increasingly unpalatable, apparently retained connections with the Quai d'Orsay, especially with Peretti de la Rocca and Seydoux, that partially undermined the premier's authority within his own ministry. To the president, the premier's previous demands for strict Treaty execution had proven unreliable. There were also indications that Millerand sounded out Tardieu in January 1923 about possibly forming a ministry. Millerand may also have initiated Loucheur's mission to London in late March 1923. Loucheur, whose goal was to persuade the British government to link war debts and reparations, discussed with Millerand a plan to exchange an Allied moratorium for German payment to France of 26 billion gold marks more than the French war debts to Britain and the United States. It also proposed that Germany accept control over its finances, end passive resistance, and concede productive guarantees. Once the program was accepted, the Ruhr could be gradually evacuated. Furthermore, the Rhineland should be demilitarized and placed under League of Nations control, but with nominal German sovereignty. Millerand, who endorsed Loucheur's plan, also wanted to create an autonomous Saar state. Apparently Poincaré accepted the plan except for Millerand's addition, but the British were not responsive. Rumor claimed that Millerand wanted to replace Poincaré with Loucheur, but its validity is difficult to test, since Millerand does not mention it and Loucheur attributes initiative for

22. A.N., F.M. 71, conversation between Millerand and Lord Derby, 17 December 1922.

the trip to Poincaré. Newspapers also hinted at conflicting currents within the French government. The semi-official *Le Temps* emphatically denied the *Daily Telegraph*'s charges that influential elements within the French government favored moderation and wanted an accommodation with Germany. To scotch the rumors and stress governmental unity, *Le Temps* insisted that no foreign journal could accurately interpret French policy.[23]

Throughout the spring of 1923, Millerand's policy toward Germany remained constant. To French envoy to Peking de Fleuriau, he insisted France would stay in the Ruhr until Germany agreed to pay, and he was skeptical about its readiness to accept French demands, despite rumors to the contrary. He was convinced the Germans would keep evading their obligations by linking German innocence to French injustice. French public opinion, he expected, would continue to back the occupation, but British opposition made the situation more complicated. He did, however, expect the British eventually to recognize that France could not evacuate the Ruhr until reparations arrived.[24]

Millerand's presidential speeches during 1923 reiterated the themes of nationalism, unity, and presidential authority while also confronting the Ruhr occupation and Franco-German relations. To the diplomatic corps on 1 January 1923, he regretted the persistent absence of genuine peace in Europe and the failure to repair wartime devastations. Motivated by neither anger nor vengeance, France wanted only its due, reparation of material damages and guarantees of future security. To the Ligue des Patriotes, he noted that his acceptance of the presidency had been solely influenced by his desire to achieve that national policy defined in November 1919. Victorious France, he insisted, only wanted conquered Germany to respect the treaties that ended the war. In Mulhouse during a presidential voyage to Alsace-Lorraine, he not only lauded the city's social and pedagogical contributions but argued that its experience of German rule allowed Alsace to guide France in dealing with an unreliable Germany. The Treaty's authorization for a creditor to seize from a defecting debtor consecrated, in Millerand's opinion, principles derived from international and traditional

23. Artaud, *Dettes interalliées*, pp. 524, 531; Maier, p. 405; McDougall, p. 265; Rupieper, p. 136; *Le Temps*, 7 April 1923.
24. A.N., F.M. 69, Millerand to de Fleuriau, Peking, 25 April 1923.

law. To the president, two wills were in conflict: the German determination to avoid payment of its debt and the French insistance that commitments be met and damages repaired.[25]

In Strasbourg, Millerand discussed the problems attendant on reintegrating Alsace-Lorraine. To him, decentralization would allow for the accommodation of local variations. Language was a particularly tricky issue. Even before 1870, the area's border character had made the imposition of French difficult, and fifty years of German domination had intensified the problem. In Metz, he noted that it would be chimerical to eliminate with a stroke of a pen forty-eight years of conquest and restore the pre-1870 situation intact to the provinces. Rather than legislative and administrative assimilation, they had to adopt an experimental approach involving a pragmatic and realistic solution to current difficulties. The degree of electoral, administrative, and judicial integration achieved in four years proved to him Alsace-Lorraine's persistent loyalty to France. For Millerand, decentralization reinforced rather than undermined French unity.[26]

Millerand considered France's policy toward Germany legitimate and inescapable. In Metz, denying any militaristic or annexationist goals, or pressures from the metallurgical industry, he attributed the move into the Ruhr to France's determination to claim the payments owed. Three years of negotiation had shown France that it confronted a government that was buying time to avoid payment and to regain its political and economic dominance. The economic sacrifices entailed by the move were necessary to avert greater suffering and to insure that France's wartime victory did not become an economic and political defeat. In Chaumont, he characterized France's commitment to freedom as the key to its German policy. Since the French assigned priority to their own freedom, they never used it to dominate their neighbors. For four years, France had fought bitterly to restore freedom to the populations forcefully removed in 1871, and since then had tried to establish the rule of law. It entered the Ruhr only to compel German respect for Treaty commitments. It therefore had to uphold a policy linked to justice. In Puy de Dome, he argued that the battle continued

25. A.N., F.M. 78, Millerand's speech of 1 January 1923 to the diplomatic corps; *ibid.*, Millerand's speech to the Comités de la Ligue des Patriotes, 24 January 1923; J.O., *Lois et décrets*, pp. 5346–7, Millerand's speech in Mulhouse, 28 May 1923.

26. *Ibid.*, pp. 5348–50, Millerand's speech in Strasbourg, 29 May 1923; *ibid.*, pp. 5354–6, Millerand's speech in Metz, 1 June 1923.

because German trickery had deprived France of the fruits of victory. It needed reparations to rebuild its ravaged departments and also to demonstrate respect for right, peace, and justice. Responsible for the war, Germany refused to pay the victims of its aggression. France, he again insisted, had no concealed militaristic or annexationist objectives for a Ruhr operation, which had the support of parliament and public opinion. Millerand urged his compatriots to abstain from domestic quarrels; a strong foreign policy required domestic unity.[27]

A celebration of Pascal's tricentennial in the Auvergne led Millerand to reiterate his basic domestic and foreign positions. Quoting Pascal's dictum that justice without force was impotent and force without justice was tyrannical, the president argued that the preceding fifty years had proven the worthlessness of law unaccompanied by strength. History showed that a democracy had to preserve an equilibrium between freedom and authority by a rigorous separation of powers. His defense of freedom included economic regionalism and decentralization. Regional economic development was essential to French economic vitality so that the rural exodus could be counteracted. Regional and individual development within the framework of republican legislation served to buttress national strength. His advocacy of economic decentralization was clearly as linked to his nationalism as it was a reflection of his libertarianism.[28]

By the end of the summer of 1923, Franco–German relations had reached a turning point. Although German passive resistance was initially effective, the French had restored production by May. An end to passive resistance became only a question of time. Throughout this period, however, Franco-British relations remained tense, with frequent critical British despatches to the Quai d'Orsay. When Gustav Stresemann became German chancellor in early September, the severe economic crisis forced the government to abandon passive resistance and order work to be resumed in the Ruhr. In

27. *Ibid.*, p. 5356, Millerand's speech in Metz, 2 June 1923; *ibid.*, pp. 5357–8, Millerand's speech in Chaumont, 3 June 1923; J.O., *Lois et décrets*, p. 6792, Millerand's speech in Puy de Dome, 8 July 1923.
28. *Ibid.*, pp. 6790–2, Millerand's speech in Clermont-Ferrand, 7 July 1923. Blaise Pascal, *Pensées* (Paris: Garnier-Flammarion, 1976), p. 137: 'La justice sans la force est impuissante: la force sans la justice est tyrannique.'

August, Millerand sent his personal secretary to the Quai d'Orsay to suggest a diplomatic initiative to capitalize on the occupation. Meeting British Prime Minister Stanley Baldwin in Paris, he agreed on the need for a Franco-British *entente*. At stake, in his opinion, was the liquidation of the war they had jointly fought, but which remained unfinished while peace commitments were not fulfilled. While the British, he believed, also wanted Germany to pay its debts, the agreement on goals broke down over means. Successive German governments resolutely denied German guilt and, since innocent, rejected payment of reparations. This German attitude had forced France to occupy the Ruhr. To Millerand, its ally should have supported France once the decision was reached, since both nations had similar goals. For the first time, he mentioned French prestige as a reason for British support in the Ruhr. At Spa in 1920, Lloyd George had hypothetically accepted an occupation if Germany defaulted on its disarmament and coal obligations. In the circumstances, therefore, France's entry into the Ruhr was legitimate and should have received British backing. The French, he promised, would evacuate the area as soon as their objectives were achieved. Only if they received German reparations could they repay their debts to Britain. The operation had double benefits for Britain, which would receive a share of German reparations as well as French debt settlement.[29]

An end to German passive resistance on 26 September 1923 brought to a head the differences between Millerand and Poincaré. To information that German chargé d'affaires von Hoesch planned to notify Poincaré officially of the German decision, Millerand responded that an end to passive resistance was the greatest event since the armistice, an unqualified French victory. The president wanted to deliver a public message emphasizing its importance, and suggested to Charles Reibel, Minister of the Liberated Regions, that general elections immediately be called to consecrate the government's Ruhr policy. He hoped the victory might lead to an alliance of the French and German economies that linked Ruhr coal and Lorraine minerals. Reibel, however, expected Poincaré to reject a presidential statement and was uncertain about the premier's reaction to the German move. Although Millerand expected Poincaré to open negotiations with the Germans, Reibel reminded

29. Chastenet, 'Ruhr,' p. 12; A.N., F.M. 69, conversation between Millerand and Baldwin at Rambouillet, 19 September 1923; McDougall, p. 289.

him that the premier had persistently evaded cabinet pressures to set France's conditions in the event of a German capitulation. Seydoux and Foch had been equally unsuccessful in getting the premier to outline a program. Given Poincaré's character, Reibel argued that he had probably not yet defined his response. To Reibel's remarks, Millerand countered that if Poincaré was not ready to negotiate with Germany, why had the French occupied the Ruhr? Reibel agreed that it was tragic that they had not asked themselves the same question. After visiting Poincaré, Reibel returned dejectedly to Millerand. The premier apparently did not plan to open negotiations with Germany in case he increased his problems with Britain. Poincaré, attributing Reibel's suggestions to Millerand, rejected them out of hand and threatened to resign if pressured. Reibel reported the president's complete discouragement (*effondrement*). When Reibel saw Foch, the marshal also commented that the premier was incapable of making decisions. To Foch, Poincaré controlled France's fate; if he did not negotiate, an opportunity would forever be lost. Although Reibel finally persuaded Foch to see the premier, the marshal was no more successful. To Reibel's suggestion of forcing a cabinet crisis, Millerand and Foch replied that a governmental collapse would only aggravate the situation. The president, who believed an excellent opportunity had been squandered, was bitter that the premier refused to negotiate directly and instead entrusted reparations issues to an international (the Dawes) commission. From René de Saint-Quentin, the French counselor of the embassy in Berlin, he later learned that German heavy industry was so thoroughly demoralized that it would have signed any agreement. The Germans were apparently convinced the French would retain the Ruhr. French Ambassador to Germany Pierre de Margerie telegraphed Poincaré that they should act quickly and capitalize on Germany's defeat to negotiate concessions from the coal and steel magnates. Poincaré, who did not inform the cabinet of the ambassador's telegram, was so irritated that he wrote in the margin that its cost should be charged to the ambassador's personal account.[30]

The end of German passive resistance revealed the serious disagreement between Millerand and Foch on the one hand and

30. Millerand, 'Souvenirs,' annexe, notes of Charles Reibel; Charles Reibel, 'Le premier drame de la Ruhr,' *Ecrits de Paris*, May 1949, pp. 24–31; Dansette, pp. 205–6; Jeanneney, *Argent*, p. 198; Chastenet, 'Ruhr,' pp. 13–15; Derfler, *President*, pp. 100–1.

Poincaré on the other. Millerand clearly wanted to capitalize on the Ruhr victory to open Franco-German negotiations that would resolve the reparations situation by payments in kind and a merger of Ruhr coal and Lorraine minerals. This powerful economic bloc would allow France to revise the Treaty so as to insure French security in the east and combine coal and mineral resources. When he failed to persuade Poincaré, Millerand considered replacing him as foreign minister with Colrat, but did not act on the idea. As he later recalled, France's incredible inertia after Germany's capitulation produced immediate results. To him, it was responsible for a revival of German confidence and the nearly fatal French financial crisis. Reibel believed France's error of September 1923 made the Ruhr occupation an issue in French domestic politics, since the Cartel des Gauches set evacuation as a principal goal. Shortly after the Cartel's victory, it carried out its electoral promise to remove French forces. The costly operation ended in August 1924 without any significant advantages for France.[31]

Poincaré's refusal to negotiate directly with Germany in September 1923 has provoked considerable controversy. By referring the matter to the Reparations Commission, he re-internationalized it. His behavior therefore respected the letter of the Versailles Treaty by returning to the inter-Allied procedures it envisaged. A reluctance to antagonize Britain, to alleviate the break caused by the Ruhr occupation, was one explanation offered for Poincaré's position. The premier also worried that a Franco-German economic combination would revive traditional British fears of French continental hegemony. He may even have wondered whether France could control that union, given its smaller population and war-ravaged condition. Furthermore, a significant current of French public opinion disliked any Franco-German collaboration. French financial problems, intensified by the occupation, also concerned the premier. Since Poincaré had always been a reluctant supporter of the occupation, his inertia in exploiting its success is comprehensible. The situation has also been explained in terms of his personality, that he experienced a form of vertigo when confronted with

31. Millerand, 'Souvenirs,' p. 116; Dansette, p. 206; McDougall, p. 289; Chastenet, *Poincaré*, p. 250; Artaud, *Dettes interalliées*, pp. 578, 615; Jolly, p. 2467; E. Bonnefous, III, p. 358. Trachtenberg, pp. 310–11, cites telegrams between de Margerie and Poincaré, A.E., Ruhr 29, 30. Reibel, pp. 30–1; Persil, pp. 152–3; Louis Guitard, *La Petite Histoire de la IIIe République. Souvenirs de Maurice Colrat* (Paris: Les Sept Couleurs, 1959), pp. 94–100.

heavy responsibilities. Perhaps German passive resistance and British opposition intimidated and paralyzed him. Even Poincaré's supporters portrayed him as lacking political imagination and frightened by his success in the Ruhr. Or perhaps he hoped a refusal to negotiate would trigger a German financial and economic collapse that would hasten Germany's disintegration and allow France to incorporate the Rhineland. If, however, he sought this goal, he did not think through the implications of his policy. François-Poncet compared him to a successful card-player, who left without collecting his winnings. Millerand was seemingly the more perceptive in this instance. As his supporters argue, the president's policy would have strengthened the Versailles system and perhaps drastically altered subsequent events.[32]

32. Reibel, p. 28; Persil, p. 153; Artaud, 'Occupation,' p. 1; Guitard, pp. 94–6; François-Poncet, 'Poincaré tel que je l'ai vu,' *Le Figaro Littéraire*, Paris, 26 June 1948; Dansette, pp. 206–7; Chastenet, *Poincaré*, p. 250; Chastenet, 'Ruhr,' pp. 16–19; E. Bonnefous, III, pp. 388–91; Derfler, *President*, p. 101. Trachtenberg, pp. 311–29, 333–5, claims Poincaré's policy during the autumn lacked any clear idea of objectives or means. Late 1923 was a turning-point: had France won the test of strength in the Ruhr, subsequent events might have followed a different course.

14
From the Evreux 'Bomb' to the Cartel Victory: Development of a Presidential Crisis

The developments in Franco-German relations of late September and Millerand's controversial speech at Evreux on 14 October 1923 were not specifically connected, but the president's frustration at the premier's refusal to exploit the German capitulation may have been the final stage in the rift between the two men. To Millerand, Poincaré had proven incapable of taking a firm stand at home or abroad. The president would have liked to extract a more satisfactory reparations arrangement from Germany's capitulation, and reinforce the Bloc National's domestic political situation. The time appeared opportune for him to deliver a presidential message highlighting the Bloc's success and launching the electoral campaign. He would have preferred to disband the current legislature before the end of its mandate in May 1924 and schedule the elections for a time when a Bloc victory could benefit the existing majority. Poincaré's refusal to negotiate with the Germans, however, deprived the Bloc National of this potential foreign policy triumph, and hints of his opposition to a presidential message deterred Millerand from delivering one. Poincaré, who did not favor early elections, was clearly reluctant to lead the Bloc National in the electoral battle. He may have preferred to remain above partisan struggles so that he could pursue a national foreign policy, or to keep open his options to the Left by avoiding a close identification with the Bloc's goals. When Poincaré abdicated political leadership of the majority, Millerand either had to leave leaderless the majority he had founded in 1919 in the electoral campaign by observing the Elysée's traditional political neutrality, or assume the role himself. The new leftist alliance was certain to exploit France's refusal to extract tangible results from the costly Ruhr occupation. Logically, therefore, Millerand's Evreux speech was directly linked to the events of 26 September and indirectly criticized the premier's response. Although the speech reiterated arguments Millerand had frequently made since 1919, it is questionable whether he would have delivered it if Poincaré had responded differently to Ruhr developments.

An official presidential voyage to the Eure gave Millerand the opportunity for a program-speech at Evreux that had the effect of a political 'bomb.' He had warned neither Poincaré nor the accompanying ministers of his intent, and refused to let his aides deter him. To Millerand, it was his duty to assume leadership of the forces which Poincaré had abandoned. Refusing to calculate the possibly adverse personal implications, he stressed publicly the Bloc National achievements over the preceding four years and urged a continuation of its national union policy. Focusing on domestic policy, he began with a homage to Gambetta that set a tone of patriotism and republicanism. Gambetta's words of 4 September 1881 and Millerand's of 1923 bore a remarkable similarity. Again, Millerand stressed the impact of the war, with the enormous sacrifices to produce France's victory and the consequent European transformation that dissolved the Austro-Hungarian empire, created a revolutionary chaos in a politically immature Russia, and reversed the injustice of 1871 by restoring Alsace-Lorraine to France. To Millerand, the Allied victory was a triumph of arms and right (*droit*). Nationalism had produced the collapse of multinational empires like the dual monarchy of Austria–Hungary and ended the subjugation of oppressed nationalities and the division of Poland. These new nations required domestic stability and external security to insure their continuity. Millerand, however, did not consider nationalist ideals incompatible with international cooperation, to which goal the League of Nations had contributed significantly. Above all, he argued, French policy was based on respect for treaties, even when it partially jeopardized its own security; 'the French people is an honest man.' Overseas, the French Republic had expanded to a prodigious degree, conquering colonial souls as much as territory. Education was, therefore, as important as force to resolve colonial problems.[1]

1. E. Bonnefous, III, p. 385; Persil, pp. 157–8; J.O., *Lois et décrets*, pp. 9917–20, 15 October 1923, Millerand's speech at Evreux, 14 October 1923; A.N., F.M. 80,

Not waiting for payment from its defaulting debtor, France had advanced over 100 billion francs to repair the devastated regions and to pay war pensions, partially covered by the 8 to 9 billion in new taxes voted by parliament. France had to protect its credit by balancing public expenditures against sufficient resources; financial caution was particularly necessary. Although Frenchmen had accepted a five-fold increase in taxation, theirs was a nation of small fortunes. Since 1789, they had recognized a duty to share public expenses; 'the fiscal duty remains above all a patriotic duty.' Expenditures also had to be cut through a reduction in the civil service and a vast administrative reorganization, encompassing the creation of economic regions that combined local initiative with central intervention. Urging an alliance of public and private initiative, he believed administrative reorganization would strengthen France's spirit of association. Chambers of commerce, industrial groups, agricultural and worker unions defended members' material and professional interests, but also served as schools of moral and civic discipline. A series of postwar economic problems had, however, threatened domestic peace, notably the strike epidemic of 1919–20. The French did not, however, plan to revoke existing social legislation but rather to expand it on the model of Alsace-Lorraine's statutes and mutualist traditions. They had, the president argued, to pursue social progress calmly and industriously; 'for, it is more important to move correctly than to move quickly.' He strongly encouraged large families in order to offset the population decline. With population linked to education, he lauded republican educational progress in the development of a strong humanities curriculum, and also technical education; to him, educational freedom was indispensable to progress. Domestic divisions must not again undermine French unity. To Millerand, renewed ties with the Vatican, important for an effective defense of French foreign interests, also promoted domestic appeasement. Confessional issues should not intrude on political disputes. The separation of church and state had demonstrated the republican determination to eliminate spiritual influences from the civil domain, thereby promoting religious neutrality. Millerand's defense of freedom of opinion led him to advocate religious toleration, provided that religion stayed a matter of personal belief, and not a spur to political action.[2]

typescript of Evreux speech; *Le Temps*, 16 October 1923; Simonsson, pp. 197–205.
   2. J.O., *Lois et décrets*, 15 October 1923, Evreux speech.

From specific concerns, Millerand turned to larger issues of freedom and authority. Orderly progress required a freedom to express all opinions under the rule of law, buttressed by a freedom of association, as guaranteed by the law of 1901. 'If freedom is the essence of the Republic, authority is no less indispensable to it than to any other form of government.' It was, he believed, slanderous to call republican France a rebel against the necessary authority. In a parliamentary regime, the legislature was supreme, but respect for popular sovereignty, the supreme law, required resistance to total legislative control. 'Rigorous separation of powers; strict observation of their attributes: freedom is at this price.' 'May the legislative power be content with legislating and controlling; may the judiciary render judgements that the law and its conscience dictates; may, under the control of the one, respectful of the independence of the other, the executive power govern and administer.' Pleading with parliament to modify proven constitutional defects, he urged it to correct its own faults. In view of the recent victory for French foreign policy, Millerand believed that the time was appropriate to tackle the constitutional revisions that would strengthen the government's ability to pursue those policies designed to enhance national prosperity and grandeur.[3]

Poincaré's hesitation had prompted Millerand to assume leadership of the Bloc National. Not only did he defend its policies, but he confronted its opponents in the new leftist coalition. He denounced the Radicals for their sectarian opposition to relations with the Vatican, refuting their claim to base their stand on Waldeck-Rousseau's 1901 Association law. The former premier had never given it a narrow sectarian interpretation, Millerand insisted. He reminded the Socialists that their prewar pacifism had been powerless to halt aggression and would remain so. His demand for constitutional revisions frightened the beneficiaries of the existing parliamentary dominance. For the first time since MacMahon, a president of the Republic violated electoral tradition to throw the weight of his office into the political balance. As an electoral gauntlet, his speech made him vulnerable to counterattack. Furthermore, Poincaré, who as president had given his premiers public support, clearly disliked Millerand's act. Privately, he noted his disagreement with the president about the appropriateness of constitutional revision. Millerand's 'bomb of Evreux' introduced a new element into the coming political struggle.

3. *Ibid.*

The Evreux speech was also seen as proof of a decisiveness which, regardless of personal consequences, had marked Millerand's entire career. Ignoring sensibilities, he unequivocally presented an apology for Bloc National centrism. The speech was also seen as a maneuver against Poincaré, whom the majority and the president considered to be too neutral and lukewarm. The premier either had to back Millerand or openly admit their differences. Seen as a sensational departure from political neutrality, Millerand's speech was criticized as an unjustified expansion of his presidential authority. His acceptance speech of 1920 had clearly indicated his intent to defend his national and social policy of 1919, making his Evreux speech a logical sequel to that earlier declaration. Millerand's supporters, calling his act courageous and praiseworthy, considered his assumption of Bloc National leadership logical in view of Poincaré's lethargy; they blamed the premier for not giving a program-speech to outline the Bloc's achievements prior to the electoral battle. Since the spring of 1923, the Right had waited in vain for such a statement. Some people argued that Poincaré feared alienating Herriot, Blum, and their Radical and Socialist colleagues.[4]

Millerand's speech was both 'an act and a program.' It was programmatic in confronting the spectrum of contemporary French concerns and indicating policy goals; it was an act in its use of the presidential right to address the nation politically. The constitution of 1875 permitted the president to deliver messages and to dissolve the legislature. Since the first of these prerogatives had fallen into disuse, and the second, discredited by MacMahon, was never exercised, the Third Republic's presidents failed to utilize even those powers they theoretically possessed. Few heads of state had such circumscribed powers. Whenever a president deviated from his largely ceremonial role, he provoked apprehension. When the National Assembly elevated an individual to this lofty post, it ensconced him in splendid isolation and powerlessness. While Millerand's speech violated no constitutional provisions, it deviated from presidential tradition.[5]

Analyses of the Left's demand for Millerand's resignation in May 1924 assign to his Evreux speech a crucial role. Expressing the

4. Millerand, 'Souvenirs,' p. 120; J. Millerand, p. 115; conversation with Jacques Millerand, 20 May 1978; E. Bonnefous, III, pp. 385–6; Jolly, p. 2467; Dansette, pp. 207–8; Maier, p. 406; Persil, pp. 157–61; Derfler, *President*, pp. 102–3.
5. *Le Temps*, 16 October 1923.

majority's views on Vatican relations, sectarianism, financial problems, and constitutional revision made him, they charged, a party leader. Spoken by the President of the Republic, they altered the head of state's neutral arbiter role. Seen as an electoral statement which Poincaré should have made, his speech evoked considerable political emotion: a threat of resignation from Poincaré and leftist satisfaction at the overt disagreement between president and premier. His act, however, made it logical later for the victorious Cartel to demand his resignation. As Socialist leader Léon Blum commented, Millerand laid his position on the line by entering the political arena. If the Bloc National were defeated, the president would fall too. Although his speech supported a policy rather than a specific ministry, his views were similar to the premier's except on two subjects: freedom of education and constitutional revision. The former, which Poincaré had not discussed, linked Millerand to the Bloc National's right wing. The latter found the premier opposed to constitutional changes. While the rift between Millerand and Poincaré did not surface officially during the autumn, mutual hostility increased. Poincaré resented Millerand's intrusion into policy-making; Millerand was frustrated by the premier's indecisiveness. Meanwhile, the Bloc National majority was increasingly upset by the premier's failure to provide electoral leadership.[6]

The Evreux speech, however, altered neither the electoral campaign nor its results, and was not debated in parliament during the elections. Nonetheless, the Left later called it a violation of the constitution. If a program-speech preempted the premier's prerogatives, it was perhaps a latent threat to parliamentarism, but it was less significant as a constitutional violation than as an act that jeopardized the president's role as a symbol of governmental permanence and stability. By arousing his political opponents to demand Millerand's resignation, the Evreux speech contradicted the spirit of the constitution. Stability of his office required a president to avoid actions that might invite pressures to resign.[7]

In an interview after the Evreux speech, Millerand, acknowledging the political nature of his speech and defending its legitimacy, reiterated his views on corporatism, constitutional revisions

6. Conversation with Jacques Millerand, 20 May 1978, his son acknowledged that the political nature of his father's speech linked him to the Bloc National; J. Millerand, p. 115; Soulié, *Cartel*, pp. 253–5; Barty, pp. 83–6; Jeanneney, *Leçon d'histoire*, p. 21; Mermiex, p. 149; Néré, p. 53; A.N., F.M. 83, *Quotidien*, 9 June 1924; Simonsson, pp. 197–205.
7. Simonsson, pp. 213–20.

to insure a separation of powers and a stronger executive, and his opposition to tyranny. Appearing 'massively solid, imperturbably calm and self-composed,' Millerand again maintained that while he could not be a party member, he could defend a policy, in his case 'liberalism.' Ministerial instability in France had precluded political or administrative continuity, he claimed. With perseverance vital to success in any area, the regime's uncertainty about the future was its greatest vice. If parliament faced new elections every time it overturned a ministry, it might behave less capriciously. Only in France, Millerand argued, was the executive so powerless relative to the legislature. A stronger executive would give reality to the fundamental democratic principle of a separation of powers, for parliament's intrusion on the executive had created a legislative monopoly of power. Any dictatorship or tyranny was 'detestable,' whether by an individual or an assembly. If the president's powers relative to the parliament's were augmented, this evil would, he believed, be mitigated. The president had the theoretical right to dissolve the Chamber with Senate consent, but was virtually incapable of securing that assent. Urging that this theoretical right be made a genuine power, Millerand also wanted to expand the electoral base of the presidency to include representatives of general councils, employer associations, worker groups, intellectuals and artists, and to expand the Senate with professional representatives, thereby introducing a corporative element. The coming electoral battle made it important, he argued, to focus the electorate's attention on essential reforms.[8]

During the winter of 1923–4, Millerand was particularly concerned about two problems: the mounting economic crisis and electoral reform. A form (albeit imperfect) of proportional representation had been substituted in 1919 for the *scrutin d'arrondissement* voting system used during most of the Third Republic. Millerand, who had long condemned that system as responsible for France's political instability, stagnation, and local corruption, had opposed its reintroduction after the Boulanger crisis (late 1880s) and, in 1910, as a member of Briand's cabinet, voted against the government of which he was a member on the electoral law issue.

The forthcoming elections revived discussion of the electoral

8. Recouly, 'Une visite,' pp. 227–31; A.E., P.B., III, p. 223, Millerand to Barrère, 24 October 1923; Derfler, *President*, p. 104.

system during 1923. Should list-voting be retained and improved or should France revert to the old single-member constituency system? The Radicals favored the old arrangement, which the Chamber rejected on 9 July 1923, and again by a smaller majority in November and December. In late November, the press reported Millerand's opposition to the *scrutin d'arrondissement* system. Bonnefous noted that Millerand told him he would demand another discussion if the Chamber passed the law; he preferred to resign rather than endorse that verdict. When the Chamber finally rejected the old system by one vote, Bonnefous reported that Millerand informed the cabinet he would veto a law to reinstitute the *scrutin d'arrondissement* system, and if his intervention did not secure the desired result, he would resign. Millerand later recalled that he informed the cabinet on 4 December that he would not countersign a law reestablishing the vote by *scrutin d'arrondissement* if the legislature passed it. Apparently, the cabinet ratified his position unanimously.

The President of the Republic seemingly posed a question of confidence by laying his own post on the line for the list-voting system. The news, which amazed the deputies, including those of the majority, secured a temporary victory for enemies of the old electoral system when Poincaré won a vote of confidence on 6 December. A favorable vote by the Senate in January for the *scrutin d'arrondissement* system prompted Millerand to warn the Senate that he would invoke presidential prerogatives to require a second reading if it backed that system over the Chamber's opposition. His preventive message, which did not actually violate the constitution, was contrary to republican traditions and spirit in curbing parliamentary freedom by a threatened presidential resignation. Since opinion in the Chamber and Senate believed that Millerand used his threat to resign to influence the parliamentary verdict, his action may have been crucial to the defeat of the *scrutin d'arrondissement* system during that legislature. His use of presidential prestige to avert an undesirable political change again testified to his active conception of the presidency, but was novel in its direct intervention in a currently controversial political issue. By linking his post to one viewpoint and threatening to veto the passage of a law against it, he essentially demanded a parliamentary vote of confidence in the president which could be viewed as a threat to parliamentarism.[9]

9. Simonsson, pp. 223–7; *Le Matin*, 2 December 1923; Millerand, 'Souvenirs,'

The second, and more critical, problem that concerned Millerand during the winter was the economic crisis. Partly because of the Ruhr occupation, France experienced mounting inflation (prices were almost two and a half times the 1914 level) and a foreign exchange crisis (the franc fell by 50 percent relative to the dollar during 1923). The combination of inflation and a severe currency deflation undermined the Bloc National; by January 1924, a monetary crisis menaced parliamentary stability. The crisis of the franc did, however, draw Poincaré closer to the majority. In mid-January, Millerand optimistically claimed that the worst of the crisis was over, but feared that the opposition would capitalize on governmental problems. Rapid and energetic decision, he insisted, had alleviated the crisis, but the incident was a useful warning to the French as well as proof to the outside world of their ability to recover.[10] Millerand's optimism was, however, premature; the currency situation, seemingly resolved in mid-January, rapidly deteriorated during the next six weeks.

Preoccupied by France's financial difficulties, Millerand argued on 3 February that its exchange and reparations difficulties were interrelated. France must, he insisted, resist attacks on its credit that had undermined its currency. Who, he queried, after examining France's postwar economic and financial recovery could doubt its credit? Agitation amongst workers, while comprehensible, had not precluded the restoration of a commercial equilibrium, rebuilding of the devastated regions, and a significant increase in taxation. Ten departments had been rebuilt and become economically active; balanced budgets had replaced prewar deficits, even though receipts did not cover outlays in the special budget for rebuilding the devastated regions and war pensions. He blamed the deficit on Germany's failure to pay the reparations that would supply receipts for that special budget.[11] Millerand's financial schizophrenia was typical of contemporary French politicians who praised balanced budgets while ignoring the enormous restoration costs not covered by revenues. This inherently inflationary situation undoubtedly

---

p. 119; E. Bonnefous, III, pp. 414–15; Soulié, *Cartel*, p. 255; *Le Temps*, 11 January 1924; François Albert, 'Chronique politique,' *Revue politique et parlementaire*, 10 January 1924, pp. 154–5.

10. A.E., P.B., III, p. 225, Millerand to Barrère, 17 January 1924; E. Bonnefous, III, pp. 396–400; Maier, pp. 459–60; Simonsson, p. 169.

11. J.O., *Lois et décrets*, pp. 1271–2, Millerand's speech to the Association of French journalists, 3 February 1924.

hurt France's currency in international money markets, but Millerand, like other French leaders, had no plans to balance the special budget except with German reparations.

By early March, the franc had fallen catastrophically; on 8 March, it hit its lowest level, 123 francs to the pound sterling. As Millerand later recalled, the franc's precipitous decline brought France to the edge of an economic collapse. He believed the only recourse was American aid. *Rapporteur* of the Chamber's finance commission Maurice Bokanowski apparently convinced Millerand that the government should intervene; he argued that a continued depressed currency would insure a left-wing electoral victory, while its restoration would benefit the Bloc National. Partisan political considerations reinforced national interest to involve Millerand.[12]

The weekend of 8–9 March was the turning-point. Millerand tried to pressure the Bank of France to use its gold reserves to bolster the currency. Convinced that France could not weather a financial crisis, he saw Poincaré and de Lasteyrie on 8 March. Their only option, he claimed, was a Bank of France pledge of its gold reserves as security for an American loan from the J.P. Morgan bank. Poincaré, who preferred to keep the Bank of France out of currency fluctuations, resented American demands for budget cuts. To the premier's threat to resign, Millerand countered that he would accept only a full cabinet resignation and then would deliver a presidential message requesting parliamentary support for measures to remedy the crisis. He seemingly considered proroguing the Chamber, but feared that a rational response from universal suffrage was unlikely during a crisis. Millerand, Poincaré, and de Lasteyrie arranged a meeting on 9 March with several governors of the Bank of France, including de Wendel and Rothschild.

At this 'historic reunion' at the Elysée on 9 March, a 'veritable war council,' Millerand, backing de Lasteyrie, pleaded with the regents of the Bank of France to cease their 'blind resistance.' Unless the Bank intervened, a financial collapse and governmental crisis would ensue. Poincaré agreed to pressure the Senate to vote the fiscal measures to consolidate the floating debt, to suspend reconstruction payments in the devastated regions, to avoid further

---

12. Millerand, 'Souvenirs,' pp. 116–17; Maier, p. 460; Stephen A. Schuker, *The End of French Predominance in Europe. The Financial Crisis of 1924 and the Adoption of the Dawes Plan* (Chapel Hill: University of North Carolina Press, 1976), p. 106.

inflation or a moratorium, and to exempt short-term treasury bonds from income tax. De Lasteyrie's and Poincaré's patriotic appeals and financial promises, which Millerand strongly endorsed, finally won over the hesitant Bank regents. The Bank pledged its gold reserves as security for the Anglo-American loan (the Bank of England contributed 4 million pounds and the Morgan Bank 100 million dollars). The financial situation experienced a rapid and dramatic improvement; by 14 March, the franc's position relative to the pound sterling was 92.35 francs, and by 13 April, its value was double the level of six weeks earlier. Strongly patriotic, Rothschild, de Wendel, and other regents were susceptible to nationalist pleas. Since the Bank had previously refused its support, Millerand's intervention may have been crucial.[13]

A dramatically improved financial situation did not resolve all governmental problems. A few weeks later, the government received a negative vote of confidence in the Chamber on a relatively minor issue. Finance Minister de Lasteyrie had mistakenly made an aspect of the pension system a question of confidence, which he claimed Poincaré had unnecessarily allowed to become a ministerial crisis. The incident became another test of the president's and the premier's relative strengths. Although Poincaré was not present during the vote, he immediately resigned. Millerand rejected the cabinet's resignation, claiming that the Conference of Experts' reparations discussions were approaching an end, a tricky situation which did not permit a change in French policy. Furthermore, he called the vote irregular, since it was an unexpected verdict on a peripheral issue unrelated to the ministry's credibility. Urging Poincaré to remain in power, he suggested a presidential statement asking for a parliamentary demonstration of confidence in the premier. Although Poincaré agreed to remain, he used the opportunity to shuffle his cabinet. Retaining Le Trocquer and Maginot, advocates of the Ruhr occupation, he eliminated the most contro-

13. Millerand, 'Souvenirs,' pp. 117–18; E. Bonnefous, III, pp. 406–9; Maier, p. 461; Schuker, p. 110; Jeanneney, *Argent*, p. 224; Jeanneney, *De Wendel*, p. 189; Simonsson, p. 196; David B. Goldey, 'The disintegration of the Cartel des Gauches and the politics of French government finance, 1924–1928,' unpublished Oxford D.Phil. dissertation, 1962, pp. 44–5. McDougall, p. 356, gives slightly different figures. Georges Lachapelle, *Les Batailles du franc* (Paris: Librairie Felix Alcan, 1928), pp. 125–6; Mermeix, p. 149; Derfler, *President*, p. 104. Kemp, p. 77, says the franc appreciated by 40 percent due to the Anglo-American loan agreement.

versial ministers – de Lasteyrie (finance), Maunoury (interior), and Chéon (agriculture) – and expanded the political composition to include two Radicals and one Left Republican. Opposed to presidential pressure on the legislature, he rejected Millerand's offer to address the Chambers. As president himself, Poincaré had delivered such statements only during the crisis of the *union sacrée* and generally disliked that procedure. He also wanted to avoid too close an identification in the public mind with Millerand's position.[14]

Unable to outline his views in a parliamentary message, Millerand used the semi-official route of a journalistic statement. On 27 March, *Le Matin* published an article generally attributed to Millerand, which asserted that fundamental French policy could only change in response to national will. Certain that Poincaré would form a new cabinet dedicated to firmness abroad, domestic order, and economic stability, he argued that France could not evacuate the Ruhr until reparations were paid, and would strive domestically for a budgetary equilibrium between expenditures and receipts and an avoidance of loans. If Poincaré proved unable to form a ministry, the president would only appoint a cabinet that accepted those national goals. Should the nation oppose that policy, the president would immediately draw the appropriate conclusions. Millerand's declaration was unprecedented for its support of a government during a ministerial crisis. It was provocative less for its content than for its seeming usurpation of the premier's role as formulator of national policy.[15]

This article provoked considerable hostility on the Left. On 28 March, the left-wing *Le Quotidien* called Millerand's message 'scandalous.' To Paul Painlevé, the declaration contradicted republican doctrine by which parliament alone approved or rejected governmental policy. It was an intolerable constraint to limit the nation's freedom to express its views, to alter the popular verdict in favor of a nationalist policy that so worried Europe. Herriot, evoking memories of Gambetta and MacMahon, maintained the national response would duplicate that of 16 May 1877 by forcing a leader

14. E. Bonnefous, III, pp. 420–1; Comte de Saint-Aulaire, 'L'Angleterre et les élections françaises de 1924,' *Ecrits de Paris*, May 1953, pp. 11–12; Dansette, pp. 208–9; Maier, pp. 471–2; Simonsson, pp. 171, 232–4; McDougall, p. 356; Schuker, p. 116; *Le Matin*, 27 March 1924.

15. *Le Matin*, 27 March 1924; Gaston Jèze, 'Chronique constitutionelle de France: la présidence de la République,' *Revue du droit public*, XLI, No. 2 (April–June 1924), pp. 244–6; Dansette, p. 209; Soulié, *Cartel*, pp. 255–7; Barty, p. 86; Jeanneney, *Leçon d'histoire*, pp. 21–2; Simonsson, pp. 241–3; Derfler, *President*, pp. 104–5.

who ignored republican wishes to resign. Léon Blum, more categorically, termed it a plebiscitary theory that negated the parliamentary system. To the *Quotidien*, Millerand's conception of his role
was the greatest danger to public freedom in fifty years; his plan to
choose a government among supporters of his policy violated the
constitution. The President of the Republic, *Le Quotidien* insisted,
could not have a personal policy or let his own preferences dictate
the choice of premier. He had to nominate a member of the
parliamentary majority and one acceptable to it. The nation should
therefore apply to Millerand the judgement against a president's
personal policy he had levied against Casimir-Périer in 1894.[16]

Millerand's statement of 29 March on the president's personal
role to the Academy of Moral and Political Sciences intensified the
emotions aroused by the article in *Le Matin*. An equilibrium between legislative and executive powers required, Millerand argued,
that the latter have a way to defend itself. Its weapon, the right of
dissolution, counterbalanced the legislature's power of the purse.
Did the executive, however, truly possess the right of dissolution?
To the president, it did, with the limitation that senatorial consent
was necessary. This statement also provoked attacks on his personal policy that contributed to the overcharged atmosphere in
which the elections would occur.[17]

The final stage of the crisis leading to Millerand's forced resignation began with the legislative elections of 11 May 1924 and the
Cartel des Gauches victory. Although the Bloc National had approximately the same popular vote as in 1919 and a numerical
majority over the Cartel, the decrease in abstentions primarily
benefited the Left, whose absolute vote increased. More importantly, the electoral system, by granting a double bonus for an
absolute majority, distorted the popular vote to give the leftist bloc
approximately fifty more seats than it would have had with genuine proportional representation. Even without the Communists,
the Cartel had a slight majority in the Chamber. The verdict has
been linked to the Bloc National's inability to solve France's severe
economic (inflation and currency depreciation) and diplomatic
problems (failure to capitalize on the Ruhr occupation to settle
reparations). The Bloc also proved singularly inept in the electoral

    16. *Le Quotidien*, 28 March 1924; Jèze, 1924, p. 246; Dansette, p. 209.
    17. Jèze, 1924, p. 246; *Le Temps*, 31 March 1924, report of Millerand's statement
to the Academy.

struggle. It was internally divided over the education issue; it lacked governmental leadership, notably from Poincaré, who held aloof from his own majority. British financial contributions to French leftist newspapers may also have played a part. As Saint-Aulaire later argued, Ramsay MacDonald was out for Poincaré's skin, but the premier, who minimized the leftist threat, discounted information about British involvement. Although Saint-Aulaire reproached himself for not warning Millerand, the significance of this British aid is difficult to assess. Nonetheless, the Cartel's victory was immediately translated into a constitutional crisis. To the victors, Millerand's partisan political stance had sacrificed the presidency's political invulnerability.[18]

Immediately after the elections, leftist journals, notably *Le Quotidien*, launched a campaign against Millerand. The *Quotidien*, which had worked for the leftist victory, was determined it would produce governmental changes; its slogan 'toutes les places et tout de suite' demanded the replacement of the president of the Chamber of Deputies, the premier and the president of the Republic by men more acceptable to the Left. Since Millerand had identified himself with the Bloc National and rejected its possible defeat, his only choice was resignation after the nation had repudiated his policies. Initially, the journal linked Millerand's involvement in the vicissitudes of the political battle to a loss of presidential invulnerability.[19]

Since the new parliament did not convene until 1 June 1924, the intervening weeks were a period of political vacuum. The old Chamber remained in power but impotent, and the new majority had not yet assumed its seats. This interregnum gave the newspapers free rein to attack the outgoing majority's policies and personalities. Poincaré, who immediately stated his plan to resign to avoid clinging to power, removed himself from the line of fire and allowed the Left to focus its attack on Millerand. At the first cabinet meeting after the elections (13 May), Poincaré tried to resign, but Millerand termed his move premature, since the current legislature's mandate did not expire until 31 May. He urged Poincaré to defend his policy to the new deputies; if rejected, the president would then turn to the new majority. Although Poincaré postponed his resig-

18. E. Bonnefous, III, pp. 434–7; Maier, pp. 475–7; Néré, p. 53; Saint-Aulaire, 'L'Angleterre,' pp. 11–14; Saint-Aulaire, *Confession*, p. 698.

19. E. Bonnefous, IV, pp. 5–7; Jèze, 1924, pp. 246–7; Dansette, p. 210; A.N., F.M. 83, *Le Quotidien*, 13 May 1924; Derfler, *President*, p. 105.

nation until 31 May, he only handled current business during the interim, and refused to appear before the new legislature.[20]

During the second half of May, leftist journals, especially the *Quotidien*, demanded Millerand's resignation almost daily. Two themes dominated their attacks on the president: his financial manipulations and his personal policy. On 14 May, the *Quotidien* claimed Millerand had never hidden his wish to alter the constitution to reinforce the presidency. Since the electorate had clearly repudiated the Bloc National's policies and personnel, including President Millerand, his moves to form a cabinet were doomed. Public opinion would, the journal claimed, force him to accept its choice. Two days later, it attributed to Millerand, not Poincaré, true responsibility for Bloc National policies, and accused him of manipulating the currency for electoral purposes, thereby depleting essential reserves. Millerand, it charged, forbade the Bank of France to back the franc after the elections hoping that a financial panic would persuade the public that chaos would follow the Bloc National's defeat. On 18 and 19 May, the journal repeated its accusations of Millerand's responsibility for manipulating the franc and diverting public funds. It compared Millerand's view of the presidency to MacMahon's, who in 1877 had nominated a premier who did not have a legislative majority. The *Quotidien*, lauding MacMahon's eventual submission to a republican majority, confidently predicted a similar fate for Millerand. Repeatedly charging him with financial skulduggery, it was unable to support its claims with facts, resorting to 'false propaganda.' Currency movements were linked rather to larger issues of supply and demand. This first blow against the Elysée failed to arouse much response, and the *Quotidien* soon turned instead to Millerand's abuse of presidential powers. Although the campaign against Millerand was launched in the newspapers, it is questionable whether they would have acted without the support of the political parties.[21]

During the period between the elections and the convening of the new legislature, two significant meetings foreshadowed the outcome of the crisis. On 19 May, Millerand met de Wendel at the

20. Millerand, 'Souvenirs,' p. 122; Dansette, p. 210; Barty, p. 35; Persil, p. 161; Maier, p. 477; Schuker, p. 127. Rouffet, pp. 367–8, quotes François-Marsal's 'Souvenirs,' pp. 12–14.

21. A.N., F.M. 83, *Le Quotidien*, 14, 16, 18, 19 and 20 May 1924; Dansette, pp. 210–11; Schuker, pp. 130–1; Mermeix, p. 156; Simonsson, p. 246; Derfler, *President*, p. 105.

Elysée. To de Wendel's complaint that nothing remained of the promises made on 9 March, Millerand replied, 'excuse me . . . there is me.' Despite this witness's (*témoin*) importance, de Wendel noted that Millerand was not the government and predicted he would no longer carry much weight. Within a week of the elections, one of his strongest supporters already foresaw an end to Millerand's influence, if not to his presidential mandate. The second, more significant meeting took place at the Elysée on 21 May, when Cartel leaders Herriot and Painlevé discussed financial matters, including the franc's defense, with Poincaré and François-Marsal. Since Herriot apparently paid little attention to the financial details, François-Marsal did not, he later recalled, expect the meeting to alleviate the tension. He did not, however, expect the leftist leaders to refuse a portfolio while Millerand was president. Although François-Marsal received warnings in late April to distance himself from the president, since the Left was determined to eliminate Millerand, he still met with him frequently during May. Leaders of the Cartel, as well as the *Quotidien*, criticized the omission of the Socialists from this Elysée meeting. They accused Millerand of trying to split the new majority and ingratiate himself with the Radicals in order to defuse pressures for his resignation. Herriot and Pierre Renaudel sounded the same theme in more nuanced terms at Hyères and Lyon on 24 and 25 May. While Socialist opposition to Millerand was clear from the start, the Radicals' position was less certain. Although Herriot hesitated throughout May, he was generally expected to accept an offer to form a cabinet.[22]

Continued attacks by the *Quotidien* charged that it would be dangerous to maintain the president in the face of the electorate's repudiation. For him to remain in the Elysée would sabotage the electoral victory and stab the new government in the back. The electoral results were viewed as a condemnation not only of the Bloc National but of Millerand as its founder and guiding force. The journal accused the president of trying to split the new majority by omitting a Socialist from the meeting at the Elysée. Theoretically above partisan political struggles, the President of the Republic had sacrificed his immunity by choosing sides. His pursuit of a personal

22. Jeanneney, *De Wendel*, p. 204; E. Bonnefous, IV, p. 9. Rouffet, pp. 368–70, cites François-Marsal, 'Souvenirs,' pp. 12–14. Barty, p. 35; Schuker, p. 127; A.N., F.M. 83, *Le Quotidien*, 22 May 1924; Simonsson, p. 248.

policy made him a traitor to democracy, it claimed. On 28 May, the *Quotidien* turned to the president's own past to buttress its argument, citing Millerand's articles in the *Petite République* in 1894 against Casimir-Périer's personal policy. Since the president had a policy and a will, Millerand had argued, those elected by universal suffrage had a right and a duty to evaluate them. Millerand should, it insisted, be removed, just as he had eliminated Casimir-Périer.[23]

The charges against Millerand fell into four categories. First, he was accused of exerting a personal influence on governmental policy and of seeking to revise the constitution to increase presidential powers. His Ba-Ta-Clan speech had specifically demanded a stronger executive and a broader presidential electoral base. His statements of 20 and 23 September 1920 had affirmed a belief in the president's right to represent a policy if not a party. At Evreux, he again pleaded for constitutional changes to insure a separation of powers and greater executive authority. Secondly, his personal intervention in governmental conduct was faulted, particularly the treatment of Briand at Cannes. Not only had he dictated policy to Briand, but, in recalling him from Cannes, he left the premier no alternative but resignation. His reversal of a cabinet that still enjoyed parliamentary confidence was a violation of the head of state's traditional political neutrality. Thirdly, he had intervened in national politics at Evreux by linking the president to the governing majority's policies, defending sectarianism and pacifism, and advocating constitutional reform and financial stringency. The *Le Matin* article of 27 March 1924 similarly defended Poincaré's government and reflected Millerand's determination to continue its policy. The defense of the Bloc National's political positions vitiated the traditionally neutral arbiter role of the head of state. His personal interviews with prefects and ministers intruded on the premier's prerogatives, while his opposition to the *scrutin d'arrondissement* linked him to the political Right. Finally, he was accused of pressuring parliament by threatening to resign.[24]

Throughout May, Millerand remained relatively calm. As François-Marsal later recalled, the president did not appear

23. A.N., F.M. 83, *Le Quotidien*, 23, 25, 27 and 28 May 1924; *La Petite République*, articles by Millerand, 5 July, 8 November 1894, 18 January 1895; Dansette, p. 211; Jèze, 1924, p. 248.

24. Dansette, p. 211; Barty, pp. 70–90; Soulié, *Cartel*, pp. 250–5; Jeanneney, *Leçon d'histoire*, pp. 19–22.

'seriously alarmed' until 2 June. On 31 May, when he launched a newspaper counter-offensive, it was, however, already too late; the new parliamentary majority had decided to exclude the president. The political vacuum of late May had helped the leftist campaign, first in the newspapers and then in parliamentary corridors. Without a genuine government, Millerand's opponents had free rein. The campaign was not led by political nonentities, counting among its leaders Briand, who had never forgiven Millerand for the Cannes incident. While Briand was not present at the group meetings during the crisis, he was clearly influential behind the scenes. He refused to bail out Millerand after all other possible premiers declined to form a ministry. Had Millerand used the month to win over the centrist deputies, a different scenario might have developed, but his repugnance for political maneuvering and corridor politics made it unlikely he would have played that game even if he had recognized the severity of the threat.

Coming to the president's defense on 31 May, the *Echo de Paris* and *Le Matin* stressed his constitutional irresponsibility; the President of the Republic was free by act and word to assume political positions. No constitutional provision forbade him to defend governmental policy, as at Evreux. Far from opposing Poincaré's program, Millerand, in his Evreux speech, had echoed the premier's statement to the Chamber of 15 July 1923. Under the constitution, the president was only responsible to the Chamber for high treason. To force his resignation on other grounds was a violation of that fundamental document. The president's fate did not reflect any party or parliamentary majority. *Le Matin*, however, recognized the gravity of the struggle, given the Socialists' determination not to support any ministry which Millerand nominated, and the likely Radical acquiescence. Millerand's defense stressed that a personal presidential policy did not violate the constitution, whereas subjecting the president to political vicissitudes did. After the Radical party's negative vote on 2 June, *Le Matin* discussed its condemnation of Millerand for support of policies which the electorate had repudiated and the view that his continuation in office offended the republican conscience and was a source of future conflict. Millerand's defenders stressed the constitution's primacy, whereas his opponents considered universal suffrage supreme. The presidency of the Republic had been a source of continuity through fifty-four years of internal wrangling and external crisis. To force his resignation would, his supporters argued, set a dangerous precedent by making nothing invulnerable to political passions.[25]

When the deputies arrived in Paris at the end of May, the campaign against Millerand moved from the press to the corridors of the Palais Bourbon. Leftist parliamentary meetings on 30 and 31 May reflected clear hostility to the president, and by 1 June an anti-presidential majority had coalesced. It termed Millerand's continued presence at the Elysée after the Bloc National's defeat an offense to the republican conscience. Despite Socialist pressures, Herriot, however, hesitated to back a Cartel statement refusing to ratify any government Millerand designated. Without direct power over the president, parliament could only control him by refusing to vote the budget or invest a government that he nominated.[26]

The crisis moved into its final stage with Poincaré's resignation on 1 June and the convocation of the legislature on 2 June. Painlevé's sizable majority in the election of the president of the Chamber of Deputies on 4 June indicated Cartel strength. After consulting the presidents of the Chamber and Senate, Millerand offered the premiership to Herriot as leader of the new majority on 6 June. Officially free to decide, Herriot felt bound by the votes of his own Radical party and his Socialist allies. Millerand later recalled that he told Herriot no current problems required disagreement between the president and the new government, although he urged him to treat Alsace-Lorraine cautiously. Herriot, however, reported that in asking him to form a cabinet, the president was aware that he would institute the Cartel's programs. Millerand thereby conceded that the president must accept an electoral verdict that had ratified a different program from the one he represented. The Elysée's official communiqué stressed agreement on a program between Herriot and Millerand, but, as the former noted, the president refused to discuss the 'presidential question.' He was not entitled to raise this constitutional issue, Herriot acknowledged, but only to accept or reject the mandate offered. He also contested Millerand's description of complete accord between them, notably on Russia. Herriot refused the premiership, he claimed, primarily because Millerand's public opposition to the Cartel removed any other choice. The painful interview still did not persuade the

25. Suarez, VI, pp. 27–8. Rouffet, p. 369, cites François-Marsal, 'Souvenirs,' p. 15. Soulié, *Cartel*, pp. 263–7; Persil, p. 162; Barty, pp. 55–61; A.N., F.M. 83, *Le Matin*, 31 May, 2 June 1924; E. Bonnefous, IV, pp. 9–10.

26. E. Bonnefous, IV, pp. 9–10; Dansette, pp. 211–12; Jeanneney, *Leçon d'histoire*, pp. 21–2; Soulié, *Cartel*, pp. 256–9; Barty, pp. 61–71.

Radical leader to form a ministry outside the leftist majority that had clearly indicated its determination to eliminate the president. The *Quotidien* argued that Millerand should have resigned immediately when Herriot refused his offer.[27]

Millerand was no more successful in persuading Painlevé or other possible candidates to accept the post, even though he explicitly agreed to respect the verdict of 11 May by installing a leftist cabinet and accepting its program. When compromise between the president and the Cartel was ruled out, Millerand's final hope was his old friend, the Radical Théodore Steeg, Minister of the Interior in 1920 and subsequently Governor-General of Algeria. A telegram from Millerand brought Steeg back to Paris, where Raoul Persil, who met his train, initially persuaded him to try to form a cabinet. After talking to Painlevé, however, Steeg recognized the uselessness of the effort. As François-Marsal reported, Steeg believed it would be politically suicidal to try to save Millerand. After François-Marsal's interview with Steeg, he claimed the president abandoned hope.[28]

Millerand then tried to find someone to read his presidential message to the Chamber and make parliament responsible for accepting or rejecting his position. He even contemplated dissolving the Chamber in the hope that new elections would produce a majority that would accept his choice of premier. When Poincaré refused to read his statement, Millerand asked his old friend, former finance minister François-Marsal, on 8 June. To François-Marsal, Poincaré had refused because of political calculation, specifically to protect his future political options by not alienating the Left. Although François-Marsal rejected the Left's program, he accepted Millerand's offer primarily as a gesture of friendship. His ministerial choices also accepted out of friendship for Millerand. Eight had been in Poincaré's cabinet and all belonged to the former majority. The sole function of his cabinet was to provoke a parliamentary debate on the presidential question. A

---

27. Millerand, 'Souvenirs,' pp. 122; Edouard Herriot, *Jadis. D'une guerre à l'autre, 1914–1936* (Paris: Flammarion, 1952), vol. 2, p. 136; E. Bonnefous, IV, pp. 9–12; Dansette, p. 212; A.N., F.M. 83, *Le Quotidien*, 7, 9 and 10 June 1924; *ibid.*, *Le Matin*, 7 June 1924; Persil, pp. 162–3; Soulié, *Cartel*, pp. 276–7; Barty, pp. 104–5; Jeanneney, *Leçon d'histoire*, p. 21; Derfler, *President*, p. 106.

28. Persil, pp. 162–3; Millerand, 'Souvenirs,' p. 122; E. Bonnefous, IV, pp. 12–13. Rouffet, p. 372, quotes François-Marsal's 'Souvenirs,' p. 15; Soulié, *Cartel*, p. 280; A.N., F.M. 83, *Le Matin*, 7 June 1924; Dansette, p. 212; Jolly, p. 2467; Maier, p. 477.

clear minority government, the ministry wanted a parliamentary decision on the presidential question, not political ultimatums. Was it legal or constitutional to force the President of the Republic's resignation by a 'ministerial strike?'[29]

On 10 June, François-Marsal read Millerand's message and his own ministerial declaration to the Chambers. The former recalled Millerand's public declarations that he had accepted the presidency only to continue his national policy of social progress, work, and union, which he had, in fact, done. Anxious for peace, work, and harmony, France wanted its security abroad guaranteed, reparations received, and the treaties establishing the new European order respected. This foreign policy required a domestic program reflecting unity among Frenchmen, respect for all beliefs, more equitable social relations, and a balance between public expenditures and receipts. According to the constitution, the President of the Republic was responsible to the Chambers only for high treason. To insure stability and continuity, it sought to safeguard the presidency from political fluctuations for a seven-year period. Millerand urged parliament to respect the constitution. It must avoid the dangerous precedent of letting a majority force a president's resignation for political reasons. Responsible for drafting legislation and insuring respect for the laws, parliament must not set the example of violating them. Dangerous advisors, influenced by partisan concerns, he believed, pressed the new legislature to open with a 'revolutionary act,' but it would surely refuse the pressures, and the Senate would abide by the constitution. To Millerand, the current crisis posed such important constitutional questions that no individual or group decision could settle it in the background.[30]

François-Marsal then read the cabinet's declaration asking for a juridical debate of the constitutional issue. The septennate, he argued, counterbalanced ministerial instability. When Charles Reibel tried to open the debate with a demand for an interpellation,

29. Millerand, 'Souvenirs,' p. 123; Rouffet, pp. 374–7; E. Bonnefous, IV, pp. 12, 14–15; A.N., F.M. 83, *Le Matin*, 4 and 8 June 1924. *Ibid.*, *Le Quotidien*, 9 June 1924, termed François-Marsal's nomination a defiance of universal suffrage. Dansette, pp. 212–13; Persil, pp. 163–4; Barty, p. 105; Jolly, p. 2467; Soulié, *Cartel*, pp. 280–8; Maier, p. 477; Derfler, *President*, p. 106.

30. J.O., *Chambre*, 11 June 1924, p. 172, quotes Millerand's presidential statement of 10 June 1924. E. Bonnefous, IV, pp. 14–15; Persil, pp. 163–4; *Revue du droit public*, XLI, No. 3 (July–September 1924), 'Chronique constitutionelle de France: la crise présidentielle de juin 1924,' pp. 462–74.

the Cartel leaders tabled a motion rejecting relations with a ministry whose composition negated parliamentary rights. Discussion should be adjourned until a government was formed that reflected the national will. Reibel countered that even though no electoral verdict had been sought on the presidential question, the new majority was determined to have the president resign. Reibel described the campaign against Millerand as revolutionary. The president's hopes for support in the Senate were dashed when the upper house voted, by a slight majority, not to deliberate the presidential message, thereby leaving the verdict to the Chamber. When the Chamber ratified Herriot's motion not to deal with a minority ministry, the debate ended without any real consideration of the issues involved.[31]

François-Marsal's inability to secure a parliamentary debate on the constitutional issue finally convinced Millerand that his departure was unavoidable. On 11 June 1924, he resigned the presidency. It was impossible for him to dissolve the Chamber without the Senate's assent. The Senate's refusal to examine the political situation had eliminated that option. The president had no way to retain his position. The ministerial strike created a political stalemate that only Millerand's resignation could break. Had Millerand persisted, the opposing majority could have convened the Chambers as a National Assembly and passed constitutional revisions that would have allowed them to depose the president. A persistent advocate of a stronger presidency, Millerand refused to weaken even further that institution. He was also too strong a democrat to contemplate seriously a move that smacked of dictatorship or anti-republicanism.[32]

After his resignation, Millerand addressed a manifesto to the nation that summarized the circumstances of his election, his political program, his collaboration with various ministries, and the Cartel's refusal to work with him. As the Republic's first magis-

31. Millerand, 'Souvenirs,' pp. 123–5, quotes one senator's remark that 'the constitution was violated without debate.' Persil, pp. 163–5, argued that had Poincaré remained neutral, Millerand might have mobilized a Senate majority. He also noted that Millerand's opponents included Briand's friends, notably Loucheur. Simonsson, p. 265, denies that Millerand could have won a majority in the Senate. Barty, p. 105; E. Bonnefous, IV, pp. 14–15; Dansette, p. 213; Soulié, *Cartel*, pp. 280–8; *Revue du droit public*, 'Crise présidentielle,' pp. 462–74.

32. Millerand, 'Souvenirs,' pp. 123–5; Persil, p. 165; Dansette, pp. 213–14. Plumyène and Lasierra, p. 29, cite an article by Taittinger in *La Liberté* of 14 November 1924 arguing that the elections altered French domestic policy and compromised Millerand's and Poincaré's patriotic work.

trate, he knew that the nation's primary domestic and foreign requirement was peace. Abroad, it implied Allied support to apply the diplomatic texts creating the new Europe, the League of Nations guarantee of international agreements, and execution of the Versailles Treaty to insure French security and reparations. Domestically, peace required elimination of prewar internal dissension to promote fraternal *entente* among all Frenchmen, and the protection of legitimate rights along with efforts to institute calmly moral and material progress. France's debt to its devastated regions and war victims had imposed a heavy burden on French taxpayers because of German defaults. The ministries that he had presided over had striven to carry out that patriotic task for four years. After the recent elections, he had agreed to collaborate loyally with the victors chosen by universal suffrage, but they had instead demanded his resignation – an 'unjustifiable pretension' that was violently contradictory to the spirit and letter of the constitution. With a separation and equilibrium of powers indispensable to public liberty, Millerand argued that the President of the Republic's mandate should devolve not simply from parliament but from an expanded electoral college representing general councils, and worker, employer, intellectual, and agricultural associations. If the constitution left the choice of president to parliament alone, it should insure that he was accountable only for high treason during his septennate – a guarantee that a partisan decision had overturned. Audacious agitators, he claimed, had used extra-parliamentary meetings to decided that a president, rejected by the new majority, should resign before the end of his legal mandate. He termed it a 'redoubtable precedent' to make the presidency a stake in electoral battles, since it indirectly introduced a plebiscitary ingredient that eliminated the constitution's only element of stability and continuity. To Millerand, such dangerous innovations were felonious, leading him to stand firm until he had exhausted all legal recourses.[33]

In interviews after he left the Elysée, Millerand conveyed a seeming detachment toward his forced resignation. To him, the final episode proved that a genuine separation or equilibrium of powers required constitutional changes. He termed the events of 10 June to be an act of parliamentary dictatorship that negated free-

---

33. Millerand, 'Souvenirs,' annexe, 'Un manifeste à la nation française!,' 11 June 1924; *Revue du droit public*, 'Crise présidentielle,' pp. 462–74; E. Bonnefous, IV, p. 16; Soulié, *Cartel*, p. 288.

dom. Only a balance of powers could insure the individual freedom against dictatorship that the Republic proclaimed. Discussing current foreign issues, Millerand feared that a reconciliation with Soviet Russia, as Herriot's cabinet urged, would strengthen the Bolshevik regime and menace France. He worried about the London conference between Herriot and British Prime Minister MacDonald, arguing that Herriot's only bargaining counter was France's occupation of the Ruhr, but reserved judgement on the Dawes Plan for reparations. With France's need for security, maintenance of its military strength had to be a primary concern. The League of Nations was not powerful enough to protect one Great Power against another. Domestically, he still endorsed a position of financial orthodoxy, whereby receipts balanced expenditures and borrowing was avoided, and a social peace among the participants in production. Advocating an administrative reform to encourage regionalism, he suggested grouping departments by economic characteristics to permit local management of regional requirements. After his resignation, he continued to endorse those programs and policies he had backed as president.[34]

Millerand's supporters viewed Poincaré's announced resignation immediately after the elections as the crucial event in the crisis. Had he remained premier and presented his program to the new parliament, he could, they insisted, have garnered sufficient support from the Center to stay in office. His defection inevitably led to Millerand's resignation. Since this argument ignores the size of the Cartel's majority and the new Chamber's mood, it is not persuasive. Not only did the Cartel want its own candidates in positions of authority, it was determined to eliminate Bloc National leadership, including Millerand. Millerand's defenders also ignore the tension that had grown during the preceding year between Millerand and Poincaré and the premier's efforts to distance himself from the Bloc National. Poincaré, who wanted to be ready if a divided nation later appealed to him, hoped to minimize disputes with the new majority and avoid identification with any narrow faction. Millerand, on the other hand, who always valued loyalty and decisiveness, linked patriotism to the Bloc National majority. Furthermore, Poincaré viewed the presidency differently from Millerand. Like the Cartel's leaders, he rejected a personal conception of the position. By spring

---

34. J. Kessel and G. Suarez, *Au camp des vaincus ou la critique du onze mai* (Paris: Editions de la Nouvelle Revue Française, 1924), pp. 17–33.

1924, personal and theoretical differences reinforced Poincaré's reluctance to support Millerand against the electoral verdict.[35]

Millerand's personal policy, rather than specific programs, caused his resignation. As he later recalled, he had long seen executive weakness as the vice of France's political regime. The Chamber's right to withhold essential credits permitted a parliamentary dictatorship whose counterweight of a right of dissolution had become a dead letter. Parliament, he claimed, had used urgent foreign policy issues to postpone constitutional revisions. As president, he tried to implement the presidential prerogatives designated by the constitution, but confronted passive resistance to a system of presidential messages countersigned by a minister. Traditional republican resistance to extensions of the executive power was, he noted, stronger than he had realized. Linking the presidency to a parliamentary majority's fate, as he had done by his Evreux speech, proved to be a tactical error. The presidential crisis of 1924 was interpreted at the time as an end to a personal presidential policy.[36]

What the nation accepted from Charles de Gaulle in 1958 after years of parliamentary wrangling, instability, and colonial disaster, it was unwilling to give to the more controversial Millerand in a less obvious crisis. Nonetheless, Millerand's constitutional reforms, proposed in his Ba-Ta-Clan speech of 1919 and frequently reiterated during his presidency, resembled the provisions of de Gaulle's constitution. Not unlike de Gaulle in temperament and political conception, Millerand wanted the presidential electoral college to include representatives of general councils and large corporations (worker and employer unions as well as intellectual groups), but Millerand never suggested a president elected by universal suffrage, as de Gaulle instituted. For his generation, the memory of Louis Napoleon was too recent. He remained a parliamentarian, endorsing a stronger executive but without a plebiscitary element.[37]

Millerand's desire for a free executive power threatened a fundamental tradition. Although the constitutional texts of 1875 gave the president the right of dissolution, it had not been used since MacMahon's time. The events of 16 May 1877 had transformed

35. Persil, pp. 161–2; Dansette, p. 214; Maier, p. 477.
36. Millerand, 'Souvenirs,' pp. 101–2; Dansette, pp. 214–15; Jèze, 1924.
37. Conversation with Jacques Millerand, 20 May 1978.

this right into a monster detested by the republicans. While the right of dissolution, constantly used in England, was not inherently undemocratic, monarchist and conservative support for MacMahon linked the procedure to the Right, giving it an anti-republican connotation. Not having to face the threat of dissolution made the task of Millerand's opponents easier. Furthermore, senatorial endorsement was a prerequisite for dissolution; the Senate refused to act in a way that seemed to reject universal suffrage. In contrast to MacMahon, however, Millerand had asked members of the new majority to form a cabinet. By staging a ministerial strike to force the president's resignation, the majority set a significant precedent. It established even more thorough legislative supremacy, further tilting the balance against the executive and jeopardizing the separation of powers proclaimed in the constitution.[38]

Since Millerand had intervened in the electoral process to support the defeated party, his departure conformed to the rules of the democratic game. Although each side charged the other with violating the constitution, the texts of 1875 were sufficiently ambiguous to make neither argument decisive. In posing a question of confidence to the nation, Millerand performed a political act. He could not therefore reasonably complain of a political response. Although Herriot's refusal to collaborate with Millerand was comprehensible, he should not have blamed his decision on party orders. In fact, Herriot, who was initially hesitant about such a categorical position, apparently did not recognize its implications. The Cartel's victory was not, however, complete; the Moderates' candidate for president, Senate president Gaston Doumergue, defeated the Cartel's choice, Chamber president Paul Painlevé.[39]

From a formal constitutional viewpoint, Millerand's arguments were valid, but the verdict is less clear for the spirit of the constitution. Since the presidential question did not play an important part in the election campaign, the results cannot be interpreted as a demand for Millerand's resignation. Nor were there any parliamentary interpellations of his controversial statements, such as

38. Fresnette Pisani-Ferry, *Le Coup d'état manqué du 16 mai 1877* (Paris: Robert Lafont, 1965), p. 326; Artaud, *Dettes interalliées*, p. 640; Soulié, *Cartel*, pp. 250–2; Jeanneney, *Leçon d'histoire*, p. 22; *Revue politique et parlementaire*, 10 May 1925, 'La révision de la constitution et les pouvoirs du président de la République,' pp. 179–80. Plumyène and Lasierra, p. 132, call Millerand an 'aventurier de passage,' but not as treacherous as Doriot.

39. Néré, pp. 53–4; Jeanneney, *Leçon d'histoire*, pp. 22–3; Barty, p. 105.

the Evreux speech or the article in *Le Matin*. Nonetheless, a defeat for the policy he represented made it logical for him to resign voluntarily. If the presidential question had been put to a popular vote, the electorate would probably have backed the new majority. With hostility to Millerand more pronounced among Socialists than Radicals, the former led the campaign to unseat him. The Radicals might have been more accommodating if they had not worried about Cartel unity. It has even been suggested that the Socialists demanded Millerand's resignation as the price of their support for a Radical government. Although the constitution did not require it, Millerand's resignation accorded with the democratic principle. Furthermore, the rules of the parliamentary game only required that he accept the electoral verdict, as he did in turning to Herriot. Delaying his resignation until his opponents accepted responsibility for their position in a parliamentary vote, Millerand protected the presidency from extra-parliamentary pressures, like the newspaper attacks. His defeat and Doumergue's election, however, restored the traditional Third Republic concept of the president as an impartial arbiter above partisan politics.[40]

The virulence of the Cartel's campaign was undoubtedly linked to Millerand's past. He was considered as a renegade Socialist who needed chastisement (the theme of *L'Humanité*'s attack). The victors of the Left feared and detested him as one of their own who had forsaken international socialism for nationalism. The Millerand affair of the beginning of the century had, therefore, extended consequences. The President of the Republic, like many former Socialists who had joined the parties of order, was far from his youthful socialism. Still a loyal democrat who hated all forms of dictatorship, he favored that domestic order and defense of France's interests abroad which the moderate parties appreciated.[41]

Millerand's personality affected his active approach to the presidency, his determination to interpret his prerogatives as extensively as possible, and the consequent opposition. Those same characteristics that made Millerand the logical choice for president in 1920 contributed to his fall in 1924. Although his style was authoritative, it was also reticent, giving the impression of massive solidity. His myopia conveyed a seeming unfriendliness. As a politician and as

40. Simonsson, pp. 273–303.
41. Soulié, *Cartel*, p. 249; Jeanneney, *Leçon d'histoire*, p. 19; Barty, pp. 40–50; Mermeix, pp. 146–7; Bariéty and Poidevin, p. 241.

president, he acted forcefully but repudiated corridor politics, the easy *camaraderie* of political coteries. His tenacious stubbornness has been likened to a wild boar's. He was still an effective speaker, able briefly to summarize the essentials of a situation. His legal training might have encouraged a scrupulousness bordering on timidity, but Millerand never lost his audacity, his readiness to take strong stands regardless of possible rebuffs. He expanded his presidential interventions beyond customary practice if not the letter of the constitution. As Reibel apparently noted to Poincaré, Millerand might wear blinders (as Poincaré charged), but he confronted problems, maturely weighed their advantages and disadvantages, made a choice, and stuck by it regardless of possible difficulties. To Reibel, Millerand, more than Poincaré, was one of the Third Republic's great statesmen.[42]

The crisis leading to Millerand's resignation has been called one of the most important in contemporary French political history. It had revolutionary implications, though bloodless, in that France replaced its deputies and altered its foreign and domestic policy, its ministers, the president of the Chamber and the President of the Republic. In retrospect, the changes appear less revolutionary and the policy changes less dramatic. Nonetheless, the month from 11 May to 11 June 1924 was significant for the Third Republic's history in its affirmation of the supremacy of popular sovereignty over personal policy. Although there were unique aspects, the situation resembled the four previous presidential resignations. In 1873, Thiers resigned when he was outvoted by the Assembly's royalist majority. MacMahon, forced after 16 May 1877 to yield to the republican majority, resigned early because of incompatibility with that majority. Grévy, who in 1887 confronted a ministerial strike similar to Millerand's, preferred resignation to a conflict with parliament. Finally, Casimir-Périer, whose personal policy Millerand denounced in 1894, left office when he could not mobilize sufficient parliamentary support.[43]

The victory of parliament over the president was perhaps most surprising in Millerand's case, since his program of constitutional reform and advocacy of a strong presidential role were precisely the reasons why the deputies and senators had urged him to accept the

---

42. Guitard, pp. 84–6; Recouly, 'Une visite,' pp. 226–8; Soulié, *Cartel*, pp. 249–50; Jeanneney, *Leçon d'histoire*, p. 19.
43. Barty, introduction, pp. 7–25.

office in 1920. Once in power, however, Millerand proved less effective than he had hoped. Furthermore, France's domestic and international position deteriorated between 1920 and 1924. Millerand became therefore an obvious scapegoat. Not really responsible for the Bloc National's policies, he was sufficiently vocal to be an easy target. Had he possessed genuine executive powers, it is questionable whether he could have provided better solutions to France's problems than the premiers he criticized. While he was perhaps one of the Third Republic's more active presidents, he was still restricted by constitutional provisions and parliamentary tradition.

15
Epilogue in the Senate

From 1924 until the outbreak of the Second World War in 1939, Millerand's policies remained consistent with those he had defined as premier and president. Still primarily interested in foreign policy, especially toward Germany and Russia, he was anxious about the progressive decline in France's strength and security. On the fringes of power, he was, however, a relatively isolated figure, a Cassandra prophesying doom but unable to influence governmental policy. A French Churchill crying in the wilderness, he was too old to save his beloved France when the long-predicted catastrophe finally arrived.

Millerand's resignation from the presidency deprived him of immediate access to political power. He resumed an active legal career and participated in the legislative section of the Academy of Moral and Political Sciences, to which he had been elected in 1918. The Cartel's electoral victory had, however, foreign policy consequences that rapidly drew Millerand back to politics. For several years, the Left had demanded that relations with Soviet Russia be restored. When Italy and Britain recognized the Soviet regime in early 1924, a decision on France's position became more pressing. When he became premier, Herriot indicated his intent to recognize the Soviet government, but waited until the autumn so that he could complete reparations negotiations and preliminary discussions with the industrial and financial groups whose prewar investments had been hurt by the Soviet nationalizations. On 28 October 1924, the French government officially recognized the Soviet government, but expressly affirmed the continuing validity of tsarist Russia's financial obligations to French citizens. Each state also promised not to intervene in the other's domestic affairs.[1]

1. Millerand, 'Souvenirs,' p. 125; E. Bonnefous, IV, pp. 31–3.

The French governmental move provoked a rightist response. Indeed, the Cartel's electoral victory had triggered an extra-parliamentary reaction on the Right; leagues were formed to mobilize popular opposition to governmental policies. Some were paramilitary organizations of former veterans with a revolutionary, fascist bent, especially during the 1930s. The league of which Millerand was a founding member belonged, however, to the traditional, nationalist Right. Its members, eminent centrist political figures, lectured against Cartel policies but did not seek to subvert the republican system. On 7 November 1924, Millerand, François-Marsal, Flandin, Maginot, Brousse and others founded the Ligue Républicaine Nationale (the L.R.N.) in response to France's recognition of the Soviet Union. Millerand often gave league-sponsored public lectures, especially before he returned to parliament in April 1925. While the L.R.N. was always a marginal force in French political life, it gave Millerand a forum in which to discuss governmental policy. His foundation of the L.R.N. marked the former president's official return to public life and also indicated conservative determination to coordinate efforts against the Cartel. The new league's manifesto criticized Herriot's evacuation of the Ruhr and his acceptance of the Dawes Plan even though the British had not supported an inter-Allied debt arrangement. It also gave an adverse picture of the financial situation in which revenues had declined, prices and taxes had increased, and the currency had become less stable since the Cartel took power, but its opposition focused on policy toward Russia.[2]

Millerand surveyed the spectrum of issues confronting France on 14 November 1924. Still primarily concerned with peace, he viewed Germany's material and moral disarmament as the basic prerequisite. The League of Nations helped maintain peace, oppose aggression, and protect French security, but unity at home was still vital; a continuation of the wartime union had to replace the luxury of prewar divisions. All citizens had, the former president insisted, a fiscal duty to pay the taxes needed to cover France's reconstruction of its devastated regions. Frenchmen must work and produce

2. Rémond, pp. 208–18; Rouffet, p. 393; Millerand, 'Souvenirs,' p. 125[1]; Jolly, p. 2467. Persil, pp. 172–3, argues that he himself feared the L.R.N. would exploit Millerand. E. Bonnefous, IV, pp. 55–7, lists the initial signatories as Millerand, Ratier, Flandin, François-Marsal, François-Poncet, Le Trocquer, Maginot, Marin, Reibel, and Brousse. He calls the L.R.N. the Right's most important initiative to regroup in the face of the Communist–Socialist menace represented by the Cartel.

in a disciplined manner. Since freedom required authority, the republican system should be altered to strengthen the executive and to restrain the legislature's encroachment; dictatorship by an assembly was as pernicious as by an individual. Millerand hoped to expand the electorate with female suffrage, give parliament professional representation, and introduce a degree of regionalism. He opposed the *école unique* because the obligation to attend the same school would violate republican educational freedom. Internationally, unity was as important as it was domestically; to force Germany to apply the Treaty required a common Allied stance. He feared Germany's admission to the League of Nations would open another channel for revisionism. Adherence to the Treaty did not, however, eliminate the need for France to maintain its own military strength; it needed all possible guarantees of its security.[3]

The former president was particularly upset by two Cartel decisions: France's recognition of the Soviet government and its termination of the Vatican embassy, both of which reversed Bloc National policies. He blamed Herriot's decision to recognize the Soviet government on domestic pressures, specifically from the communists. He expected the move to strengthen the Third International's efforts to foment world-wide revolution with its subversive cells in the French army and labor unions. His charges of communist manipulation of the government are difficult to substantiate, but Herriot, probably pushed by his Socialist allies, clearly hoped recognition would resolve Franco-Russian economic and political problems. If Socialist ideology influenced the recognition of Russia, the Radicals' anticlerical heritage affected the withdrawal of France's embassy to the Vatican in February 1925. Throughout the period of the Bloc National legislature, the Left had attacked diplomatic ties to the Vatican. For Millerand, domestic rather than foreign considerations also explained the decision to withdraw the embassy. In 1920, he had defended France's representation in a forum where religious matters affecting its colonial, Middle Eastern, and Rhineland interests were discussed. His experience in Alsace-Lorraine convinced him that the Republic needed an ambassador to give it prestige when negotiating with the Vatican about the provinces' religious issues. Anxious to perpetuate the wartime union by ending confessional disputes, he expected

3. Millerand, 'Souvenirs,' p. 126; A.N., F.M. 91, Millerand's speech to the Union chrétienne des jeunes gens de Paris, 14 November 1924; Persil, pp. 170–2.

French Catholics to view the elimination of the embassy as a provocation, perhaps reviving the old religious disputes.[4]

Millerand's famous speech of 16 December 1924 at Luna Park officially launched the Ligue Républicaine nationale. Its focus was anti-communist, a denunciation of the Cartel for recognizing the Soviet government. 'By what criminal aberration, when a wounded but victorious France needs a calm convalescence, does a government establish itself openly in Paris under the crossed standard of the hammer and sickle, the general staff of the revolution?' A 'prisoner' controlled by an audacious and unscrupulous political party, the government was, he charged, compelled to apply socialist programs. Unless they halted the dictatorship by the 'regime of civil war' which their government had supposedly recognized for economic reasons, Frenchmen courted destruction. Even as a Socialist, Millerand had urged his colleagues to subordinate party concerns to national interest. He blamed his exclusion from the Socialist party in 1903 on his support for War Minister André's prohibition for soldiers to join labor exchanges that were spreading antimilitarism. Perceiving France and its republican system in danger in 1924, Millerand and his L.R.N. colleagues had launched a rallying-cry of alarm to the nation, public opinion, and republicans of all philosophical and religious persuasions. Although critical of the Cartel's misguided military, financial, and foreign policy decisions, Millerand hoped France would respond positively to his league's nationalist appeal.[5]

The conservative groups that emerged after the Cartel's electoral victory sought to improve the parliamentary system and strengthen the executive. Specifically, they wanted a genuine separation of powers, restoration of the president's right of dissolution, an electoral system based on proportional representation, and a prohibition against simultaneous participation in parliament and the government. With these objectives in mind, Millerand's L.R.N. launched a propaganda campaign against the Cartel that was designed to secure a conservative victory in the municipal elections of May 1925. The former president gradually aligned the various factions behind his banner, but, as a contemporary noted, the practical effects of his league were questionable. Lacking both the flair and the black horse of a Boulanger, Millerand had too

4. *Ibid.*
5. E. Bonnefous, IV, pp. 33, 57; Persil, p. 172; A.N., F.M. 89, Millerand's speech for the L.R.N. at Luna Park, 16 December 1924.

recently been on the other side of the barricades. Unlike Mussolini, he restricted himself to after-dinner speeches at elegant banquets. A man unable to retain his own position seemed an unlikely savior for France.[6] Perhaps most importantly, Millerand remained a committed republican who would never adopt extra-legal means to achieve his ends. While he never captured public imagination like Boulanger or utilized Mussolini's strong-arm tactics, Millerand nonetheless effectively re-grouped the Right's scattered forces.

Millerand's speech for the L.R.N. of 11 January 1925 in Rouen was the opening salvo of the campaign against the Cartel. He again attacked the government for increasing the communist peril by recognizing the Soviet regime. Although anti-communism was the ideological cement for the conservative counter-thrust, Millerand viewed financial problems as most pressing because of the deterioration that had followed the leftist victory. A restoration of confidence alone could end the flight of capital. After his resignation, Millerand had acknowledged that the currency must be restored, but claimed the magnitude of wartime devastation invalidated a comparison between 1871 and 1919. France's obligation to repair its devastated departments had saddled it with a huge debt. To him, the war, not postwar inept financial management, accounted for the franc's depreciation. German reparations payments, the only remedy, were still the key to French financial stability in 1925 as they had been in 1919. He feared that France's obligation to evacuate the Ruhr a year after the signature of the London agreement would only jeopardize its security, but insisted that troops remain in the Rhineland so that Germany executed the Treaty's financial and military clauses. He did not want military service reduced or the powers of the League of Nations restricted. Refuting charges of a clerical menace, he still opposed withdrawal of the Vatican embassy. Finally, he repeated his demand to restore the president's right of dissolution and to enact an administrative reform that would permit greater regionalism.[7]

6. Louis Marcellin, *Voyage autour de la Chambre du Cartel des gauches* (Paris: Nouvelle Librairie Nationale, 1925), p. 256; E. Bonnefous, IV, p. 58. Robert Soucy, *French Fascism: The First Wave, 1924–1933* (New Haven: Yale University Press, 1986), pp. 30–1, 39, 174, calls Millerand a non-fascist conservative who kept his distance from anti-parliamentary groups like Rédier's Légion and refused to attend a Faisceau demonstration at Rennes in 1926. He told Faisceau leader Valois that the idea of dictatorship 'repelled' him. In 1925, at the height of the conservative backlash to the Cartel, L.R.N. support was estimated at 300,000.

7. A.N., F.M. 86, Millerand's response to a speech by Charles Dupuis at the

When the Chamber passed the government's bill to suppress the Vatican embassy on 2 February 1925, the religious question again became a political concern. It implemented Herriot's and the Radicals' electoral commitment. Determined to preserve a secular state, they believed that representation at the Vatican buttressed the Catholics' domestic position and blurred the distinction between temporal and spiritual responsibilities. They discounted any damage to France's international prestige or to its ability to protect French missionary interests in the East. However, the Council of State's verdict that the Concordat still applied in Alsace-Lorraine forced the Cartel to appoint a *chargé de mission* to handle the provinces' concerns in Rome.[8]

The government's move fueled the conservative propaganda campaign against the Cartel and augmented Catholic opposition to the government. The political battle assumed a significant religious dimension for the first time since the war. Millerand accused the government of falsifying the results of Franco-Vatican relations to justify the rupture and of ignoring the consequent foreign dismay. Perceiving French unity as vital to national security, he attacked the government for a policy of 'sectarianism, disorder, and menace' that aided only revolutionary socialism. He viewed this 'incoherent' religious policy, harking back to the bitter, narrow sectarianism of an earlier anticlericalism, as a declaration of war against the Catholics. While Millerand attributed the Cartel's religious policy to its Radical component, he blamed the Socialists for the recognition of the Soviet Union. A desire to promote revolution, not economic benefits, influenced the Bolsheviks, he charged. The Cartel was playing charades with the Russians that hurt French domestic and foreign security. To counter the Cartel's divisive religious and diplomatic moves, he hoped the L.R.N. would serve as a force of republican integration. That league by-passed parliamentary intrigues to address its ideological propaganda directly to the public, urging all Frenchmen to participate in postwar France's daunting struggle. The wartime virtues of self-denial, discipline, and unity alone could defeat Cartel sectarianism and German militarism. Indeed, the war's legacy made discord among

Institut de France, 28 June 1924; A.N., F.M. 91, interview of Millerand by Hutin in the *Echo de Paris*, 1 September 1924; A.N., F.M. 89, Millerand's speech for the L.R.N. at Rouen, 11 January 1925; A.N., F.M. 90, Millerand's speech for the L.R.N. at Luna Park, 14 November 1925.
    8. E. Bonnefous, IV, pp. 60–2.

Frenchmen 'sacrilegious' and 'impious.' Citing Gambetta's salvation of the Republic after the crisis of 16 May 1877, he pleaded with twentieth-century republicans to unite and reap the harvest of their wartime victory.[9]

Although Millerand spoke under L.R.N. auspices for several years, he soon recognized his need for a parliamentary base if his attack on the Cartel was to be effective. He found his opportunity when the death of Paul Magny, senator for the department of the Seine, forced a by-election for his seat in 1925. Millerand's Senate campaign stressed his long parliamentary career and his specific contributions as premier and minister of commerce. As premier, he believed in 1925, his most noteworthy achievements had been the revived ties to the Vatican, the repression of the revolutionary strikes, and the rescue of endangered Poland – the activities most likely to appeal to the Right. The current government, he charged, had reversed that earlier policy of order, freedom, and social progress to obey revolutionary dictates which undermined French confidence just when it needed unity to implement social reforms. Stressing his history of support for reform, Millerand cited his decrees of 1899 and 1900 on salaries, length of the work day, and retirement pensions and the addition in 1920 of a Ministry of Public Hygiene and an under-secretariat for technical education. His dedication to social reform justified, he maintained, his attack on the Cartel's divisive tactics. Communism, a minority current, had used governmental weakness to encourage domestic divisions, undermine authority, threaten freedom, and endanger diverse interests. Millerand's remarks obviously contained much electoral rhetoric, but won for him an easy victory in the department of the Seine. Indeed, the Cartel had already been defeated in other by-elections. Millerand's victory in the election of 5 April 1925 may have reflected not only his own and the former Bloc National's revived prestige, but also some public disenchantment with ten months of Cartel leadership.[10]

In parliament, Millerand continued to oppose the Cartel. He portrayed the current situation in dismal tones, arguing that the

9. A.N., F.M. 92, Millerand's speech for the L.R.N. in Marseilles, 1 March 1925.
10. E. Bonnefous, IV, pp. 58–9; Millerand, 'Souvenirs,' p. 126; Jolly, p. 2467; Persil, p. 173; A.N., F.M. 84, Millerand's electoral speech, 8 March 1925.

electoral promises of peace and financial stability had evaporated in the reality of higher living costs, a depreciated currency, and virtual civil strife. The L.R.N.'s attack had, he believed, yielded results, but a restoration of confidence was necessary to avert imminent financial collapse. Although the new finance minister, Joseph Caillaux, never forgave Millerand for his passing attack, the latter viewed the choice of Caillaux, a disciple of Germany and a wartime defeatist, for a ministerial position as an example of the Cartel's compliance *vis-à-vis* its neighbor across the Rhine. By April 1925, French security particularly worried Millerand. Problems connected with German disarmament and occupation of the Rhineland had prompted new British and German proposals that eventually culminated in the Locarno accords of October 1925. A critic of Locarno even before it was formally ratified, Millerand would remain a foe throughout the interwar period, fearing German expansionism in the east through union with Austria or revision of the German–Polish frontier. Since Locarno only guaranteed Germany's western frontiers, it seemed to encourage eastern ambitions that violated the postwar treaties. For the same reason, he opposed French evacuation of the demilitarized zone until Germany met its Treaty commitments.[11]

Millerand often reflected on the war to provide lessons for the difficult postwar period. While its legacy of horror reinforced pressures for peace, it had also elicited positive characteristics like courage, sacrifice, and honor that the postwar world desperately needed. Joffre's calm confidence or Belgian King Albert's courage and stature had inspired soldiers and doomed Germany's hegemonic drive. Permanent peace, however, required respect for the institutions that guaranteed to all nations their political and territorial integrity. The League of Nations must be able to enforce its decisions even against national wishes. However desirable general disarmament was for a climate of peace, France had to preserve its own security by maintaining its military force and occupying German territory until peace conditions were applied. Anxious for normal Franco-German economic and political relations, Millerand still considered the Locarno accords a poor solution to international tension, since they encouraged an eastern revisionism which could require French aid to Poland or Czechoslovakia.[12]

11. E. Bonnefous, IV, pp. 79–82, 92–3; Persil, p. 173; A.N., F.M. 90, Millerand's speech for the L.R.N. at the Cirque de Paris, 23 April 1925.
12. A.N., F.M. 91, Millerand's speech in Brussels, 9 December 1924, 'De la

Millerand did not address the Senate for more than a year after his election. His speech of 3 June 1926 termed the Locarno guarantees insufficient. A Russo-German pact of 25 April 1926 created an uncertain atmosphere for the Senate debate on Locarno. To Millerand, a fundamental ambiguity (*une équivoque*) characterized the accords. France hoped reconciliation would make the peace arrangements more palatable, but Germany saw the *rapprochement* as the first step to revision. Indeed, Germany's contrasting attitude toward its eastern and western frontiers had, Millerand believed, prompted the Locarno initiative. Citing Cardinal de Retz, the former president observed that politics required an ability to choose between grave disadvantages. To him, Locarno's debits outweighed the alleged reinforcement of French security which had evaporated when the United States did not ratify the peace treaties. The Locarno accords transformed Britain and Italy from allies into neutral arbiters in a Franco-German dispute. While Britain, like France, wanted to preserve the current Rhine territorial status, the pact, in protecting Germany against France as much as the reverse, precluded an alliance with Britain and made it more difficult to establish Treaty violations. To Millerand, Locarno essentially disarmed France *vis-à-vis* Germany. Furthermore, since Germany had persistently disregarded all formal commitments, its signature could not be trusted. He believed Germany wanted to enter the League only to alter its Treaty obligations. Locarno would not preclude a Russo-German alignment, as had been recently demonstrated. In the interest of world peace, Millerand urged tighter links between France and the small East European states. Citing Mirabeau, he termed Locarno's illusion of eternal peace its greatest danger, since it could tempt France to disarm before an armed Europe. They must rebuff such perilous chimeras and back moral strength with material force.[13] Millerand's eloquent plea elicited little response from his Senate colleagues, who overwhelmingly endorsed the Locarno accords. Millerand himself, despite grave reservations, refused to compromise France's international position

guerre à la paix'; A.N., F.M. 92, interview with Hutin in the *Echo de Paris*, 1925, about the evacuation of the Rhineland; A.N., F.M. 93, Millerand's speech at the Franco-Polish celebration at Vincennes, 27 February 1926; *ibid.*, Millerand's speech at Champenoux (Nancy), 12 September 1926, 'Le souvenir français.' A.N., F.M. 86, Millerand's speech at the Institut, 25 October 1931, called Joffre the 'savior' of France during the battle of the Marne.

13. Wolfers, p. 65; E. Bonnefous, IV, pp. 136–7; Persil, p. 176; J.O., *Sénat*, 3 June 1926.

by voting against the pact. Foreign Minister Briand described Locarno as a move toward peace, but still promised to maintain French military strength. In 1926, pacifism did not displace security in France's foreign policy hierarchy, although the latter was not specifically defined in the wake of Locarno. Would Briand have seen an eastern revision as prejudicial enough to French security to require a forceful response? The question was not officially confronted.

France experienced a devastating financial crisis in the second half of 1926. Poincaré formed a 'great ministry' in July with a program of economy and rationalization to avert a total collapse. His stabilization of the franc in November 1926 at approximately one-fifth of its 1914 value was hailed as a heroic salvation of the currency. Crucial, in Millerand's opinion, to the original panic and later euphoria was the psychological dimension. The 'Poincaré experience' confirmed his belief that a restoration of confidence was the prerequisite for a financial recovery. Although a national government restored financial peace, it did not eliminate France's other problems: its need for German reparations to pay war debts to the United States, rebuild French territory, fortify the eastern frontier, or re-model the army. Financial and foreign preoccupations did not, however, obliterate Millerand's interest in constitutional revisions for a stronger executive or his opposition to a return to the *scrutin d'arrondissement* electoral system, which he termed a ballot of 'immorality' and 'corruption.'[14]

Millerand lost his Senate seat in the elections of January 1927 to 'republican socialist' Pierre Laval. He later blamed his defeat, the first of his political career, on the Communists, whose alliance with the other leftist parties in the Seine department had given the Left an almost total victory. The Communists had already been victorious in the Parisian municipal elections, and Millerand's rebuff transferred that municipal verdict to the national level. The former president's defeat undoubtedly stemmed from his specific personality and program, overt anti-communism and outspoken independence, but also demonstrated the effective leftist electoral alliance and a shift in the political complexion of the Paris region with its 'red belt' suburbs. In general, the larger leftist component in the

14. E. Bonnefous, IV, pp. 180–2; A.N., F.M. 89, Millerand's speech for the L.R.N. at the Salle Wagram, 26 November 1926; A.N., F.M. 93, Millerand's speech to the Société industrielle de Mulhouse, 5 June 1926; A.N., F.M. 90, Millerand's speech for the L.R.N. at Melun, 9 May 1927.

new Senate was at the expense of the conservative parties.[15]

Although Millerand was resigned to accept an end to his political career, he actually served another twelve years in the Senate. A former colleague in the Chamber, Henry Roulleaux-Dugage, persuaded him in August 1927 to run for the Senate seat from the Orne department that Robert Leneveu's death had opened. He was elected on 30 October 1927 and reelected in 1935. In Alençon, Millerand cited his record of opposition to the Cartel through his extra-parliamentary activities for the L.R.N., an organization which he described as dedicated to 'freedom' and 'fatherland' (*liberté et patrie*). Its non-sectarian program reflected his conviction that the wartime experience had made the prewar domestic struggles 'puerile' and 'loathsome.' Pleading for religious freedom, avoidance of internecine struggles, and a greater degree of regional influence, he also urged a balanced budget and spending cuts by reducing the number of civil servants. Although he blamed the currency's near collapse on the Cartel, he portrayed foreign policy as its most serious shortcoming, particularly the recognition of the Soviet government. Since peace required Poland's territorial integrity as much as Alsace-Lorraine's protection, Locarno presented serious drawbacks. He concluded with a plea for a constitutional revision to guarantee a genuine separation of powers. Again linking authority and freedom as equally vital to a healthy democracy, he repeated his demand that the presidential right of dissolution be implemented to end the legislature's total domination.[16]

Although foreign policy was Millerand's dominant interest, he occasionally addressed domestic issues such as financial stringency, constitutional revision, production, social reform, and regionalism. In Clermont-Ferrand in 1928, for example, he argued that increased production along with lower costs would best enable France to compete effectively at the international level. Frenchmen must share the burden of public expenditures, but the state must use all resources and eliminate unnecessary expenses. Social peace and prosperity were the prerequisites for an effective economy and social reform; the two remained symbiotically entwined. Councils

15. E. Bonnefous, IV, pp. 201–2. Millerand, 'Souvenirs,' p. 127, noted that friends and adversaries saw his defeat as the end of his political career. A.N., F.M. 90, Millerand's speech for the L.R.N. at Melun, 9 May 1927. Persil, pp. 174–5, blamed the defeat on backstairs intrigues and Communist votes.

16. Millerand, 'Souvenirs,' p. 127; E. Bonnefous, IV, p. 358; A.N., F.M. 94, Millerand's speech in Alençon, 15 September 1927, part of his Senate campaign for the Orne; also in A.N., F.M. 85.

of all producing groups permitted direct worker–employer contact that promoted social harmony. He hoped urban benefits could be extended to agricultural laborers to counteract the serious social threat presented by the rural exodus. Better hygiene to improve the quality of rural life might lower the death rate and stem the exodus. Millerand believed stronger economic regions would foster national prosperity and political decentralization; local freedom would counteract the dictatorship of Parisian centralism. He still blamed the degradation of public customs on the *scrutin d'arrondissement*, which the Chamber had restored on 12 July 1927. To continue to deny the suffrage to women was, he argued, a violation of republican popular sovereignty made possible by the total legislative control that had replaced a genuine executive–legislative equilibrium.[17] The fact that Millerand represented a department with a significant rural component, instead of a Parisian *arrondissement*, might have influenced his advocacy of regionalism and rural reform, but his views on those issues long predated his election to the Senate from the Orne.

Although reelected to the Senate in October 1927, Millerand did not speak again until July 1929 during the debate on the Young Plan. Criticizing Foreign Minister Briand's 'dangerous' encouragement of a national pacifist mentality, he termed France's acceptance of Germany's proposals of February 1925 a turning-point which established a disequilibrium between Germany's eastern and western frontiers. Millerand, who backed a Franco-German *entente*, refused to sanction the end to a Rhineland occupation, the only safeguard of French security and insurance that Germany would obey the Treaty's military and reparations clauses. He rejected the link between the Young Plan, a reparations arrangement, and a Rhineland evacuation. Furthermore, he termed it 'iniquitous' for France to pay a former associate (the United States) more than it received from a former enemy (Germany). The Young Plan reduced German obligations but did not alter France's. Again, Millerand failed to persuade his Senate colleagues against endorsing governmental foreign policy by an overwhelming majority.[18]

17. A.N., F.M. 94, Millerand's speech in Clermont-Ferand, 30 September 1928, in the departmental councilors' campaign; E. Bonnefous, IV, pp. 223–7.

18. J.O., *Sénat*, 24 July 1929; Persil, pp. 178–80; E. Bonnefous, IV, pp. 358–9; A.N., F.M. 94, Millerand's speech to the Société des conférences, 18 January 1929.

Concern for France's international position eventually won Millerand's reluctant vote for the Young Plan as it had for the Locarno pacts; a strong parliamentary endorsement of French foreign policy would buttress the government's international negotiating position. Although Foreign Minister Briand cited Millerand's own correspondence with the British in 1920 to justify France's evacuation of the Rhineland, Millerand denied the parallel. Insisting he was neither bellicose nor systematically anti-German, he cited his previous support for normal Franco-German relations. To him, however, France's failure to repudiate Germany's frontier proposals in 1925 was a dangerous deviation that increased French security but simultaneously made war more likely by undermining eastern stability. Making Britain and Italy judges instead of allies had compounded the error. Millerand argued that the new reparations and evacuation plans of 1929 surrendered French prerogatives while hiding behind pacific statements. With peace dependent on Treaty execution, it was an inexcusable illusion to depend on pious statements like the Kellogg–Briand pact. In his opinion, it was premature simultaneously to evacuate the third Rhineland zone and to initiate the Young Plan. Since his colleagues apparently did not share his fears, Millerand finally decided not to vote against the government when it pleaded for the Senate to ratify the Chamber's virtually unanimous endorsement of its foreign policy. Although Millerand still wanted France to base its foreign policy on Treaty execution, he was increasingly a voice in the wilderness, unable to halt the government's abandonment of its remaining guarantees against German defaults.[19] Millerand's votes for the Locarno accords and the Young Plan could be viewed as proof of intellectual cowardice, a willingness to oppose verbally but to act as the government wished. His recognition of the danger which these agreements posed for France's international position yielded, however, to his belief that France would be strengthened if it could present a united front to the outside world.

Over the next two years, Millerand saw his fears become reality as the American stock-market crash plunged the world into depression. To him, the ensuing grave domestic and international problems gave national interests a priority over particular concerns.

19. E. Bonnefous, IV, p. 378. Wolfers, p. 43, quotes Millerand's statement to the Chamber of 13 April 1920 and Briand's statement of 8 November 1929. J.O., *Sénat*, 20 December 1929; *ibid.*, 5 April 1930; A.N., F.M. 94, Millerand's speech to the Union du commerce et de l'industrie pour la défense sociale, 11 December 1929.

The world crisis further complicated reparations and war debts, but France, though anxious for American friendship, still wanted its debt to the United States linked to its credit with Germany. When the economic and financial crisis showed no signs of slackening by 1932, Millerand urged budget cuts and moves to streamline production. Even during the world-wide depression, he was reluctant to abandon the nineteenth-century liberal commitment to laissez-faire economics, relying primarily on private initiative and turning to the government only in exceptional situations. Nor did Millerand expect the world economic conference scheduled to be held in London in 1933 to solve France's economic problems. To France, the connection between war debts and reparations meant that a moratorium for one implied one for the other. The United States, however, still denied the French equation, demanding its due despite German reparations defaults. He did, however, believe that France's strong resource base would allow it to survive the economic crisis. A growing peace mystique, as reflected in the League of Nations or the Kellogg–Briand pact, was, however, accompanied by the reality of receding disarmament. Germany had denounced or evaded, Millerand maintained, the Treaty's military stipulations and had passed larger military budgets than France while pressuring for general disarmament. In the face of persistent German bellicosity, France had given up its only guarantee of security, the Rhineland occupation. An equally serious Soviet menace matched the German peril. The German–Soviet pacts of Rapallo (1922) and Berlin (1926), stemming from a common hatred of Poland, illustrated Germany's belief that the Versailles Treaty's injustices could only be reversed in Moscow. French support for existing pacts, especially with the smaller nations, alone enabled France to thwart Soviet and German designs against the West. To Millerand, therefore, peace and disarmament were dangerous illusions that concealed a threatening reality.[20]

The advent to power in Germany of Adolf Hitler opened a new phase in Franco-German relations that culminated in war six years

---

20. A.N., F.M. 95, Millerand's speech to the Jeunesses patriotes, 6 March 1931; *ibid.*, Millerand's speech in Brussels honoring Foch, 25 April 1930; J.O., *Sénat*, 30 June 1931; A.N., F.M. 96, Millerand's speech to the Société des conférences, 'Au seuil d'une année difficile,' 15 January 1932, also delivered with the title 'La situation de la France,' 2 March 1932; A.N., F.M. XIII, Millerand's article, 'Désarmement,' 1932, written while Von Schleicher was chancellor; A.N., F.M. 96, Millerand's speech in Flers, 4 June 1933, opening the foire–exposition.

later. During 1933, Millerand's warnings about German intentions became increasingly vehement. To him, France's reduction of its military service obligation to one year illustrated its pacific intention, but Stresemann's memoirs had proven that the apparent Franco-German *entente* of the late 1920s was a fiction at whose base was the reality of frequent Treaty violations. The period of unlimited confidence in Germany that culminated in the premature evacuation of the last Rhineland zone had simply aided Germany in evading its financial and military obligations without winning its friendship for France. Maintenance of peace required not only fulfillment of international obligations but a reduction of national armaments compatible with national security. Seldom had a victor been as moderate as France in 1919, Millerand claimed, but it had progressively relinquished its guarantees of German Treaty observation; the concessions of Locarno, the Dawes and Young Plans, the Hoover Moratorium, and the Disarmament Conference had all eroded the initial resolve to exact strict compliance. The victors, he believed, had to share the blame for the treaties' collapse with the vanquished. Idealistic illusions had helped to destroy the Versailles Treaty settlement by 1933, and Millerand expected more violent German attempts at Treaty revision with Hitler in power, with war the inevitable result.[21]

The situation in Eastern Europe seemed to Millerand the greatest threat to permanent peace. Ever since the Versailles negotiations, Germany had denounced its eastern frontiers, particularly the German–Polish boundary. Would an adjustment of those borders truly guarantee peace, Millerand wondered? Since an independent Polish state needed access to the sea to survive, a corridor terminating in the free city of Danzig appeared to be the only viable solution. Germany had, however, complained unceasingly about the corridor, and had backed all local clashes and minority complaints. In Upper Silesia, it had refused any compromise, even when the Allies tried to ascertain local sentiments by a plebiscite. German pressures to alter the eastern frontiers clearly confronted

21. A.N., F.M. XIII, Millerand's article, 'L'attitude de la France à l'égard de l'Allemagne,' sent to Winkler, New York, 28 March 1933; *ibid.*, Millerand's article, 'L'entente franco-allemande,' sent to Chambrun, New York, 30 January 1933; A.N., F.M. 96, Millerand's speech in Brussels, 'Idéalistes et idéologues, 1919–1933,' 8 February 1933; Alexandre Millerand, 'La paix et la révision des traités,' *Revue de France*, Vol. 13, No. 4 (15 July 1933), pp. 231–50, is virtually identical to the Brussels speech.

East European determination to preserve the treaties' borders. Russo-German collaboration, which linked revisionist states, made the eastern situation especially precarious in Millerand's opinion. Russia, like Germany, wanted to destroy the 'scraps of paper,' the treaties, that created the new East European states. Millerand did not expect Hitler's advent to alter Russo-German relations significantly.[22]

The persistent economic depression accompanied the ever-more threatening foreign situation. Domestic financial and foreign military pressures began to pull in opposite directions. To balance the budget, the government suggested military cutbacks, but, to Millerand, disarmament was inconceivable in the current international climate. Since 1932, Germany had suspended reparations payments and agreed to attend the disarmament conference only if other states also disarmed. Millerand feared that his prediction that they were heading toward war under the flag of peace would become a reality. To him, a strong French army was the best guarantee of European peace, but Premier Daladier saw general disarmament as the more effective route.[23]

By 1934, intensified German rearmament convinced Millerand that Europe truly faced the menace of war. Since domestic and international unity were necessary to thwart the German revisions of the Treaty, he begged his compatriots to lay aside their ancient quarrels. Claiming innocence to justify fifteen years of efforts to alter the 'unjust' Treaty, Germany, Millerand argued, used its insistence on Treaty fulfillment to conceal its own rearmament and to demand general disarmament. It had capitalized on France's myopia to subvert the Treaty; its progressive rearmament and annexationist pressures toward Austria had paralleled France's abandonment of its own guarantees and reduction of its military force. The French government must, Millerand insisted, preserve France's armed strength. *Mein Kampf* clearly stated Hitler's hatred of France and his war plans. France must not let pacific statements lull its watchfulness, even though the First World War's enormous human and territorial devastation made all pacific developments from the League to the Locarno and Kellogg–Briand pacts particu-

22. A.N., F.M. XIII, Millerand's article, 'Les frontières orientales allemandes,' sent to Chambrun, New York, 21 January 1933; *ibid.*, Millerand's article, 'The Soviet peril,' sent to Chambrun, New York, 6 January 1933, revised for publication in March.
23. J.O., *Sénat*, 22 and 27 February 1933.

larly appealing. A union of the small East European states to defend their frontiers against German aggression would, Millerand believed, be a more effective guarantee of peace than an eastern Locarno. Although he argued that war would be vastly more expensive than an armed peace, his persistent warnings had seemingly little effect on France's leaders.[24]

The plebiscite of 1935 which gave Saar back to Germany led Millerand to reevaluate France's foreign and domestic situation. He argued that continuity had characterized French foreign policy since 1919, despite varying methods, specifically a desire to eradicate the specter of war. However, the initial tactic of preserving peace by demanding German compliance with the stipulations of the Versailles Treaty and guaranteeing French security by the occupation of the Rhineland had yielded after 1924 to efforts to insure a Franco–German *entente*. To Millerand, France had been so hypnotized by the chimera of that Franco–German accord that it had evacuated the Rhineland ahead of schedule, ignored friends with common interests like Poland, and pursued a vague foreign policy in the face of the Hitlerian menace. With Britain once again committed to a policy of splendid isolation, France had only its other alliances and its military strength to rely on. Although Millerand supported the Maginot line, he wanted a two-year military service obligation restored to counteract the reduced manpower resulting from the wartime casualties. Calling Millerand a truly great statesman (*de très grande classe*), General de Gaulle noted in June 1935 the former president's support for a professional army. Domestically, Millerand suggested a more rational organization of French finances. Unable to raise taxes, France could only apply a deflationary policy of reduced expenditures. To him, however, the lack of executive leadership was the root of France's problems. He traced the explosion of 6 February 1934 back to the Cartel's decision of 1924 to force his resignation or a *coup d'état*. Although the appeal to Doumergue had averted civil war, Millerand still believed a genuine solution required the restoration of governmental authority, specifically the right of dissolution as the vital counterpart to parliament's financial sovereignty.[25]

24. J.O., *Sénat*, 16 January 1934; Persil, p. 181; Jolly, p. 2468; A.N., F.M. XIII, Millerand's article, 'La politique de la France,' 8 March 1934; *ibid.*, Millerand's article, 'Sur les chemins de l'Europe,' 28 June 1934; *ibid.*, Millerand's article, 'Le Locarno orientale,' 26 July 1934.
25. A.N., F.M. 98, Millerand's speech to the Société des conférences, 'La

The Ethiopian war and Germany's re-militarization of the Rhineland sealed Millerand's disillusionment with the League of Nations and his conviction of German bellicosity. The ineffectiveness of the League's sanctions against Italy proved to Millerand the illusion of collective security, leading him to conclude sadly that only an alliance of all states supporting the postwar European settlement could preserve peace and French security. Since France's true interests lay in Europe, it must shelve idealistic support for new overseas nations like Ethiopia when that aid conflicted with European considerations. The premise of successful sanctions was a willingness to fight for peace, a risk that no nation could incur unless its vital interests were at stake or its independence threatened. France had therefore to maintain its material strength to guard its vital interests against Hitler's Germany. Germany's re-militarization of the Rhineland in March 1936 even prompted Millerand to alter his position on the Soviet Union. He reluctantly supported a Franco-Soviet pact and feared a vote against it in the French parliament would imply that it violated Locarno.[26]

Although Millerand occasionally discussed general domestic issues like decentralization and constitutional reform, he addressed only one specific social reform in his Senate years: the settlement of labor disputes. He contrasted the principles behind Waldeck-Rousseau's proposals of 15 November 1900 with Léon Blum's and Camille Chautemps' laws of 1936 and 1938. The arbitration provisions of Blum's law were, he claimed, too favorable to the C.G.T. Waldeck-Rousseau had tried to avert the civil war represented by strikes by encouraging potential belligerents to discuss their differences and seek solutions acceptable to both parties. In the interest of social peace and greater national production, employers would have relinquished some of their formerly inviolable rights and transformed the factory's absolute monarchy into a type of parliamentarism. This 'revolutionary' reform would have provided for arbitration if no consensus emerged, with strikes only a tactic of last resort that required a majority vote. To Millerand, Blum's

situation,' 1 February 1935, later published in the *Revue hebdomadaire*; J.O., *Sénat*, 20 March 1935; Persil, p. 183; Millerand, 'Souvenirs,' pp. 127–8; Charles de Gaulle, *Lettres, notes et carnets de 1919–juin 1940* (Paris: Plon, 1980), II, p. 392; Charles de Gaulle, *The Complete War Memoirs of Charles de Gaulle* (New York: Simon and Schuster, 1967), p. 18.

26. A.N., F.M. 98, Millerand's speech to the Conférence de presse franco-étrangère, 25 November 1935; J.O., *Sénat*, 12 March, 25 June 1936; Jolly, p. 2468.

proposal was an unsatisfactory substitute for the earlier unratified law of 1900. Giving the C.G.T. a dominant position on the workers' side made numerous unaffiliated workers fear for syndical freedom. The former president reacted negatively to Chautemps' arbitration and conciliation law of 1938, which he also viewed as less satisfactory than the proposal of 1900. Since that project had never been officially enacted, Millerand's criticism of the new law on the ground that it provided less than Waldeck-Rousseau envisaged is not persuasive. In part, his opposition may have stemmed from the belief that the economic climate was unpropitious; Millerand had always been convinced that a prosperous economy was a prerequisite for social reform.[27]

Even on foreign affairs, Millerand's statements became increasingly rare. As a member of the Senate's Foreign Affairs Commission, he backed the government's non-intervention in the Spanish Civil War. To him, Germany's reoccupation of the Rhineland marked the beginning of the end. As he bitterly concluded in his autobiographical memoirs, 'we went to war under the flag of peace.' His final speech in the Senate of 7 February 1939 noted France's desire for peace, but added sadly that it did not depend on France alone. He divided the preceding twenty years into three distinct periods. From 28 June 1919 to 11 May 1924, the focus on Treaty application involved the use of constraint, for example the occupations of German territory in 1920, 1921, and 1923, and the signature of treaties of alliance with Poland and Czechoslovakia, new European states committed to the status quo. From May 1924 to January 1933 was a time of confidence in Germany, culminating in the Rhineland's premature evacuation. From 1933 to the Munich pact of September 1938, Germany steadily subverted the Versailles Treaty by re-militarizing the Rhineland, annexing Austria, and partly absorbing Czechoslovakia. To Germany, clearly, formal Treaty commitments were simply scraps of paper. Convinced of German hegemonic ambitions, Millerand pessimistically predicted additional moves in the East. France's only recourse was greater military strength, alliances with states sharing material and moral interests, and especially avoidance of hazardous ventures. He strongly criticized postwar British policy for trying to prevent any

27. Jolly, p. 2468; Millerand, 'Souvenirs,' p. 128; J.O., *Sénat*, 15 December 1936; A.N., F.M. XIII, Millerand's article, 'La leçons d'hier,' late 1938; J.O., *Sénat*, 27 February 1938.

nation from establishing continental hegemony and for dismantling
its military force, but also blamed French pacifism for abandoning
French guarantees in the face of a rearming Germany.[28]

France thus reaped the harvest it had sown by ignoring those,
including Millerand, who had long foreseen the potential menace.
At eighty years old, Millerand was unable physically to play a
leadership role, even though his contemporary Marshal Pétain
would attempt it. Furthermore, the nation was not ready to heed
his warnings. When the National Assembly voted Pétain full
powers on 10 July 1940, former president Millerand was absent.
Millerand's life ended at his home in Versailles on 6 April 1943. He
did not long outlive the Republic to which he had dedicated his
lengthy political career and with so many of whose dramatic
moments he had been so intimately associated.[29]

    28. Millerand, 'Souvenirs,' pp. 129–30; J.O., *Sénat*, 7 February 1939; A.N., F.M.
XIII, Millerand's article, 'Les leçons d'hier,' late 1938.
    29. Jolly, p. 2468; J. Millerand, p. 111; Basdevant, p. 3; Persil, p. 11.

Conclusion

A striking consistency of ideas and personality traits characterized Alexandre Millerand's unusually full and diverse life. A description of the young Millerand bears a notable similarity to a posthumous assessment. In 1889, Henry du Basty noted a reforming spirit implemented by a cold, serious, though eloquent, speaking style. His legal training emerged as he skillfully argued the case for those ideals he sought to implement by legislation. Basty predicted that Millerand would be one of the 'great personalities of the future.' A decade later, President Loubet apparently described Millerand as the most promising of younger French statesmen. To Loubet, an obstinate, painstaking dedication to his objectives and a reliability of verbal commitments made him an unusual Frenchman; such characteristics were more common among the British. Basdevant's survey of Millerand's life and accomplishments in 1955 gave the subsequent details of that promising career but stressed its basic consistency. He, too, compared Millerand's speeches to legal briefs, logical, orderly, persuasive, using reason rather than sentiment to convince. To Basdevant, Millerand's organizational ability, industriousness, and quiet, determined patriotism characterized the aged senator warning France against the looming German menace as much as the youthful deputy pursuing social reform. Indeed, from an organizational point of view, the 'imposing figure' of Alexandre Millerand often 'dominated' the first quarter of the century. He not only reorganized the ministries of commerce, public works and war, but continued his battle for organization in the Elysée and parliament. His resignation from the presidency was termed a serious setback for this organizational current (*courant organisateur*). His fundamental goal was to improve the human condition through better working conditions and social solidarity within the framework of national strength and prosperity. A hatred

of dictatorship and persistent faith in a democratic Republic encouraged his support for public order and peace as well as a
willingness to use force domestically and internationally in the
national interest. Always a libertarian as well as a social reformer,
his dedication to a democratic, republican France made him a
nationalist above all. His prominence within the French parliament,
significant cabinet posts, active presidential role, and participation
in vital French developments for half a century clearly merited the
appellation of great personality predicted at the outset.[1]

A prominent political position and distinguished career did not
shield Millerand from controversy and crisis. Critical assessments
spanning the length of his career balanced those designations of
'great' personality, minister, or president. Clemenceau could fault
Millerand's disloyalty to a former mentor in the Boulanger affair,
resent his criticism of governmental actions toward strikers in
1907, attack him for blind abdication to the High Command in
1915, and feel bitter at his acceptance of the premiership in 1920.
But Clemenceau valued Millerand sufficiently to offer him the
justice ministry in 1906 and the post of Commissioner-General in
Strasbourg in 1919, and to designate him as premier when he
sought the presidency. Poincaré could denounce Millerand's ambition in seeking a cabinet post for a Socialist in 1899, his stubborn,
silent defense of Joffre in 1915, his proposal of an active presidential
role in 1920, or his usurpation of the premier's political leadership
with the Evreux speech of 1923. Yet Poincaré, too, often viewed
his former school friend more positively. Millerand's decisiveness
in the railroad strike of 1910 persuaded Poincaré to name him war
minister in 1912. Even in 1915, he recognized that Millerand was
often the scapegoat for others' mistakes. He clearly endorsed the
president's strong stand toward Germany during the Cannes conference of 1922 even though he proved no more able than Briand to
sustain that position the following year. Poincaré's or Clemenceau's
views probably reflected the changing times and vicissitudes of
their own careers as much as Millerand's behavior.

Other negative assessments were not tempered by positive
evaluations. Combes, whom Millerand attacked for excessive anticlericalism, never forgave him, and Combes' charges of cupidity

1. A.N., F.M. XI, Henry du Basty, 'Les hommes politiques français: M. Miller-
and,' *Revue d'histoire contemporaine*, 20 January 1889; Basdevant; Derfler, *Millerand*;
Persil, p. 185; Thomas Barclay, 'Monsieur Millerand and his programme,' *The
Nineteenth Century*, Vol. 58, No. 525 (November 1920), pp. 803–4; Rials, pp. 158–63.

and illegality proved surprisingly persistent and difficult to repudiate. A similar charge of avarice and greedy acceptance of huge fees
surfaced again after he left the presidency. Caillaux denigrated him
as simply a lawyer, able to present clear, logical arguments, but
lacking the true intuition and judgement of greatness.[2] Yet, Caillaux, too, had borne the brunt of Millerand's criticism for his
pro-German pacifism. It is therefore reasonable to conclude that
their evaluations reflected resentment at personal injury or career
setbacks as much as a dispassionate assessment of Millerand's
personality or behavior. Similarly, Briand's abandonment of Millerand in 1910 and his corridor intrigues against the war minister in
1915 and the president in 1924 stemmed from personal ambition
and resentment at Millerand's independent position on electoral
reform, loyal support for Joffre, or strong stance about Cannes
developments as much as Briand's genuine disagreement with
specific programs. Contemporary and retrospective assessments of
Millerand's personality and activities illuminated the character and
situation of the analysts as much as the subject. Impartial objec-
tivity is as elusive in the study of a personality as it is in the
evaluation of any historical phenomenon.

Likewise, the responses of political or social organizations to
Millerand illustrated the current situation. Socialists acknowledged
Millerand's leadership in the 1890s and ratified his reformist position of Saint-Mandé as a basic minimum program, because socialism appeared likely to achieve its objectives by universal suffrage
and legislative action not because of Millerand's personal charisma.
The rejection of Millerand personally and ministerialism generally,
and the return to a revolutionary line, also stemmed from broader
phenomena like frustration at the ballot-box, working-class pressures, and international socialist developments more than a change
in Millerand's ideas or actions. On the other hand, those same
nationalists who detested the Millerand who fought Boulanger or
held a post in the government that curbed the church and republi-
canized the army after the Dreyfus Affair admired his work as war
minister in 1912 and 1914 and loyally supported the Bloc National
under his leadership in 1919, a transformation dramatically illustrated by Barrès's presence alongside Millerand on the same electoral list. While Millerand, as part of the new nationalism that

2. Octave Homberg, *Les Coulisses de l'histoire. Souvenirs, 1898–1928* (Paris:
Librairie Arthème Fayard, 1938), pp. 201, 216; Lefranc, *Le Mouvement socialiste*,
p. 89, quoting Caillaux.

promoted a strong army and repression of domestic dissent, had adopted some of the positions that the late nineteenth-century nationalists represented, he remained an opponent of personal dictatorship and a loyal republican. A change in circumstances from the peaceful decades of the late nineteenth century to the menacing prewar years and wartime crisis also influenced the different evaluation of Millerand by the nationalists. Millerand's famous Ba-Ta-Clan speech of 1919, the keynote of the Bloc National, bore a remarkable similarity to the Socialist program enunciated at Saint-Mandé twenty-three years before, even though Socialists and nationalists would have rejected the connection. The emphasis in 1919 had indeed shifted to nationalism rather than the socialism of 1896, but the key ingredients remained constant. The nation, which still claimed its citizens' first loyalty, required a burial of internecine quarrels and a common effort to achieve its social, economic, and political goals. Freedom and security in all their dimensions occupied the same key place for Millerand in 1919 as in 1896. Millerand's fundamental consistency of ideas emerged through the shifting political labels and altered circumstances.

Millerand has been described as a 'pioneer on the well-travelled road to fame and power which winds its tortuous way from Left to Right.'[3] Around 1910, his emphasis altered to the nationalist aspects of his program rather than the socialist. While his position in the 1890s was on the Left of the political spectrum and in the postwar years on the Right, that change indicated less different ideas than a different political climate which led him to use the same words to justify different actions. In part, his more conservative location derived from the success of his earlier goals; as he achieved his objectives, he sought to preserve them. In part, his altered relative stance reflected the elimination of the monarchist, clerical forces from the Right and the expansion of the revolutionary groups on the Left. Finally, his different position stemmed from the vastly altered problems confronting postwar France from its prewar concerns. Foreign policy and France's response to the wartime legacy reinforced Millerand's nationalistic focus rather than the social issues that had dominated the nation's concerns during the preceding generation. External circumstances more than the conservatism of advancing age or personal political ambition produced the altered emphasis from socialism to nationalism with its conse-

3. Philip M. Williams, *Wars, Plots and Scandals in Post-War France* (Cambridge: Cambridge University Press, 1970), p. 24.

quent Left–Right implications. Nonetheless, the Millerand who repressed strikers in 1910 or 1920 because he believed national interests dictated the preservation of social order was hardly the Socialist Millerand who defended strikers in the 1890s. While his career reflected consistency of personality traits and ideas, the change in emphasis from socialism to nationalism produced actions by the older Millerand that were at odds with those of the young reformer.

Millerand not only provoked vastly different views of his personality and actions but triggered a number of crises that revealed significant aspects of contemporary French history. His acceptance of the commerce ministry in 1899 provoked a crisis in French socialism that not only altered the parliamentary behavior of Socialists for the next thirty-seven years, but deprived a growing segment of the French population of the influence it might otherwise have exerted within the political system. Repudiation of reformism and ministerialism in favor of the absolutist, revolutionary route had far greater implications for France than the mere exclusion of one Socialist from his party's ranks.

Millerand's split with the Briand cabinet in 1909–10 over electoral reform and the premier's subsequent exclusion of him from the reshuffled cabinet illustrated not only Millerand's independence and commitment to principles even at the cost of personal damage, but, more importantly, the resilience of the Third Republic's *scrutin d'arrondissement* electoral system and the persistence of vested interests in fighting for their fiefs. Millerand's failure to win the battle for a proportional list-voting system presaged the ultimate failure of the political system to reform itself and permit consideration of those larger national issues which transcended parish-pump politics.

Millerand's forced resignation from the war ministry over the du Paty de Clam affair in 1913 demonstrated not only his own loyalty to commitments and legalism, but the hold which issues of the past exerted on the present. As some historians have argued, not only did France always seem prepared to fight every previous war, but it continued to fight past political battles. The Dreyfus Affair still pitted Right against Left in 1913 as it had in 1899 and as it would in altered form down to Vichy. Furthermore, Millerand, who failed to appreciate sufficiently the hold of such legacies, could not compete effectively in the France of 1913 any more than he could in the France of 1924 when the Cartel des Gauches evoked those charges of dictatorship that he himself had levelled against Casimir-Périer in 1894–5. The more politically astute Briand or Poincaré, with their recognition of the realities of the French political game, emerged successfully from those crises that dealt setbacks to Millerand.

Similarly, the hostility that Millerand provoked in 1915 as Minister of War indicated the relative importance of civil and military forces in a democracy in wartime. Millerand's specific defense of Joffre against the efforts of civilian politicians to share in the war's direction proved not only his loyalty to the general but his belief that military crises necessitated a significant degree of autonomy for the soldiers in the field. His defeat had far more extensive implications than the elimination of a given war minister. The constant expansion of civilian control not only eroded the status of the military as a somewhat separate entity within society, but drew non–specialist civilians ever more closely into the military decision-making process. The implications of this civil–military crisis extended considerably beyond the events of 1915 to influence not only the conduct of the First World War but also the interwar period and the events of 1940. Clearly, numerous other factors affected those later developments, but the trend toward civilian domination that Millerand's departure initiated played its part.

Millerand's premiership and presidency were significant for French interwar foreign policy and constitutional developments. The collapse of the firm stand toward Germany that his departure represented presaged the eventual collapse of the initially victorious France before a restored, aggressive neighbor. Finally, the presidential crisis of 1924 not only ended a specific politician's political effectiveness, it shifted power from the right-of-center Bloc National to a left-wing coalition. More significantly, it dealt a setback to efforts to reform France's political system by counterbalancing the instability of parliamentary domination with the consistency of an effective executive. France's fear of dictatorship, a legacy of its Napoleonic past which Millerand shared, far outweighed its desire for leadership. His resignation in 1924 insured that France would muddle along with its incompetent leaders and inefficient parliament until external disaster intervened. Perhaps endorsement of a stronger presidential role in 1924 would not have protected France from the European and colonial defeats of the next quarter-century, but it might have enabled the nation to confront them more effectively. A study of Millerand, whose career illuminates many significant developments in recent French history, validates the observation that biography provides a window on history, a means of reintegrating the scattered pieces left by the specialists.

Bibliography

Archives and Personal Papers

Archives du Ministère de la Guerre

Série N, 1872–1919
1. Cabinet du Ministre
   5N 4, 8, 10, 11, 12, 13, 14
2. Fonds Buat
   6N 7, 9, 10, 15, 18, 22, 25, 28–35

Archives du Ministère des Affaires Etrangères

1. *Papiers d'Agents*
   Sous-Série Millerand – 118
   1–12: Questions intérnationales
   13–53: Allemagne (réparations)
   54–55: Balkans
   58–60: Grande Bretagne
   61–65: Orient
   66: Palestine
   67–93: Russie
   94: Suisse
   95: Notes Personnelles
   Papiers Barrère
   vol. 3
2. Série Guerre 1914–1918
   867: Turquie, Syrie, Palestine
3. Série z Europe, 1918–1929
   ss Grande Bretagne: 44, 45
   ss Allemagne: 385, 522
   ss Belgique: 57, 58

ss Pologne: 130
ss Saint-Siège: 14–16
4. Série Amérique
  ss Etats-Unis: 39, 61, 226
5. Série E Levant 1918–1929
  ss Syrie-Liban-Cilicie: 22–33
  ss Turquie: 162, 169, 170
6. Série y Internationale 1918–1940
  Conférernces Aix-les-Bains, Lausanne 1920: 682
  Conférence de Cannes, 1922: 21

Archives Nationales de France

1. Série des Archives personnelles et familiales
  470 A.P. Fonds Millerand (inventory still provisional)
    1–13: 1885–1914
    14–32: Ministère de la guerre, 1914–1915
    33–43: 1915–1919
    44–47: Commissariat général à Strasbourg
    48–65: Premier et Ministre des Affaires Etrangères
    66–83: Président de la République
    84–99: 1924–1940
    I–XV: Don Supplémentaire, mélanges
2. Comptes-Rendus des Commissions Parlementaires
  1885–1889
  C5376: Army
  C5381: Budget
  1889–1893
  C5454: Chemin de fer
  C5443: Budget
  1893–1898
  C5548: Budget
  C5555: Budget
  C5613^2: Travail
  1898–1902
  C5618: Army
  C5624–5629: Budget
  C5673: Travail
  1902–1906
  C7278: Assurance et prévoyance sociale
  C7310–7311: Enquêtes parlementaires
  1906–1910
  C7343: Assurance et prévoyance sociale
  C7349: Budget

C7353: Travaux publics
C7414: Travail
1910–1914
C7421: Army
C7424: Budget
C7486: Travail
1914–1919
C7488: Affaires étrangères
C7494–7501: Army
C7533, 7543–7545: Budget
3. Ministère du Travail
F²² 543: Inspection du travail

Archives Parlementaires

1. Chambre des Députés, Palais Bourbon
   Commission des affaires étrangères, 1920
2. Sénat, Luxembourg
   Commission de l'armée, boîte 158, 1915
   Commission des affaires étrangères, 1920

Bibliothèque de l'Institut

Général Edmond Buat, 'Souvenirs,' I, 1914–1918

Private Papers

Millerand family, Sèvres, France
Alexandre Millerand, 'Mes souvenirs (1859–1941) – contribution à l'histoire de la Troisième République,' Versailles, 22 April 1941. Unpublished memoir.

Official Publications

France, *Documents diplomatiques français (1871–1914).* 3ᵉ Série, vol. V. Paris: Imprimerie Nationale, 1933.

France, *Journal officiel de la République française. Lois et décrets.* Paris: Imprimerie Nationale, 1885–1940.

France, *Journal officiel de la République française. Débats parlementaires. Chambre des Députés.* Paris: Imprimerie Nationale, 1885–1940.

France, *Journal officiel de la République française. Débats parlementaires. Sénat.* Paris: Imprimerie Nationale, 1885–1940.

Great Britain, *Documents on British Foreign Policy, 1919–1939.* Edited by

Rohan Butler and J.P.T. Bury. First Series, vols. VII, VIII, IX, XI, XIII. London: Her Majesty's Stationery Office, 1958–1963.
United States, *Papers Relating to the Foreign Relations of the United States.* Vol. III, 1920. Washington: United States Government Printing Office, 1936.

Newspapers

L'Echo de Paris
Le Matin
Mouvement Socialiste
La Petite République
Le Quotidien
La Revue socialiste
Le Temps

Books and Articles

d'Abernon, Edgar Vincent, Viscount. *Diary of An Ambassador.* New York: Doubleday, Doran & Co., Inc., 1929.
——. *The Eighteenth Decisive Battle of the World.* Warsaw, 1920. Westport, Conn.: Hyperion Press, Inc., 1977.
Adam, M. 'Confédération danubienne ou petit entente,' *Acta Historica*, XXV (1979), pp. 61–113.
Albert, François. 'Chronique politique,' *Revue politique et parlementaire*, 10 February 1922, pp. 277–87.
—— 'Chronique politique,' *Revue politique et parlementaire*, 10 January 1924, pp. 153–70.
Allain, Jean-Claude. *Joseph Caillaux.* Paris: Imprimerie Nationale, 1978, 1981. 2 vols.
Anderson, Malcolm. *Conservative Politics in France.* London: George Allen & Unwin, Ltd., 1974.
Andler, Charles. *Vie de Lucien Herr (1864–1926).* Paris: Editions Rieder, 1932.
Andrew, Christopher. 'Déchiffrement et diplomatié: le cabinet noir du Quai d'Orsay sous la Troisième République,' *Relations internationales*, No. 5, 1976, pp. 37–64.
Andrew, Christopher M., and Kanya-Forstner, A.S. *France Overseas. The Great War and the Climax of French Imperial Expansion.* London: Thames and Hudson, 1981.
Antonucci, A. *Le Bilan des réparations et la crise mondiale.* Paris: Editions Berger-Levrault, 1935.

Artaud, Denise. 'A propos de l'occupation de la Ruhr,' *Revue d'histoire moderne et contemporaine*. XVII (January–March 1970), pp. 1–21.

—— *La Question des dettes interalliées et la reconstruction de l'Europe (1917–1929)*. Lille: Atelier reproduction des thèses, 1978, 2 vols., dactylographié.

Asquith, H.H. *Letters to Venetia Stanley*. Oxford: Oxford University Press, 1982.

Auffray, Bernard. *Pierre de Margerie (1861–1942) et la vie diplomatique de son temps*. Paris: Librairie C. Klincksieck, 1976.

Badié, Vincent. *Les Principaux Aspects du socialisme réformiste en France*. Montpellier: Imprimerie du progrès, 1931.

Baechler, Christian. *Le Parti catholique alsacien, 1890–1939. Du Reichsland à la République jacobine*. Paris: Editions Ophrys, 1982.

Barclay, Thomas. 'Monsieur Millerand and his programme,' *The Nineteenth Century*. Vol. 58, No. 525 (November 1920), pp. 803–12.

Bardoux, Jacques. *De Paris à Spa*. Paris: Librairie Félix Alcan, 1921.

Bariéty, Jacques. *Les Relations franco-allemandes après la première guerre mondiale*. Paris: Editions Pedone, 1977.

—— 'Les Réparations allemandes, 1919–1924: objet ou prétexte à une politique rhénane de la France,' *Bulletin de la société d'histoire moderne*, 15e série, no. 6 (1973), pp. 21–33.

—— and Poidevin, Raymond. *Les Relations franco-allemandes (1815–1975)*. Paris: Armand Colin, 1977.

Barrère, Camille. 'La Conférence de San Remo,' *Revue des deux mondes*, 1 August 1938, pp. 510–14.

Barrès, Maurice. *Mes cahiers*. Vols. XII (*1919–1920*) and XIII (*1920–1922*). Paris: Librairie Plon, 1949.

Barthélemy, Joseph. 'Chronique de politique extérieure,' *Revue politique et parlementaire*, 10 February 1922, pp. 288–304.

—— *La Conduite de la politique extérieure dans les démocraties*. Paris: Publications de la conciliation intérnationale, Dotation Carnegie, 1930.

Barty, Jacques. *L'Affaire Millerand*. Paris: Longin, 1924.

Basdevant, Jules. 'Notice sur la vie et les travaux de Alexandre Millerand,' *Publications de l'Institut de France*, No. 23 (Paris, 28 November 1955).

du Basty, Henry. 'Les Hommes politiques français: M. Millerand,' *Revue d'histoire contemporaine*, 20 January 1889.

Baumont, Maurice. *La Faillite de la paix (1918–1939)*. Paris: Presses Universitaires de France, 1967.

Baumont, Michel. 'Abel Ferry et les étapes du controle aux armées, 1914–1918,' *Revue d'histoire moderne et contemporaine*, XV (Jan.–Mar. 1968), pp. 162–208.

Beau de Loménie, E. *Les Responsibilités des dynasties bourgeoises*. Vol. III. Paris: Editions Denoël, 1954.

Becker, Jean-Jacques. *Le Carnet B*. Paris: Editions Klincksieck, 1973.

—— 'Les "Trois Ans" et les débuts de la première guerre mondiale,' *Guerres mondiales et conflits contemporains*, No. 145 (January 1987), pp. 7–26.

Bergmann, Carl. *The History of Reparations.* Boston: Houghton Mifflin Co., 1927.

Bernard, Philippe, and Dubief, Henri. *The Decline of the Third Republic, 1914–1938.* Cambridge: Cambridge University Press, 1985.

Bernard, Phillipe. *La Fin d'un monde, 1914–1929.* Paris: Editions du Seuil, 1975.

Bompard, Jacques. 'Un ministre de la guerre: M. Alexandre Millerand,' *Revue politique et parlementaire*, 10 January 1914 (Paris), pp. 30–52.

Bonnefous, Georges and Edouard. *Histoire politique de la Troisième République.* Vols. I, II, III. Paris: Presses Universitaires de France, 1956–68.

Bonnefous, Edouard. *Avant l'oubli. La vie de 1900 à 1940.* Paris: Laffont/ Nathan, 1985.

Bonnet, Georges. *Le Quai d'Orsay sous trois Républiques.* Paris: Librairie Arthème Fayard, 1961.

—— *Vingt ans de vie politique. 1918–1938. De Clemenceau à Daladier.* Paris: Fayard, 1969.

Bourdeau, J. 'La crise du socialisme et la fin d'une doctrine,' *Revue des deux mondes*, 15 September 1899 (Paris), pp. 241–64.

Bourgin, Georges. *La Troisième République, 1870–1914.* Paris: Armand Colin, 1967.

Bournazel, Renata. *Rapallo: naissance d'un mythe. La Politique de la peur dans la France du Bloc national.* Paris: Armand Colin, 1972.

Bradley, John. *Allied Intervention in Russia.* London: Weidenfeld & Nicolson, 1968.

Brécot, Jean (pseud. Monmousseau). *La Grande grève de mai 1920.* Paris: Librairie du Travail, nd.

Bresler, Harvey J. 'The French railway problem,' *Political Science Quarterly*, XXXVII, No. 2 (June 1922), pp. 211–26.

Brogan, D.W. *The Development of Modern France, 1870–1939.* New York: Harper & Row, 1966. 2 vols.

Bugnet, Charles. 'Joffre et M. Millerand,' *Revue des deux mondes*, 15 April 1936, pp. 785–819.

—— *Rue St.-Dominique et G.Q.G. ou les trois dictatures de la guerre.* Paris: Librairie Plon, 1937.

Cairns, John C. 'International politics and the military mind: the case of the French Republic, 1911–1914,' *The Journal of Modern History*, XXV, No. 3 (Chicago, September 1953), pp. 273–85.

—— 'Politics and foreign policy: the French Parliament, 1911–1914,' *The Canadian Historical Review*, XXXIV, No. 3 (Toronto, September 1953), pp. 245–76.

Calmette, G. *Les Dettes interalliées.* Paris: Alfred Costes, 1926.

Cambon, Paul. *Correspondance. 1870–1924.* Vol. III. Paris: Grasset, 1946.

Capéron, Louis. *L'Invasion laïque*, Paris: Desclée, 1935.

Carroll, E. Malcolm, *French Public Opinion and Foreign Affairs, 1870–1914.*

London: Frank Cass & Co., Ltd., 1931.

—— *Soviet Communism and Western Opinion, 1919–1921*. Chapel Hill: University of North Carolina Press, 1965.

Cassar, George H. *The French and the Dardanelles*. London: George Allen & Unwin, Ltd., 1971.

Challener, Richard D. *The French Theory of the Nation in Arms, 1866–1939*. New York: Russell & Russell, Inc., 1965.

Chapman, Geoffrey William. 'Decision for war: the domestic political context of French diplomacy, 1911–1914.' Unpublished Ph.D. dissertation, Princeton University, 1971.

Chapman, Guy. *The Dreyfus Trials*. London: B.T. Batsford, 1972.

Charlet, Georges, *Les Rapports entre haut commandement militaire et pouvoirs publics en France durant la guerre 1914–1918*. Lille: Imprimerie G. Sautai, 1930.

Chastenet, Jacques. *Cent ans de République*. Vol. 3 Paris: Jules Tallandier, 1970.

—— *La France de M. Fallières*. Paris: Librairie Arthème Fayard, 1949.

—— *Histoire de la Troisième République*. Vols. III, IV, V. Paris: Librairie Hachette, 1960–1970. 2nd edn.

—— *Raymond Poincaré*. Paris: René Juillard, 1948.

—— 'Une occasion manquée: l'affaire de la Ruhr,' *La Revue de Paris*, July 1959, pp. 5–19.

Clemenceau, Georges. *Grandeurs et misères d'une victoire*. Paris: Librairie Plon, 1930.

Cobban, Alfred. *A History of Modern France*. Vol. III: *1871–1962*. Baltimore: Penguin Books, 1967.

Colton, Joel. *Léon Blum: Humanist in Politics*. Cambridge, Mass.: The M.I.T. Press, 1966.

Combarieu, Abel. *Sept ans à l'Elysée avec le Président Emile Loubet*. Paris: Librairie Hachette, 1932.

Combes, Emile. *Mon ministère. Mémoires, 1902–1905*. Paris: Librairie Plon, 1956.

Coornaert, E. 'Les Présidents de la IIIe République,' *Politique*, 15 May 1931, pp. 399–416.

Cornilleau, Robert. *De Waldeck-Rousseau à Poincarè*. Paris: Editions Spes, 1927.

—— *Du Bloc national au front populaire*. Paris: Editions Spes, 1939.

Cramaussel, Jean. *Les Messages présidentiels en France*. Paris: Jouve et Cie., Editeurs, 1928.

Dansette, Adrien. *Histoire des présidents de la République*. Paris: Amiot-Dumont, 1953.

David, Robert. 'Une grande carrière politique: M. Jonnart,' *La Revue hebdomadaire*, 22 October 1927, pp. 463–77.

Davray, Henry D. 'M. Alexandre Millerand,' *The Anglo-French Review*, IV, No. 5 (December 1920), pp. 470–9.

De Gaulle, Charles. *The Complete War Memoirs of Charles de Gaulle.* New York: Simon and Schuster, 1967.

—— *Lettres, notes et carnets de 1919–juin 1940.* Vol. II. Paris: Librairie Plon, 1980.

Delcros, Xavier. *Les Majorités de reflux à la Chambre des Députés de 1918 à 1958.* Paris: Presses Universitairies de France, 1970.

Derfler, Leslie. *Alexandre Millerand: The Socialist Years.* The Hague: Mouton, 1977.

—— 'Le "cas Millerand"': une nouvelle interprétation," *Revue d'histoire moderne et contemporaine,* April–June 1963, pp. 81–104.

—— *President and Parliament. A Short History of the French Presidency.* Boca Raton: University Presses of Florida, 1983.

Dolléans, Edouard. *Histoire du mouvement ouvrier.* Vol. 2: *1871–1936.* Paris: Librairie Armand Colin, 1948.

Dollot, René. *Diplomatie et présidence de la République.* Paris: Editions Pedone, 1955.

Doty, C. Stewart. *From Cultural Rebellion to Counterrevolution: The Politics of Maurice Barrès.* Athens: Ohio University Press, 1976.

Doukas, Kimon A. *The French Railroads and the State.* New York: Columbia University Press, 1945.

Dreyfus, François G. 'Le malaise politique,' in *L'Alsace de 1900 à nos jours,* edited by P. Dollinger. Toulous: Privat, 1979, pp. 99–133.

—— *La Vie politique en Alsace, 1919–1936.* Paris: Armand Colin, 1969.

Dreyfus, Mathieu. *L'Affaire telle que je l'ai vécue.* Paris: Bernard Grasset, 1978.

Dubech, Lucien. 'M. Alexandre Millerand,' *La Revue universelle,* III, No. 13 (Paris, 1 October 1920), pp. 116–22.

Duroselle, Jean-Baptiste. *Clemenceau.* Paris: Fayard, 1988.

—— *Histoire diplomatique de 1919 à nos jours.* Paris: Dalloz, 1978.

—— *La France et les français.* Vol. I: *La France de la Belle Epoque, 1900–1914.* Vol. II: *Histoire de la grande guerre, 1914–1920.* Paris: Editions Richelieu, 1972.

Du Sault, Jean. *La Vie et l'œuvre de Charles Jonnart.* Paris: Imprimerie Moderne, nd.

—— 'Les relations diplomatiques entre la France et le Saint-Siège,' *Revue des deux mondes,* October 1971, pp. 115–22.

Dutton, David. 'The union sacrée and the French cabinet crisis of October 1915,' *European Studies Review,* Vol. 8, No. 4 (October 1978), pp. 411–24.

Ellis, Jack D. *The Early Life of Georges Clemenceau, 1841–1893.* Lawrence: The Regents Press of Kansas, 1980.

Elwitt, Sanford. *The Third Republic Defended. Bourgeois Reform in France 1880–1914.* Baton Rouge: Louisiana State University Press, 1986.

Escaich, René. 'L'influence des présidents de la République,' *Ecrits de Paris,* May 1965, pp. 64–76.

412   Bibliography

Estèbe, Jean. *Les Ministres de la République, 1871–1914.* Paris: Presses de la Fondation Nationale des Sciences Politiques, 1982.

Farrar, Marjorie M. *Conflict and Compromise: The Strategy, Politics and Diplomacy of the French Blockade, 1914–1918.* The Hague: Martinus Nijhoff, 1974.

—— 'Politics versus patriotism: Alexandre Millerand as French minister of war', *French Historical Studies*, XI, No. 4 (Fall 1980), pp. 577–607.

—— 'Victorious nationalism beleaguered: Alexandre Millerand as French premier in 1920,' *Proceedings of the American Philosophical Society*, Vol. 126, No. 6 (1982), pp. 481–519.

Favez, Jean-Claude. *Le Reich devant l'occupation Franco-Belge de la Ruhr en 1923.* Geneva: Librairie Droz, 1969.

Felix, David. *Walther Rathenau and the Weimar Republic: The Politics of Reparations.* Baltimore: The Johns Hopkins Press, 1971.

Ferras, Henry. *Le Rôle du président de la République dans la direction de la politique extérieure.* Paris: Presses Universitaires de France, 1935.

Ferry, Abel. *Les Carnets secrets d'Abel Ferry 1914–1918.* Paris: Bernard Grasset, 1957.

Fiechter, Jean-Jacques. *Le Socialisme français: de l'affaire Dreyfus à la grande guerre.* Geneva: Librairie Droz, 1965.

Fink, Carole. *The Genoa Conference. European Diplomacy, 1921–1922.* Chapel Hill: University of North Carolina Press, 1984.

Flandin, Pierre-Etienne. 'La politique et la vie. La démission de M. Briand–M. Poincaré et sa politique,' *Revue de France*, 15 February 1922, pp. 838–47.

François-Poncet, André. 'Poincaré tel que je l'ai vu,' *Le Figaro littéraire*, 26 June 1948.

—— *De Versailles à Potsdam.* Paris: Flammarion, 1948.

—— *La Vie et l'œuvre de Robert Pinot.* Paris: Librairie Armand Colin, 1927.

Gallieni, J.S. *Mémoires du Maréchal Gallieni.* Paris: Payot, 1920.

Gagnon, Paul A. *France since 1789.* New York: Harper & Row, Publishers, 1972.

Garçon, Maurice. *Histoire de la justice sous la IIIe République.* Vol. I. Paris: Librairie Artème Fayard, 1957.

Godfrey, John F. *Capitalism at War. Industrial Policy and Bureaucracy in France, 1914–1918.* Leamington Spa: Berg Publishers Ltd., 1987.

Goguel, François. *La Politique des partis sous la IIIe République.* Paris: Editions du Seuil, 1946.

Goldberg, Harvey. *The Life of Jean Jaurès.* Madison: University of Wisconsin Press, 1962.

Goldey, David B. 'The disintegration of the Cartel des gauches and the politics of French government finance, 1924–1928.' Unpublished D.Phil. dissertation, Oxford University, 1962.

Goulut, L. *Le Socialisme au pouvoir.* Paris: Marcel Rivière et Cie., 1910.

Guitard, Louis. *La Petite Histoire de la IIIe République. Souvenirs de Maurice Colrat*. Paris: Les Sept Couleurs, 1959.

Hankey, Lord Maurice. *Diplomacy by Conference. Studies in Public Affairs, 1920–1946*. London: Ernest Benn, Ltd., 1946.

Hardach, Gerd. 'La mobilisation industrielle en 1914–1918: production planification et idéologie,' in *1914–1918, l'autre front*, edited by Patrick Friedenson (Cahiers du mouvement social, No. 2). Paris: Les Editions Ouvrières, 1977, pp. 81–109.

Harvey, Donald J. *France Since the Revolution*. New York: The Free Press, 1968.

Hatzfeld, Henri. *Du paupérisme à la sécurité sociale. Essai sur les origines de la sécurité sociale en France 1850–1940*. Paris: Librairie Armand Colin, 1971.

Hauser, Fernand. 'M. Alexandre Millerand,' *Politica*, February 1924, pp. 67–75.

Helmreich, Jonathan. 'The negotiation of the Franco-Belgian military accord of 1920,' *French Historical Studies*, Spring 1964, pp. 360–78.

Helmreich, Paul C. *From Paris to Sèvres. The Partition of the Ottoman Empire at the Peace Conference of 1919–1920*. Columbus: Ohio State University Press, 1974.

Hennebicque, Alain. 'Albert Thomas et le régime des usines de guerre, 1915–1917,' in *1914–1918, l'autre front*, edited by Patrick Friedenson (Cahiers du mouvement social, No. 2). Paris: Les Editions Ouvrières, 1977, pp. 111–44.

Herbillon, Colonel Emile. *Souvenirs d'un officier de liaison pendant la guerre mondiale*. Paris: Editions Jules Tallandier, 1930. 2 vols.

Herriot, Edouard. *Jadis. D'une guerre à l'autre, 1914–1936*. Vol. 2, Paris: Flammarion, 1952.

Hogenhuis-Seliverstoff, Anne. *Les Relations franco-soviétiques (1917–1924)*. Paris: Publications de la Sorbonne, 1981.

Hoisington, William A., Jr. *The Casablanca Connection: French Colonial Policy, 1936–1943*. Chapel Hill: University of North Carolina Press, 1984.

Homberg, Octave. *Les Coulisses de l'histoire. Souvenirs, 1898–1928*. Paris: Librairie Arthème Fayard, 1938.

Horne, Alastair. *The French Army and Politics, 1870–1970*. New York: Peter Bedrick Books, 1984.

Howorth, Jolyon. *Edouard Vaillant. La création de l'unité socialiste en France*. Paris: Edi Syros, 1982.

Huc, Arthur. *Hommes et doctrines*. Paris: Editions Bernard Grasset, 1935.

Huddleston, Sisley. 'French politics to-day,' *The New Europe*, 20 July and 5 August 1920, pp. 59–62, 85–8.

—— 'French policy in Middle Europe,' *The New Europe*, 16 September 1920, pp. 20–6.

—— 'M. Millerand – the man and his meaning,' *Fortnightly Review*,

December 1920, pp. 899–909.

—— *Those Europeans.* New York: G.P. Putnam's Sons, 1924.

Hughes, Judith M. *To The Maginot Line. The Politics of French Military Preparation in the 1920s.* Cambridge, Mass.: Harvard University Press, 1971.

Humbert, Charles. *Chacun son tour.* Paris: L'Ile de France, 1925.

Ignace, Edouard. In *L'Echo national*, 4, 8, 9, 10 February 1922, series of articles on Millerand's intervention in the affair of the Banque Industrielle de Chine.

Ignotus. 'Etudes et portraits: M. Alexandre Millerand,' *La Revue de Paris*, 1 November 1921, pp. 49–58.

Jacobson, Jon. 'Strategies of French foreign policy after World War I,' *Journal of Modern History*, Vol. 55, No. 1 (March 1983), pp. 78–95.

Jeanneney, Jean-Noël. *L'Argent caché.* Paris: Fayard, 1981.

—— *François de Wendel en République. L'argent et le pouvoir 1914–1940.* Paris: Editions du Seuil, 1976.

—— *Leçon d'histoire pour une gauche au pouvoir. La faillite du Cartel 1924–1926.* Paris: Editions du Seuil, 1977.

Jèze, Gaston. 'Chronique constitutionnelle de France: la présidence de la République,' *Revue du droit public*, October–December 1920, pp. 574–87.

—— 'Chronique constitutionnelle de France: la présidence de la République,' *Revue du droit public*, XLI, No. 2 (April–June 1924), pp. 242–8.

Joffre, Joseph J.C. *Mémoires du Maréchal Joffre (1910–1917).* Paris: Librairie Plon, 1932. 2 vols.

Johnson, Douglas. *France and the Dreyfus Affair.* London: Blandford Press, 1966.

Jolly, J. (ed.) *Dictionnaire des parlementairies français.* Vol. 7. Paris: Presses Universitaires de France, 1972.

Jones, Adrian. 'The French railway strikes of January–May 1920: new syndicalist ideas and emergent communism,' *French Historical Studies*, XII, No. 4 (Fall 1982), pp. 508–40.

Jordan, W.M. *Great Britain, France, and the German Problem, 1918–1939.* London: Oxford University Press, 1943.

Keiger, John F.V. *France and the Origins of the First World War.* New York: St. Martin's Press, 1983.

Kemp, Tom. *The French Economy 1913–39. The History of a Decline.* London: Longman, 1972.

Kessel, J. and Suarez, G. *Au camp des vaincus ou la critique du onze mai.* Paris: Editions de la Nouvelle Revue Française, 1924.

Khoury, Philip. *Syria and the French Mandate. The Politics of Arab Nationalism, 1920–1945.* Princeton: Princeton University Press, 1987.

King, Jere Clemens. *Generals and Politicians.* Berkeley: University of California Press, 1951.

Kovacs, Arpad F. 'French military legislation in the Third Republic

1871–1940,' *Military Affairs*, XIII, 1949, pp. 1–13.

Konvits, Joseph. 'Biography: the missing form in French historical studies,' *European Studies Review* 6, 1976, pp. 9–20.

Kriegel, Annie. *Aux origines du communisme français, 1914–1920.* Vol. I. Paris: Mouton et Co., 1964.

Krumeich, Gerd. *Armaments and Politics in France on the Eve of the First World War.* Trans. by Stephen Conn. Dover, N.H.: Berg Publishers Ltd., 1984.

Kuisel, Richard F. *Capitalism and the State in Modern France.* Cambridge: Cambridge University Press, 1981.

Lachapelle, Georges. *Les Batailles du franc.* Paris: Librairie Félix Alcan, 1928.

Laroche, Jules. *Au Quai d'Orsay avec Briand et Poincaré, 1913–1926.* Paris: Hachette, 1957.

—— 'La grande déception de Cannes (Souvenirs de 1922),' *Revue de Paris*, June 1957, pp. 39–51.

—— 'Quelques aspects de l'affaire de la Ruhr,' *Revue d'histoire diplomatique*, 1949, pp. 180–2.

Lavy, A. *L'Œuvre de Millerand. Un ministre socialiste (juin 1899–janvier 1902).* Paris: Librairie Georges Bellais, 1902.

Lebovics, Herman. 'Protection against labor troubles. The campaign of the Association de l'industrie française for economic stability and social peace during the great depression, 1880–96,' *International Review of Social History*, XXXI, part 2, 1986, pp. 147–65.

Lecanuet, R.P. *Les Signes avant-coureurs de la séparation.* Paris: Librairie Félix Alcan. 1930.

Lefebvre, Georges. *The Coming of the French Revolution.* Trans. by R.R. Palmer. Princeton: Princeton University Press, 1947.

Lefranc, Georges. *Le Mouvement socialiste sous la Troisième République (1875–1940).* Paris: Payot, 1963.

—— *Le Mouvement syndical sous la Troisième République.* Paris: Payot, 1967.

Lesourd, Jean-Alain. 'Romain Rolland, témoin de son temps,' *L'Information historique*, No. 1, 1959, pp. 41–3.

—— *Les Présidents de la République dans l'histoire de la France.* Paris: Les Editions Inter-nationales, 1960.

Ligou, Daniel. *Histoire du socialisme en France, 1871–1961.* Paris: Presses Universitaires de France, 1962.

Lloyd George, David. *War Memoirs.* Vol. I. Boston: Little Brown & Co., 1933.

Loucheur, Louis. *Carnets secrets. 1908–1932.* Brussels: Editions Brepols, 1962.

McDougall, Walter A. *France's Rhineland Diplomacy 1914–1924: The Last Bid for a Balance of Power in Europe.* Princeton: Princeton University Press, 1978.

McMillan, James F. *Dreyfus to De Gaulle. Politics and Society in France, 1898–1969.* London: Edward Arnold, 1985.

Maier, Charles S. *Recasting Bourgeois Europe.* Princeton: Princeton University Press, 1975.

Malliavin, René. *La Politique nationale de Paul Deschanel.* Paris: Librairie Ancienne Honoré Champion, 1925.

Mandell, Richard D. *Paris 1900.* Toronto: University of Toronto Press, 1967.

Marcelet and Mulson. *La Famille Millerand de Roche.* Saint-Dizier: André Brulliard, 1923.

Marcellin, Louis. *Politique et politiciens pendant la guerre.* Paris: La Renaissance du Livre, 1922–4. 4 vols.

—— *Voyage autour de la Chambre du Cartel des gauches.* Paris: Nouvelle Librairie Nationale, 1925.

Martin, Auguste. 'Péguy et Millerand,' *L'Amitié Charles Péguy*, No. 78 (15 June 1960) and No. 79 (August 1960), pp. 10–29; pp. 1–23.

Martin, Benjamin F. *Count Albert de Mun. Paladin of the Third Republic.* Chapel Hill: University of North Carolina Press, 1978.

Masson, Stéphane. 'C'était l'actualité . . . il y a 20 ans: 6 Avril 1943, mort du Président Alexandre Millerand,' *Aux carrefours de l'histoire*, No. 64, April 1963, pp. 130–2.

Mayeur, Jean-Marie. *La Vie politique sous la Troisième République. 1870–1940.* Paris: Editions du Seuil, 1984.

Mazgaj, Paul. *The Action Française and Revolutionary Syndicalism.* Chapel Hill: University of North Carolina Press, 1979.

Mélot, Ernest. 'L'evolution du régime parlementaire,' *La Revue générale*, 15 April 1935, pp. 468–80.

Mermeix. *Histoire du franc depuis le commencement de ses malheurs.* Paris: Albin Michel, 1926.

Messimy, General Adolphe. *Mes souvenirs.* Paris: Librairie Plon, 1937.

Michel, Marc. *L'Appel à l'Afrique.* Paris: Publications de la Sorbonne, 1982.

Michon, Georges. *La Préparation à la guerre. La loi de trois ans (1910–1914).* Paris: Marcel Rivière, 1935.

Millerand, Alexandre. 'Août 1914–août 1918,' *Revue des deux mondes*, 1 August 1918, pp. 481–6.

—— 'Au secours de la Pologne (août 1920),' *La Revue de France*, 12ᵉ Année, IV (15 August 1932), pp. 577–93.

—— *Le Contrat de travail.* Association nationale française pour la protection légale des travailleurs. 4ᵉ série. Séance of 18 January 1907. Paris: Félix Alcan, 1907.

—— 'La crise de l'arbitrage obligatoire,' *Revue politique et littéraire (Revue bleue)*, 5 March 1927, p. 129.

—— *Deux discours.* Paris: Librairie Marcel Giard, 1923.

—— 'Les deux méthodes,' *Les Annales politiques et littéraires*, No. 2492 (20 April 1934), p. 425.

—— 'Le devoir de demain,' *Revue politique et littéraire*, 14–21 April 1917, pp. 225–31.

—— 'En attendant une constitution,' *Revue de Paris*, 15 October 1930, pp. 721–39.

—— 'L'enseignement technique ou professionnel,' in *Enseignement et démocratie*. Paris: Félix Alcan, 1905.

—— 'La France unie,' *Le Parlement et l'opinion*, 1924.

—— *La Grève et l'organisation ouvrière*. Paris: Félix Alcan, 1906.

—— *La Guerre libératrice*. Paris: Librairie Armand Colin, 1918.

—— 'La loi de trois ans,' *Le Parlement et l'opinion*, 20 July 1913, pp. 3–9.

—— 'Un nouveau chiffon de papier?,' *Les Annales politiques et littéraires*, No. 2508, 10 August 1934, pp. 149–50.

—— 'Les origines française du B.I.T.,' *Revue des deux mondes*, 1 April 1932, pp. 588–601.

—— 'La paix et la révision des traités,' *Revue de France*, Vol. 13, No. 4 (15 July 1933), pp. 231–50.

—— *Politique de réalisations*. Paris: Bibliothèque Charpentier, 1911.

—— 'La politique extérieure', *Revue des deux mondes*, 1 April 1935, pp. 526–34.

—— 'La politique sociale d'un état moderne,' *Le Parlement et l'opinion*, 30 October 1913, pp. 1–7.

—— *Pour la défense nationale. Une année au ministère de la guerre (14 janvier 1912–12 janvier 1913)*. Paris: Bibliothèque Charpentier, 1913.

—— 'Le problème de l'autorité: la révision de la constitution,' *Revue bleue*, 5 May 1934, pp. 321–9.

—— 'Psychologie des belligérents,' *Revue politique et littéraire*, 24 November–1 December 1917, pp. 705–11.

—— *Le Retour de l'Alsace-Lorraine à la France*. Paris: Bibliothèque Charpentier, 1923.

—— 'La situation,' *La Revue hebdomadaire*, 16 February 1935, pp. 263–82.

—— *Le Socialisme réformiste français*. Paris: Librairie Georges Bellais, 1903.

—— Interviewed by *Le Temps*, 27 May and 1 August 1912.

—— *Travail et travailleurs*. Paris: Bibliothèque Charpentier, 1908.

—— *Union républicaine sociale et nationale*. Paris: Imprimerie 'Le Papier', 1919. Ba-Ta-Clan speech of 7 November 1919.

Millerand, Jacques, 'Alexandre Millerand,' *L'Histoire*, No. 8, 1979, pp. 108–15.

Milza, Pierre. 'Quand Millerand restreignait l'immigration . . .' *L'Histoire*, No. 16, October 1979, pp. 96–7.

Miquel, Pierre. *Poincaré*. Paris: Librairie Arthème Fayard, 1961.

Mitrakos, Alexander S. *France in Greece during World War I. A Study in the Politics of Power*. East European Monographs, No. 101. New York:

Columbia University Press, 1982.

Mourin, Maxime. *Les Relations Franco-Soviétiques 1917–1967*. Paris: Payot, 1967.

Nast, E. 'A propos de la liquidation des biens des congrégations,' *Revue politique et parlementaire*, LIV, 10 October 1907, pp. 46–84.

Neilson, Keith. *Strategy and Supply. The Anglo-Russian Alliance, 1914–17*. London: George Allen & Unwin, 1984.

Nelson, Keith. *Victors Divided. America and the Allies in Germany, 1918–1923*. Berkeley: University of California Press, 1975.

Néré, Jacques. *La Troisième République, 1914–1940*. Paris: Librairie Armand Colin, 1967.

Nevakivi, Jukka. *Britain, France and the Arab Middle East 1914–1920*. London: The Athlone Press, 1969.

Noblemaire, Georges. 'Une ligne droite, Alexandre Millerand,' *La Revue hebdomadaire*, 9 October 1920, pp. 125–45.

Noland, Aaron. *The Founding of the French Socialist Party (1893–1905)*. Cambridge, Mass.: Harvard University Press, 1956.

Northedge, F.S. *The Troubled Giant. Britain Among the Great Powers 1916–1939*. London: G. Bell & Sons, Ltd., 1966.

Offerlé, Michel. 'Les socialistes et Paris, 1881–1900.' Unpublished political science thesis, University of Paris I, 1979. 2 vols.

Orry, Albert. *Les Socialistes indépendents*. Vol. III of *Histoire des partis socialistes en France*, published under the direction of A. Zévaès. Paris: Marcel Rivière et Cie., 1911.

Paillat, Claude. *Dossiers secrets de la France contemporaine*. Vol. 2: *La Victoire perdue 1920–1929*. Paris: Editions Robert Laffont, 1980.

Paléologue, Maurice. *Au Quai d'Orsay à la veille de la tourmente. Journal, 1913–1914*. Paris: Plon, 1947.

Le Parlement et l'opinion. 23 September 1920 (Paris), pp. 1649–1766. Special issue on Alexandre Millerand.

Parson, Léon. *Le Cas Millerand et la décision du congrès socialiste de Paris*. Paris: Libre d'edition des gens de lettres, 1900.

Partin, Malcolm O. *Waldeck-Rousseau, Combes and the Church: The Politics of Anti-Clericalism 1899–1905*. Durham: Duke University Press, 1969.

Paul, Harry W. *The Second Ralliement: The Rapprochement Between Church and State in France in the Twentieth Century*. Washington, D.C.: Catholic University of America Press, 1967.

Paul-Boncour, J. *Entre deux guerres. Souvenirs sur la III' République*. Paris: Plon, 1945. Vols. 1 and 2.

Payen, Fernand. *Raymond Poincaré*. Paris: Editions Bernard Grasset, 1936.

Pédoya, Jean. *La Commission de l'armée pendant la grande guerre*. Paris: Ernest Flammarion Editeur, 1921.

Pedroncini, Guy. 'Stratégie et relations internationales: la séance du 9 janvier 1912 du Conseil Supérieur de la Défense Nationale,' *Revue d'histoire diplomatique*, 91ᵉ année, janvier–juin 1977, pp. 143–58.

Péguy, Charles. *Victor-Marie Comte Hugo*. *Cahiers de la Quinzaine*. XIIe Série No. 1 Paris: 1910.

Pellier, H. *Le Président Millerand dans le nord africain*. Paris: Librairie Hachette, 1922.

Perrot, Michelle. *Le Socialisme français et le pouvoir*. Paris: Etudes et documentation internationale, 1966.

Persil, Raoul. *Alexandre Millerand (1859–1943)*. Paris: Société d'éditions françaises et internationales, 1949.

Petit, Lucien. *Histoire des finances extérieures de la France. Le règlement des dettes interalliées (1919–1929)*. Paris: Berger-Levrault, 1932.

Pinkney, David. 'The dilemma of the American historian of modern France,' *French Historical Studies*, Vol. I, No. 1, 1958, pp. 11–25.

Pinot, Robert. *Le Comité des forges de France au service de la nation (août 1914–november 1918)*. Paris: Librairie Armand Colin, 1919.

—— 'Les industries metallurgiques et la guerre,' in Zolla, Daniel, ed., *La Guerre et la vie économique*. Paris: Félix Alcan, 1916, pp. 197–239.

Pisani-Ferry, Fresnette. *Le Coup d'état manqué du 16 mai 1877*. Paris: Robert Laffont, 1965.

Plumyène, J. and Lasierra, R. *Les Fascismes français, 1923–1963*. Paris: Editions du Seuil, 1963.

Poincaré, Raymond. 'Chronique de la quinzaine,' *Revue des deux mondes*, 1 February 1921, pp. 661–72.

—— *A la recherche de la paix, 1919*. Vol. IX of *Au service de la France*. Paris: Librairie Plon, 1974.

—— *Au service de la France*. Vols. I–VII. Paris: Librairie Plon, 1926–31.

—— *La Victoire et la paix*. Paris: H. Daragon, 1921.

—— *Questions et figures politiques*. Paris: Bibliothèque Charpentier, 1907.

Porch, Douglas. *The March to the Marne. The French Army 1871–1914*. Cambridge: Cambridge University Press, 1981.

Prelot, Marcel. *L'Evolution politique du socialisme français, 1789–1934*. Paris: Editions Spes, 1939.

'La Présidence de la République,' *Revue du droit public*, October–December 1923, pp. 632–44.

Ralston, David B. *The Army of the Republic. The Place of the Military in the Political Evolution of France, 1871–1914*. Cambridge, Mass.: M.I.T. Press, 1967.

Rappoport, Charles. *Socialisme de gouvernement et socialisme révolutionnaire*. Paris: Bibliothèque du parti ouvrier français, nd.

Rebérioux, Madeleine. *La République radicale? 1898–1914*. Paris: Editions du Seuil, 1975.

Reboul, C. *Mobilisation industrielle*. Paris: Berger-Levrault, 1925.

Reclus, Maurice. *La Troisième République de 1870 à 1918*. Paris: Librairie Arthème Fayard, 1945.

Recouly, Raymond. *Joffre*. Paris: Editions des Portiques, 1931.

—— 'Une visite au Président Millerand,' *La Revue de France*, 15 November

1923, pp. 225–37.

Reibel, Charles. 'Le premier drame de la Ruhr,' *Ecrits de Paris*, May 1949, pp. 24–31.

Reid, Donald. *The Miners of Decazeville. A Genealogy of Deindustrialization.* Cambridge, Mass.: Harvard University Press, 1985.

—— 'Putting social reform into practice: labor inspectors in France, 1892–1914,' *Journal of Social History*, Vol. 20, No. 1, 1986, pp. 67–87.

Rémond, René. *La Droite en France.* Paris: Aubier, Editions Montaigne, 1963.

Renard, Georges. 'Millerand: quelques souvenirs,' *La Revue socialiste*, January–February 1950, pp. 94–110.

Renouvin, Pierre. *La Crise européene et la première guerre mondiale.* Paris: Presses Universitaires de France, 1934, 1962.

—— *Les Formes du gouvernement du guerre.* Paris: Presses Universitaires de France, 1925.

—— *Histoire des relations internationales.* VII. *Les Crises du XXᵉ siècle, I, de 1914 à 1929.* Paris: Librairie Hachette, 1957.

Revue du droit public. 'Chronique constitutionnelle de France: la crise présidentielle de juin 1924,' XLI, No. 3 (July–September 1924), pp. 462–74.

Revue politique et parlementaire. 'La révision de la constitution et les pouvoirs du président de la République,' 10 May 1925, pp. 177–89.

La Revue universelle. 1 October 1920, pp. 116–22.

Rials, Stéphane. *Administration et organisation 1910–1930.* Paris: Editions Beauchesne, 1977.

Ribot, Alexandre. *Lettres à un ami.* Paris: Editions Bossard, 1924.

Ries, J. 'Combes, Millerand et Jaurès en 1904,' *La Revue socialiste*, July 1964, pp. 209–17.

Roberts, Stephen H. *The History of French Colonial Policy 1870–1925.* Hamden, Conn.: Archon Books, 1963.

de la Rocca, Comte de Peretti. 'Briand et Poincaré,' *Revue de Paris*, 15 December 1936, pp. 767–88.

Rogers, Lindsay. 'The French president and foreign affairs,' *Political Science Quarterly*, XL, December 1925, pp. 540–60.

Rouanet, Gustave. 'La Crise du parti socialiste,' *La Revue socialiste*, August–September 1899, pp. 200–15, 347–71.

Rouffet, Michel. 'Frédéric François-Marsal.' Unpublished doctoral thesis, University of Paris I, 1982.

Rupieper, Hermann J. *The Cuno Government and Reparations 1922–1923.* The Hague: Martinus Nijhoff, 1979.

Saint-Aulaire, Comte de. 'L'angleterre et les élections françaises de 1924,' *Ecrits de Paris*, May 1953, pp. 9–19.

—— *Confession d'un vieux diplomate.* Paris: Flammarion, 1953.

Saint-Quentin. René de. 'L'occasion manquée de la Ruhr (septembre 1923),' *Revue d'histoire diplomatique*, 1949, pp. 177–9.

Sarrail, Général Maurice. *Mon commandement en orient (1916–1918)*. Paris: Ernest Flammarion Editeur, 1920.

Sauvy, Alfred. *Histoire économique de la France entre les deux guerres (1918–1931)*. Paris: Fayard, 1965.

Scham, Alan. *Lyautey in Morocco. Protectorate Administration, 1912–1925*. Berkeley: University of California Press, 1970.

Schmidt, Royal J. *Versailles and the Ruhr: Seedbed of World War II*. The Hague: Martinus Nijhoff, 1968.

Schuker, Stephen A. *The End of French Predominance in Europe. The Financial Crisis of 1924 and the Adoption of the Dawes Plan*. Chapel Hill: University of North Carolina Press, 1976.

Schuman, Frederick L. *War and Diplomacy in the French Republic*. New York: Howard Fertig, 1969.

Seager, Frederic H. *The Boulanger Affair*. Ithaca: Cornell University Press, 1969.

—— 'Joseph Caillaux as premier, 1911–1912: the dilemma of a liberal reformer,' *French Historical Studies*, XI, No. 2, (Fall 1979), pp. 239–57.

Sementéry, Michel. *Les Présidents de la République française et leur famille*. Paris: Editions Christian, 1982.

Sforza, Count Carlo. *Makers of Modern Europe*. London: Ekin Mathews & Marrot, 1930.

Shapiro, David, ed. *The Right in France, 1890–1919. Three Studies*. Carbondale: Southern Illinois University Press, 1962. St. Antony's Papers, No. 13.

Sherwood, John M. *Georges Mandel and the Third Republic*. Stanford: Stanford University Press, 1970.

Shorter, Edward, and Tilly, Charles. *Strikes in France, 1830–1968*. London: Cambridge University Press, 1974.

Shorrock, William I. *French Imperialism in the Middle East. The Failure of Policy in Syria and Lebanon, 1900–1914*. Madison: University of Wisconsin Press, 1976.

Silverman, Dan P. *Reconstructing Europe After the Great War*. Cambridge, Mass.: Harvard University Press, 1982.

Simonsson, Ragnar. *Millerands Presidentur. En Studie över Presidentmakt och parlamentarism i Frankrike*. Uppsala: Almquist & Wikells Boktryckeri -A.-B., 1938.

Smith, Adolphe. 'Millerand, Briand and the French Socialist Party,' *The Fortnightly Review*, June 1921, pp. 1014–23.

Soltau, Roger H. *French Parties and Politics*. London: Humphrey Milford, 1922.

Sonolet, Louis. *La Vie et l'œuvre de Paul Deschanel, 1855–1922*. Paris: Librairie Hachette, 1926.

Sorlin, Pierre. *Waldeck-Rousseau*. Paris: Armand Colin, 1966.

Soucy, Robert. *French Fascism: The First Wave, 1924–1933*. New Haven: Yale University Press, 1986.

Soulié, Michel. *Le Cartel des gauches*. Paris: Jean Dullis, 1974.

—— *La Vie politique d'Edouard Herriot*. Paris: Armand Colin, 1962.

Soutou, Georges. 'Une autre politique? Les tentatives françaises d'entente économique avec l'allemagne, 1919–1921,' *Revue d'Allemagne*, VIII, No. 1 (January–March 1976), pp. 21–34.

—— 'L'impérialisme du pauvre: la politique économique du gouvernement français en Europe centrale et orientale de 1918 à 1929,' *Relations internationales*, No. 7, Autumn 1976, pp. 219–39.

—— 'Les mines de Silésie et la rivalité franco-allemande, 1920–1923,' *Relations internationales*, No. 1, 1974, pp. 135–154.

—— 'La politique économique de la France en Pologne (1920–1924),' *Revue historique*, January–March 1974, pp. 85–116.

—— *L'Or et le sang. Les buts de guerre économiques de la première guerre mondiale*. Paris: Fayard, 1989.

—— 'Problèmes concernant le rétablissement des relations économiques franco-allemandes après la première guerre mondiale,' *Francia*, 2, 1974, pp. 580–96.

Sternhell, Zeev. *Maurice Barrès et le nationalisme français*. Paris: Armand Colin, 1972.

—— *Ni droite ni gauche. L'idéologie fasciste en France*. Paris: Editions du Seuil, 1983.

—— 'Paul Déroulède and the origins of modern French nationalism,' *Journal of Contemporary History*, Vol. 6, No. 4 (1971), pp. 46–70.

Stone, Judith. *The Search for Social Peace: Reform Legislation in France, 1890–1914*. Albany: State University of New York Press, 1985.

Strauss, Paul. *Les Fondateurs de la République*. Paris: La Renaissance du Livre, 1934.

Strowski, Fortunat. 'M. Alexandre Millerand, écrivain et homme politique,' *La Renaissance politique, littéraire, artistique*, 21 April 1923, pp. 18–19.

Suarez, Georges. *Briand: sa vie – son œuvre*. Vols. II, V. Paris: Librairie Plon, 1938, 1941.

Sumler, David E. 'Domestic influences on the nationalist revival in France, 1909–1914,' *French Historical Studies*, VI, No 4 (Fall 1970), pp. 517–37.

—— 'Opponents of war preparedness in France, 1913–14,' in Solomon Wank, ed., *Doves and Diplomats*. Westport, Conn.: Greenwood Press, 1978.

—— 'Polarization in French politics, 1909–1914.' Unpublished Ph.D. dissertation, Princeton University, 1968.

Tanenbaum, Jan Karl. *France and the Arab Middle East 1914–1920. Transactions* of the American Philosophical Society. Vol. 68, Part 7. Philadelphia: October 1978.

—— *General Maurice Sarrail 1856–1929: The French Army and Left-Wing Politics*. Chapel Hill: University of North Carolina Press, 1974.

Terrail, Gabriel (Mermeix). *Au sein des commissions*. Paris: Librairie Ollendorff, 1924.

Thomson, David. *Democracy in France Since 1870.* New York: Oxford University Press, 1964. 4th edn.

Tint, Herbert. *The Decline of French Patriotism, 1870–1940.* London: Weidenfeld & Nicolson, 1964.

Tirard, Paul. *La France sur le Rhin. Douze années d'occupation rhénane.* Paris: Librairie Plon, 1930.

Trachtenberg, Marc. *Reparation in World Politics: France and European Economic Diplomacy 1916–1923.* New York: Columbia University Press, 1980.

Ullman, Richard H. *The Anglo-Soviet Accord.* Vol. III of *Anglo-Soviet Relations, 1917–1921.* Princeton: Princeton University Press, 1972.

Vérecque, Charles. *Trois années de participation socialiste à un gouvernement bourgeois.* Paris: Bibliothèque du parti socialiste de France, 1904.

Vindex, Ch. *Le Ministère Waldeck–Millerand.* Paris: Bloud, 1902.

Viviani, René. 'M. Alexandre Millerand,' *Revue des deux mondes,* 1 November 1920, pp. 84–95.

Wandycz, Piotr S. *France and her Eastern Allies 1919–1925.* Minneapolis: University of Minnesota Press, 1962.

Watson, David R. *Georges Clemenceau. A Political Biography.* London: Eyre Metheun Ltd., 1974.

Weber, Eugen. *Action Française.* Stanford: Stanford University Press, 1962.

—— 'France,' in *The European Right,* edited by Hans Rogger and Eugen Weber. Berkeley: University of California Press, 1966, pp. 71–127.

—— *France: fin de siècle.* Cambridge: Harvard University Press, 1986.

—— *The Nationalist Revival in France, 1905–1914.* Berkeley: University of California Press, 1968.

Weill-Raynal, Etienne. *Les Réparations Allemandes et la France.* Paris: Nouvelles Editions Latines, 1938. Vol. 1.

Weygand, Maxime. *Mémoires.* Vol. II. Paris: Flammarion, 1957.

Willard, Claude. *Les Guesdistes. Le mouvement socialiste en France, 1893–1905.* Paris: Editions sociales, 1965.

Williams, Philip M. *Wars, Plots and Scandals in Post-War France.* Cambridge: Cambridge University Press, 1970.

Williamson, Samuel R., Jr. *The Politics of Grand Strategy. Britain and France Prepare for War, 1904–1914.* Cambridge, Mass.: Harvard University Press, 1969.

Willis, James F. *Prologue to Nuremberg. The Politics and Diplomacy of Punishing War Criminals of the First World War.* Westport, Conn.: Greenwood Press, 1982.

Winnacker, R.A. 'The Delégation des Gauches: a successful attempt at managing a parliamentary coalition,' *The Journal of Modern History,* IX, No. 4 (December 1937), pp. 449–70.

Winock, Michel. 'Socialisme et patriotisme en France (1891–1894),' *Revue d'histoire moderne et contemporaine,* July–September 1973, pp. 376–421.

Wohl, Robert. *French Communism in the Making, 1914–1924*. Stanford: Stanford University Press, 1966.

Wolfers, Arnold. *Britain and France Between Two Wars*. New York: W.W. Norton & Co., 1940, 1966.

Wright, Gordon. *Between the Guillotine and Liberty*. New York: Oxford University Press, 1983.

—— *France in Modern Times*. Chicago: Rand McNally, 1974, 2nd edn.

—— *Raymond Poincaré and the French Presidency*. Stanford: Stanford University Press, 1942.

Zeldin, Theodore. *France, 1848–1945*. Oxford: Clarendon Press, 1973, 1977. 2 vols.

Zévaès, A. *Histoire de la IIIe République. 4 septembre 1870–21 octobre 1945*. Paris: Editions de la Nouvelle Revue Critique, 1946.

—— *Ombres et silhouettes. Notes et souvenirs d'un militant*. Paris: Editions Georges-Anquetil, 1928.

Ziebura, Gilbert. *Léon Blum et le parti socialiste 1872–1934*. Paris: Armand Colin, 1967.

Index